iOS Animations by Tutorials

Seventh Edition

By Marin Todorov

iOS Animations by Tutorials

Marin Todorov

Notice of Rights

Notice of Liability

Trademarks

ISBN: 978-1-950325-65-8

Table of Contents

Book License

By purchasing *iOS Animations by Tutorials*, you have the following license:

- You are allowed to use and/or modify the source code in *iOS Animations by Tutorials* in as many apps as you want, with no attribution required.
- You are allowed to use and/or modify all art, images and designs that are included in *iOS Animations by Tutorials* in as many apps as you want, but must include this attribution line somewhere inside your app: "Artwork/images/designs: from *iOS Animations by Tutorials*, available at www.raywenderlich.com".
- The source code included in *iOS Animations by Tutorials* is for your personal use only. You are NOT allowed to distribute or sell the source code in *iOS Animations by Tutorials* without prior authorization.
- This book is for your personal use only. You are NOT allowed to sell this book without prior authorization, or distribute it to friends, coworkers or students; they would need to purchase their own copies.

All materials provided with this book are provided on an "as is" basis, without warranty of any kind, express or implied, including but not limited to the warranties of merchantability, fitness for a particular purpose and noninfringement. In no event shall the authors or copyright holders be liable for any claim, damages or other liability, whether in an action of contract, tort or otherwise, arising from, out of or in connection with the software or the use or other dealings in the software.

All trademarks and registered trademarks appearing in this guide are the properties of their respective owners.

Before You Begin

This section tells you a few things you need to know before you get started, such as the hardware and software you'll need, where to find the project files for this book and more.

What You Need

To follow along with the tutorials in this book, you'll need the following:

- **A Mac running macOS Monterey or later.** You'll need this to be able to install the latest version of Xcode and use Xcode previews.
- **Xcode 13.0 or later.** Xcode is the main development tool for iOS. You'll need Xcode 13.0 or later for all tasks in this book. You can download the latest version of Xcode from Apple's developer site here: https://developer.apple.com/develop/
- Basic knowledge of Swift and iOS development. This book is about animations specifically; to understand the animation code and how the accompanying demo projects work you will need at least a basic understanding of Swift and UIKit.

If you want to try things out on a physical iOS device, you'll need a developer account with Apple, which you can obtain for free. However, all the sample projects in this book will work just fine in the iOS Simulator bundled with Xcode, so the developer account is completely optional.

Book Source Code & Forums

Where to Download the Materials for This Book

The materials for this book can be cloned or downloaded from the GitHub book materials repository:

- https://github.com/raywenderlich/iat-materials/tree/editions/7.0

Forums

We've also set up an official forum for the book at https://forums.raywenderlich.com/c/books/ios-animations-by-tutorials. This is a great place to ask questions about the book or to submit any errors you may find.

"To my father."

— *Marin Todorov*

About the Author

Marin Todorov is the author of this book. Marin is one of the founding members of the raywenderlich.com team and has worked on eight of the team's books. He's an independent contractor and has worked for clients like Apple, Realm, Roche and others. Besides crafting code, Marin also enjoys blogging, teaching and speaking at conferences. He happily open-sources code. You can find out more about Marin at www.underplot.com.

About the Editors

Rich Turton is an editor of this book. He is an iOS developer for MartianCraft and long-time contributor to raywenderlich.com. When he's not in front of a computer he is usually trying to play the piano, trying to make fancy cocktails, or trying to play elaborate Lego games with his daughters. Sometimes all at the same time..

Introduction

There's no denying it: Creating animations is one of the most enjoyable parts of iOS development!

Animations are fun to create, they breathe life into your user interface, and most importantly, they make your interface a delight to use. Who doesn't love an app that gives you a little visual thrill when you open a menu or swipe right?

You've probably seen impressive animations in many third-party apps, as well as in Apple's own built-in apps. When used properly, animations can convey information to your users and draw their attention to important parts of the interface.

To create responsive and attractive user interfaces, you'll need to use all kinds of animations, from very subtle effects, to extremely expressive ones that leap off the screen.

In this book, you'll learn about various iOS animation techniques, from simple view animations, to vivid 3D animations, to view controller animations that make the navigation in your app look and feel great.

By the end of this book, you'll have worked through the chapter content and you'll have hands-on experience solving the challenges at the end of the chapters — and you'll be well on your way to coming up with stunning animations for your own apps!

Who this book is for

This book is for iOS developers who already know the basics of iOS and Swift, and want to dive deep into animations.

If you are a complete beginner to iOS development, we recommend you read through *The UIKit Apprentice* first. Otherwise this book may be a bit too advanced for you.

- https://www.raywenderlich.com/books/uikit-apprentice

This book does require some basic knowledge of Swift. If you do not know Swift, you can still follow along with the book because all of the instructions are in step-by-step format. However, there will likely be parts that are confusing due to gaps in your knowledge.

Before beginning this book, you might want to go through our *Swift Apprentice* series, which covers the basics of Swift development:

- https://www.raywenderlich.com/books/swift-apprentice

As with raywenderlich.com, all the tutorials in this book are in Swift.

How to use this book

Each chapter in this book includes a starter project and covers a small number of animation techniques in detail; this lets you work through the chapters in the book in any order.

However, for beginners, we do suggest that you work through the chapters in order, since the concepts build upon each other. Also, remember you'll get the most out of the book if you follow along with the tutorials and perform the hands-onchallenges.

For advanced developers, there's still value in the early chapters since that cover the basics, since you might not yet be familiar with the Swift syntax for these familiar animation APIs. However if you're comfortable with that, feel free to jump ahead to the topics that interest you the most.

What's in store

This book is divided into seven sections. You can find more details on each section in its introduction, which also includes a short description of its chapters. Here's a brief overview.

Section I: Animations With SwiftUI

SwiftUI is a modern, cross-platform, declarative UI framework introduced by Apple in iOS13. It's a big departure from how you used to build UI and animations in earlier iOS versions but it's also a lot of fun to work with and you will quickly get to build some truly stunning effects.

Section II: View Animations

UIKit View animations are the most common type of animations in iOS, but still very powerful; you can easily animate almost any view element and change things such as its size, position and color.

Section III: Auto Layout

Auto Layout is becoming more common in apps, and there are some special techniques to animate views that are sized and positioned with auto layout constraints. This section provides a crash course in Auto Layout and then covers theanimation techniques that play nicely with Auto Layout.

Section IV: Layer Animations

Views on iOS are backed by layers, which offer a lower-level interface to the visual content of your apps. When you need more flexibility or performance, you can use layer animations rather than view animations. In this section, you'll learn about layers and the Core Animation API.

Section V: View Controller Transition Animations

Animating views and layers is impressive, but you can dial it up to 11 and animate entire view controllers! In this section, you'll learn the techniques for transitioning between view controllers, as well as transitioning between changes in device orientations, all in the same view controller.

Section VI: Animations With UIViewPropertyAnimator

`UIViewPropertyAnimator`, introduced in iOS10, and helps developers create interactive, interruptible view animations. Since all APIs in UIKit just wrap that lower level functionality, there won't be many surprises for you when looking at `UIViewPropertyAnimator`. This class does make certain types of view animations a little easier to create, so it is definitely worth looking into.

Section VII: 3D Animations

In this section, you'll move beyond two dimensions and learn about 3D animations and effects with CATransform3D. Although Core Animation isn't a true 3D framework, it lets you position things in 3D-space and set perspective – which leads to some very slick and impressive effects!

Section I: Animations With SwiftUI

SwiftUI is a modern cross-platform declarative UI framework from Apple. SwiftUI supports all Apple platforms so, as a cool bonus, you can apply anything you learn in this section to any of your tvOS, macOS, iPadOS and watchOS apps!

In this section, you'll work through several different animations including some beautiful thumbnail zoom transitions and a modern-looking SwiftUI spinner.

Chapter 1: Introduction to Animations With SwiftUI

SwiftUI is the new paradigm from Apple for building your app UI declaratively. It's a big departure from the existing UIKit and AppKit frameworks.

When using UIKit and AppKit, you need to constantly micro-manage your data model and your views to keep them in sync. That's exactly what dictates the need to use a view controller in the first place – you need that class to be the "glue" between the state of your views (aka, what the user sees onscreen) and the state of your data (aka, what's on disk or in memory).

And of course, you need to monitor user input, like touches or other gestures, and react to those, too. You end up in a never-ending cycle of updating your model and updating the user interface via a multitude of asynchronous callbacks. A lot of this code is *very* repetitive and prone to errors.

When using SwiftUI, on the other hand, you need to adopt a new approach towards building user interfaces. And let me put you at ease – that new approach is much better than what I just described. In this brave new world, you do not explicitly create views and add them on your screen; instead, you create a view model that SwiftUI renders for you automatically.

Since SwiftUI derives the rendered user interface from your data, you can never have an inconsistent state onscreen – the only source of truth is your data. What's rendered onscreen is simply a function of that data, so you don't need to sync states back and forth.

Long story short – you update your data and SwiftUI makes sure that everything looks perfect onscreen.

I realize that if you have solid experience with UIKit or AppKit, SwiftUI might sound like magic, but I can assure you there's nothing magical about it. It's a rock-solid, modern-day UI framework.

If you want to learn SwiftUI in depth, check out the book SwiftUI by Tutorials (https://bit.ly/2L5wLLi) from raywenderlich.com.

> **Note**: If you'd like to make the most out of the frameworks that Apple introduced in 2019, I recommend using Combine alongside SwiftUI. You can learn about Combine in detail in Combine: Asynchronous programming with Swift (https://bit.ly/2ItbdXa).

In this book, you are going to focus on animations *only*. Therefore, getting some understanding of SwiftUI before you get to work on the next two chapters would be beneficial. However, even if you don't have any experience with SwiftUI, you can still work through the chapters and create some beautiful animations.

It's time to get started!

SwiftUI Basics

As you established in the previous section, when using SwiftUI, you describe your user interface declaratively and leave the rendering to the framework.

Each of the views you declare for your UI (those can be anything, like text labels, images or shapes) adheres to the `View` protocol. `View` requires each view struct to feature a property called `body`.

Any time you change your data model, SwiftUI asks each of your views for their current body, which might change according to changes in your latest data model. It then builds the view hierarchy to render onscreen. In a sense, SwiftUI makes "snapshots" triggered by changes in the data model.

Since SwiftUI can identify all views in your view hierarchy, it's not difficult for it to animate any changes to your views. If in the current snapshot of your views, a given view is 100 pixels to the right, it's a piece of cake for SwiftUI to animate this change.

It works the same way if your view is larger than it used to be or if it's now purple where it used to be pink. SwiftUI keeps track of the state in the previous snapshot and, if you need it to, can animate any changes you declare for your views.

Doesn't that sound just amazing?

Having covered the very basics of SwiftUI, try some animations in Xcode and see how it works in practice.

Your First SwiftUI Animation

To get started, open the **starter** project provided for this chapter of the book. The project consists of two parts – a simple playground view, where you'll try some basic animations, and a more complete example called Savanna Tours, where you're going to try some real-life UI animations.

SwiftUI introduces some new tools in Xcode. To be able to work through the next two chapters, you'll need a basic understanding of these new tools.

Xcode has a handy Editor mode called **Canvas**. A Canvas editor displays your code visually and in real-time and allows you to re-run your code very quickly.

The basic controls that you'll need to master for this chapter are as follows:

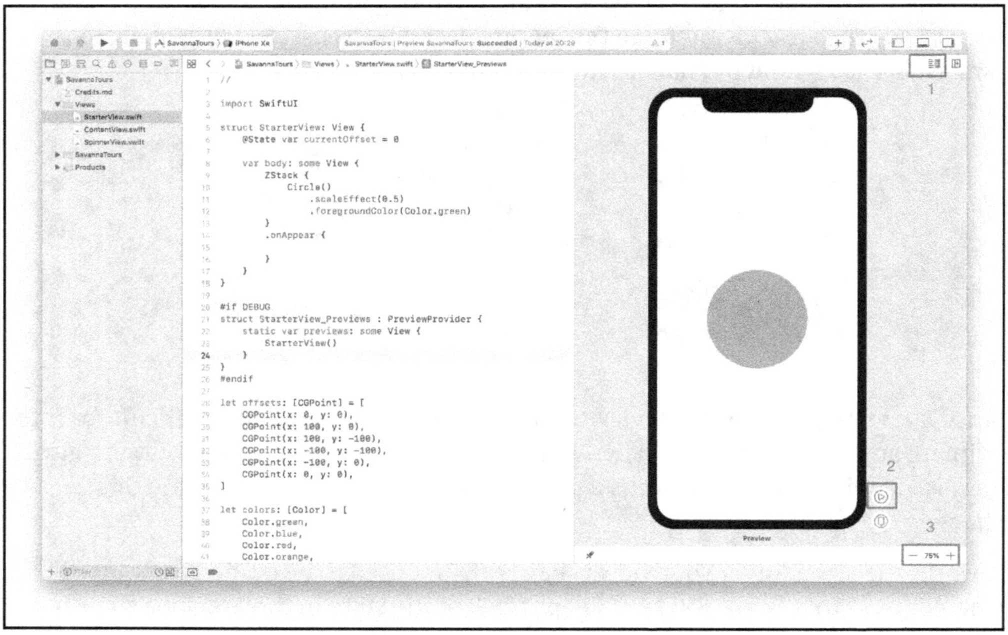

1. **Adjust Editor Options**: A drop-down menu that allows you to enable the new live-preview Xcode editor called **Canvas.**

2. **The Canvas Run button**: Allows you to switch between static and interactive previews of your code.

3. **The Canvas zoom**: Helps you zoom out the preview and see your view layout in full, or to zoom into particular view you want to see in detail.

To get into the `SwiftUI` workflow, select **StarterView.swift** in the Project Navigator and make sure you see the Editor Canvas. To do that, click **Adjust Editor Options** in the drop-down menu and click **Editor and Canvas** from the list of options:

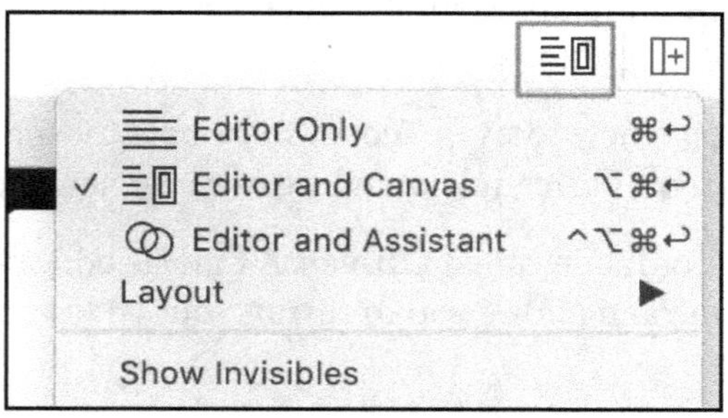

Now, you should see a split editor with StarterView.swift on the left-hand side and a nice green circle on the right-hand side. That circle is the preview of your layout.

It's important to notice that Xcode currently displays a static preview of the layout. You cannot interact with the preview and, most importantly for you, you will not see any animations in action. The static preview makes an initial snapshot of your layout and displays that onscreen.

To switch to interactive previewing, click the **Canvas Run** button. That will make Xcode compile `StarterView` and run an interactive preview. To give you a visual hint that you are now running your code interactively, Xcode changes the background color of the Canvas and switches the play icon on the Canvas Run button to a stop icon. Clicking the button again will switch back to static previewing.

For the next two chapters, you'll need to enable interactive previewing, since you will be playing with animations. Speaking of which, it's finally time to try some code!

Look at the code of the `body` property inside `StarterView` – this is where you declare your UI, which is currently a simple green circle:

```
Circle()
  .scaleEffect(0.5)
  .foregroundColor(Color.green)
```

Next, extract the circle foreground color into a state property and try to animate it. Add a new property to `StarterView` called `color`:

```
@State var color = Color.green
```

Marking properties as `@State` will trigger a new snapshot of your view each time they're modified. To update your user interface, you don't adjust your views directly; instead, you modify state properties. That triggers a new render of your layout automatically for you.

Next, use the new state property instead of the fixed foreground color. Replace the `foregroundColor(...)` modifier on your circle with:

```
.foregroundColor(color)
```

Now, each time you modify `color`, SwiftUI will create a new snapshot of the circle with its new foreground tint. To see that in action, add a little timeout after adding the circle onscreen and change the `color` property.

Inside onAppear, insert the code that changes the circle color so that it looks like this:

```
.onAppear {
  delay(seconds: 2) {
    self.color = .red
  }
}
```

delay(seconds:block:) is a helper function declared in the starter project that executes a closure after a given amount of seconds. In the case above, you say that 2 seconds after the circle appears onscreen, you'd like to change the color state property's value to red.

As you keep adding code throughout the chapter, you could confuse the Xcode build system, as it will eagerly try to show your changes onscreen and in real time. If it gets too confused, Xcode will pause the previewing and you might see a banner like this on top of the Canvas:

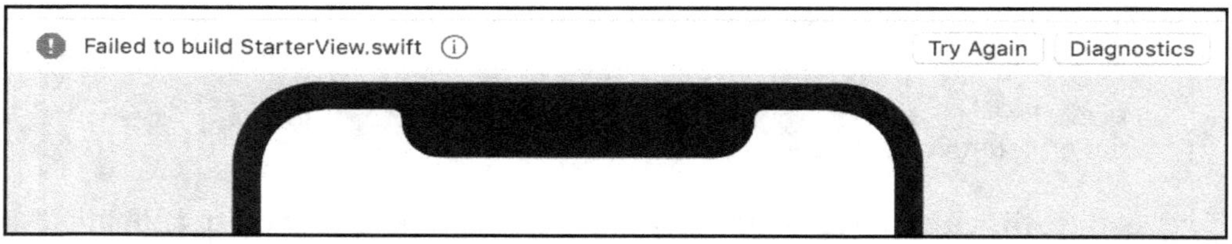

In that case, just press **Try again** or **Resume** to get the preview running again. You could also press **Diagnostics** to get additional information about why the preview got stuck. Oftentimes, it's an issue with your code like a failed type inference or something along those lines.

Once the interactive preview is running in the Canvas editor (make sure you've clicked the Canvas Run button), you'll see the green circle turn into a red circle after a small delay:

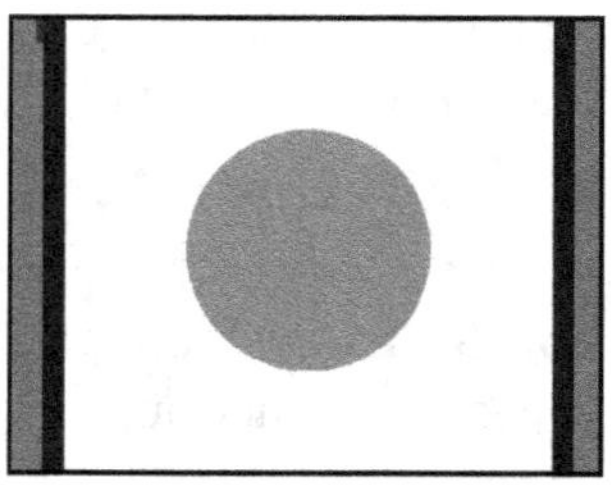

Note: Congrats, you've just accidentally drawn the Japanese flag!

Next, you need to add another modifier on your circle view to let know SwiftUI that you'd like it to animate the layout changes.

Append the following line just after the line where you call `foregroundColor(_)`:

```
.animation(.default, value: self.color)
```

`animation(_:value:)` sets the default animation to apply to layout changes when the second parameter's value changes. In this case, SwiftUI will use a default animation with pre-defined parameters any time you change the `color` property.

As soon as you save your code changes, Xcode re-runs the interactive preview. You should see the circle color animate with a nice crossfade transition from green to red:

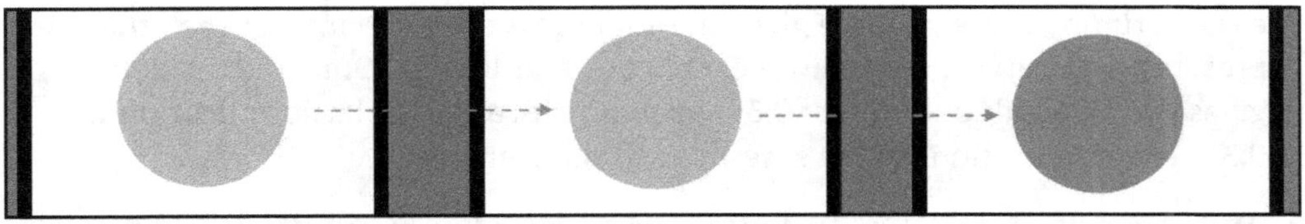

Sadly, in more recent versions of Xcode previews will not show animations but don't worry about it. Run the project and inspect the animation in the iPhone simulator instead if that's the case for you:

Congratulations, you've created your first SwiftUI animation!

The Animation Type

You easily created an animation by adding the `animation(_:value:)` modifier, but what is the `.default` value that you passed as the parameter?

`animation(_:value:)` takes an `Animation` as a parameter, which defines the properties of the resulting animation effect. These properties include the duration (how long the animation takes), the timing curve (you'll learn more about timing curves in Chapter 3, "Getting Started With View Animations") or whether it should be a spring-driven animation (you'll cover springs in detail in Chapter 4, "Springs").

You create an `Animation` using one of the following static methods:

- **Animation.easeIn(duration:)**: A method that produces a basic animation with ease-in timing curve, and the given duration. There are variants for the other preset timing curves: `.easeOut`, `.easeInOut` and `linear`. Omitting the duration gives you a default duration of 0.35 seconds. `.default` is a basic animation with 0.35 seconds duration and an ease-in-ease-out timing curve.
- **Animation.interpolatingSpring(mass:stiffness:damping:initialVelocity)**: This method creates a spring-driven animation which interpolates between the previous and current states of your view, but depending on its parameters, could overshoot its final value to produce "bouncy" animations. You can learn much more about spring-driven animations in chapters 4 and 13.
- **Animation.spring(response:dampingFraction:blendDuration:)**: A method that creates a different type of spring-driven animations which have a different configuration that allows you to create more "fluid" effects.

Once you create your animation instance, you can use the following modifiers to change the animation even more:

- **delay(_)**: Adds a delay of a specific amount of time before the animation starts.
- **repeatCount(_:autoreverses:)**: Configures the animation to repeat a given number of times. If `autoreverses` is set, it plays the effect forwards and backwards instead of restarting the animation on each repeat.
- **repeatsForever(autoreverses:)**: Like above, this modifier makes the animation repeat, but it repeats indefinitely instead of a given number of times.
- **speed(_)**: Allows you to speed up or slow down the animation.

This sounds amazing, especially if you've created animations before with other frameworks. But with SwiftUI, custom animations for views, controls and shapes is really easy. You just have to create an animation instance by choosing one of the the factory methods, applying any of the few modifiers you just learned about and adding the animation to a view by using the `animation(_:value:)` modifier!

You'll create a few more animations throughout this chapter and the next one, so you'll see there's no other secret sauce to SwiftUI's animations. It's a real joy to quickly iterate and experiment with your layout and UI effects.

Next – back to finishing that first SwiftUI animation you had going earlier. You're going to quickly explore a couple more ideas and then move on to building a full-blown real-life app animation.

As you saw, creating animations is just a matter of changing properties that you've declared as your view's state. SwiftUI automatically knows how to detect the differences between the current and previous snapshots of your UI and how to apply animations to the views featuring the `animation(_:value:)` modifier.

The starter code in `StarterView` includes a list of colors that you can easily cycle through. Using it makes for a more interesting animation.

Delete the code inside `onAppear { ... }` and replace it with:

```
for index in 1..<offsets.count {
  delay(seconds: Double(index)) {
    self.currentOffset = index
  }
}
```

This schedules a number of changes to `currentOffset` over time, like so:

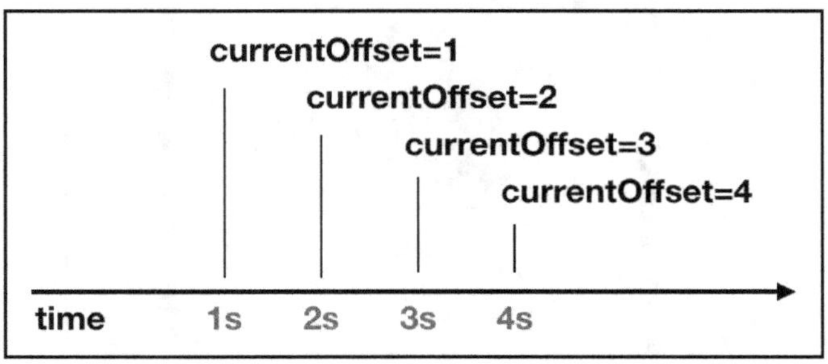

Now instead of using the `color` property for your circle you'll use the values predefined in `colors`. To do that, find `foregroundColor(_)` and replace it with:

```
.foregroundColor(colors[currentOffset])
```

Finally, since now the animation isn't driven by the `color` property but by `currentOffset`, you need to change the animation modifier as well. Change the modifier from:

```
.animation(.default, value: self.color)
```

to:

```
.animation(.default, value: self.currentOffset)
```

When you run the project, you'll observe the circle crossfade into a number of colors before ending on its initial green shade. As your last step in building your first SwiftUI animation, you'll send your circle view on a trip around the ... screen!

Views in SwiftUI have a modifier called `offset(x:y:)`. You'll use this modifier to feed your circle different offsets over time and make it move around.

The starter code already includes an array of offsets called `offsets` and you've already set your `currentOffset` state property. So the only thing that's left to do is to add the `offset` modifier and be on your way.

Add this on the line below the `animation(_:value:)` modifier:

```
.offset(x: offsets[currentOffset].x,
  y: offsets[currentOffset].y)
```

Each time you modify `currentOffset`, SwiftUI grabs the current offset from `offsets` and animates the circle to its next location onscreen. Check the preview and you'll see your circle animate through both colors and offsets:

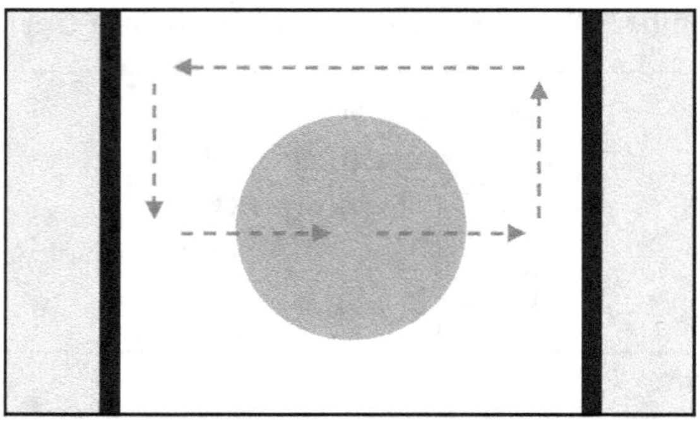

With that, your first SwiftUI animation is complete. Time to take on the world! I mean – time to play with a real-life animation and learn about animating even more SwiftUI modifiers.

Exploring More View Modifiers

For this section of the chapter, you'll work on a project called **Savanna Tours**. Since this project caters to both the introduction in this chapter and the tutorial part, it's important for you to make a little source change first.Open **SavannaToursApp.swift** and replace the line `StarterView()` with:

```
ContentView()
```

That will change the initial view from the test starter view to `ContentView` which you will need for what ensues next.

Click **ContentView.swift** in the Project Navigator to open that file and you'll see the initial layout of that view in the Canvas on the right side of the split:

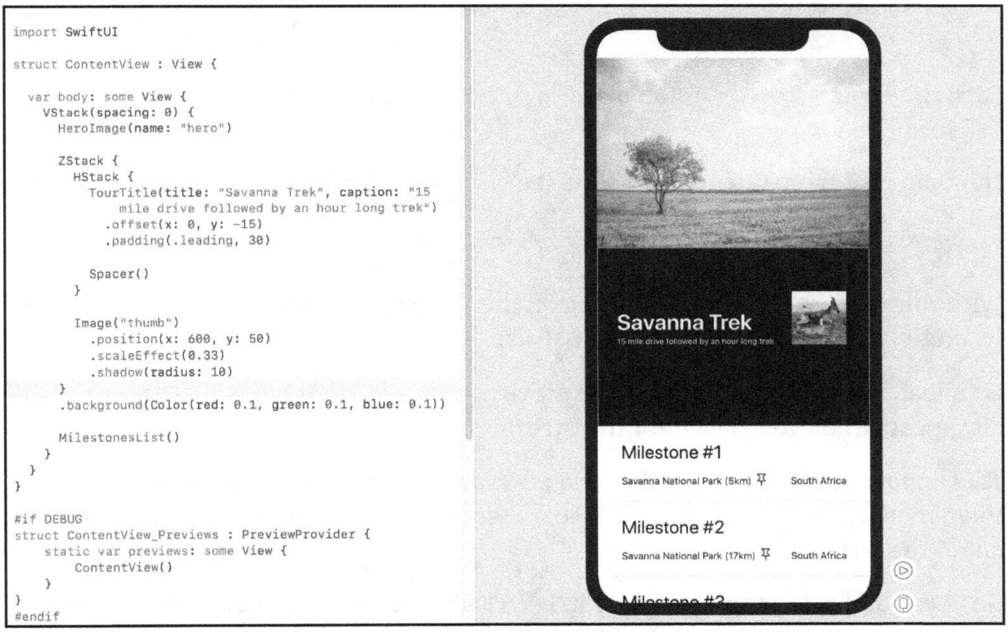

`ContentView` is part of an app that offers tours in the African savanna. In the Canvas Editor, you can see each tour's details including a title, a short description, a large photo, and a list of the tour's milestones.

Click the **Canvas Run** button to run an interactive preview and you'll see the only interactivity available at the moment is scrolling through the tour's milestones.

In this section of the chapter, you'll make the tour thumbnail, which you can find on the right side of the tour's title, interactive. Your app's users will be able to tap on the thumb and see a larger version of it onscreen presented, and dismissed, with a neat animation.

First of all, just like in the previous example, you'll need a property to hold some of your state. Namely, whether the thumbnail is zoomed or not. A simple Boolean state property suffices for that purpose, so add this to `ContentView`:

```
@State var zoomed = false
```

To toggle between zoomed-in and -out states, add `onTapGesture {...}` to the thumbnail. Add this code directly below `.shadow(radius: 10)`:

```
.onTapGesture {
  self.zoomed.toggle()
}
```

Each time you tap on the thumbnail view, the zoomed state will alternate between `false` and `true`.

Now, put that new state to work. Find the current `scaleEffect(_)` and change it to:

```
.scaleEffect(self.zoomed ? 1.33 : 0.33)
```

With this modifier, each time you tap on the thumb it will alternate between `33%` of its original size and `133%` of its original size.

Go ahead and click the thumb in the preview... oh, no! What happened? The thumb disappears when you click it for the first time.

This happens because the hard-coded position of `(600, 50)` works only when the thumbnail is scaled down to its `33%` size. Once the image is in full size, it repositions out of the screen.

Go ahead and patch this for now; you'll find a better solution later in the chapter. Replace the current `position(x:y:)` with:

```
.position(x: self.zoomed ? 220 : 600, y: 50)
```

Now, click through the zoomed-in and zoomed-out states and you should see that it works just fine now. Although you may have noticed that the zoomed-in version is not centered onscreen.

That's a bit annoying, but you'll fix that later on.

The last step to get your animation going is, just like in the previous section, adding `animation(_:value:)` on the view you'd like to animate.

Right below `.shadow(radius: 10)` add:

```
.animation(.default, value: self.zoomed)
```

Click a few times on the thumbnail and observe the animation. Notice how SwiftUI automatically interpolates the multiple animations you're running on the same thumb view:

1. The first animation scales the thumb way up, which pushes its location to the right. If you weren't changing its position as well, it would've animated out of the screen.

2. The second animation animates the thumb's position leftwards to keep it inside the screen while it scales up.

SwiftUI interpolates the changes of both animations. The final result is a neatly curving motion that starts rightwards but turns around and ends to the left of its starting point. That builds a very nice zoom effect!

To make that zoom even more slick, replace the default animation with a spring-driven animation:

```
.animation(.spring(), value: self.zoomed)
```

The default spring animation uses a harmonic oscillator under the hood with some default presets to deliver a very nice timing curve for your animations. You'll learn more about the mechanics of spring animations later in this book.

Click the thumbnail again and enjoy the new effect. Click repeatedly in quick succession and you'll notice interrupting the current animation never gives you a "broken" layout. All animations in SwiftUI are interruptible and reversible by default, and you get this for free out of the box.

Next, you're going to add another animation to yet another view on your screen. This way, you'll see how to drive multiple animations onscreen from a single state change.

In the code, scroll up to find the `TourTitle` view, which displays the tour's title and description onscreen. Add the following right after `.padding(.leading, 30)` to animate that view:

```
.offset(x: self.zoomed ? 500 : 0, y: -15)
.animation(.default, value: self.zoomed)
```

The code is similar to what you've done before. You add `animation(_:value:)` to the view and you change the value of `offset(x:y:)` based on your current state.

Clicking the thumb will now hide the tour title under the scaling-up thumb, resulting in a nice transition back and forth from the zoomed state.

Go back to the thumb view next and experiment with more modifiers. Right below the line `Image("thumb")` (the order of modifiers matters), add:

```
.clipShape(RoundedRectangle(cornerRadius: self.zoomed ? 40 : 500
))
```

This will clip the thumbnail to the shape you give as a parameter:

Since the corner radius of the clip rectangle is bigger than half its side's length, SwiftUI rounds the rectangle to a circle. Now, the thumbnail looks really nice!

Even better, when you click the thumb, it will animate its clipping shape to a rounded rectangle with a smaller corner radius and give the thumb a completely different shape:

And of course, all the changes to the thumb's layout are nicely animated with a fluid spring animation.

SwiftUI makes drawing and animating shapes really easy, because you apply the same basic principles to both views and shapes. You don't need to differentiate between them and they're both first-class citizens of your UI.

You'll learn much more about working with shapes in the next chapter, but first, add one more animation in your current project to add even more glow to the thumbnail view.

Below your `clipShape(_)` modifier insert:

```
.overlay(
  Circle()
    .fill(self.zoomed ? Color.clear : Color(red: 1.0, green:
1.0, blue: 1.0, opacity: 0.4))
    .scaleEffect(0.8)
  )
```

This code is somewhat meta, so it might take a while to grasp. You're using `overlay(_)` on your thumb view, which adds another view as an overlay over your original view.

overlay(_) takes yet another view as its parameter; you just create a Circle inline and set its modifiers, then pass it onto overlay(_). The circle overlay is 80% of the size of its parent (the thumb) and it's filled with a semi-transparent white color. This makes it look more like a nice badge than a flat thumbnail:

When you zoom the thumbnail, the circular overlay will disappear as you animate its white fill to a transparent clear color.

Now, add one more modifier directly after the one you just added:

```
.saturation(self.zoomed ? 1 : 0)
```

saturation(_) modifies the color saturation of the current view. The code you just added will desaturate the thumb completely when it's small and will animate it to full-color beauty when it zooms in.

Aaaand congratulations – you've built a beautiful animation by using a single state property and by leveraging SwiftUI's animation super-powers!

In this chapter, you learned a bit about SwiftUI and building user interfaces declaratively. While this book focuses specifically on animations, you saw that SwiftUI is a modern, declarative and, let's be honest, an easy-to-use UI framework.

Besides being able to quickly iterate and build your UI, creating eye-stunning animations with SwiftUI is pure joy!

This chapter includes a couple of quick exercises to iterate over your newly acquired skills; you'll learn more about creating more complex animations in the next chapter.

Key Points

- SwiftUI lets you build your UI declaratively and ask it to animate any changes between "snapshots" of your view hierarchy.
- You add animations via the `.animation(_:value:)` modifier on your views. You can provide a default or custom animation as the parameter.
- You animate various view modifiers via changes to the view's state properties, which trigger a new snapshot and which ask SwiftUI to interpolate between the previous and current layout.

Challenges

Challenge 1: Adding a Rotation Animation

To try one more type of animation, try adding a `rotationEffect(_)` to your thumb. Alternate between `0` and `90` degree angles for the rotation, depending on whether the thumb is zoomed in or not. If you'd like a tip – insert the rotation modifier before you adjust the position and scale of the thumb.

The initial state of the UI should look like this:

Challenge 2: Center the Zoomed Thumbnail

In this challenge, you'll learn how to animate views' positions onscreen based not on a relative offset, but rather on its relative position to the screen size. This will finally let you center that thumbnail horizontally on the screen.

To access the geometry (or the position and size) of a parent view in SwiftUI, use `GeometryReader` to access the thumb's container view width and to animate the thumb right in its horizontal center when scaled up.

To do that, wrap `Image("thumb")` and **all its modifiers** inside a block like this:

```
GeometryReader { geometry in
  < your existing code here >
}
```

Inside the closure, you have access to an object called `geometry`, which gives you the size and position of the thumb's parent view.

Now you can replace the original thumbnail `position(x:y:)` with:

```
.position(
  x: self.zoomed ? geo.frame(in: .local).midX : 600,
  y: 60
)
```

You keep the thumbnail at an x position of `600`, but when scaled up, you move it to the `midX` coordinate of its parent frame.

This way, when you click the thumb one last time, you'll see it neatly centered onscreen:

And that's a wrap! Get ready for the next chapter, which will lead you through building animation effects that will simply make your head spin...

Chapter 2: Intermediate SwiftUI Animations

You hopefully completed the previous chapter successfully and worked through the exercises too — you're on the path to becoming a great SwiftUI animator!

As you remember, SwiftUI works by you declaring how your UI should look for a given set of data. If the data changes, your UI is rebuilt. You can add modifiers to part or all of the UI to let the framework know that, if those parts change, you'd like the change to be animated. Your job is mostly to describe what kind of animation (basic or spring) you would like for SwiftUI to automatically apply between the "snapshots" of your view hierarchy when you make changes to your state data.

There is not much more than this basic principle to learn in order to create stunning animations with SwiftUI! That's a rather stark difference when comparing with animations via UIKit or AppKit.

In this chapter, you will iterate over drawing shapes and animating them on screen. You will also learn about view transitions, and will create a more complex, interactive multi-stage animation.

Getting Started

The final animation you will build by working through the end of this chapter will be a modern, fluid spinner-view that will look like this:

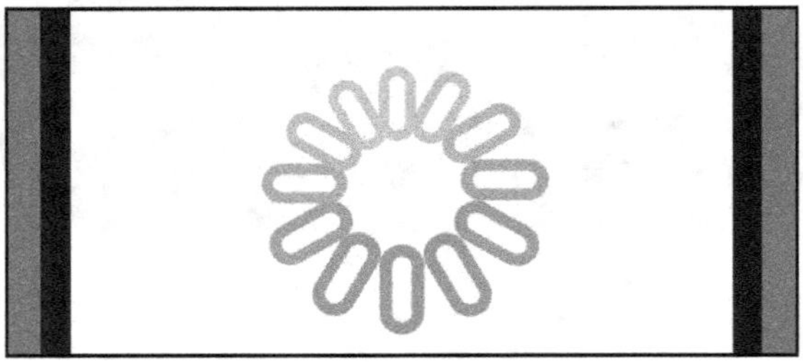

The beginnings of that spinner, however, are rather humble. To get started, open the starter project for this chapter and click **SpinnerView.swift**. Then, check out the starter view layout in the Editor Canvas:

This is where you start on your path to the spinner view you saw earlier. Currently on screen, you see a single ellipse shape that we'll call a "leaf" throughout this chapter.

Have a look at the starter code of `SpinnerView` and observe that:

- `Leaf` is a view type nested inside `SpinnerView` — since views are just structs, you can treat them as any other type in your code base. You can nest views, make them public or private, make them conform to further protocols besides `View`, etc.
- `Leaf` draws itself by using a view type called `Capsule`. `Capsule` along with `Circle`, `RoundedRectangle` and `Rectangle` allow you to easily draw shapes, or use them as clipping masks.
- The `SpinnerView` body is currently very simple, it includes a single leaf shape and, once added on screen, calls its `animate(_:value:)` method which is currently empty.

The code is all set for you to jump in and add some coolness.

Drawing the Spinner

Your first task is to draw the static spinner on screen. This will give you some insight into how to compose shape views and hopefully give you ideas how to design your own shape animations in future.

First of all, find the line of code which adds the initial leaf on screen `Leaf()` and delete it. In its place insert a loop which creates as many leaves as the `leavesCount` constant:

```
ForEach(0..<leavesCount) { index in
  Leaf()
}
```

Cool! That code will draw twelve identical leaves on screen. In fact all of them are so identical that when drawn over each other they look exactly the same as that initial identical leaf:

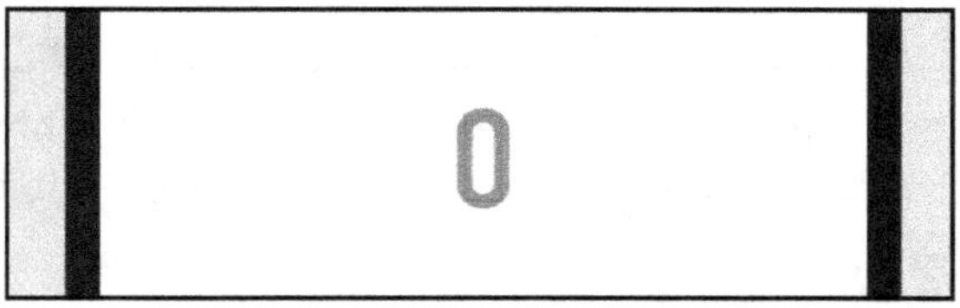

No worries, a few more tweaks and the spinner view will start taking shape. First of all, in order to see more than a single leaf drawn on screen, let's rotate each one slightly off the previous.

First, add a property on the `Leaf` type which will help us set the rotation of the capsule shape. Add inside `Leaf`:

```
let rotation: Angle
```

Swift will automatically generate a `Leaf(rotation:)` initializer for your leaf view and you will need to adjust the code that creates the leaves accordingly. Scroll down a bit and, inside the `ForEach` closure, replace `Leaf()` with:

```
Leaf(rotation: Angle(degrees:
  (Double(index) / Double(self.leavesCount)) * 360.0)
)
```

This will calculate the delta angle between each of the leaves so that, when all of them are drawn on screen, they will form a full circle.

You don't see on screen any "full circle" right now, though, since you haven't added the rotation view modifier yet. Move over to the code in the leaf's `body` property and add directly after the `frame(width:height:)` modifier:

```
.rotationEffect(rotation)
```

This modifier will apply the injected rotation to the view.

Now you will finally see something change in the Editor Canvas (you might need to click the **Resume** button towards the top of the canvas in case Xcode paused updates while you were adding your code.)

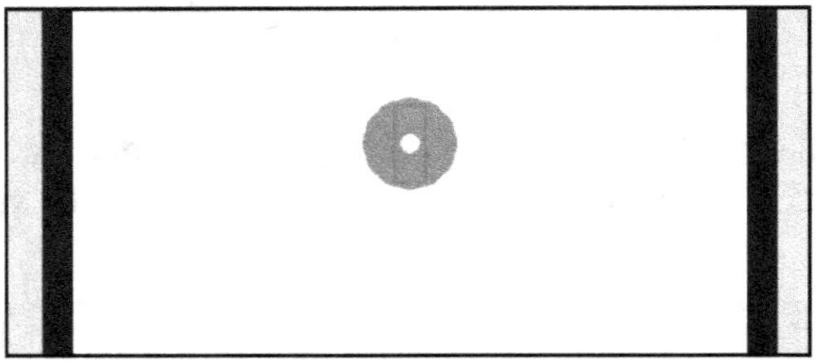

You can definitely see a bunch of the leaves drawn over each other. To make them even more distinguishable, blow them apart slightly by giving them some offset off their original center.

Insert this line just before the rotation modifier:

```
.offset(x: 0, y: 70)
```

This will first offset each leaf and then rotate it to produce this nice flower-like layout:

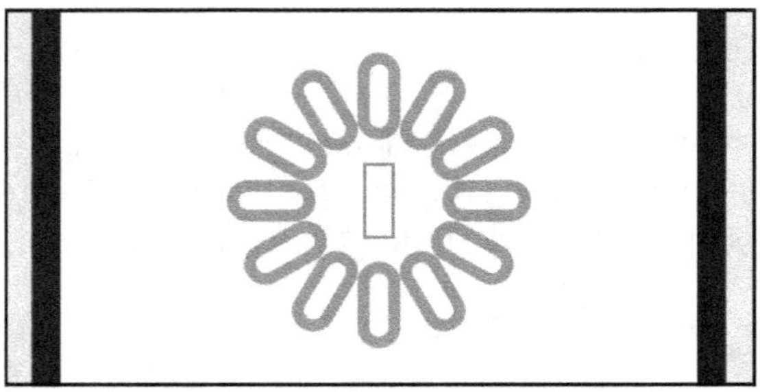

Great! This gives you a nice base to work off and create a beautiful animation. If you haven't done that so far, it's time you switch to the interactive preview in your Editor Canvas, by clicking the play button next to the preview.

Creating the Basic Spinning Animation

To get an animation going, you will use a timer so you can repeatedly make changes to your state over time. Each time the timer fires you will animate a different leaf, creating a wave-like effect that goes round and round.

In your `SpinnerView` add a new state property:

```
@State var currentIndex: Int?
```

This is the property you will be updating continuously from your timer's callback. Move down to the empty `animate()` method and start the animation code by creating a new timer:

```
Timer.scheduledTimer(withTimeInterval: 0.15, repeats: true)
{ timer in

})
```

You create a new `Timer` instance and configure it to fire each `0.15` seconds — this an arbitrary value I chose for that animation that you can adjust to your taste later on, if you wish.

Now, it's time to set the current leaf index from within the timer callback block. Insert this code into the closure you just added:

```
if let current = self.currentIndex {
  self.currentIndex = (current + 1) % self.leavesCount
} else {
  self.currentIndex = 0
}
```

This code will increment the value of `currentIndex` each time the timer fires and reset the value back to `0` when you reach the total number of leaves. This will allow you to iterate over each of the leaves repeatedly.

Next, you need to inject that state into the `Leaf` view so it can render itself differently depending on whether it's the one to currently animate.

Add this new property to `Leaf`:

```
let isCurrent: Bool
```

As this modifies the automatically generated `Leaf` initalizer you also need to update the code where you create your leaf views. Find the place inside `ForEach` where you create each leaf and adjust the code to also include the `isCurrent` property like so:

```
Leaf(rotation: Angle(degrees:
  (Double(index) / Double(self.leavesCount)) * 360.0),
  isCurrent: index == self.currentIndex
)
```

Now, you can adjust the `stroke(_:lineWidth:)` modifier on `Capsule()` to draw the leaf differently in case it should animate. Change the line `.stroke(_:lineWidth:)` to:

```
.stroke(isCurrent ? Color.white : Color.gray, lineWidth: 8)
```

This should get your basic animation going:

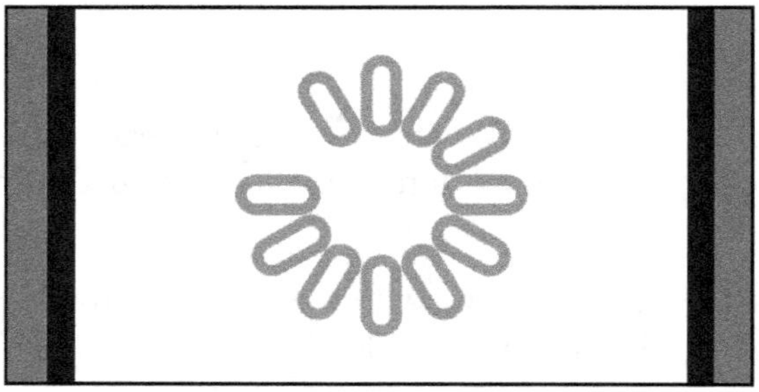

See how the current leaf "goes around" and keeps animating indefinitely.

However, this "animation" is not being animated by SwiftUI. It's being driven by your timer. Since the state changes occur pretty quickly (between 6 and 7 times per second) they look sort-of animated, but you can do better!

Next, you're going to invite SwiftUI to the party as well. Since you'd like to animate the changes to each separate leaf add a new modifier to the `Leaf.body` code (e.g. right after the `rotationEffect(_)` line you added there earlier):

```
.animation(.easeInOut(duration: 0.5), value: isCurrent)
```

You intentionally set an animation duration longer than the timer interval in order to have at least a few leaves animating on screen at the same time.

Unlike before, now you can see a very fluid and clean crossfade effect on each animating leaf:

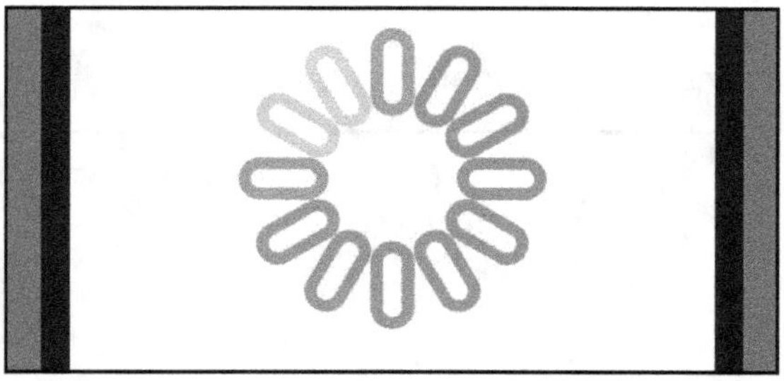

If I have to be completely honest — this spinner animation is *already* quite pleasant. I mean, I'd take that spinner in my app any day!

But you *have* to believe that you can do even better! Let's keep iterating over the current result and you can make this spinner view truly stunning.

First, adjust the duration of the animation to `1.5` seconds like so:

```
.animation(.easeInOut(duration: 1.5), value: isCurrent)
```

This will make the fade effect much more subtle than before, but that's okay because you will add few more effects and you wouldn't like any of them to dominate the composite animation. Find the line where you add an `offset(x:y:)` modifier to the capsule shape and adjust it so that the current leaf will animate slightly towards the spinner center:

```
.offset(x: isCurrent ? 10 : 0, y: isCurrent ? 40 : 70)
```

This change will make the leaves float slightly during the animation much like a sea anemone's tentacles float in the water:

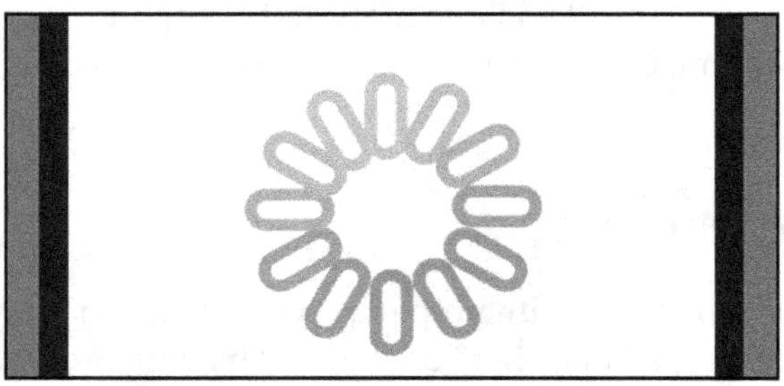

To finish off the current part of the animation, you'll scale the leaves as they move as well.

Insert a new scale effect modifier just before the `rotationEffect(_)` one:

```
.scaleEffect(isCurrent ? 0.5 : 1.0)
```

This will make the leaves *flow* even more:

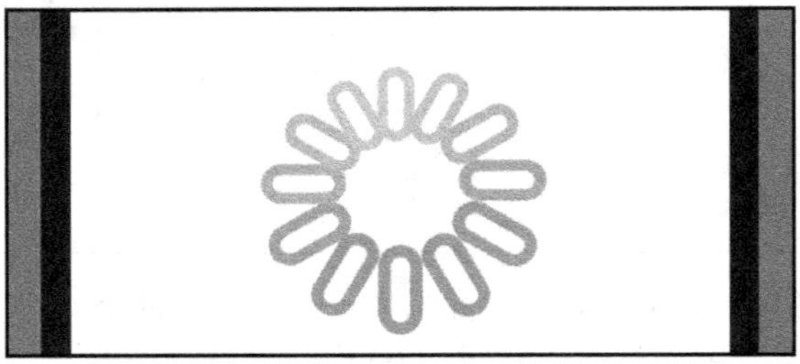

With that last change your basic animation, driven by a timer with the help of SwiftUI, is completed! Next, you will look into how to add multiple separate stages to that animation.

Adding Multiple Animation Stages

I bet you still remember that all layout changes on screen in SwiftUI are triggered by changes to your state. Currently, you have a single state property which sets which leaf is currently animated.

SwiftUI can cope with more complex state though. It's re-rendering everything anyway, so it's no problem to add more state properties to your spinner view and implement even more complex logic based on that.

In this section, you will make your spinner assemble whenever it has completed its purpose on screen. For example, the network operation that the spinner represents visually has completed. You will add one more state property to distinguish between being in an "active" animating state and being in the state of completion.

Add a new state property to the `SpinnerView`:

```
@State var completed = false
```

Just as with the `currentIndex` state property, every change of the value of `completed` will re-trigger a "snapshot" of your UI and animate any desired changes.

For the purpose of this chapter, you will simply change to "completed" state after the timer has fired `60` times. This will make for a few seconds of spinning before completing.

Scroll down to `animate()` and insert this line at the beginning of the method:

```
var iteration = 0
```

You will use `iteration` to keep track of how many times the timer has fired so far and check it's value to determine when to switch to completed state.

Next, add this, still inside the closure, at the end of the timer callback closure:

```
iteration += 1
if iteration == 60 {
  timer.invalidate()
  self.completed = true
}
```

Resume the interactive preview in the Editor Canvas. You will see that, after a few seconds, the spinner stops animating leaves. After the ones that were already animating all settle down, you have the "completed" state render looking like this:

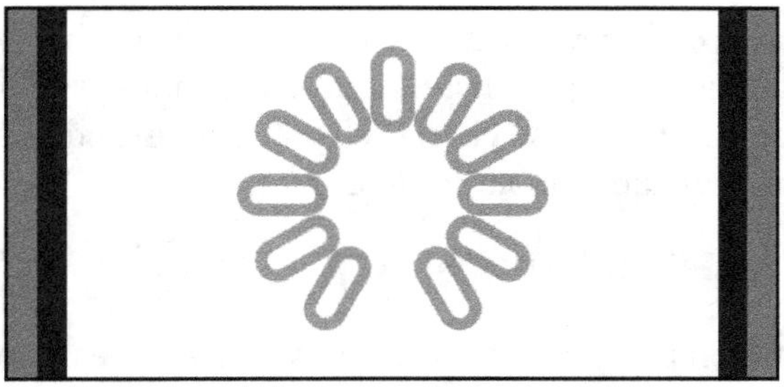

Notice how the leaf that ended being the current one when you switched to completed state is drawn in white. That's why you have that little hole in there at the bottom of the shape. So now, you have two stages to your animation that are driven by your state. Let's reflect that in a more prominent way on screen.

You will make all leaves perform a custom transition when you switch them to completed state. To achieve that first you will need to inject the completed state into the `Leaf` type.

Add to `Leaf`:

```
let isCompleting: Bool
```

And again, just like before, you need to update the place in the code where you create leaves, since the automatically generated initializer has been changed to include an `isCompleting` parameter.

Adjust your code to include that new parameter as well:

```
Leaf(
  rotation: Angle(degrees:
  (Double(index) / Double(self.leavesCount)) * 360.0),
  isCurrent: index == self.currentIndex,
  isCompleting: self.completed
)
```

OK, now that your leaf code knows whether it's being rendered in the completing stage of the animation, you can adjust some of its modifiers to create the new transition.

First, let's reset each leaf's rotation whenever you switch to completed state. That will animate all leaves back to the initial leaf's location. Modify the rotation modifier on the `Capsule` instance to:

```
.rotationEffect(isCompleting ? .zero : rotation)
```

The animation so far is driven by changes to `isCurrent` so when you modify `isCompleting` that doesn't trigger an animation. Fret not — add one more modifier to instruct the view to animate also changes to `isCompleting`. Just below the existing `animation(_:value:)` modifier in `Leaf` add:

```
.animation(.easeInOut(duration: 1.5), value: isCompleting)
```

Wait until the animation plays out and you will see the leaves neatly fold up at the end of the animation:

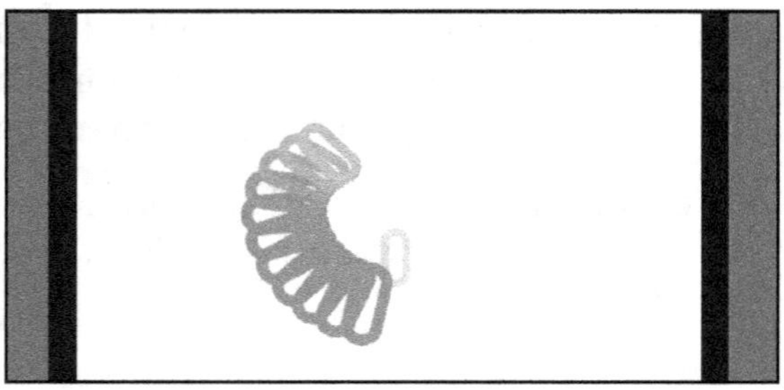

Let's keep iterating on this effect and make the capsule shapes also morph into circles. You can do this by setting the same width and height for the capsule which will effectively morph it into a circle. Change the `frame(width:height:)` modifier to:

```
.frame(width: 20, height: isCompleting ? 20 : 50)
```

If you play through the animation few times you will notice a little artifact during the last moments of the animation. There is one leaf that seems to move towards the center and fade out instead of moving with the others. What gives?

This is the one leaf that ended up being the current one when you switched to completed state. Since it's the only white leaf it causes a bit of a glitch towards the end of the completion effect. Fixing that isn't all that difficult, you have the correct state after all - you just need to derive your UI correctly from it. In the timer closure, after you set `self.completed = true`, add the following:

```
self.currentIndex = nil
```

This means none of the leaves are current, so the animation ends cleanly on a single gray circle:

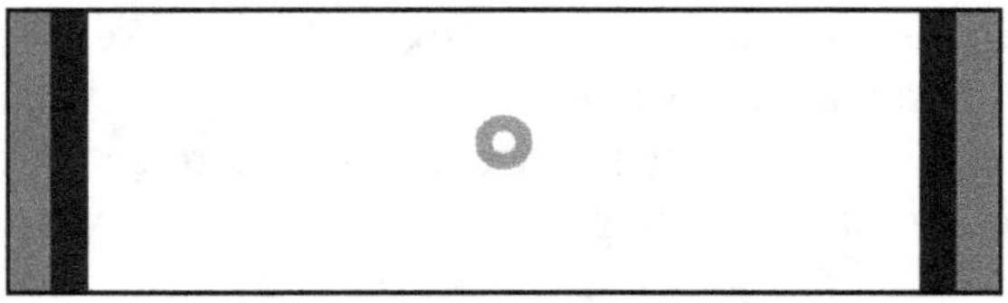

This final state looks nice but it's time to add one last stage to the animation and learn about view transitions.

Adding View Transitions

You've seen how to create SwiftUI animations between different states of views in your view hierarchy. But you can also create animation effects called transitions which deal with the situations when you add or remove a view to/from your view hierarchy.

Those types of animation effects are created slightly differently because you don't have two states to interpolate between. When you add or remove a view you don't have either a previous or current state, since the view is not in the view hierarchy.

In this section, once your spinner animation completes, you will remove the spinner view from the view hierarchy and add a transition to animate its way out of the screen. To achieve this, you will add one more state property to keep track of the spinner's presence in the view hierarchy.

Add the following to `SpinnerView`:

```
@State var isVisible = true
```

While `isVisible` is set to `true`, which is your initial state, you will render the spinner on screen. Once you set `isVisible` to `false`, you will remove the view and that will trigger the "exit" transition animation.

Find the `ZStack` type inside the `body` property of `SpinnerView` and wrap the call and its modifier inside an `if` statement. Your code should now look like this:

```
if isVisible {
  ZStack {
    ForEach(0..leavesCount) { index in
      ...
    }
  }.onAppear(perform: animate)
}
```

This way, when you toggle the `isVisible` property, you will remove the spinner from the body of `SpinnerView`. The best place to toggle `isVisible` is from within the final timer callback. Scroll a bit down and find the line where you set your state to completed: `self.completed = true`. Since the logic here gets a bit more comple, let's extract the code in a separate method.

First, add the following method to `SpinnerView`:

```
func complete() {
  guard !completed else { return }

  completed = true
  currentIndex = nil
  delay(seconds: 2) {
    withAnimation {
      self.isVisible = false
    }
  }
}
```

Next, from within the timer closure, replace the lines where you set `completed` and `currentIndex` with:

```
self.complete()
```

When you replay the animation you will see all leaves fold up and finally disappear when you remove the stack from the view hierarchy.

Next, you will add a transition effect to the view using the `transition(_)` modifier. There are a few predefined transitions you can use, and you can also create a custom transition based on a combination of a few others.

The `transition(_)` modifier takes an argument of type `AnyTransition` which is a type erased transition. Just like with `Animation`, you can use a few predefined transitions and some handy factory methods to create your own:

- `AnyTransition.opacity`: A cross fade effect which either fades in or out of the view.
- `AnyTransition.slide`: A transition that slides in views from the left when added, and to the right side when removed.
- `AnyTransition.move(edge:)`: Creates a transition that moves a view in and out towards the given edge of the screen.
- `AnyTransition.offset(_)`: Creates a transition which moves the view by a given offset.
- `AnyTransition.scale(scale:anchor:)`: Creates a transition which scales the view up or down.

Additionally, you can combine a number of transitions to create your own custom transition by using the `.combined(with:)` method. Or, for more advanced timing curves and custom duration, you can combine a transition with an animation by using the `animation(_)` modifier on a transition instance.

Give one of those transitions a try. Add the following modifier to the `ZStack` in your `SpinnerView`:

```
.transition(.move(edge: .top))
```

Now, when you replay the animation, instead of disappearing in place, the spinner should first move up a little bit, and then fade out.

This move transition could be better. It is only moving the collapsed leaves to the top edge of the spinner itself, which is only the size of a single leaf. The spinner is the center piece of the screen and it would be much nicer if it transitioned out of the screen bounds instead. This is the perfect opportunity to give creating custom transitions a try.

Add a new property to `SpinnerView`:

```
let shootUp = AnyTransition
  .offset(CGSize(width: 0, height: -1000))
```

Your custom transition is called `shootUp` and, as you probably guessed already, animates the view up and out of the screen by moving it `1000` points upwards.

To give your custom transition a more interesting timing curve, which will make the animation start slower and speed up towards the edge of the screen, you can combine the `offset(_)` transition with an animation using a `.easeIn` timing curve.

Append:

```
.animation(.easeIn(duration: 1.0))
```

The last step you need to make in order to see the new transition on screen is to replace `.transition(.move(edge: .top))` with:

```
.transition(shootUp)
```

With that, the third and last stage of your spinner animation is finished:

Take a moment to enjoy the amazing result you achieved by writing some 50 or so enjoyable lines of code!

Interactive Animations

At this point, you know plenty about creating animations with SwiftUI but there is one last topic you will cover in this chapter: Creating beautiful animations driven by the user.

You will add a drag gesture to the spinner control to give the user the ability to cancel the operation that the spinner represents — i.e. if the spinner shows up while a network request is taking place, swiping down on the spinner will cancel the network operation and hide the spinner view.

First of all, add a new state property to `SpinnerView` to keep track of the user's drag gesture translation whenever a gesture is in progress:

```
@State var currentOffset = CGSize.zero
```

Now, add a `gesture(_)` modifier to your `ZStack`:

```
.gesture(
  DragGesture()
    .onChanged { gesture in
      self.currentOffset = gesture.translation
    }
    .onEnded { _ in
      if self.currentOffset.height > 150 {
        self.complete()
      }
      self.currentOffset = .zero
    }
)
```

Using the `gesture(_)` modifier, you add a new gesture to the view by instantiating `DragGesture`. Alongside the initialization, you add an `onChanged(_)` handler to react to changes in the position of the drag gesture and `onEnded(_)` to handle the end of a drag.

During the gesture, you constantly update `currentOffset` with the current gesture translation and, in `onEnded(_)`, you reset that translation which will animate the spinner back to its original place.

In case the user swiped more than `150` points down, you call `complete()` to switch the spinner to its completed state.

The code is so simple that you actually create everything in-place and don't bother with any local variables or helper functions.

To wrap up add three more modifiers on your `ZStack` which will apply effects to the view during a drag gesture:

```
.offset(currentOffset)
.blur(radius: currentOffset == .zero ? 0 : 10)
.animation(.easeInOut(duration: 1.0), value: currentOffset)
```

You apply the current drag offset to the view position and additionally, once the user starts a drag, you add a blur to the spinner for even more visual feedback.

Play the animation one last time and try dragging the spinner around and then releasing it:

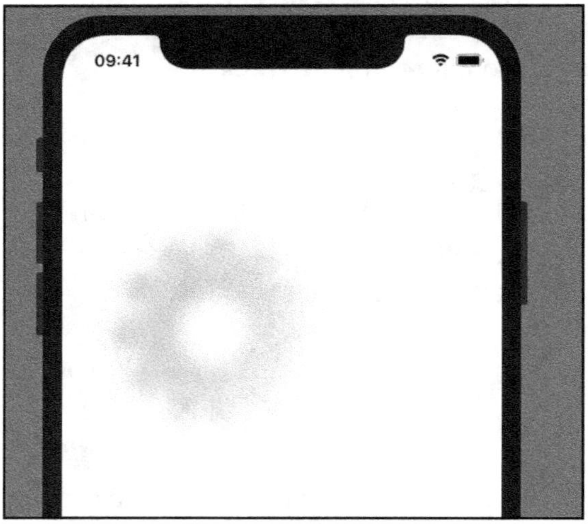

If you dragged upwards or sideways, the spinner animates back to its original place. In case you dragged it down and for more than `150` points, that kicks off the completion stage animation right away.

With that last addition of a gesture driven, interactive animation, your tour of SwiftUI is complete!

Key Points

- Shapes in SwiftUI adhere to the `View` protocol so you can build intriguing animations including transforming, fading in and out and morphing shapes just like you do for any other animation in your UI.
- You can add more state to your view types to be able to drive more complex, potentially multi-stage animations.
- Incorporating gesture input in your view state is a matter of adding few more modifiers to your views so building user interactive animations is a piece of cake.

Where to Go From Here?

So far in this book, you learned how to create basic and spring animations with SwiftUI. You've built quite complex visual effects that span over different stages, and that are also driven by the user. You're on a good path to building engaging user interfaces with SwiftUI.

If you'd like to learn Apple's SwiftUI framework in depth, the best resource to look into is the "SwiftUI by Tutorials" book on raywenderlich.com: SwiftUI by Tutorials (https://bit.ly/2L5wLLi).

As mentioned in this section's introduction, SwiftUI is only available on iOS13, and newer. If your business case demands compatibility with iOS12, or older, you will still need to use Auto Layout and Core Animation to build your app's UI and visual effects.

Well, good news everyone! The rest of this book is designed to turn you into a master of animations with those technologies — just turn the page over and get started!

Section II: View Animations

This section will introduce you to the animation API of UIKit. Though simple to use, the UIKit animation API provides you with lots of flexibility and power to handle most, if not all, of your animation requirements.

Animations are visible, onscreen effects that apply to all of the views, or visible objects, in your user interface. You can animate *any* object onscreen that ultimately inherits from `UIView`. This includes `UILabel`, `UIImageView`, `UIButton` and any custom classes you've created yourself.

Chapter 3: Getting Started With View Animations

In the previous chapters you got a taste of what creating animations with SwiftUI feels like but now it's time to go a level deeper into the system and get your hands dirty with some UIKit code.

In this chapter and accompanying project, you'll learn how to do the following:

- Set the stage for a cool animation.
- Create move and fade animations.
- Adjust the animation easing.
- Reverse and repeat animations.

There's a fair bit of material to get through, but I promise it will be a lot of fun. Are you up for the challenge?

Your First UIKit Animation

Open the starter project located in the Resources folder for this chapter. Build and run your project in Xcode; you'll see the login screen of a fictional airline app like so:

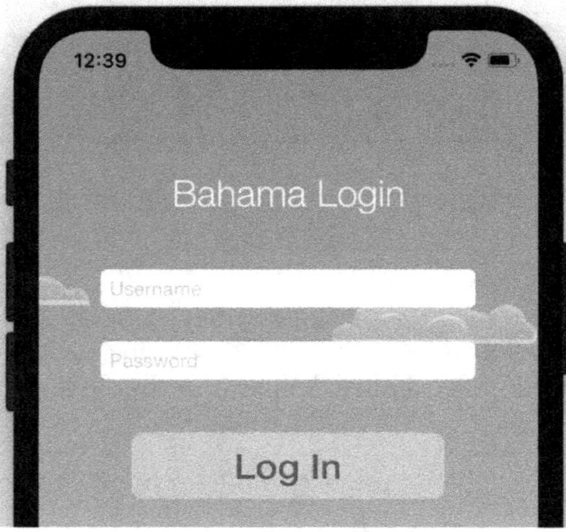

The app doesn't do much right now; it just shows a login form with a title, two text fields, and a big friendly button at the bottom.

There's also a nice background picture and four clouds. The clouds are already connected to outlet variables in the code named `cloud1` through `cloud4`.

Open **ViewController.swift** and have a look inside. At the top of the file you'll see all the connected outlets and class variables. Further down, there's a bit of code in `viewDidLoad()` which initializes some of the UI. The project is ready for you to jump in and shake things up a bit!

Enough with the introductions — you're undoubtedly ready to try out some code!

Your first task is to animate the form elements onto the screen when the user opens the application. Since the form is now visible when the app starts, you'll have to move it off of the screen just before your view controller makes an appearance.

Add the following code to `viewWillAppear()`:

```
heading.center.x  -= view.bounds.width
username.center.x -= view.bounds.width
password.center.x -= view.bounds.width
```

This places each of the form elements outside the visible bounds of the screen, like so:

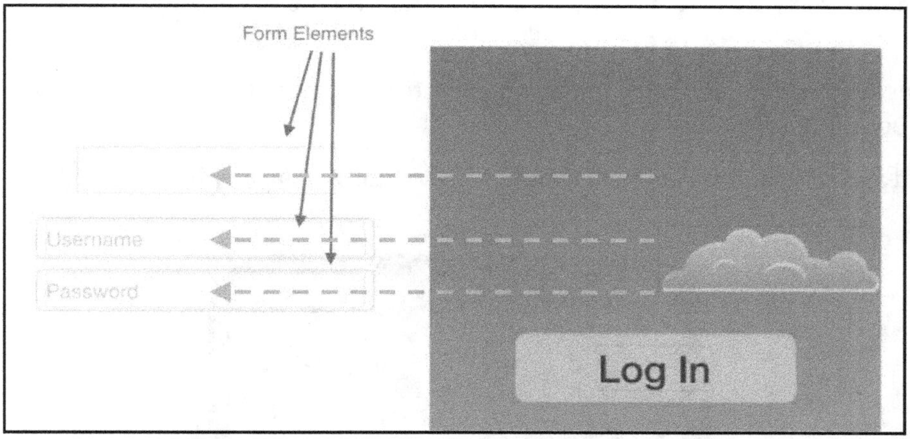

Since the code above executes before the view controller appears, it will look like those text fields were never there in the first place. Build and run your project to make sure your fields truly appear offscreen just as you had planned:

Perfect — now you can animate those form elements back to their original locations via a delightful animation.

Add the following code to the end of `viewDidAppear()`:

```
UIView.animate(withDuration: 0.5) {
  self.heading.center.x += self.view.bounds.width
}
```

To animate the title into view you call the `UIView` class method `animate(withDuration:animations:)`. The animation starts immediately and animates over half a second; you set the duration via the first method parameter in the code.

It's as easy as that; all the changes you make to the view in the animations closure will be animated by UIKit.

Build and run your project; you should see the title slide neatly into place like so:

That sets the stage for you to animate in the rest of the form elements.

Since `animate(withDuration:animations:)` is a class method, you aren't limited to animating just one specific view; in fact you can animate as many views as you want in your animations closure.

Add the following line to the animations closure:

```
self.username.center.x += self.view.bounds.width
```

Build and run your project again; watch as the username field slides into place:

Seeing both views animate together is quite cool, but you probably noticed that animating the two views over the same distance and with the same duration looks a bit stiff. Only kill-bots move with such absolute synchronization!

Wouldn't it be cool if each of the elements moved independently of the others, possibly with a little bit of delay in between the animations?

First **remove** the line you just added that animates `username`:

```
self.username.center.x += self.view.bounds.width
```

Then add the following code to the bottom of `viewDidAppear()`:

```
UIView.animate(withDuration: 0.5, delay: 0.3, options: [],
  animations: {
    self.username.center.x += self.view.bounds.width
  },
  completion: nil
)
```

The class method you use this time looks familiar, but it has a few more parameters to let you customize your animation:

- `withDuration`: The duration of the animation.
- `delay`: The amount of seconds UIKit will wait before it starts the animation.
- `options`: Lets you customize a number of aspects about your animation. You'll learn more about this parameter later on, but for now you can pass an empty array `[]` to mean "no special options".
- `animations`: The closure expression to provide your animations.
- `completion`: A code closure to execute when the animation completes. This parameter often comes in handy when you want to perform some final cleanup tasks or chain animations one after the other.

In the code you added above you set `delay` to 0.3 to make the animation start just a hair later than the title animation.

Build and run your project; how does the combined animation look now?

Ah — that looks much better. Now all you need to do is animate in the password field.

Add the following code to the bottom of `viewDidAppear()`:

```
UIView.animate(withDuration: 0.5, delay: 0.4, options: [],
  animations: {
    self.password.center.x += self.view.bounds.width
  },
  completion: nil
)
```

Here you've mostly mimicked the animation of the username field, just with a slightly longer delay.

Build and run your project again to see the complete animation sequence:

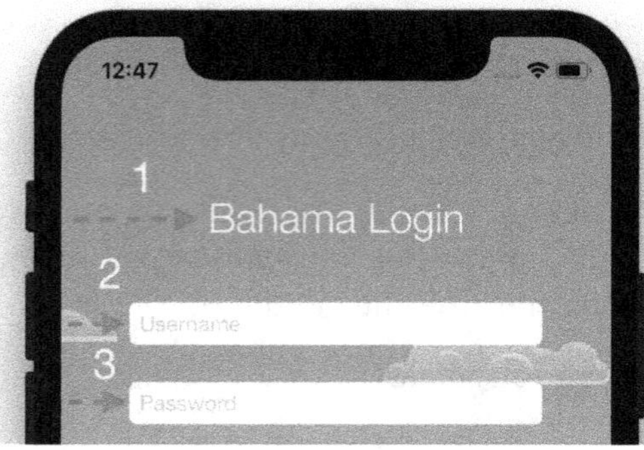

That's all you need to do to animate views across the screen with a UIKit animation!

That's just the start of it — you'll be learning a few more awesome animation techniques in the remainder of this chapter!

Animatable Properties

Now that you've seen how easy animations can be, you're probably keen to learn how else you can animate your views.

This section will give you an overview of the animatable properties of a `UIView`, and then guide you through exploring these animations in your project.

Not all view properties can be animated, but all view animations, from the simplest to the most complex, can be built by animating the subset of properties on a view that *do* lend themselves to animation, as outlined in the next section.

Position and Size

You can animate a view's position and frame in order to make it grow, shrink, or move around as you did in the previous section. Here are the properties you can use to modify a view's position and size:

- **bounds**: Animate this property to reposition the view's content within the view's frame.
- **frame**: Animate this property to move and/or scale the view.
- **center**: Animate this property when you want to move the view to a new location on screen.

Don't forget that in Swift, several **UIKit** properties such as `size` and `center` are mutable . This means you can move a view vertically by changing `center.y` or you can shrink a view by decreasing `frame.size.width`.

Appearance

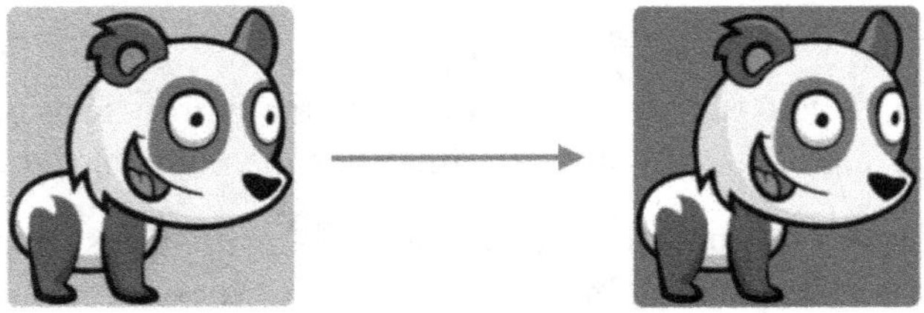

You can change the appearance of the view's content by either tinting its background or making the view fully or semi-transparent.

- **backgroundColor**: Change this property of a view to have UIKit gradually change the background color over time.
- **alpha**: Change this property to create fade-in and fade-out effects.

Transformation

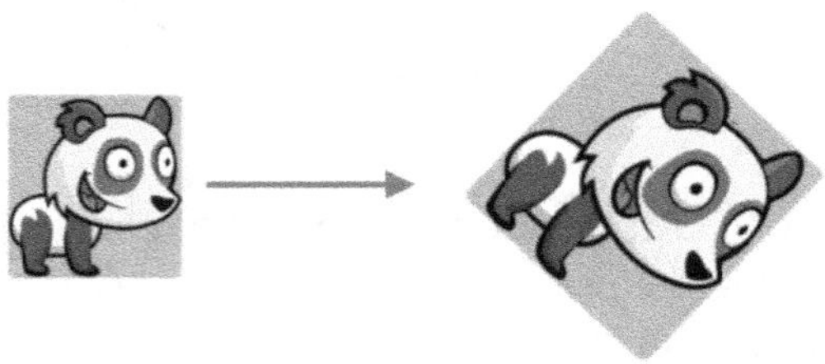

Transforms modify views in much the same way as above, since you can also adjust size and position.

- **transform**: Modify this property within an animation block to animate the rotation, scale, and/or position of a view.

These are affine transformations under the hood, which are much more powerful and allow you to describe the scale factor or rotation angle rather than needing to provide a specific bounds or center point.

These look like pretty basic building blocks, but you'll be surprised at the complex animation effects you're about to encounter!

Animation Options

Looking back to your animation code, you were always passing `[]` in to the options parameter. `options` lets you customize how UIKit creates your animation. You've only adjusted the duration and delay of your animations, but you can have a lot more control over your animation parameters than just that.

Below is a list of options declared in the `UIView.AnimationOptions` set type that you can combine in different ways for use in your animations.

Repeating

You'll first take a look at the following two animation options:

- `.repeat`: Include this option to makes your animation loop forever.
- `.autoreverse`: Include this option only in conjunction with `.repeat`; this option repeatedly plays your animation forward, then in reverse.

Modify the code that animates the password field `viewDidAppear()` to use the `.repeat` option as follows:

```
UIView.animate(withDuration: 0.5, delay: 0.4,
  options: .repeat,
  animations: {
    self.password.center.x += self.view.bounds.width
  },
  completion: nil
)
```

Build and run your project to see the effect of your change:

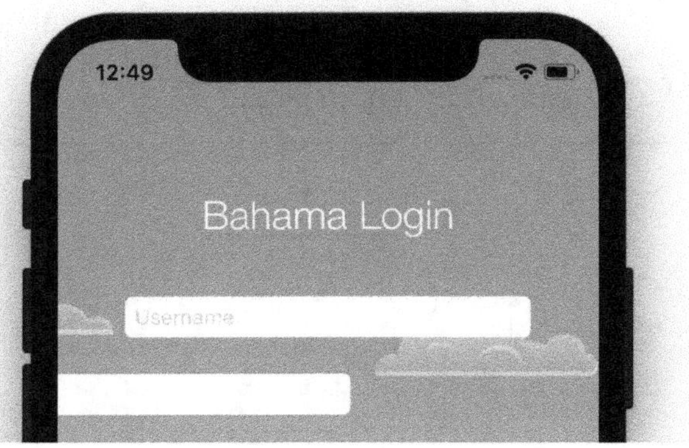

The form title and username field fly in and settle down in the center of the screen, but the password field keeps animating forever from its position offscreen.

Modify the same code you changed above to use both `.repeat` and `.autoreverse` in the `options` parameter as follows:

```
UIView.animate(withDuration: 0.5, delay: 0.4,
  options: [.repeat, .autoreverse],
  animations: {
    self.password.center.x += self.view.bounds.width
  },
  completion: nil
)
```

Note how if you want to enable more than one option you need to use the set syntax and list all options separated with a comma and enclose the list in square brackets.

> **Note**: If you only need a single option, Swift allows you to omit the square brackets as a convenience. However, you can still include them in case you add more options in the future. That means `[]` for no options, `[.repeat]` for a single option, and `[.repeat, .autorepeat]` for multiple options.

Build and run your project again; this time the password field just can't make up its mind about staying on the screen!

Animation Easing

In real life things don't just suddenly start or stop moving. Physical objects like cars or trains slowly accelerate until they reach their target speed, and unless they hit a brick wall, they gradually slow down until they come to a complete stop at their final destination.

The image below illustrates this concept in detail:

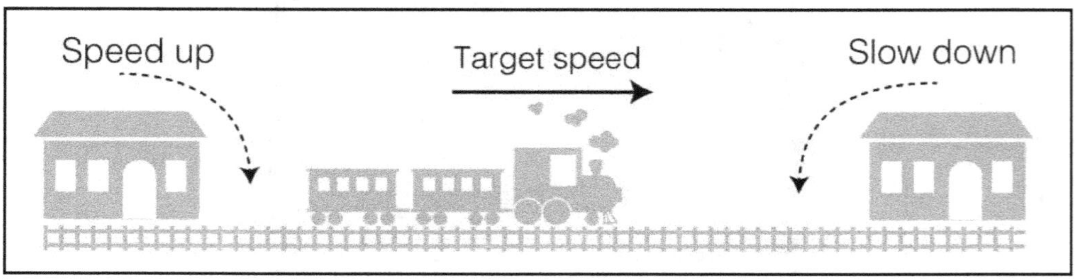

To make your animations look more realistic, you can apply the same effect of building momentum at the beginning and slowing down before the end, known in general terms as **ease-in** and **ease-out**. You can choose from four different easing options:

- `.curveLinear`: This option applies no acceleration or deceleration to the animation. The only time in this book you'll use this option is in the final challenge of Chapter 5: "Transitions".
- `.curveEaseIn`: This option applies acceleration to the start of your animation.
- `.curveEaseOut`: This option applies deceleration to the end of your animation.
- `.curveEaseInOut`: This option applies acceleration to the start of your animation *and* applies deceleration to the end of your animation.

To better understand how these options add visual impact to your animation, you'll try a few of the options in your project.

Modify the animation code for your password field once again with a new option as follows:

```
UIView.animate(withDuration: 0.5, delay: 0.4,
  options: [.repeat, .autoreverse, .curveEaseOut],
  animations: {
    self.password.center.x += self.view.bounds.width
  },
  completion: nil
)
```

Build and run your project; notice how smoothly the field decelerates until it reaches its rightmost position, before returning to the left side of the screen:

This looks much more natural since that's how you expect things to move in the real world.

Now, try the opposite. Ease-in the animation when the field is still outside of the screen by modifying the same code as above to change the `.curveEaseOut` option to `.curveEaseIn` as follows:

```
UIView.animate(withDuration: 0.5, delay: 0.4,
  options: [.repeat, .autoreverse, .curveEaseIn],
  animations: {
    self.password.center.x += self.view.bounds.width
  },
  completion: nil
)
```

Build and run your project; observe how the field jumps back from its rightmost position with robotic vigor. This looks unnatural and isn't as visually pleasing as the previous animation.

Finally give `.curveEaseInOut` a try. It combines the two options you already know into one very natural looking easing. `.curveEaseInOut` is also the default easing function UIKit applies to your animations.

You've seen how the various animation options affect your project and how to make movements look smooth and natural.

Before you move on, change the options on the piece of code you've been playing with back to `[]`:

```
UIView.animate(withDuration: 0.5, delay: 0.4, options: [],
  animations: {
    self.password.center.x += self.view.bounds.width
  },
  completion: nil
)
```

Now that you know how basic animations work, you're ready to tackle some more dazzling animation techniques.

Key Points

- You create an animation by using one of the variations of `UIView.animate(...)`.
- Within the `animations` closure you set the **final** state of the desired animation and UIKit will automatically create a smooth animation between the current and final states.
- You customize your animations by providing `UIView.AnimationOptions` values to set easing, repeating, and autoreversing properties.

Challenges

If this chapter is the first time you've animated a view in iOS, your head might be spinning a little. Don't worry, though, because no matter your initial skillset, you'll be well on your way to animation mastery in just a few chapters. For now though, there's one very simple challenge waiting for you where you'll create an animation of your very own.

Challenge 1: Fade in the Clouds

In **ViewController** you have four outlets: `cloud1`, `cloud2`, `cloud3`, and `cloud4`. Your task is to fade those in when the application starts.

You can pretty much decide on the exact form your solution will take, but here's a list of the basic steps you'll need to follow:

1. Set the `alpha` property to `0.0` for all four cloud views in `viewWillAppear()`.
2. In `viewDidAppear()`, make four separate calls to `animate(withDuration:delay:options:animations:completion:)`. You'll get a nice-looking effect if you use a duration of `0.5` for all four animations and delays of `0.5`, `0.7`, `0.9`, and `1.1` respectively.
3. In each `animations` closure change the `alpha` of the respective cloud view to `1.0`. This will fade the cloud in.

When you run the project you should see a nice transition effect that animates the clouds, one after another:

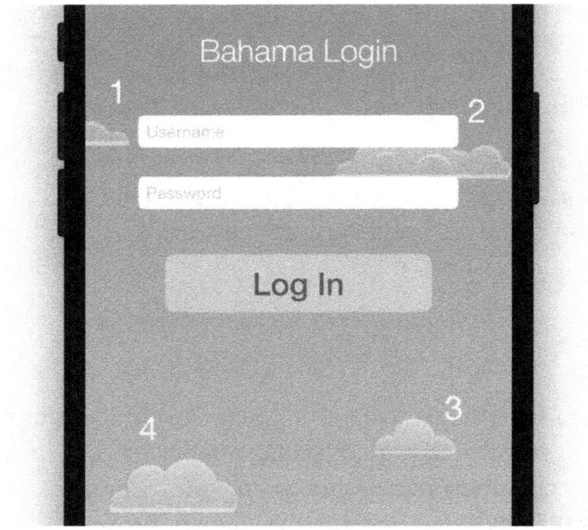

All views on the screen should animate nicely. Well almost...the Log In button isn't animating! Don't worry — you'll fix that in the next chapter.

Chapter 4: Springs

Springs in UIKit provide more polish and aesthetics to view animations. Apple themselves use springs for a wide number of system animations as well as in their own applications. Springs are usually responsible for any bouncing views you see on screen, but in fiddling with the spring animation parameters you will see that this API allows you to create a variety of pleasing animations.

So far, your animations have been fluid movements in a single direction. When you animated a view's position, it was a straightforward movement from point A to point B, like so:

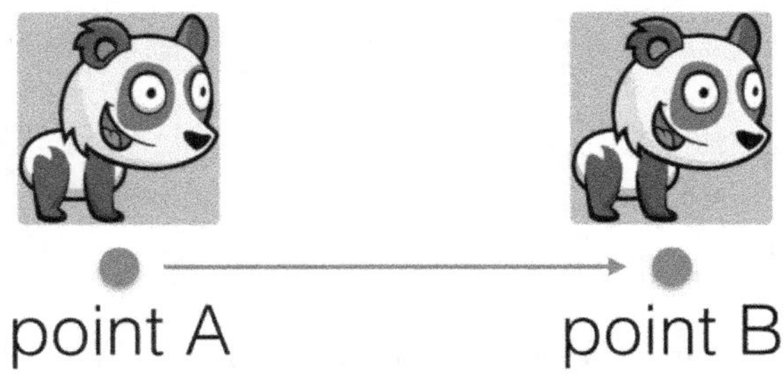

In this chapter you'll learn how to create more complex animations, which move views as if they were attached to a spring, as demonstrated below:

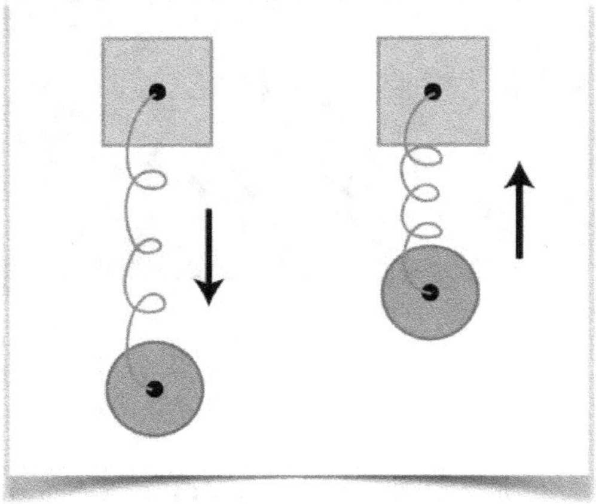

If you took the basic animation from point A to point B and added a bit of springiness to it, the motion of the animation would follow a path indicated by the red arrows below:

The view heads from point A to point B, but overshoots point B by a small amount. The view then heads back to point B and overshoots by a little less this time. This back-and-forth oscillation repeats until the view has come to rest at point B.

It's a nice effect; it adds a snappy, real-world feel to your animations. This chapter will show you how to use this effect to add a little bit of playfulness to your UI.

Spring Animations

You'll continue on with the project from the previous chapter; if you didn't complete the exercises in Chapter 3 (including the challenge at the end of the chapter), then grab the starter project from the Resources folder for Chapter 4 and start from there.

Build and run your project; you should see the views on screen (except the Log In button) animate as soon as the app opens like so:

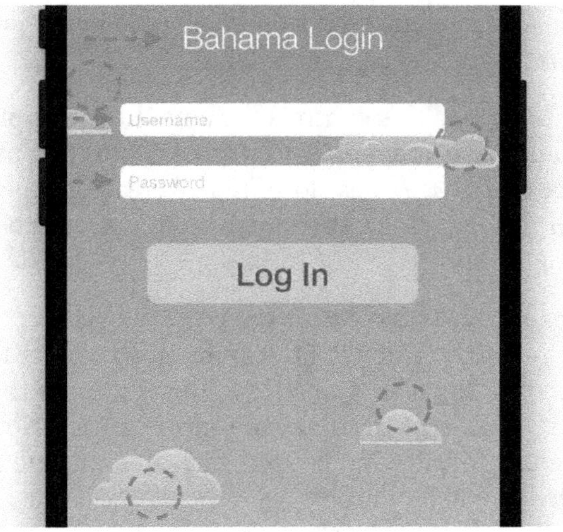

Your job is to take care of the last non-animated element on this screen: the Log In button.

Open **ViewController.swift** and add the following code to the bottom of `viewWillAppear()`:

```
loginButton.center.y += 30.0
loginButton.alpha = 0.0
```

Just as you did in the previous chapter, you set the start position of the button a bit lower on the y-axis and set its alpha value to zero so that it will start out as invisible.

Now move to `viewDidAppear()` and add the following code:

```
UIView.animate(withDuration: 0.5, delay: 0.5,
usingSpringWithDamping: 0.5, initialSpringVelocity: 0.0,
options: [], animations: {
  self.loginButton.center.y -= 30.0
  self.loginButton.alpha = 1.0
}, completion: nil)
```

There are two key points in this piece of code.

First, you've animated two different properties at the same time! That was easier than you thought, right?

Second, you used a new animation method for the first time: `animate(withDuration:delay:usingSpringWithDamping:initialSpringVelocity:options:animations:completion:)`. Saying that method name too quickly just might injure your tongue!

The previous method looks much like the ones you used in the previous chapter of the book, but it sports a couple of new parameters:

- `usingSpringWithDamping`: This controls the amount of damping, or reduction, applied to the animation as it approaches its final state. This parameter accepts values between `0.0` and `1.0`. Values closer to `0.0` create a bouncier animation, while values closer to `1.0` create a stiff-looking effect. You can think of this value as the "stiffness" of the spring.
- `initialSpringVelocity`: This controls the initial velocity of the animation. A value of `1.0` sets the initial velocity of the animation to cover the total distance in the span of one second. Bigger and smaller values will cause the animation to have more or less velocity, and will affect how the spring settles. Note however that the initial velocity is soon amended by the spring calculation, and the animation will always finish by the end of `duration`.

Build and run your project; check out how the button moves now:

Since your animation has an initial velocity of `0.0` and a neutral damping of `0.5`, the animation doesn't look very eye-catching.

You should be able to dress up this animation a little by trying some different values for the velocity and damping.

Change the duration to `3.0` and the damping to `0.1`. This is just to let you observe the effect of your changes in slow motion instead of at normal speed.

Build and run your project again; note how the opacity of the button changes as it moves up. This is because the spring behavior affects **all** properties you animate; in your case, this affects *both* the vertical position of the button *and* its alpha value.

Now set `initialSpringVelocity` to `1.0` and build and run your project again:

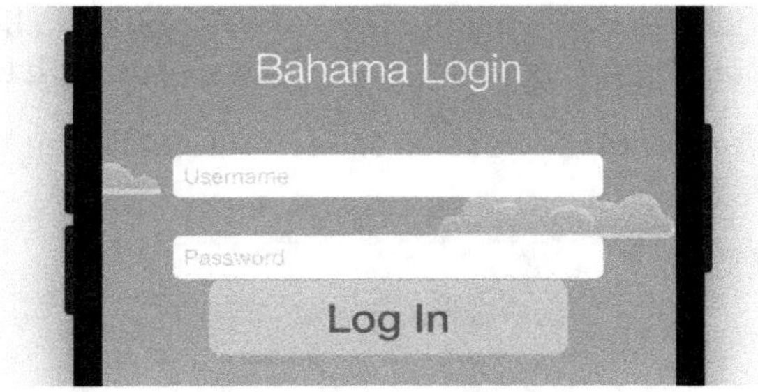

You'll notice that the button bounces a bit more when it animates and moves beyond the password field; this is because it has more momentum at the beginning of its movement.

Play around with some different values for damping and velocity until you understand how changes in these parameters affect the look and feel of your animation.

When you're done, set the values for the velocity and damping back to their original values, like so:

```
UIView.animate(withDuration: 0.5, delay: 0.5,
usingSpringWithDamping: 0.5, initialSpringVelocity: 0.0,
options: [], animations: {
  self.loginButton.center.y -= 30.0
  self.loginButton.alpha = 1.0
}, completion: nil)
```

Animating User Interactions

You don't have to limit your spring animations to the initial placement of your views. In fact, animating views in response to user input can really make your interface come alive. In this section you'll animate the Log In button in response to a tap.

Add the following code to `login()`:

```
UIView.animate(withDuration: 1.5, delay: 0.0,
usingSpringWithDamping: 0.2, initialSpringVelocity: 0.0,
options: [], animations: {
  self.loginButton.bounds.size.width += 80.0
}, completion: nil)
```

The above animation increases the button's width by `80` points over a duration of a second and a half. The button will bounce around a fair bit as well since the damping is set to just `0.2`. Increasing the bounds grows the frame on its left and right sides.

Build and run your project; tap the button to see your animation in action:

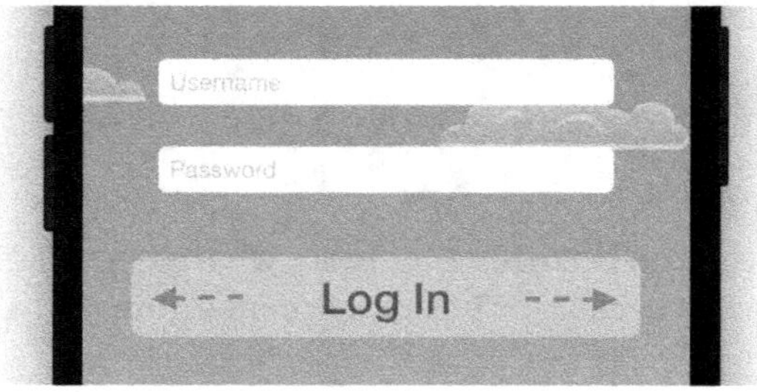

The button grows and bounces in a blobby fashion when you tap it; it's a neat way to provide tap feedback to the user.

Next you'll combine this animation with a few more spring movements to really bring the button to life.

Add the following code to the end of `login()`:

```
UIView.animate(withDuration: 0.33, delay: 0.0,
usingSpringWithDamping: 0.7, initialSpringVelocity: 0.0,
options: [], animations: {
  self.loginButton.center.y += 60.0
}, completion: nil)
```

The above animation moves the button `60` points down when tapped. Notice that the duration for this animation is much shorter than the one that animates the button width.

This is intentional, since the desired effect is to make the button jump away from the tap and bounce a bit once it's settled into its new vertical position.

Build and run your project; tap the button and see how it moves in response to your touch this time:

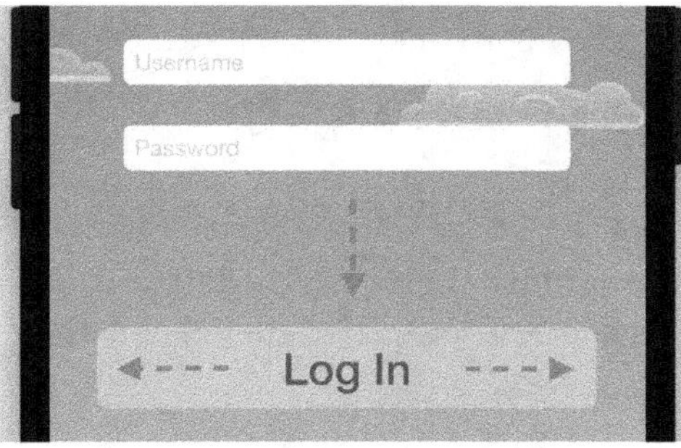

That looks really nice — but you're quickly becoming an animation master and you *know* that you can do even better!

Another great way of providing user feedback is through color change. You'll tint the button as it moves by animating the `backgroundColor` property of the button.

Add the following code to the last animation you added, inside the `animations` closure expression:

```
self.loginButton.backgroundColor =
UIColor(red: 0.85, green: 0.83, blue: 0.45, alpha: 1.0)
```

Build and run your project again; you'll see the button move, change shape *and* change color, all at the same time:

There's one last bit of feedback to add here: an activity indicator. The Log In button is supposed to start a user authentication activity over the network, so it would be nice to show an activity indicator to the user to let them know that there's an action in progress.

Scroll up and have a look at `viewDidLoad()` and find the existing code for the progress indicator. `spinner` contains an instance of `UIActivityIndicatorView` that's all ready for your use. You haven't seen it on the screen yet because its alpha is set to `0.0`.

Head back to `login()` and add the following code to the last `animations` closure expression:

```
self.spinner.center = CGPoint(
  x: 40.0,
  y: self.loginButton.frame.size.height/2
)
self.spinner.alpha = 1.0
```

This animation moves the spinner slightly to the left and fades it in. This should be enough to attract the user's attention and let them know their request is being processed.

Build and run your project; check out the final version of your spiffy new animation:

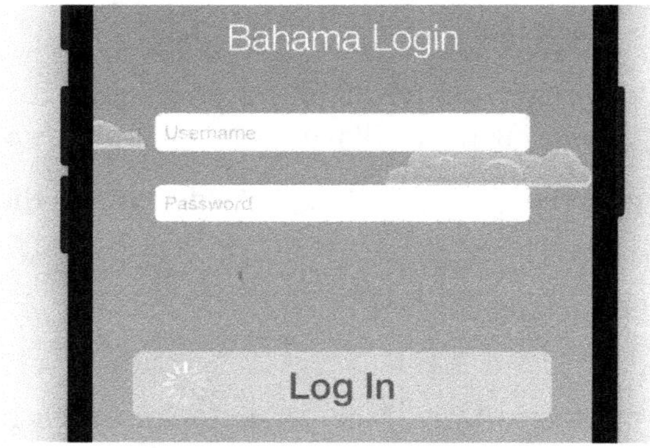

Take a moment to reflect on what you've accomplished here. You've added three simultaneous animations to the button view to make it grow in width, move down the screen, and change color.

You've also animated and faded in an activity spinner, which is itself a subview of the button view.

All animations are combined automatically by UIKit and run flawlessly to create one fluid visual effect.

There's no need for you to worry about the implementation details of your animations; you can instead focus on designing great animations and wowing your users thanks to UIKit!

Key Points

- You can create visual feedback for user interaction by creating animations in response to the user's actions.
- You create spring animations in a very similar manner to "standard" animations — the additional parameters are the spring damping and initial velocity.
- Combining various animations (with springs or without) creates rich visual experiences.

Challenges

Challenge 1: Convert Text Field Animations to Spring-animations

The spring animation APIs in UIKit are quite similar in usage to their standard animation counterparts. Thus it shouldn't be much of a problem for you to convert the animations you have running on the `username` and `password` fields to spring animations.

To complete this challenge you will need to do the following:

1. Add the `usingSpringWithDamping` and `initialSpringVelocity` parameters to the animation for the username field. Use `0.0` for the spring initial velocity. Try out `0.2`, `0.6` and `0.9` for the spring damping and choose the value that looks most like a pleasant and subtle spring effect to you.
2. Repeat the same for the `password` field animation using the damping and velocity of your choice.

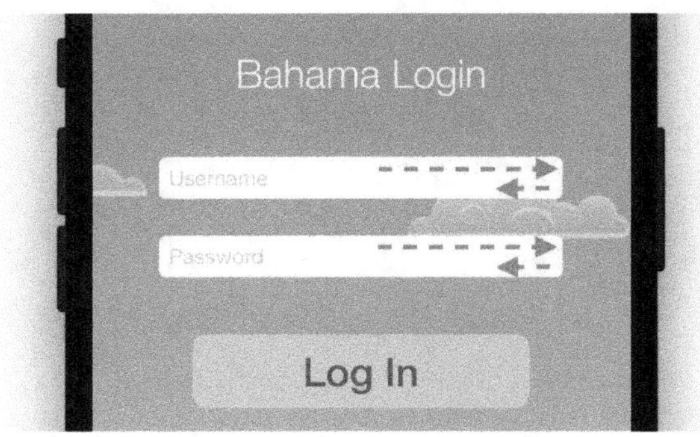

By this point in the book you've gained a solid foundation of spring animation. The more you play with this type of animation, and the more you experiment with different combinations of damping and velocity, the more comfortable you'll be designing the perfect spring animation for the views in your own apps.

Are you ready to *spring* into the next chapter? In Chapter 5, you'll learn about the next type of animation in UIKit: **transitions**.

Chapter 5: Transitions

Transitions are predefined animations you can apply to views. These predefined animations don't attempt to interpolate between the start and end states of your view (like the animations you created in the previous two chapters). Instead, you'll design the animations with the transitions API so that the various changes in your UI appear natural.

Example Transitions

To better understand when you'd use transitions, this section walks you through the various animation scenarios where you could make use of transition animations.

Adding a New View

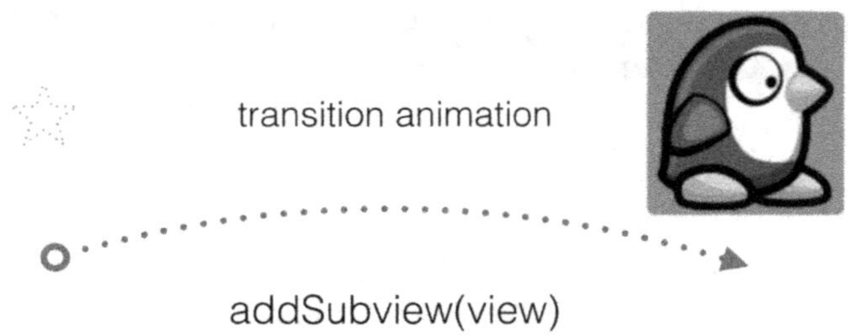

To animate the addition of a new view on the screen, you call a method similar to the ones you used in the previous chapters. The difference this time is that you'll choose one of the predefined transition effects and animate what's known as an **animation container view**.

The transition animates the container view, and any new views you add to it as subviews appear while the animation runs.

To better explain how you'd animate container views and when you'd execute the transition between subviews, read the following code snippet (you don't need to type this in anywhere):

```
var animationContainerView: UIView!

override func viewDidLoad() {
  super.viewDidLoad()
  //set up the animation container
  animationContainerView = UIView(frame: view.bounds)
  animationContainerView.frame = view.bounds
  view.addSubview(animationContainerView)
}

override func viewDidAppear(_ animated: Bool) {
  super.viewDidAppear(animated)

  //create new view
  let newView = UIImageView(image: UIImage(named: "banner"))
  newView.center = animationContainerView.center

  //add the new view via transition
```

```
    UIView.transition(with: animationContainerView,
      duration: 0.33,
      options: [.curveEaseOut, .transitionFlipFromBottom],
      animations: {
        self.animationContainerView.addSubview(newView)
      },
      completion: nil
    )
  }
```

In this hypothetical situation, you create a new view named `animationContainerView` in `viewDidLoad()` of your view controller. You then position and add this container to the view.

Later, when you want to create an animated transition, you create a new view to animate; here it's named `newView`.

To create the transition, you call `transition(with:duration:options:animations:completion:)`. This is almost identical to the standard **UIView** animation method, but in this case you supply an extra parameter `view`, which serves as the container view for the transition animation.

There's a new animation option here, `.transitionFlipFromBottom`, which you haven't seen yet. This is one of the predefined transitions discussed in the introduction of this chapter. `.transitionFlipFromBottom` flips the view over with the bottom edge of the view serving as the "hinge" around which the view flips.

Finally, you add a subview to your animation container within your animations block, which causes the subview to appear during the transition.

The full list of predefined transition animation options are as follows:

- `.transitionFlipFromLeft`
- `.transitionFlipFromRight`
- `.transitionCurlUp`
- `.transitionCurlDown`
- `.transitionCrossDissolve`
- `.transitionFlipFromTop`
- `.transitionFlipFromBottom`

Removing a View

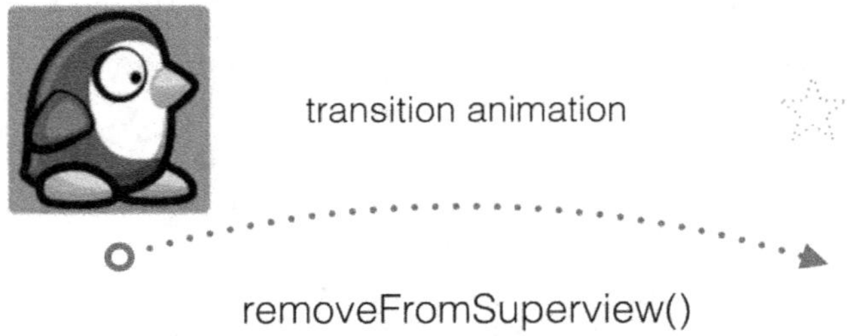

Removing a subview from the screen with a transition animation works much like adding a subview. To do this with a transition animation, you simply call `removeFromSuperview()` inside the animation closure expression like so (again, this is an example, you don't need to enter this code):

```
//remove the view via transition

UIView.transition(with: animationContainerView, duration: 0.33,
  options: [.curveEaseOut, .transitionFlipFromBottom],
  animations: {
    someView.removeFromSuperview()
  },
  completion: nil
)
```

The wrapper transition will perform the flip animation and `someView` will disappear at the end of it all.

Hiding/Showing a View

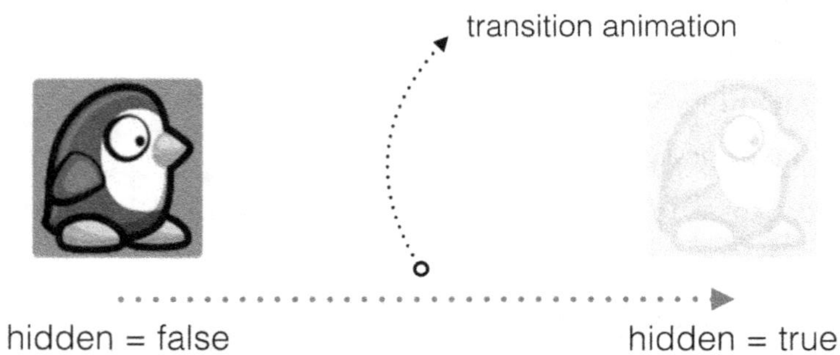

So far in this chapter, you've learned only about transitions that alter the view hierarchy. That's why you needed a container view for the transitions — this puts the hierarchy change in context.

In contrast, you don't need to worry about setting up a container view to hide and show views. In this case, the transition uses the view *itself* as the animation container.

Consider the following code to hide a subview using a transition:

```
//hide the view via transition

UIView.transition(with: someView, duration: 0.33,
  options: [.curveEaseOut, .transitionFlipFromBottom],
  animations: {
    someView.alpha = 0
  },
  completion: { _ in
    someView.isHidden = true
  }
)
```

Here you pass in the view you intend to show or hide as the first argument to `transition(with:duration:options:animations:completion:)`. All you do after that is set the `alpha` property of your view in the animations block and *voilà*, the transition animation kicks off.

Replacing a View With Another View

Replacing one view with another view is also an easy process. You simply pass in the existing view as the first argument and set the `toView:` parameter as the view you wish to replace it with as shown below:

```
//replace via transition
UIView.transition(from: oldView, to: newView, duration: 0.33,
  options: .transitionFlipFromTop, completion: nil)
```

It's becoming quite apparent how much of the heavy lifting UIKit does for you! In the remainder of this chapter, you'll work on showing and hiding UI elements via transitions and learn some new animation skills you can bring into your own projects!

Mixing in Transitions

You'll continue to work on the Bahama Air login screen project in this chapter; you've already created a number of compelling animations to the views on this screen to add a bit of pizzazz to the login form and to make the button react to being tapped.

Next, you're going to simulate a bit of user authentication and animate several different progress messages. Once the user taps the Log In button, you'll show them messages including "Connecting...", "Authorizing..." and "Failed."

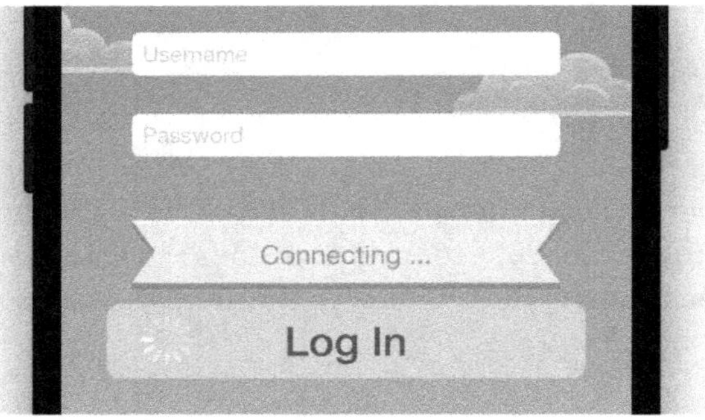

If you haven't worked through the previous chapters, you can begin with the starter project in the Resources folder for this chapter. If you've followed the examples in the last few chapters in your own project, great job! You can simply continue working with your existing project.

Open **ViewController.swift** and look at `viewDidLoad()`. Part of this method adds a hidden image view stored in the class variable status. The code then creates a text label and adds it as a sub-view to `status`.

You'll use `status` to show the progress messages to the user. The messages are sourced from the messages array, which is another class variable included in the starter project.

Add the following method to `ViewController`:

```
func showMessage(index: Int) {
  label.text = messages[index]

  UIView.transition(with: status, duration: 0.33,
    options: [.curveEaseOut, .transitionCurlDown],
    animations: {
      self.status.isHidden = false
    },
```

```
      completion: { _ in
        //transition completion
      }
    )
  }
```

This method takes one parameter called `index`, which you use to set the value of `label` to the contents of messages based on `index`.

Next you call `transition(with:duration:options:animations: completion:)` to animate the view. To show the banner as it transitions you set `isHidden` to `false` within the animations block.

There's another new animation option above: `.transitionCurlDown`. This transition animates the view like a sheet of paper being flipped down on a legal pad and looks like the following:

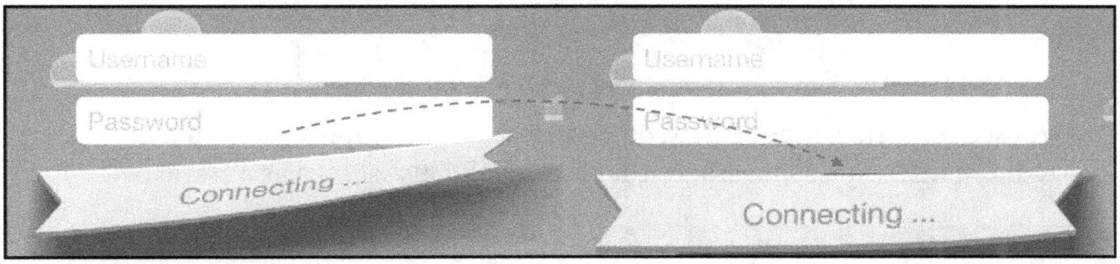

It's time to exercise your new `showMessage(index:)` method. Find the following block of code in `login()`:

```
animations: {
  self.loginButton.bounds.size.width += 80.0
}, completion: nil)
```

This is your existing animations block that makes the login button bounce when the user taps it. You'll add something new — a completion closure — to this animation that calls `showMessage(index:)`.

Replace the completion's `nil` argument value with the following closure expression:

```
completion: { _ in
  self.showMessage(index: 0)
}
```

The closure takes one `Bool` parameter, which tells you whether the animation finished successfully or was cancelled before it ran to completion.

> **Note**: The completion closure above has a single parameter for `completed`. Because you don't care whether it finished or not, Swift allows you to skip binding the parameter by putting "_" in its place.

Inside the closure you simply call `showMessage` with index `0` to show the very first message from the messages array.

Build and run your project; tap the Log In button and you'll see the status banner appear with your first progress message.

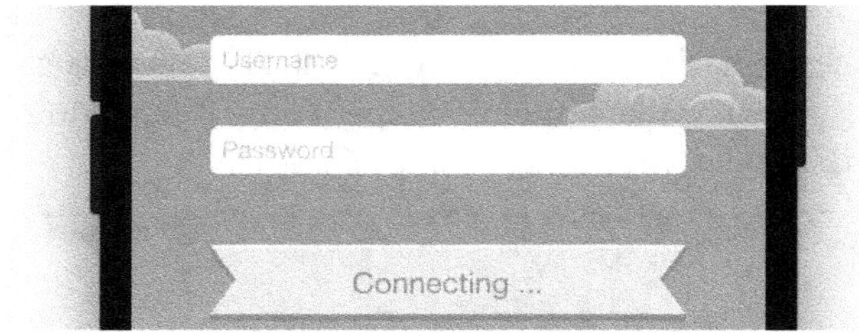

Did you see how the banner curled down like a sheet of paper? That's a really nice way to bring attention to messages that are usually just shown as a static text label.

> **Note**: Some of your animations seem to run really quickly, don't they? Sometimes it's tricky to ensure the animation happens at just the right location, and in the correct sequence. Or maybe you just want things to happen slower so you can appreciate the effect!
>
> To slow down all animations in your app without changing your code, select **Debug/Toggle Slow Animations** in **Frontmost App** from the iPhone Simulator menu. Now tap the Login button in your app and enjoy the animations and transitions in vivid slow motion!

For the next animation, you'll first need to save the banner's initial position so you can place the next banner in just the right spot.

Add the following code to the end of `viewDidLoad()` to save the banner's initial position to the property called `statusPosition`:

```
statusPosition = status.center
```

Now you can begin to devise a mixture of view animations and transitions.

Add the following method to remove the status message from the screen via a standard animation:

```
func removeMessage(index: Int) {
  UIView.animate(withDuration: 0.33, delay: 0.0, options: [],
    animations: {
      self.status.center.x += self.view.frame.size.width
    },
    completion: { _ in
      self.status.isHidden = true
      self.status.center = self.statusPosition

      self.showMessage(index: index + 1)
    }
  )
}
```

In the code above you use your old friend `animate(withDuration:delay:options:animations:completion:)` to move `status` just outside of the visible area of the screen.

When the animation completes in the `completion` closure, you move status back to its original position and hide it. Finally you call `showMessage` again, but this time you pass the index of the next message to show.

Combining standard animations with transitions is quite easy: you simply call the appropriate API and UIKit calls the corresponding Core Animation bits in the background.

Now you need to complete the chain of calls between `showMessage` and `removeMessage` to mimic a real authentication process.

Find `showMessage(index:)` and replace the comment `//transition completion` with the following code:

```
delay(2.0) {
  if index < self.messages.count - 1 {
    self.removeMessage(index: index)
  } else {
    //reset form
  }
}
```

Once the transition completes, you wait for `2.0` seconds and check if there are any remaining messages. If so, remove the current message via `removeMessage(index:)`. You then call `showMessage(index:)` in the completion block of `removeMessage(index:)` to display the next message in sequence.

> **Note**: `delay(_:completion:)` is a convenience function that runs a block of code after an elapsed delay; it's defined at the top of **ViewController.swift**. Here you're using it to simulate the usual network access delay.

Build and run your project once more; enjoy the resulting animation sequence, which updates the authentication progress messages like so:

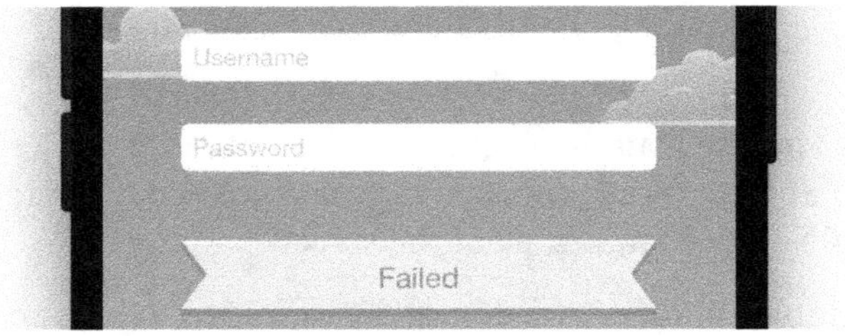

Transitions are a small but important subset of animation knowledge to keep in your figurative toolbox, since they're the only way to create 3D-styled animations in UIKit.

If you're looking forward to learning more elaborate 3D effects, you'll have the opportunity to do that in Section VI, "3D Animations", which discusses Core Animation and 3D layer transformations in detail.

Before you move on to the next section, give the challenges in this chapter a try. Since you've learned so much about animation in the last three chapters, one challenge isn't enough — I've given you three!

These challenges give you the chance to wrap up development on your Bahama Air login screen — and also to take on your first über haxx0r challenge. Woot!

Key Points

- Apple provides a set of predefined animations called transitions you can use to handle special changes in your app's UI state.
- Transitions are targeted towards adding, removing, and replacing views in the view hierarchy.
- When you are designing animations, you can enable **Debug ▸ Toggle Slow Animations** in the Simulator to be able to observe them in slow motion.

Challenges

Challenge 1: Pick Your Favorite Transition

So far you've seen only one of the built-in transition animations. Aren't you curious to see what the others look like?

In this challenge you can try out all the other available transition animations and use your favorite to animate the progress message banner.

Open `ViewController` and find the line in `showMessage(index:)` where you specify the transition animation `.transitionCurlDown`:

```
UIView.transitionWithView(status, duration: 0.33, options:
  [.curveEaseOut, .transitionCurlDown], animations: …
```

Replace `.transitionCurlDown` with any of the other transition animations available, then build and run your project to see how they look. Here's the list of available transitions:

```
.transitionFlipFromLeft
.transitionFlipFromRight
.transitionCurlUp
.transitionCurlDown
.transitionCrossDissolve
.transitionFlipFromTop
.transitionFlipFromBottom
```

Which one do you think works best with the other animations on this screen?

In case you don't have a favorite, try my favorite transition: `.transitionFlipFromBottom`. I think it fits really well with the banner graphic:

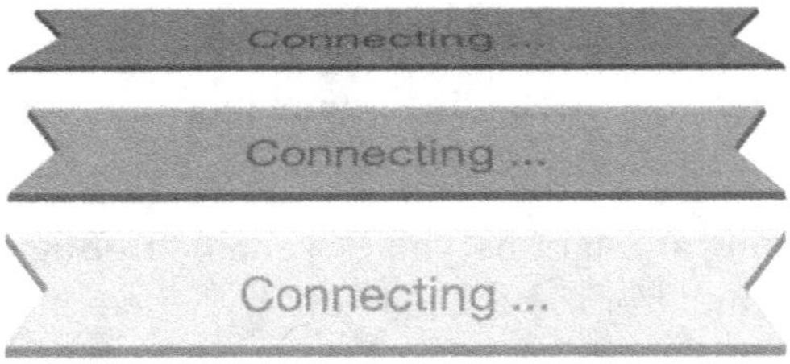

Challenge 2: Reset the Form to Its Initial State

For this challenge, you'll reset the form to its initial state by undoing all the animations that run once you tap the Log In button. That way, if the login fails, the user would see all of the animations happen again when they tap the Log In button a second time.

Here's a list of the general steps you'll need to complete this challenge:

1. Create a new empty method `resetForm()` and call it from your code where the placeholder comment `//reset form` lives.

2. In `resetForm()` use `transition(with:duration:options:animations:completion:)` to set the visibility of status to hidden and center to `self.statusPosition`. This should reset the banner to its initial state. Use a `0.2` seconds duration for that transition.

3. It would be nice if the transition that hides your banner uses the exact opposite animation of the one that shows the banner. For example, if you show the banner via `.transitionCurlDown`, then use `.transitionCurlUp` to hide it. The reverse of `.transitionFlipFromBottom` would be `.transitionFlipFromTop` ...and so forth.

4. Next, add a call to `animate(withDuration:delay:options:animations:completion:)` in `resetForm()`. Make the following adjustments inside the animations closure block:

- Move `self.spinner` — the activity indicator inside the Log In button — to its original position of `(-20.0, 16.0)`.

- Set the alpha property of `self.spinner` to `0.0` to hide it.

- Tint the background color of the Log In button back to its original value: `UIColor(red: 0.63, green: 0.84, blue: 0.35, alpha: 1.0)`.
- Continue to reset all changes you made to the Log In button and decrease the `bounds.size.width` property by `80.0` points.
- Finally, move the button back up to its original spot under the password field and decrease `center.y` by `60.0` points.

If you precisely reversed all of the animations in the authentication process, the screen should animate as below once all authentication messages have displayed:

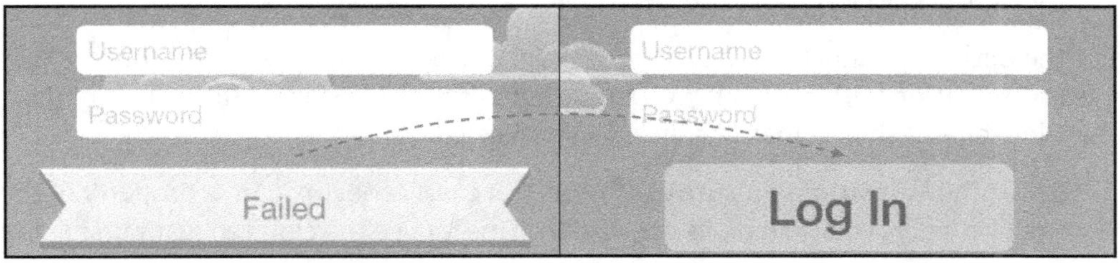

Well done! And now for this chapter's final challenge...

Challenge 3: Animate the Clouds in the Background

Wouldn't it be cool if those clouds in the background moved slowly across the screen and reappeared from the opposite side?

Yeah, it would totally be cool — and that's your challenge!

The four cloud image views are already wired to four outlets in `ViewController` so you're good to go. You can try to make the clouds move on your own, using your newfound knowledge of transition animations, or you can follow the recipe below:

1. Create a new method with signature `animateCloud(cloud: UIImageView)` and add your code inside that.
2. First, calculate the average cloud speed. Assume the cloud should cross the entire length of the screen in about `60.0` seconds. Call that constant `cloudSpeed` and set it to `60.0 / view.frame.size.width`.

3. Next, calculate the duration for the animation to move the cloud to the right side of the screen. Remember, the clouds don't start from the left edge of the screen, but from random spots instead. You can calculate the correct duration by taking the length of the path the cloud needs to follow and multiplying the result by the average speed: `(view.frame.size.width - cloud.frame.origin.x) * cloudSpeed`.

4. Then call `animate(withDuration:delay:options:animation:completion:)` with the duration you just calculated above. You'll need to create an instance of `TimeInterval` from it as the compiler won't have decided the correct type for you: `TimeInterval(duration)`.

For the options parameter use `.curveLinear`; this is one of the very few times you'll use an animation with no easing. Clouds are naturally quite far in the background, so their movement should look absolutely even-keeled.

5. Inside the animations closure expression set the `frame.origin.x` property of the cloud to `self.view.frame.size.width`. This moves the cloud to just outside the screen area.

6. Inside the completion closure block move the cloud to just outside the opposite edge of the screen from its current position. Don't forget to skip the closure parameter by using "_" as you did earlier in this chapter. To position the cloud properly set its `frame.origin.x` to `-cloud.frame.size.width`.

7. Still working in the completion closure, add a call to `animateCloud()` so that the cloud re-animates across the screen.

8. Finally, add the following code to the end of `viewDidAppear()` to start the animations for all four clouds:

```
animateCloud(cloud1)
animateCloud(cloud2)
animateCloud(cloud3)
animateCloud(cloud4)
```

This should make all four clouds traverse the screen slowly to create a nice, unobtrusive effect.

If you completed the challenges for this chapter, congratulations! They were tough!

The past few chapters had a lot of information to digest, but you took a stiff, static login form and turned it into an eye-catching and fun experience for the user:

It's time to take a short break from new material and put all your view animation knowledge to the test! In the next chapter, you'll use a wide assortment of the practical things you've learned to add some serious polish to the Bahama Air app.

Chapter 6: View Animations in Practice

Looking at the reference of available animation APIs, it's easy to fall into the trap of thinking view animations are limiting to fading in or out and moving views around the screen. In this chapter, you will work through three practical examples of combining different animations in order to create more complex, non-trivial visual effects.

Having said that, please note that this chapter is *optional*. If you would like to keep on learning about new APIs, feel free to skip to the next chapter — no hard feelings!

In this chapter you are going to add some cool animations to dress up a flight summary screen, like the one shown below:

There are a few new effects to be found in this chapter that build on the animation foundations you learned in the previous chapters:

1. **Crossfade animation:** An animation that blends one image into another.
2. **Cube transition animation:** A transition animation that creates a faux 3D transition effect.
3. **Fade and bounce transition:** A slightly different take on the combination of simple animations, auxiliary views and everything else you learned up to this point.

This chapter is juicy with code, so head on in to the next section to get started right away!

Crossfading Animations

Open the starter project from the **Resources** folder for this chapter. Build and run your project to get acquainted with what you have to work with. The app currently shows the flight summary for a trip from London to Rome with a layover in Paris.

The flight summary screen alternates between the two connecting flights and shows items such as the destination, flight number and gate number:

Your first task is to smoothly transition, or **blend**, between the two background images.

Your first instinct might be to simply fade out the present image and then fade in the new one. But this approach would show the content behind the image as the alpha approached zero; you want the content behind this screen to remain hidden during the entire animation.

Fading the images out, then fading them in again would result in an odd-looking transition like the following:

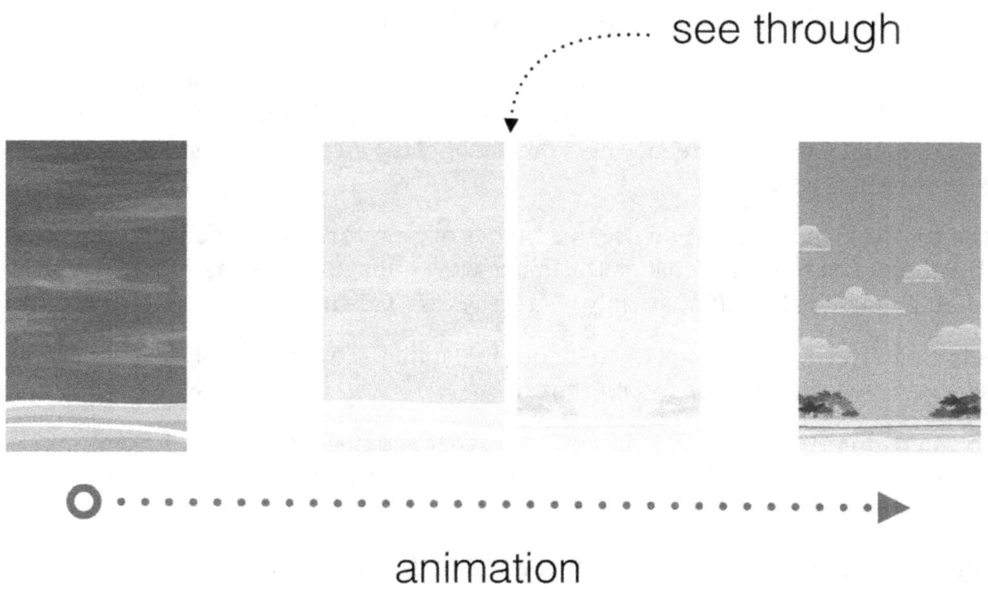

Obviously, you'll need a different approach to solve this problem.

Open **ViewController.swift** and add the following new method to handle your new crossfade effect:

```
func fade(imageView: UIImageView, toImage: UIImage, showEffects:
Bool) {
  UIView.transition(with: imageView, duration: 1.0,
    options: .transitionCrossDissolve,
    animations: {
      imageView.image = toImage
    },
    completion: nil
  )

  UIView.animate(withDuration: 1.0, delay: 0.0,
    options: .curveEaseOut,
    animations: {
      self.snowView.alpha = showEffects ? 1.0 : 0.0
```

```
    },
    completion: nil
  )
}
```

The method takes the following three parameters:

1. `imageView`: This is the image view you are going to fade out.
2. `toImage`: This is the new image you want visible at the end of the animation.
3. `showEffects`: This is a boolean flag indicating whether the scene should show or hide the snowfall effect. The snowfall animation should only run on the first connecting flight's screen, where presumably the airport is experiencing bad weather.

The transition animation you use this time is of type `.transitionCrossDissolve` — this allows you to simply change the image view's image to the one supplied as a parameter and UIKit automatically creates a cross-fade transition.

Additionally, you fade `snowView` in or out in parallel with the rest of the animation depending on the value of `showEffects`.

So where do you trigger `fade(imageView:,toImage:,showEffects:)` from? Currently `changeFlight(to:)` switches all the data about the two connecting flights.

Since you are going to eventually animate all of the UI elements on this screen, update the signature of that method as follows:

```
func changeFlight(to data: FlightData, animated: Bool = false) {
```

Above, you supply a default value of false for the new animated parameter so that existing calls to this method work as they did before, with no animation.

Next, find the code inside `changeFlight(to:,animated:)` that updates both the image view and the snow view:

```
bgImageView.image = UIImage(named: data.weatherImageName)
snowView.isHidden = !data.showWeatherEffects
```

Wrap it in an `if` statement that optionally animates the transition as shown below:

```
if animated {
  fade(imageView: bgImageView,
    toImage: UIImage(named: data.weatherImageName)!,
```

```
    showEffects: data.showWeatherEffects)
} else {
  bgImageView.image = UIImage(named: data.weatherImageName)
  snowView.isHidden = !data.showWeatherEffects
}
```

This method calls `fade(imageView:, toImage:, showEffects:)` when `animated` is true and passes in the proper parameters from `data`.

If you want to see what's inside of data, have a look inside **FlightData.swift**. The FlightData structure is the model that represents a single flight; there's two of those flights already pre-defined in **FlightData.swift**: `londonToParis` and `parisToRome`.

Back in **ViewController.swift** you still need to make one more change before you can see the crossfade effect on screen You need to add the animated parameter to the line where you call `changeFlight(to:, animated:)`.

In `changeFlight(to:animated:)` change the call to `self.changeFlight` near the end of the method inside the delay call as follows:

```
self.changeFlight(to: data.isTakingOff ?
  parisToRome : londonToParis, animated: true)
```

Build and run your app; you should now see the image views transition smoothly:

The images blend beautifully into each other, and since you fade the snow effect at the same time, the animation looks seamless. You can even see it snow in Rome for a split second!

You've learned an important technique here: transitions can be used to animate changes to non-animatable properties of your views.

> **Note**: If you want to have some fun, you can try also some of the transition effects from the previous chapter. Keep in mind that transitions like `.transitionFlipFromLeft` are simply too distracting for the current project. `.transitionCrossDissolve` is a subtle "background" effect which only enhances the animations, which will happen in the foreground.

That takes care of the image view, but the text labels for the flight number and gate number look like they could use some creative animation:

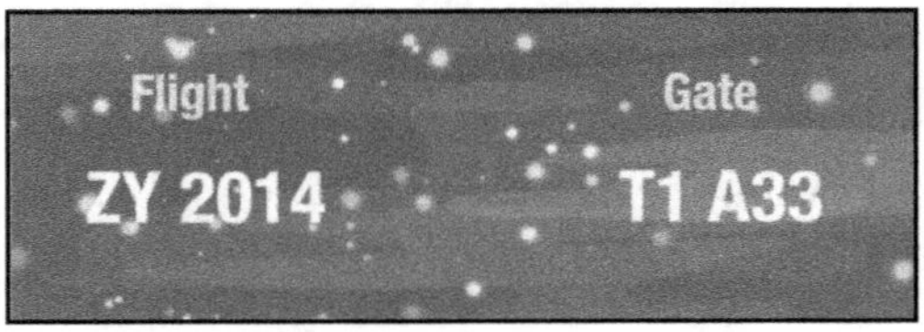

You'll take care of those next with a faux-3D transition.

Cube Transitions

The effect you are going to build in this section makes it look like the flight and gate information is on adjacent sides of a cube that rotates around its center to reveal the next value. When complete, your animation will work as illustrated below:

This is not a real 3D effect, but it looks pretty close and it's a great opportunity for you to try animations featuring auxiliary views.

Your approach will be to add a temporary label, animate the heights of the two labels simultaneously, remove the temporary label and, in the end, clean up after yourself.

This will be also the first animation you create that has a **direction**, since you'll play it both forwards and backwards. The direction will determine whether the temporary label appears from the top or bottom.

Start by adding the following enumeration inside the `ViewController` class:

```
enum AnimationDirection: Int {
  case positive = 1
  case negative = -1
}
```

Your animation method will take a parameter that sets the animation direction.

Next, add the initial version of that method as shown below:

```
func cubeTransition(label: UILabel, text: String, direction:
AnimationDirection) {
  let auxLabel = UILabel(frame: label.frame)
  auxLabel.text = text
  auxLabel.font = label.font
  auxLabel.textAlignment = label.textAlignment
  auxLabel.textColor = label.textColor
  auxLabel.backgroundColor = label.backgroundColor
}
```

The method takes three parameters:

1. `label`: The label that you want to animate.
2. `text`: The new text to display on the label.
3. `direction`: The location from where you animate the new text label; this is either the top or the bottom of the view.

To start, you'll create a new label `auxLabel` and copy all key properties of the existing label to it, including `frame`, `font`, and `alignment`.

The single difference between the two labels is the text they each contain: the auxiliary label will contain the new text.

Having the two labels appear at the same position is not what you want. Instead, you need to move the auxiliary label away from the existing view and make it really tiny.

Keep going with the transition! Add the following code to end of `cubeTransition`:

```
let auxLabelOffset = CGFloat(direction.rawValue) *
  label.frame.size.height/2.0

auxLabel.transform =
  CGAffineTransform(translationX: 0.0, y: auxLabelOffset)
  .scaledBy(x: 1.0, y: 0.1)
)

label.superview?.addSubview(auxLabel)
```

In the code above, you first calculate the vertical offset for the auxiliary label. The raw value of `direction` is either `1` or `-1`, which gives you the proper vertical offset to position the temporary label.

Next, you adjust the transform of the auxiliary label to create a faux-perspective effect. When you scale the text on its Y-axis alone, it'll look squashed like you're viewing the plane of the text on edge:

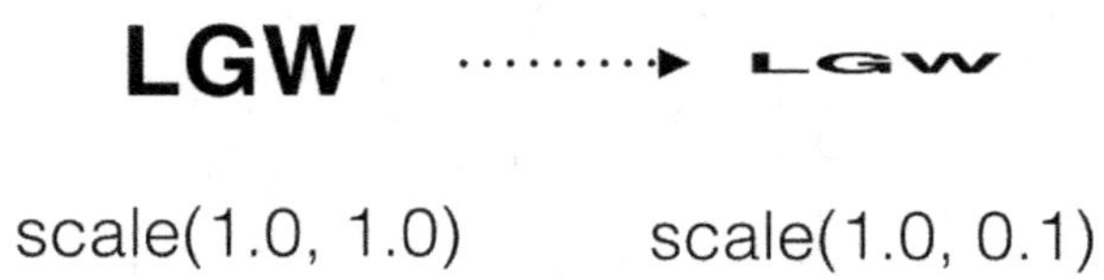

Finally, you add the newly created label at the same level in the hierarchy as the existing label.

Next add the following animation code to the end of `cubeTransition`:

```
UIView.animate(withDuration: 0.5, delay: 0.0,
options: .curveEaseOut,
  animations: {
    auxLabel.transform = .identity
    label.transform =
      CGAffineTransform(translationX: 0.0, y: -auxLabelOffset)
      .scaledBy(x: 1.0, y: 0.1)
    )
  },
  completion: { _ in
    label.text = auxLabel.text
    label.transform = .identity

    auxLabel.removeFromSuperview()
  }
)
```

In the `animations` block you reset the `transform` of `auxLabel`; this makes the new text grow in height and positions it exactly on top of the old one.

Speaking of the old text, you also apply a transform to label that scales it down and moves it in the direction opposite to where the new text appears.

Insert the following code in `changeFlight(to:animated:)` inside the `if` statement, just below where you call `fadeImageView`:

```
let direction: AnimationDirection = data.isTakingOff ?
  .positive : .negative

cubeTransition(label: flightNr, text: data.flightNr, direction:
direction)
cubeTransition(label: gateNr, text: data.gateNr, direction:
direction)
```

In the same method, **move the existing code** that sets the `flightStatus`, `flightNr`, `gateNr`, `departingFrom`, `arrivingTo` text **inside** the `else` statement, otherwise those statements will change the label's text immediately and spoil your animation.

The completed `else` block should look now like this:

```
} else {
  bgImageView.image = UIImage(named: data.weatherImageName)
  snowView.isHidden = !data.showWeatherEffects

  flightNr.text = data.flightNr
  gateNr.text = data.gateNr

  departingFrom.text = data.departingFrom
  arrivingTo.text = data.arrivingTo

  flightStatus.text = data.flightStatus
}
```

Build and run your project; enjoy the results of your labor as you watch the gate number and flight number animate via your fancy faux-3D transition.

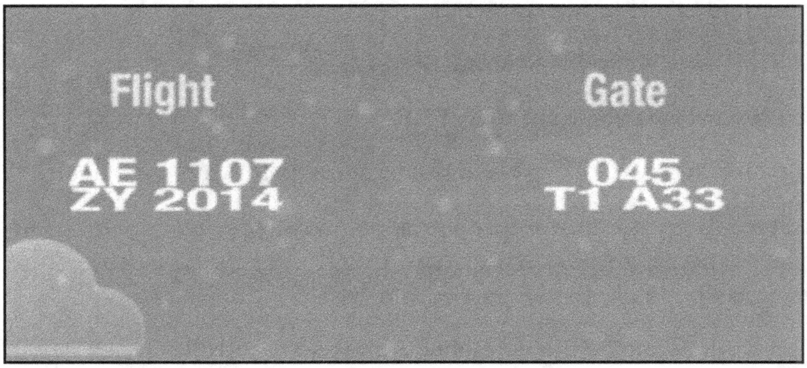

Notice how running the animation both forwards and backwards gives a real impression that you're switching between two alternate states. This screen is becoming more and more alive, thanks to you!

You're not quite done yet; you'll finish off this chapter by adding a composite animation to the three-letter airport codes on the screen to make the screen transitions feel organic and snappy!

Fade and Bounce Transitions

The final animation in this chapter makes use of labels, auxiliary views, and everything else you've learned up to this point. Consider it a chapter review, if you will!

Start by adding the following new method for the new transition animation:

```
func moveLabel(label: UILabel, text: String, offset: CGPoint) {
  let auxLabel = UILabel(frame: label.frame)
  auxLabel.text = text
  auxLabel.font = label.font
  auxLabel.textAlignment = label.textAlignment
  auxLabel.textColor = label.textColor
  auxLabel.backgroundColor = .clear

  auxLabel.transform = CGAffineTransform(translationX: offset.x,
y: offset.y)
  auxLabel.alpha = 0
  view.addSubview(auxLabel)
}
```

The new method takes three parameters:

1. `label`: The label you want to animate.
2. `text`: The new text you want to display.
3. `offset`: The arbitrary offset you'll use to animate the auxiliary label.

The code above is pretty simple: just as you did in the previous section, you create an auxiliary label and copy all properties to it from the existing one. To create the label transform, you simply use the `offset` parameter.

Finally, just before you add the new label to the view controller's view, you hide it by setting its `alpha` property to `0.0`.

That sets the stage for your animations. Next you're going to exchange the places of the original and auxiliary labels. This time, instead of using the same animation for both labels, you'll create separate animations for each and move them independent of each other. This will result in an interesting and organic visual effect.

First add the following code to the end of `moveLabel`:

```
UIView.animate(withDuration: 0.5, delay: 0.0,
  options: .curveEaseIn,
  animations: {
    label.transform = CGAffineTransform(translationX: offset.x,
```

```
y: offset.y)
    label.alpha = 0.0
  },
  completion: nil
)
```

This animation moves the label away from its original position and fades it out.

Next, add the following code to animate the auxiliary label:

```
UIView.animate(withDuration: 0.25, delay: 0.1,
options: .curveEaseIn,
  animations: {
    auxLabel.transform = .identity
    auxLabel.alpha = 1.0
  },
  completion: { _ in
    //clean up
  }
)
```

You reset the auxiliary label's transform above, effectively moving it to its original location. You also fade the text in by animating its alpha value.

Note that this animation kicks off after a `0.1` second delay and it lasts only `0.25` seconds. This means that the two labels will overlap while exchanging places, creating a subtle yet pleasing "ghost" effect.

Before you can test your new animation, you need to add the code to remove the auxiliary label when the animation is complete.

Find the comment `//clean up` in the completion block of the code you just added and replace it with the following code:

```
auxLabel.removeFromSuperview()
label.text = text
label.alpha = 1.0
label.transform = .identity
```

This wraps up the transition nicely, returns the label to its initial state and sets the new text of the label.

Now find `changeFlight(to:,animated:)` and add the following code to the bottom of your `if animated {` statement:

```
let offsetDeparting = CGPoint(
  x: CGFloat(direction.rawValue * 80),
  y: 0.0)

moveLabel(label: departingFrom, text: data.departingFrom,
  offset: offsetDeparting)

let offsetArriving = CGPoint(
  x: 0.0,
  y: CGFloat(direction.rawValue * 50))

moveLabel(label: arrivingTo, text: data.arrivingTo,
  offset: offsetArriving)
```

This new method takes an arbitrary offset as a parameter. This lets you create two different animations for the departure and arrival airports.

For the departure label, you create a horizontal movement; for the arrival airport, you create a vertical movement instead.

That's all the code you need! Build and run your app to see all labels animate via your snappy new transition effect.

Take a moment to appreciate that even in this impressive-looking animation, you've *still* only animated a few properties on any given view. You've worked with bounds, frame, center, transform, `backgroundColor` and alpha — but you've managed to create some very impressive animations with those properties alone!

Animating each property on its own might not always result in mind-blowing effects, but using a combination of a number of simple animations and using subtle yet powerful techniques such as adding auxiliary views and transitions can produce impressive visual effects.

Let your imagination... take flight!

Key Points

- You are not limited to animating a single view property from a single animation call; you can combine and overlap animations freely.
- To create complex effects you might use any and all "tricks" you feel the task at hand calls for, including creating temporary views for the duration of the animation.

Challenges

Challenge 1: Animate the Flight Status Banner

So far there's still one UI element that doesn't animate when the screen switches between the two connecting flights — the flight status:

The piece of text on the banner saying "Boarding" is a `UILabel`; as such, you can use either of the two label animations you created in this chapter to show the alternate flight statuses.

I believe you can figure out how to animate the banner on your own; use the `flightStatus` outlet to access the label and `data.flightStatus` to get the new text to animate to.

Feel free to experiment and play around further. The more experience you gain, the better understanding you will have of animations in UIKit!

Now that you're a pro at animations and transitions, it's time for the final topic on view animations — combining multiple animation steps together with **keyframes**.

Chapter 7: Keyframe Animations

Keyframe animations are the a special sort of view animation that, instead of going from point A to point B, let you create animations with multiple milestones. Keyframes are another building block of complex, eye pleasing animations which allow you to upgrade from simple one-shot animations to designing complex animations sequences.

Let's see how it would look like if you wanted to chain multiple simple animations together and move a view in a rectangular pattern:

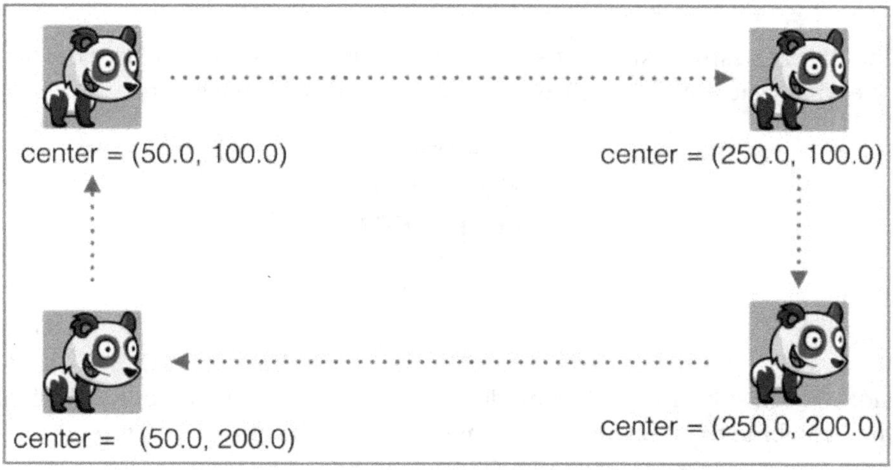

To achieve this you could chain several animations and completion closures together like so:

```
UIView.animate(withDuration: 0.5,
  animations: {
    view.center.x += 200.0
  },
  completion: { _ in
    UIView.animate(withDuration: 0.5,
      animations: {
        view.center.y += 100.0
      },
      completion: { _ in
        UIView.animate(withDuration: 0.5,
          animations: {
            view.center.x -= 200.0
          },
          completion: { _ in
            UIView.animate(withDuration: 0.5,
              animations: {
                view.center.y -= 100.0
              }
            )
          }
        )
      }
    )
  }
)
```

Look at all that nesting! And that's for a simple rectangle-shaped path; can you imagine what that would look like for a more complicated movement?

There must be a better way...

Instead, you can split the total animation into four distinct stages, or **keyframes**, and then combine the individual keyframes into a **keyframe animation**.

Keyframe animations

Consider another animation that depicts the take-off sequence of a plane. The distinct stages of this animation would look like the following:

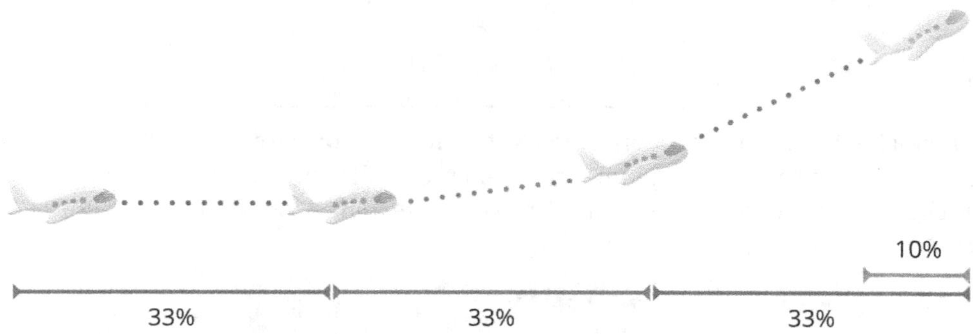

The first stage of the animation sequence accelerates the plane on the runway. The second stage gives the plane a little altitude and tilts it upward. The third stage continues to tilt the plane and boosts the plane skyward at a much faster rate.

There's a fourth and final stage in the final 10% of the animation that fades the plane out of view, as if it were moving behind some low-hanging clouds.

The complete animation could be overwhelming to create, but breaking down the animation into the various stages makes it a lot more manageable. Once you've defined the keyframes for each stage, you've got the problem mostly solved.

You'll learn about keyframes and how to assemble them into a keyframe animation by creating an airplane animation similar to the above — but it will be far more complex. Don't worry, you're more than capable of handling this!

Setting up Your Keyframe Animation

If you worked through the project in the last chapter, you can use that as your starting point; if you didn't do that, or if you want to start fresh, you can use the starter project for this chapter.

Build and run your project; you should see the two alternating connecting flights:

You'll make the airplane take off from its starting position, circle around, then land and taxi back to the starting point. This animation will run each time the screen switches between connecting flights. The complete animation will look something like this:

Open **ViewController.swift**; all the code for this animation will live in a new class method named `planeDepart()`.

Find `changeFlight(to:,animated:)` and you'll see an `if animated` statement near the top containing all of the animated changes. Add the following line at the top of the `if` block (be careful to place it *inside* the block):

```
planeDepart()
```

Now add the following initial version of your new animation method `planeDepart()` as shown below:

```
func planeDepart() {
  let originalCenter = planeImage.center

  UIView.animateKeyframes(withDuration: 1.5, delay: 0.0,
    animations: {
      //add keyframes
    },
    completion: nil
  )
}
```

You store the original position of the airplane in `originalCenter` so you'll know where your animation should finish.

You also use `animateKeyframes(withDuration:delay:options:animations:completion:)` to create your first keyframe animation. The parameter list is identical to the ones you've used all along in this book to create your view animations. You set the duration to `1.5` seconds, add no other options and add an empty `animations` closure.

The options for keyframes are different; they come from the `UIViewKeyFrameAnimationOptions` enumeration instead of `UIViewAnimationOptions`. You'll learn about the fine details of keyframe options a little later in this chapter.

Adding Keyframes

It's time to add your first keyframe. Replace the `//add keyframes` comment with the following code:

```
UIView.addKeyframe(withRelativeStartTime: 0.0, relativeDuration:
0.25,
  animations: {
    self.planeImage.center.x += 80.0
    self.planeImage.center.y -= 10.0
  }
)
```

This is the first of several calls to `addKeyframe(withRelativeStartTime:relativeDuration:animations:)` you'll be adding.

The animation keyframe above is little different than the animation methods you've used so far.

`addKeyframe(withRelativeStartTime:relativeDuration:animations:)` is the first time you've used relative durations in the animations in this book. The start time of the keyframe, as well as its duration, are expressed as percentages relative to the entire duration of the animation. For example, `0.1` would be 10%, `0.25` would be 25%, and `1.0` would be 100% of the total duration.

Working with relative values lets you specify that a keyframe should last for a fraction of the total time; UIKit takes the relative durations of each keyframe and automagically figures out the exact durations for each keyframe, saving you a ton of work.

In the final bit of code above you set the start time to `0.0` — meaning "immediately" — and the duration to `0.25`, representing 25% of the total animation time:

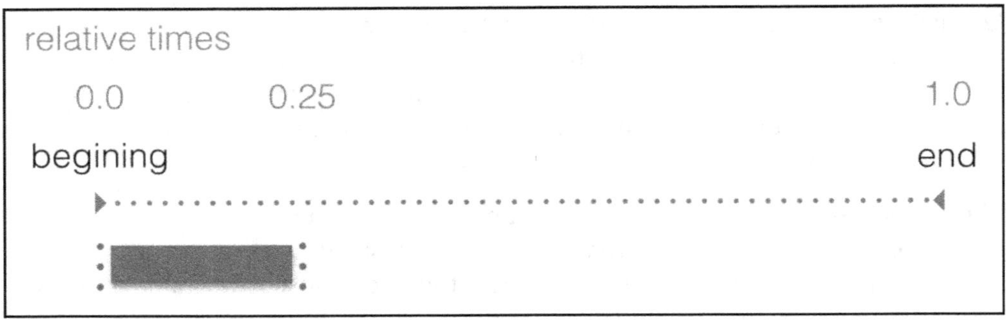

Since you set the duration of the complete animation to `1.5` seconds, the first keyframe will last for approximately `0.375` seconds. Later on, if you decide to modify the total duration of the animation to a different value, the individual keyframe animations will recalculate their duration times accordingly.

Build and run your project and check out the first frame of your animation:

Running the first keyframe sets in motion the code in the animations closure: the airplane moves `80` points to the right and `10` points up.

This is, of course, only the first step in creating the complete animation sequence. To create the second keyframe, add the following code to the keyframe block, underneath the previous `addKeyframe` call:

```
UIView.addKeyframe(withRelativeStartTime: 0.1, relativeDuration:
0.4) {
  self.planeImage.transform = CGAffineTransform(rotationAngle:
-.pi / 8)
}
```

The second keyframe starts 10% of the way into the animation and lasts for 40% of the total duration. This keyframe rotates the airplane as it moves off the runway:

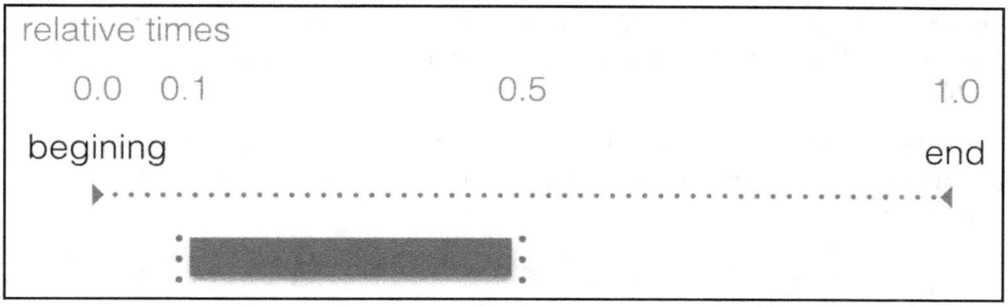

Build and run your project now and see how the two keyframes look when they run together:

Keep building your sequence by adding the third keyframe as follows:

```
UIView.addKeyframe(withRelativeStartTime: 0.25,
relativeDuration: 0.25) {
  self.planeImage.center.x += 100.0
  self.planeImage.center.y -= 50.0
  self.planeImage.alpha = 0.0
}
```

In this stage of the animation, you keep the airplane moving along but start to fade it out.

Build and run your project and see how the three keyframes in your animation look:

The plane flies out of sight and disappears. Now you'll need to bring it back and land it safely on the next connecting flight screen.

Before you show the airplane on the screen, you'll have to reset the orientation of the plane — that is, undo the rotation you've applied — and move it to the left of the visible area.

Since the airplane is invisible with its alpha set to `0` for the moment, you can move it around without the user seeing anything. Add the following keyframe to your animation:

```
UIView.addKeyframe(withRelativeStartTime: 0.51,
relativeDuration: 0.01) {
  self.planeImage.transform = .identity
  self.planeImage.center = CGPoint(x: 0.0, y: originalCenter.y)
}
```

This keyframe runs after all three previous frames have completed and lasts just a small fraction of a second; it resets the plane transform and moves it to the left edge of the screen.

Now you can add the final keyframe and taxi the airplane frame and taxi back to the original location:

```
UIView.addKeyframe(withRelativeStartTime: 0.55,
relativeDuration: 0.45) {
  self.planeImage.alpha = 1.0
  self.planeImage.center = originalCenter
}
```

This keyframe fades the airplane back in while moving it to the original starting point of the animation.

Build and run your project to see the completed animation sequence as shown below:

Take a minute to review the code you wrote. It's easy to follow and decode; you can modify, rearrange or alter the timing of any of the sections above without too much work on your part.

It's a short step to imagine your animation as a series of separate animations with delays in between, or even as a set of animations triggered from completion closures. Keyframes are an incredibly useful and flexible way to design and control your animations.

Calculation Modes in Keyframe Animations

Keyframe animations don't support the built-in easing curves that are available in standard view animations. This is by design; keyframes are supposed to start and end at specific times and flow into each other.

If each stage of your animation above had an easing curve, the plane would jerk around instead of moving smoothly from one animation into the next. If you *could* apply easing to the entire animation, that would result in your animation durations being ignored — and that's not what you want.

Instead, you have several **calculation modes** to choose from; each mode offers a different method to calculate intermediate frames of the animation as well as different optimizers for smooth movement and even pacing. Check out the documentation by searching for `UIViewKeyframeAnimationOptions` for more details.

Now that you know how to group together any number of simple animations using keyframe animations, you can build just about any sequence that comes to mind. If you want to test your knowledge of keyframes and keyframe animations, give the challenge below a try before moving on to the next section.

Key Points

- You can "chain" animations by using keyframes much easier than using the `completion` closure on the standard APIs to produce sequences.
- Keyframe animations not only allow you to "chain" animations but also to "overlap" them, and group them in general in any way you wish.
- Don't forget all keyframe timing values are relative to the complete animation, whereas the API defining the complete sequence uses absolute time.

Challenges

Challenge 1: Animate the Flight Departure Times

There's still one UI element on screen that isn't animated: the black flight summary status bar at the top of the screen that shows the flight departure times.

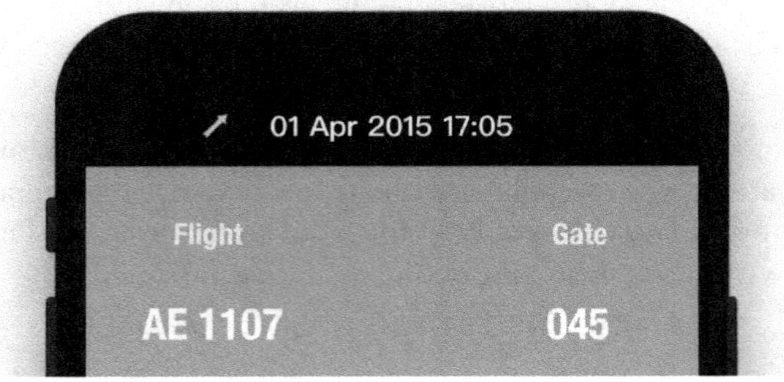

Your challenge is to add a keyframe animation to move the summary offscreen each time the connecting flight data changes.

Then you'll change the text to reflect the departure time of the next flight animate it back on screen like so:

The departure summary label is already connected to an outlet called `summary`.

If you need a general structure for your solution, here's a basic recipe you can follow:

- Create a new method `summarySwitch(to: String)` to animate the summary label.
- Inside the method, define a keyframe animation with two keyframes — one to animate the text out of the screen and another to animate it back in.
- Finally, make a call to `delay(seconds:completion:)` outside of the keyframe animation and change the text of the summary label in the closure parameter. You need to time the text change to happen exactly when the label is offscreen.
- Call `summarySwitch(to)` from within the "animated" part of `changeFlight(to:,animated:)`

Don't forget to move the existing non-animated call inside the `else` statement.

How did you do? If you succeeded, congratulations! You've managed to animate every single UI element in the project.

The next section of this book delves into the seemingly complex world of Auto Layout and animations; you'll learn that Auto Layout isn't nearly as mystifying as you might have thought, and you'll learn to animate constraints just as easily as you animate views!

Section III: Auto Layout

You'll need a slightly better understanding of the Auto Layout paradigm than the average iOS developer to make your animations play nicely with Auto Layout. Fortunately, you'll find working with Auto Layout constraints in code isn't as hard as it sounds at first. In fact, it's a fairly straightforward process once you work through a few examples.

By the end of this section, you'll have tamed Auto Layout and will know how to bend it to your will to create some really amazing animations.

Chapter 8: Introduction to Auto Layout

Auto Layout is a system of APIs that allow developers to express the dimension and position of UI elements in terms relative to the size of the screen and/or various device treats.

Auto Layout allows for a wide range of UI customizations, from slight variations of views' widths to aesthetically fill the space of various screens, to completely rearranging the UI layout from rows to columns when switching between portrait and landscape orientations.

This chapter is for the readers that need an *iOS Animations by Tutorials* crash course on Auto Layout. You will need to have the skills taught in this chapter in order to proceed to the next one, where you'll learn about animations in Auto Layout.

If you are already well-versed in building Auto Layout interfaces, you can skip ahead to Chapter 9, "Animating Constraints."

For those of you out there still reading and eager to dive into using Auto Layout, imagine first, if you will, a world *without* Auto Layout...

You're in charge of creating a new app for your company.

Your design, built with Interface Builder, would look like something like the following:

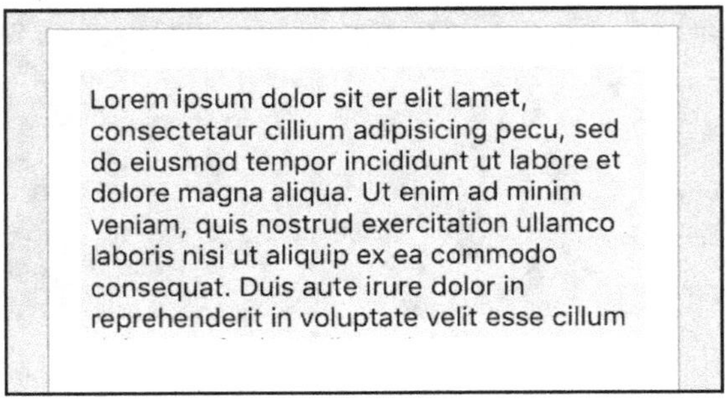

With the view positioned exactly as you want it, you then check its frame in the Size Inspector.

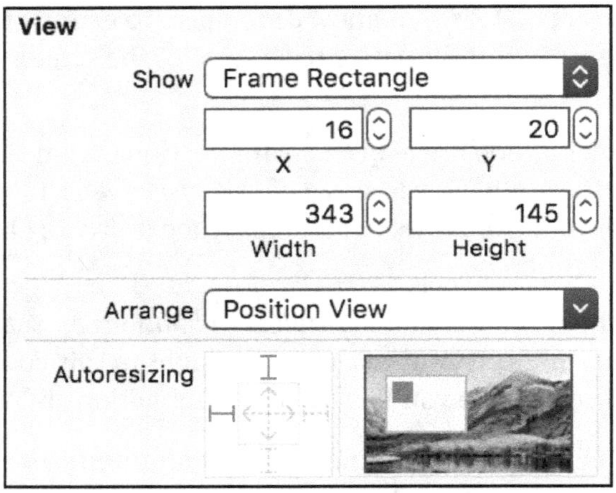

The position and size of your view are expressed in absolute values of points. That *looks* okay, so you launch the iPhone 8 Simulator to see your beautiful app in action:

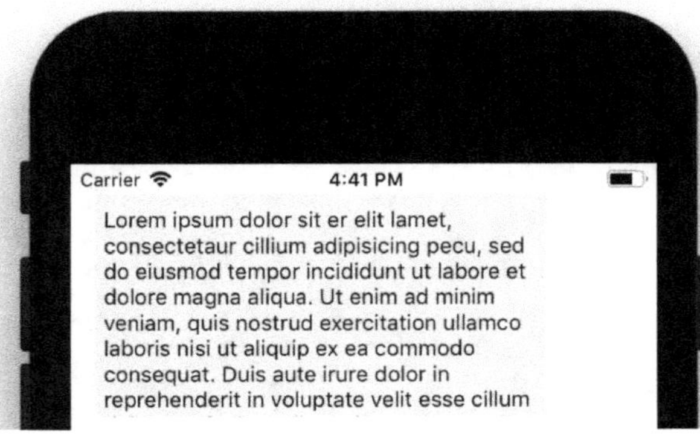

What happened? You view is no longer centered. The problem is that the view's position is expressed in points; you had designed your app in Interface Builder with the iPhone SE in mind, but since the iPhone 8 has a different screen resolution, your view appears off-center.

When you press Cmd + Right arrow to rotate the Simulator, the situation gets even worse:

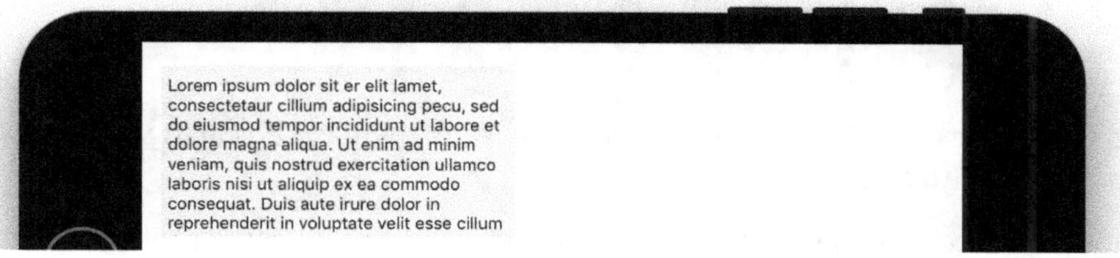

The auto-resizing and re-positioning system in Interface Builder provides a partial solution to these kinds of problems. However, if you're serious about creating dynamic and beautiful user interfaces that work with multiple device sizes and orientations, then you'll need to start using Auto Layout.

Auto Layout to the Rescue

Since you're no longer living in the Twilight Zone and Auto Layout is a reality, consider the same project from before, but this time using Auto Layout:

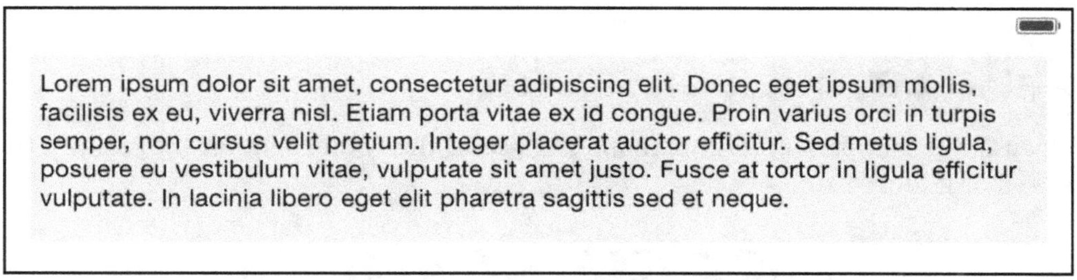

With Auto Layout it's easy to indicate that the `center.y` property of the text view should equal the `center.y` value of its superview. This means the text view will *always* be centered within its superview – independent of the screen on which the app runs.

You could also choose to set the width of the text view to 90% of the width of its superview; this leaves a nice 5% margin of white space around the text.

With this simple set of rules in hand, Auto Layout happily rearranges the elements in your UI to look good on any device, in any orientation.

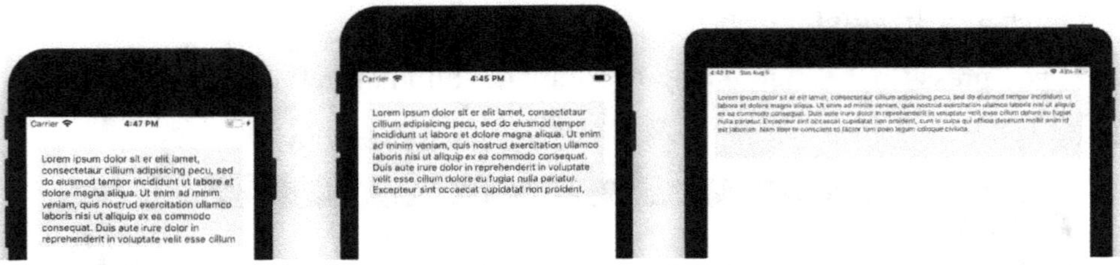

"So what's the catch?" you might be thinking. Well, there isn't a catch *per se*, it's just that you need to *think differently*.

Once you place your app in the hands of Auto Layout, you no longer set the bounds, frame or center properties of a view. If you were to try, UIKit will force a layout pass on your UI using Auto Layout, which will set everything back to the positions and sizes determined by your constraints.

Not being able to change these properties means that you can't *animate* those properties either! Therefore to move your views around or change their shape, you'll instead alter the Auto Layout rules — or *constraints* — that define where a view appears as well as its size.

But before you can animate constraints, you first need to learn how to create constraints, and more importantly, how they work.

Auto Layout Constraints

Open the starter project for this chapter in Xcode, then build and run your project to see what it looks like:

That's right — the project has no UI at all. Your job in this chapter is to build a simple interface with Auto Layout and learn how constraints work.

The project *does*, however, include some starter code:

- **ViewController.swift**: This class contains a few outlets to be connected to the views you'll create in Interface Builder. Further, it contains table view delegate and data source methods, which you will use once you add a table view to the user interface.
- **HorizontalItemList.swift**: This is a scroll view subclass, which shows a scrollable list of images. You'll use this class in the next chapter.

Your goal is to build a very simple dynamic UI, which will have the following appearance on different devices and orientations:

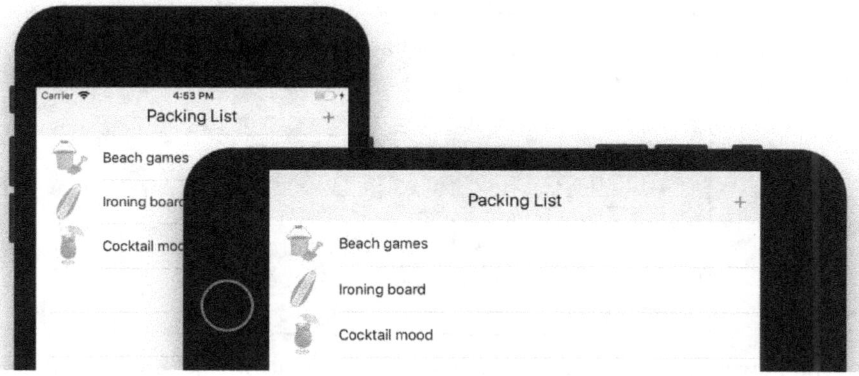

Adding the Top Menu

First you're going to add the top menu to the interface file. Visually, the menu will resemble a navigation bar.

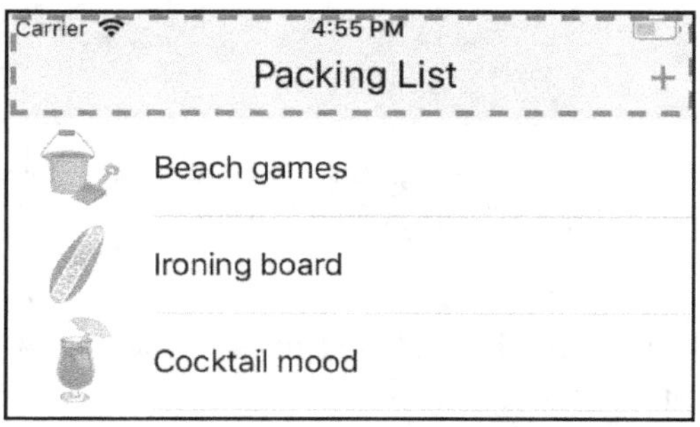

In the next chapter, you're going to make it expand and contract, and offer the user much more than a plain old navigation bar.

Open **Main.storyboard** and drag a custom view onto the existing view controller:

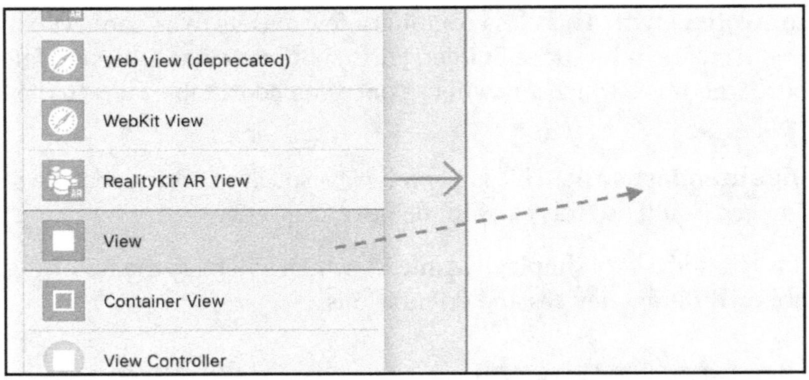

Use the Attributes Inspector to change the background color of the view to **Group Table View Background Color**:

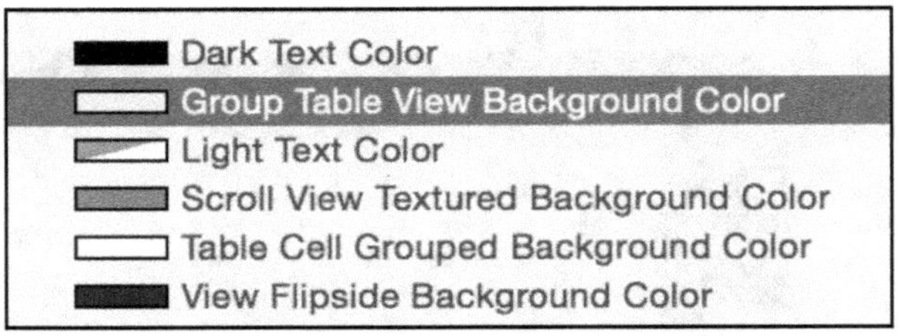

Resize the new view to more or less resemble a navigation bar in size; you don't need to worry about the exact dimensions right now. Make sure to snap the view to the top, left and right edges of the safe area:

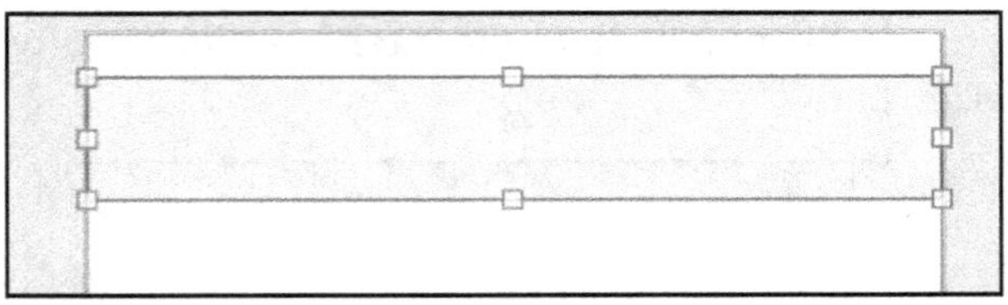

Now that you can actually see the view, you can constrain it to stay always in that top area where you mocked it up in Interface Builder.

> **Note**: Be sure to position the bar on the top of the safe area. This will make sure it looks right on all device types.

Creating Your First Constraint

Select the view, and then click on the **Pin** button — the middle button — in the toolbar in the bottom right corner of Interface Builder (a.k.a. the square TIE fighter button):

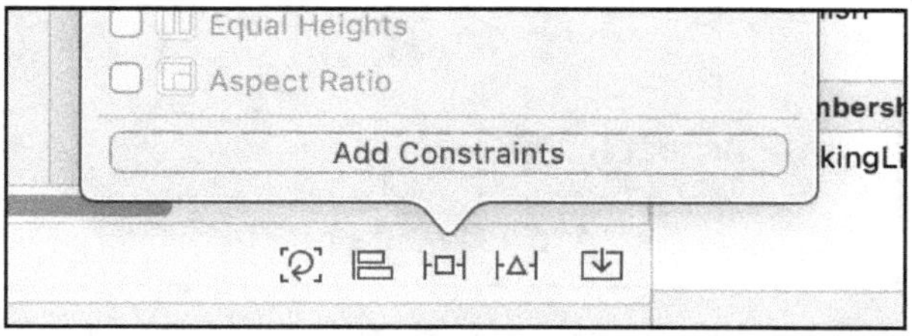

In the resulting popup menu, uncheck **Constrain to margins** and click the **left**, **top**, and **right** indicators to create three constraints:

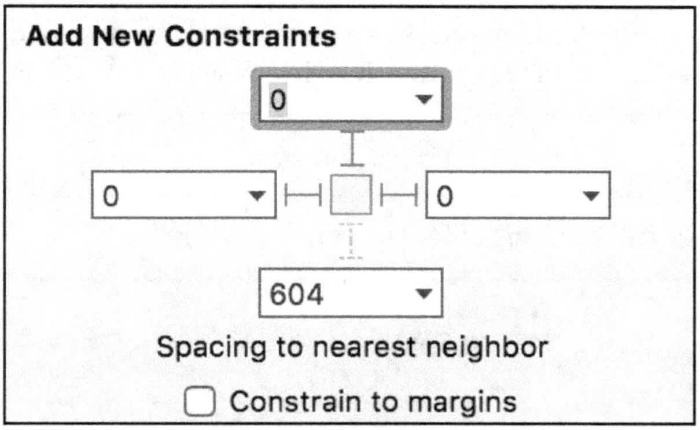

Click the **Add 3 Constraints** button to add them to your view and close the popup.

Each constraint is a relationship expressed as an equation; the top constraint you just created would be represented like so:

```
View.Top = 1 * Safe Area.Top + 0
```

The top position of your new view will always be `0` pt from the top of the safe area.

Constraining the Menu Height

Select your view again and click again on the **Pin** button to get the constraints popup. This time you want to create a constraint to fix the **Height** of the menu view to a constant value. In the popup, you will see the height of the view you set while positioning the view.

Check the checkbox next to **Height** and then click **Add 1 Constraint** at the bottom.

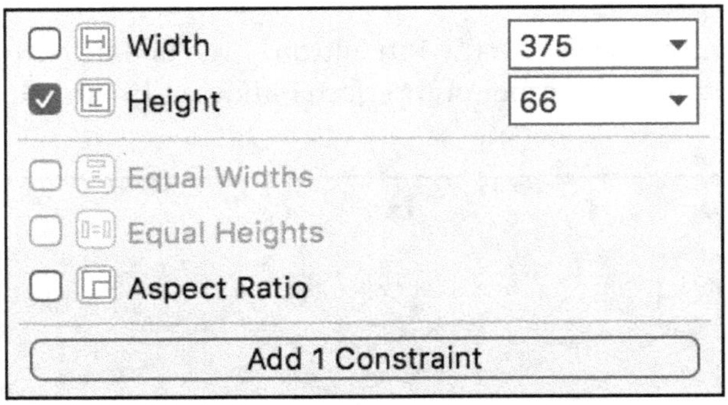

Now you've fixed the height of your menu bar forever. However, what if you wanted the height to be precisely `44pt`? Let's look into how to edit the already created Height constraint.

Deselect the current UI element and select your view once more then switch to the Size Inspector, the second tab from the right in the assistant editor:

Here, you'll see all the constraints for the selected view:

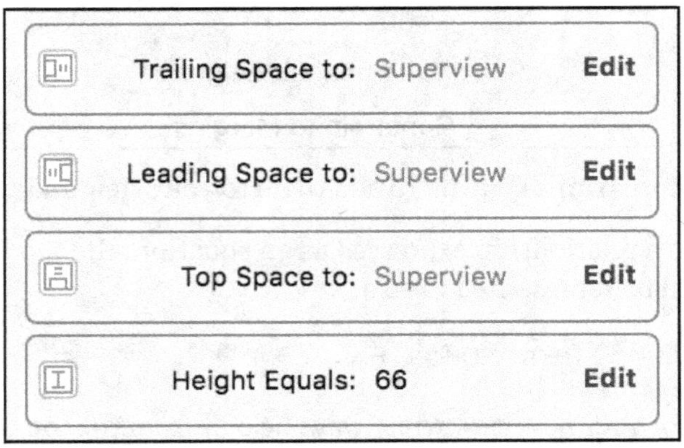

You probably don't have the Height fixed to `44pt` so let's fix that.

Click the **Edit** button on the offending constraint and set it to **44pt**, like so:

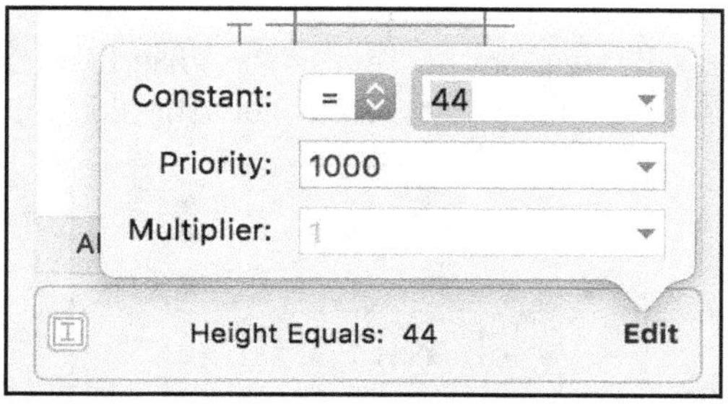

As soon as you do that you'll see the menu resize accordingly:

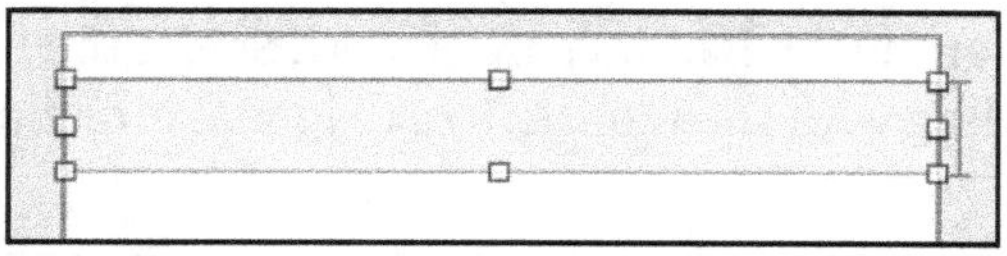

Use **View as:** at the bottom of the storyboard to see that the layout is preserved across different screen sizes:

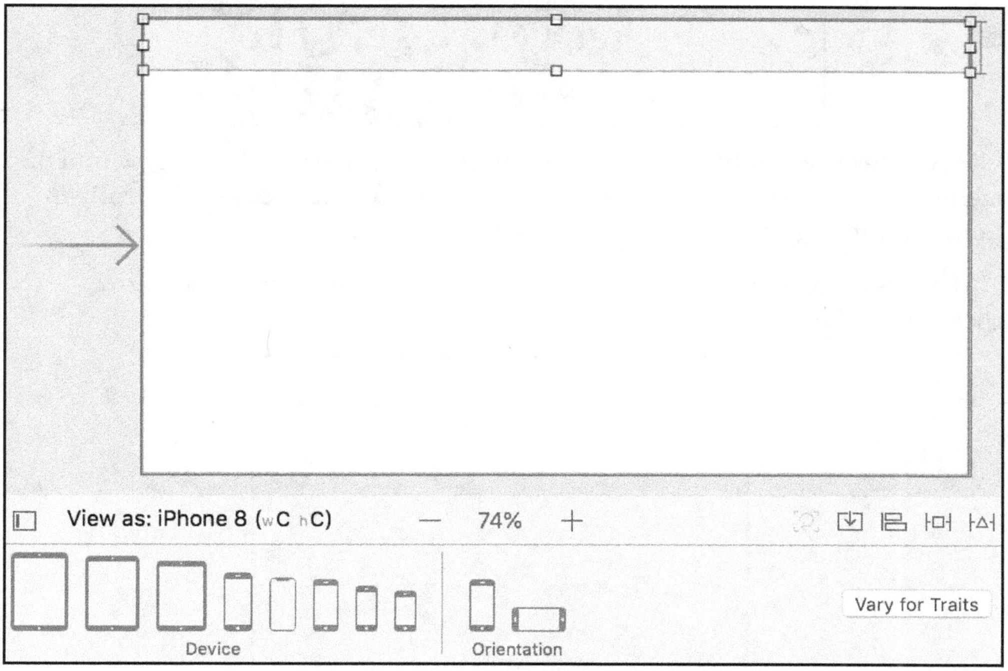

It works! The menu view is always pinned to the top and sides and has a height of `44pt`. And even better — you *understand* how it works. Now you can start to populate that menu.

Adding the Menu Title

Drag a label onto the menu view, set its Text to **Packing List**, the Alignment to **Center**, and the Font size to **21.0** points. Your label should look as follows:

Now you need to center the label in its parent view. Select the label, and while holding the Ctrl key, drag with the mouse (in a diagonal direction) to the menu bar like so:

Click **Center Horizontally in Container** to center the label horizontally within the menu. Then, while holding the Ctrl key, drag again and click **Center Vertically in Container** to align the label vertically within the menu.

This creates constraints that fix the label's center coordinate to the center coordinate of the menu:

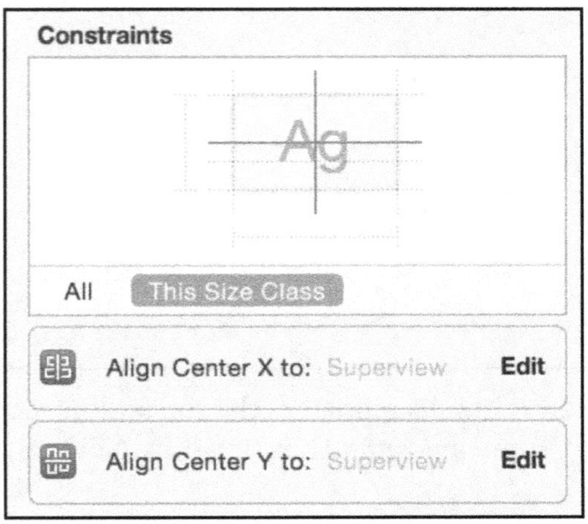

Things don't look quite right in Interface Builder; unless you placed the label precisely in the center of the menu view you'll probably see something like the following:

Resolving Auto Layout Issues

While designing in Interface Builder it's possible that dragging views around can result in a difference between where views are placed in Interface Builder, and where your constraints would place them at runtime (i.e. the view is positioned manually on a spot that doesn't reflect the applied constraints).

In the image above, the label just happens to be placed precisely in the vertical center of the menu, so Interface Builder notes this with a **blue guide** indicating the vertical constraint has been satisfied.

The **orange guide**, however, indicates that the horizontal alignment constraint is "broken". Interface Builder shows you the current frame of your view in solid orange along with the frame that the constraint expects in a dashed orange line.

To fix this, ensure the label is selected, then click the **Update frames** button in the bottom right corner of Interface Builder as shown below:

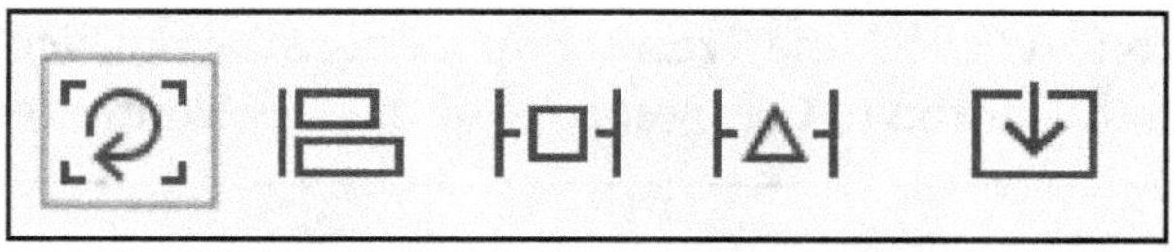

Your label will automatically jump to the correct position and size:

The two new constraints on your label translate to the following equations:

```
UILabel.CenterX = 1.0 * Superview.CenterX + 0.0
```

```
UILabel.CenterY = 1.0 * Superview.CenterY + 0.0
```

Next, you'll add the + button on the right hand side of the screen.

Adding a Menu Button

Drag a button onto the menu view. Set its Title to +, Font Size to **27.0**, and align it as shown below:

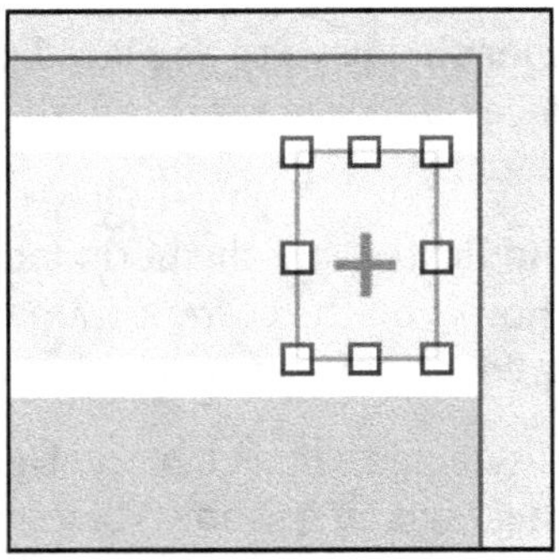

Click the Pin button and check the **Trailing Space** constraint. Click **Add 1 Constraint** to pin the button to the right edge of the view controller.

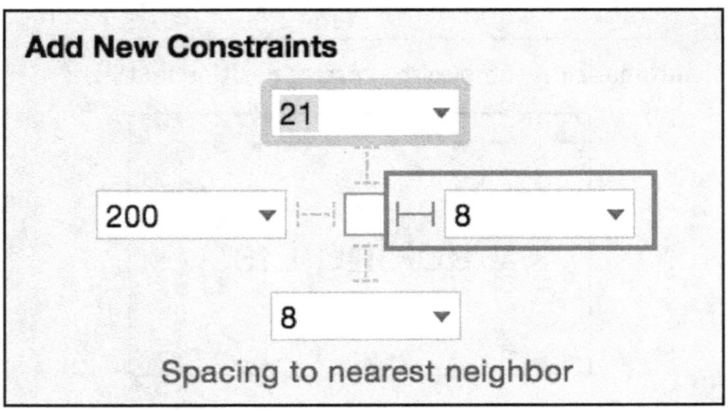

So far you've created only constraints between a view and its superview. But you don't have to *constrain* yourself in this way anymore — pardon the pun! You can create relationships between views on the same level of the view hierarchy as well.

For example, it would be a good idea to vertically align the + button to the title label. This way they will always line up, even if you move the title label.

Aligning Views With Auto Layout

Select the button and hold Ctrl on your keyboard as you drag with the mouse from the button to the label. Release the mouse button when the label activates and you will see a popup menu like so:

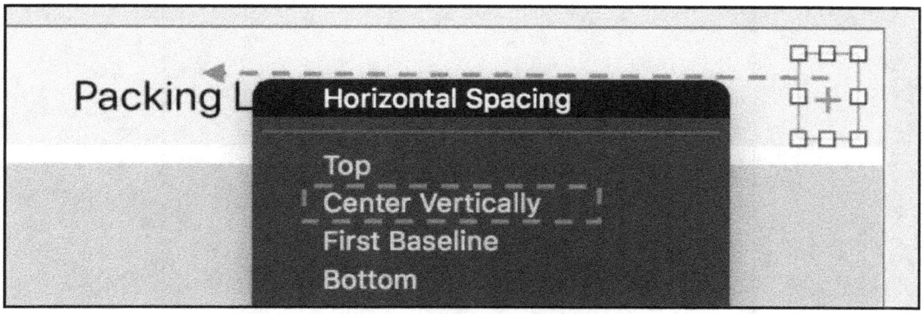

Click on **Center Vertically** to align the button vertically to the label.

Make sure the constant is **0** (zero) and the **First Item** of the new constraint is the + button, as shown in the image below:

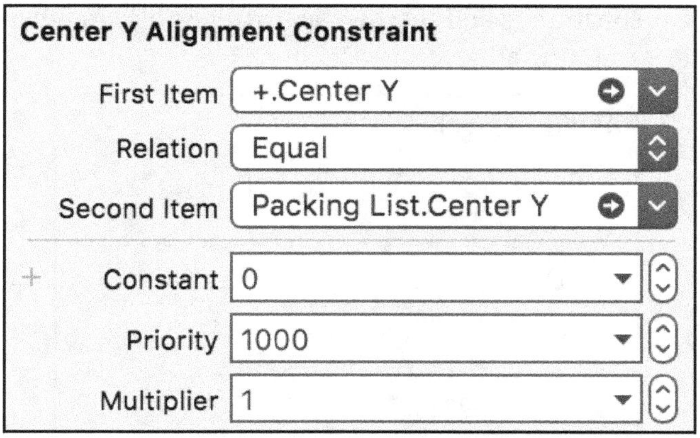

This is important because you want to attach the button to the title, instead of vice versa. If you see **Packing List.Center Y** as the first item, click on the drop down next to it and then click **Reverse First and Second Item** to switch the two items.

Now select the button again and click on the **Update frames** button, if it's enabled. This ought to remove any warnings in Interface Builder (if there were any). You are almost done with creating the user interface; the only missing element is the table view.

Adding and Constraining a Table View

Drag a table view and drop it in the empty view controller space:

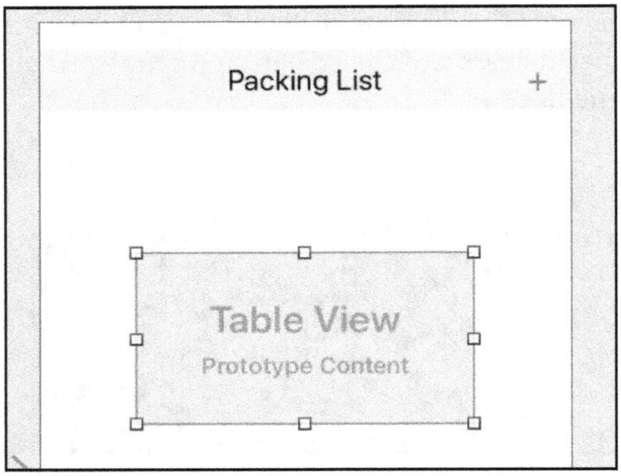

Since you're getting quite skilled at using Auto Layout in Interface Builder, you'll likely breeze through the steps to set up your table view.

Click the **Pin** button and uncheck **Constrain to Margins**, enable the **top**, **left**, **bottom**, and **right** constraints and set them all to **0**; just be careful *not* to press Enter prematurely before entering all values:

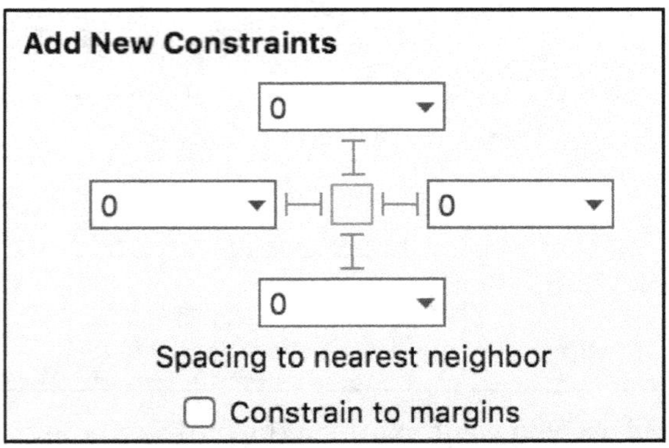

Click **Add 4 Constraints** to add the constraints to your view and close the popup:

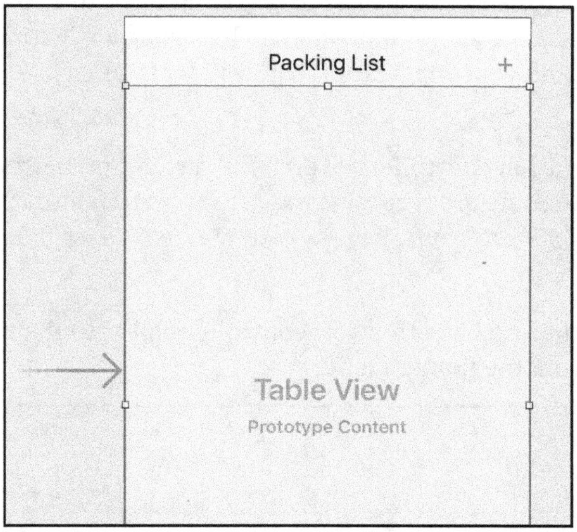

Note that the constraints you create via the **Pin** button popup relate to the table's nearest neighbor, not necessarily its parent view. In the case of the left, right, and bottom constraints above this is the superview — the view controller's view.

In the case of the top constraint above, there's a neighboring view closer to the table's top – the menu. So Interface Builder automatically picks up that view for the top constraint.

You're done setting up the basic constraints for your app! You now have a good understanding of how Auto Layout works and how to setup constraints and relationships between views in Interface Builder. Thanks to these new skills of yours, you'll get to create some cool new animations for your Packing List project in the next chapter.

Finalizing the UI

There's just two more things to take care of before you move on: cleaning up what white bar at the top, and connecting the existing outlets to their corresponding UI elements.

The white bar is because you're using safe area layout guides. That area at the top will be taken up by the status bar and / or notch on applicable devices. You don't want to put any of your content in there, but you don't want it to stand out as a separate color either.

Select the white area, which will select the main view of the view controller. Open the attributes inspector and change the background color to **Group Table View Background**, which is the same color you used for your navigation bar. The white area will disappear and your "navigation bar" will look taller.

> **Note**: Real navigation controllers stretch the navigation bar to the top of the screen and use the safe area margins to position their content, but that's a little advanced for this chapter!

Ctrl-drag with the mouse from the view controller object to the table view, then select **tableView** from the popup menu:

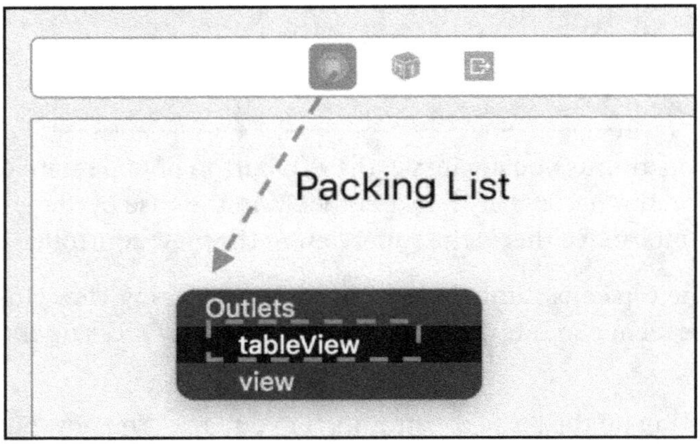

Then **Ctrl-drag** from the view controller to the title and select **titleLabel**:

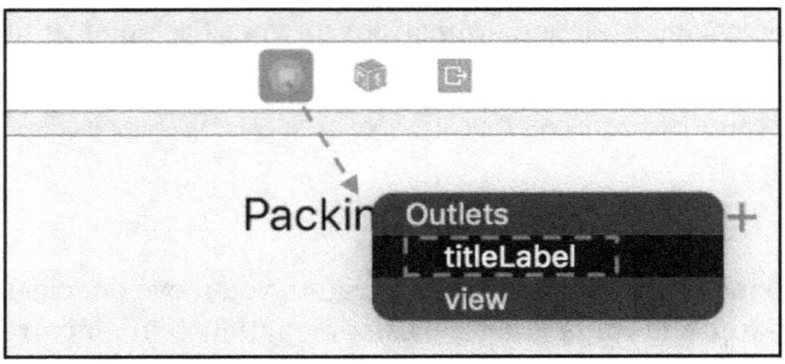

Do the same for the + button and select **buttonMenu**:

Now **Ctrl-drag** from the button back to the view controller and select **actionToggleMenu**.

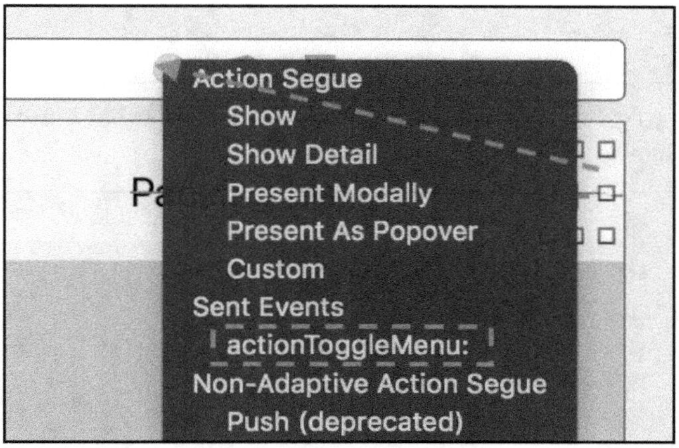

Next, drag from the table view to the view controller and select **dataSource**:

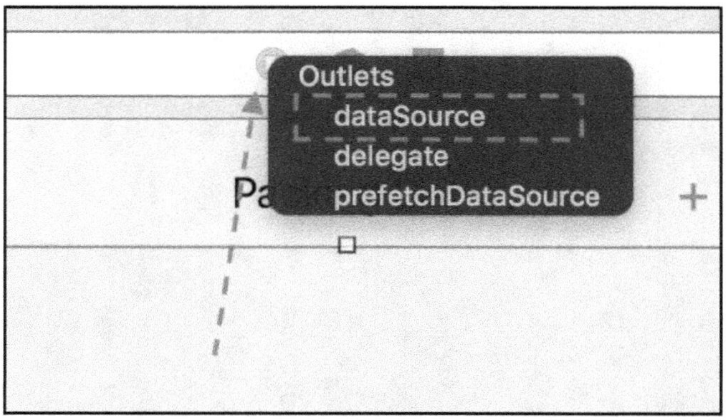

Once again, **Ctrl-drag** from the table view to the view controller but this time select **delegate**:

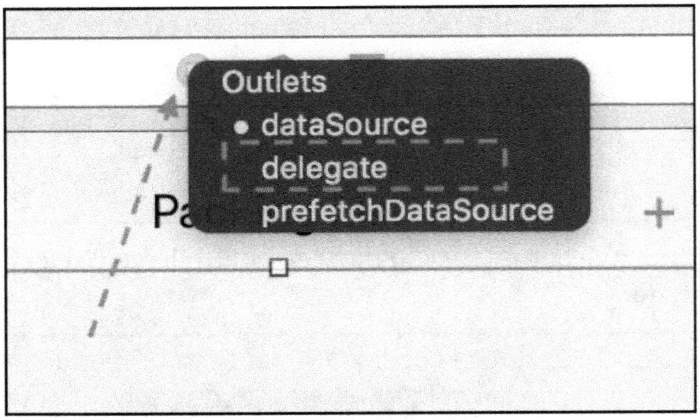

All that's left is to give your table a prototype cell. Drag a **table view cell** object onto the table view, like so:

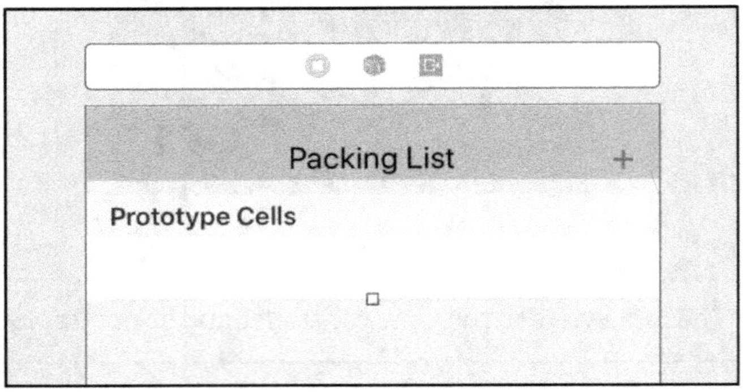

Then open the Attributes Inspector and enter **Cell** for the **Identifier**:

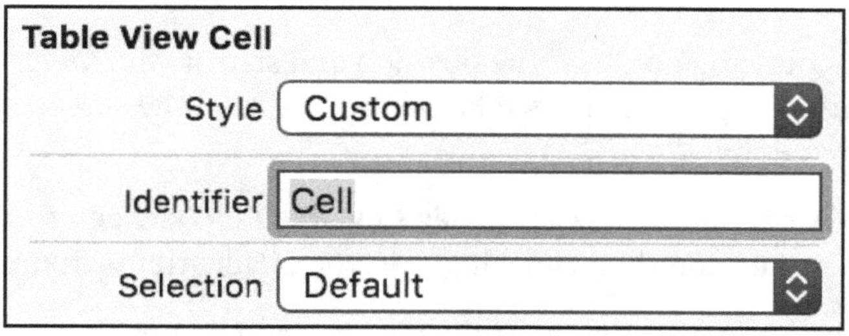

At long last, build and run your project; the existing table view code in **ViewController.swift** will pick up the newly connected outlets and populate the table with data:

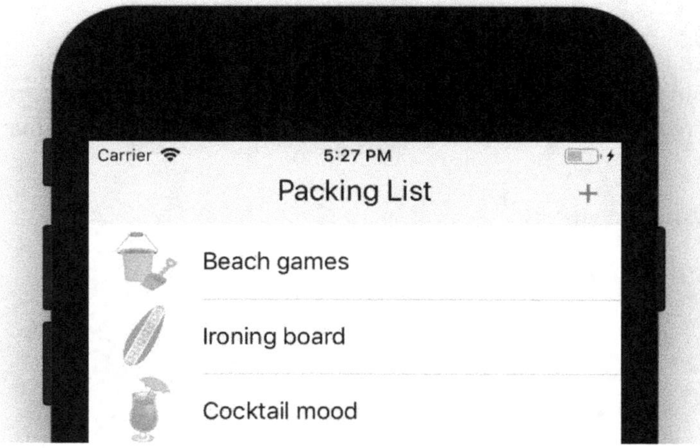

The app not only *looks* good, but it has a rock-solid layout thanks to Auto Layout. Give the app a whirl in different Simulators — both iPhone (notched and non-notched) and iPad — and change the orientation to check it out for yourself!

Key Points

- With Auto Layout, you don't set the position and size of your views in absolute values but rather express them as relative to the size of the screen or other views in the view hierarchy.
- You create new constraints between views by dragging between them while holding the Ctrl key and then choosing the type of constraint from a popup menu.
- Once a view has its constrains set (fully determining its position and size) it will be automatically laid out on any screen size by Auto Layout.

Challenges

Your challenge this time is simple: simply head on in to the next chapter! By now you understand Auto Layout in some detail, which is an important prerequisite for the work you're about to do in the next chapter, which deals with animations and Auto Layout.

See you in the next chapter!

Chapter 9: Animating Constraints

In the previous chapter, you learned how to use Auto Layout to create a responsive user interface for your Packing List project. You'll take it up a notch in this chapter and add a number of bouncy animations to your app. You've learned that in order for Auto Layout to work properly, you can't fiddle directly with the view's frame or center properties. Instead, you have to work with the layout constraints to create your desired animations.

So far you've seen how to animate view properties: you can animate numeric properties, such as `alpha`, from one float value to another. Instances of `CGPoint`, like in the case of the center property, can be modified progressively until the center value reaches the target position. Naturally, your next question would be "That's great — but how do I animate a *constraint*?"

Animating constraints is no more difficult than animating properties; it's just a little different. Usually you simply replace an existing constraint with a new one and let Auto Layout animate the UI between the two states.

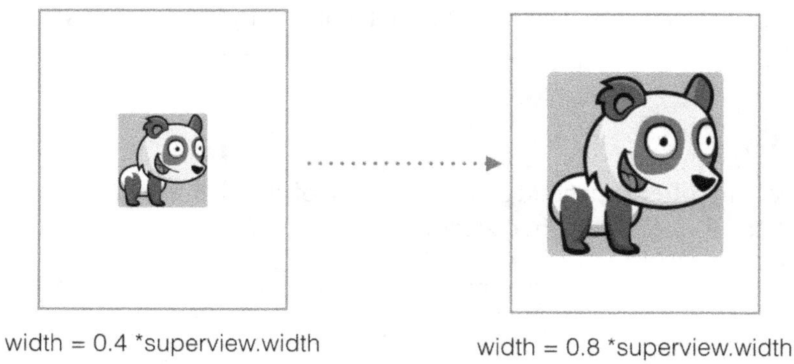

The sole exception is when you **only** need to change a single property of the constraint, such as `constant`, in the constraint's equation. In that case, you simply modify the constraint directly in code and animate the change.

In this chapter, you'll add an animation to expand the Packing List menu bar and reveal a list of items; the user can then tap an item to add it to their packing list as shown below:

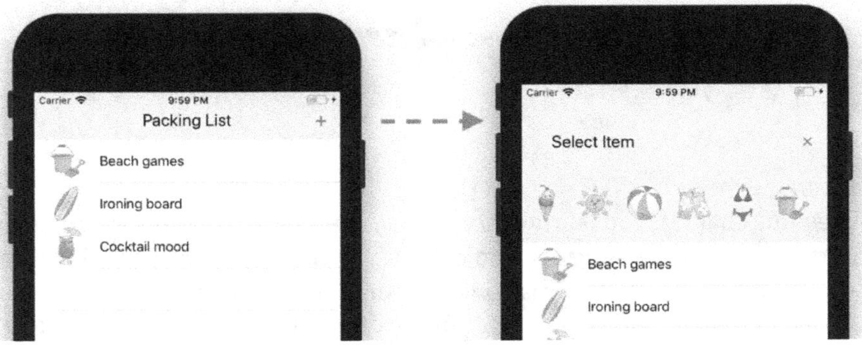

This interaction — as well as a few more visual treats — will be driven by fluid and eye-catching animations.

What are you waiting for? Time to get packing!

Animating Interface Builder Constraints

If you completed the project from the previous chapter, you can carry on where you left off; otherwise, you can use the starter project from this chapter.

Your first task is to expand the menu when the user taps the **+** button. In order to do that, you'll need to change the height of the menu bar by animating its height constraint.

Making the Menu Expand

Open **ViewController.swift** and scroll to the top of the class. Under the rest of the outlets add the following line of code:

```
@IBOutlet weak var menuHeightConstraint: NSLayoutConstraint!
```

`NSLayoutConstraint` is the class that represents the constraints you create in Interface Builder. Just like any other button, image view, or label, you can also create an outlet to a constraint.

Open **Main.storyboard** and select the menu view:

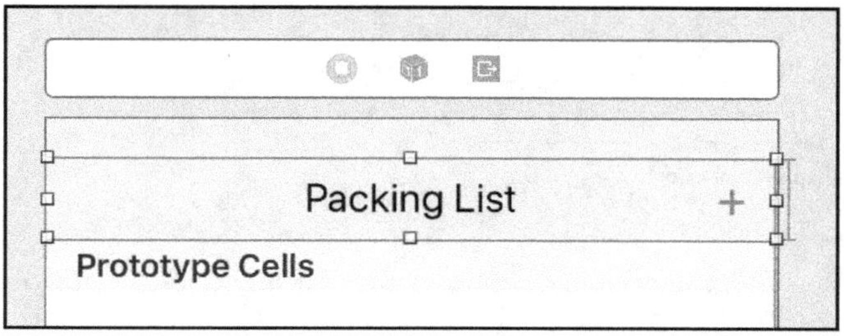

Open the Size Inspector tab and double click on the Constraint that says **Height Equals: 44**. This will open the familiar view of the constraint's equation:

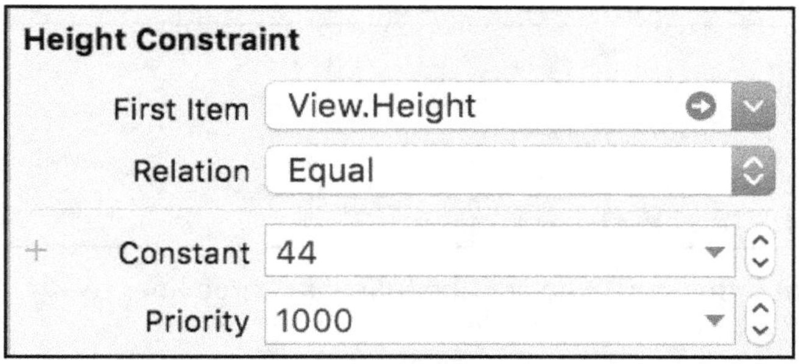

Switch to the last tab on the right — the **Connections Inspector**:

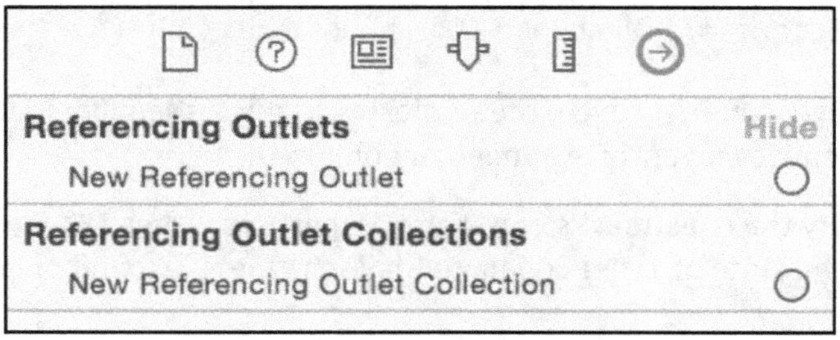

From here you can connect the constraint to its outlet in ViewController.

Drag from the small circle next to **New Referencing Outlet** to the view controller object:

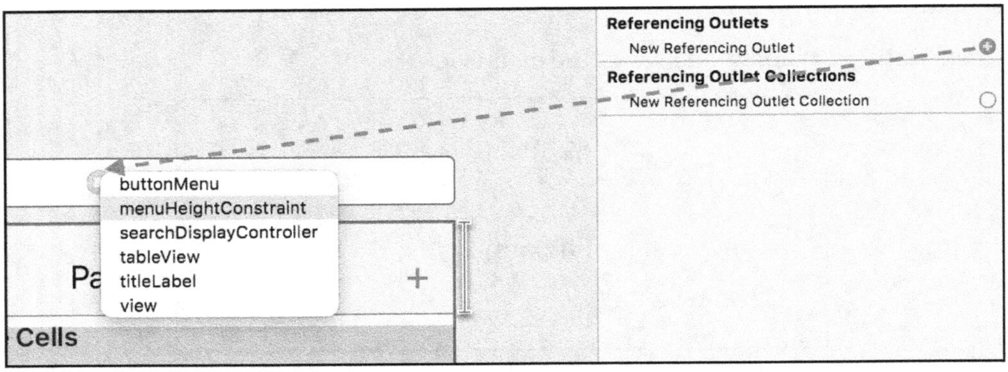

From the popup menu, select the only available option: **menuHeightConstraint**. You've now created your outlet, as shown in the image below:

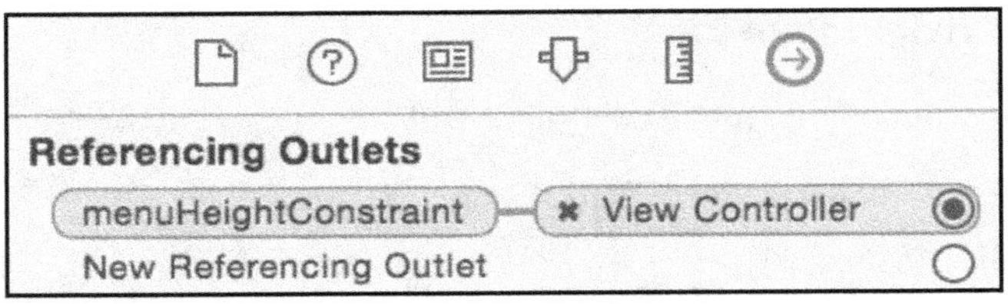

Open **ViewController.swift** and add the following three lines to `actionToggleMenu()`:

```
isMenuOpen.toggle()
menuHeightConstraint.constant = isMenuOpen ? 184.0 : 44.0
titleLabel.text = isMenuOpen ? "Select Item" : "Packing List"
```

In the code above, you first toggle the Boolean variable `isMenuOpen`, which tracks whether the menu is currently expanded or collapsed.

Next, you modify the constraint's `constant` property to either 184.0 pt or 44.0 pt, depending on the state of `isMenuOpen`, to make the menu expand or collapse as required.

In the final line of code you toggle the menu title between **Packing List** and **Select Item** as appropriate.

Build and run your project; tap the + button a few times and the menu should expand and contract as you had planned:

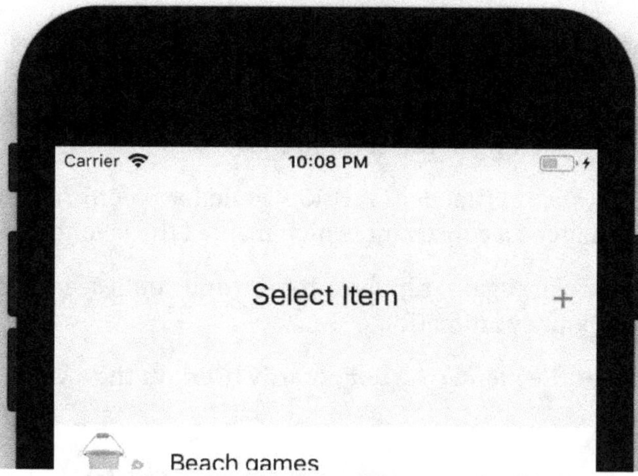

To animate the layout changes, you'll need your old friend `animate(withDuration:animations:)` or any of the similar APIs.

Animating Layout Changes

Add the following code to the bottom of `actionToggleMenu`:

```
UIView.animate(withDuration: 1.0, delay: 0.0,
  usingSpringWithDamping: 0.4, initialSpringVelocity: 10.0,
  options: .curveEaseIn,
  animations: {
    self.view.layoutIfNeeded()
  },
  completion: nil
)
```

In the code above, you create a spring animation (just as you learned about in Chapter 4, "Springs") and force an update of the layout from within the animations closure. This is all it takes to animate your constraint modifications.

Still a little fuzzy on what's happening above? Here's a bit more background on how the animation works.

When you modify pertinent view properties inside an animation closure, they'll be animated as you would expect, and Auto Layout will still set the `bounds` and `center` of your views once it finishes its calculations.

In this case, you've already updated the constraint value, but iOS hasn't had a chance to update the layout yet. By calling `layoutIfNeeded()` from within the animation closure, you set the center and bounds of *every* view involved in the layout. That's it — there's no magic happening in the background!

If you *hadn't* called `layoutIfNeeded()`, UIKit would have performed a layout anyway since you changed a constraint, which marked the layout as **dirty**.

Build and run your project again; tap the + button and you'll see the menu expand and contract with a bouncy animation.

You can even see that the menu title temporarily overlays the system menu on its way back up:

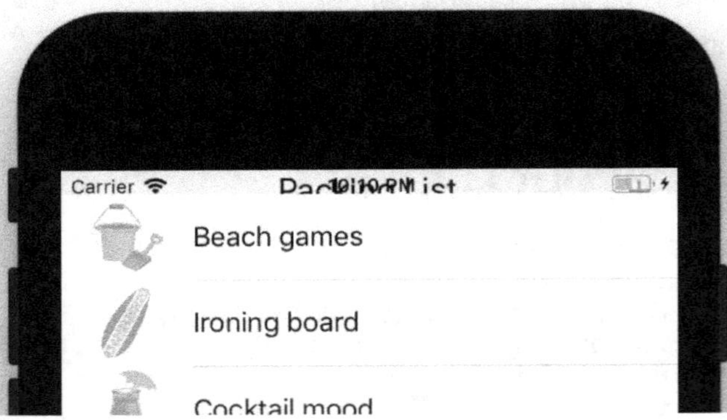

Of course, once the animation settles down it all looks good again.

Did you notice that the table view *also* shrank and grew along with the menu? Instead of covering up the table, the menu actually *pushed* the table view away as it expanded.

This is because of the existing constraint you added in the previous chapter that attaches the top of the table to the bottom of the menu. When the menu grows, the table shrinks to satisfy the constraint. Two animations for the price of one!

To spice things up a bit, you'll now mix constraint animations with some non-constraint animations to see what new effects you can create.

Your next task is to rotate the + button by 45 degrees when the menu expands so it resembles an **x** — i.e. a close button.

Rotating View Animations

Since you already know how to rotate views by adjusting their transform, add the following code to the final `animations` closure:

```
let angle: CGFloat = self.isMenuOpen ? .pi / 4 : 0.0
self.buttonMenu.transform = CGAffineTransform(rotationAngle:
angle)
```

When the menu expands, you set the angle of the rotation to 45 degrees (or π/4 radians); when it contracts, you simply set the rotation back to 0. Then you update the transform on the button to set the view in motion.

Build and run your project; tap the + button to see how the rotation animation looks alongside the call to `layoutIfNeeded()`:

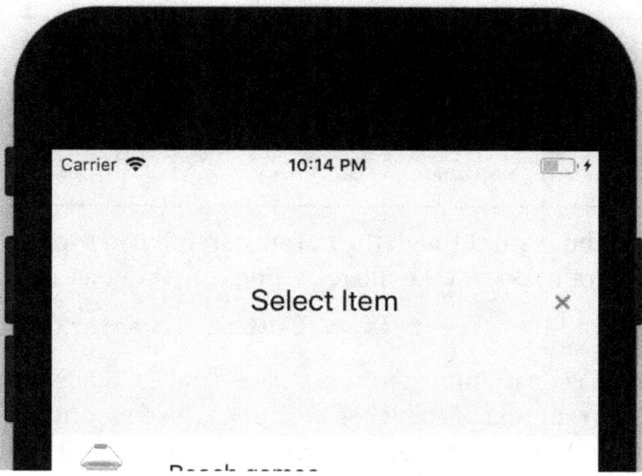

The animation looks gorgeous; you can temporarily set the animation duration to 5–6 seconds to see exactly how the + sign rotates to become an **x**. You can also see the button bounce around its center thanks to the spring animation that drives both the constraint and rotation animations.

Inspecting and Animating Constraints

Working with outlets in a visual fashion is a relatively easy way to connect up your outlets, but sometimes you can't use Interface Builder to connect all the bits of your UI to your outlets. You might add constraints from code, or maybe you just don't want to Control-drag and create a massive number of outlets!

In these cases, you need to inspect the existing constraints at runtime and modify in code the ones you want to animate.

Luckily, the `UIView` class has a property named `constraints`, which gives you a list of all constraints that affect the given view. How convenient is that?

Add the following code to the top of `actionToggleMenu()`:

```
titleLabel.superview?.constraints.forEach { constraint in
  print(" -> \(constraint.description)\n")
}
```

This one-liner loops over all constraints affecting the menu bar view and prints them one by one to Xcode's output console.

Build and run your project; tap the + button to see all constraints neatly listed like so:

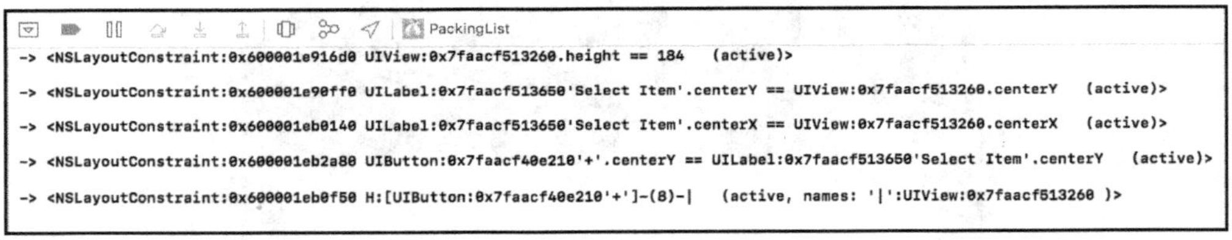

It looks a bit messy, but read through the output carefully and you'll be able to figure out what each constraint does. Take the following constraint as an example:

```
UILabel:...'Select Item'.centerX == UIView:...centerX
```

It's clear that this is a constraint between a `UIView` and a `UILabel`; the description also includes the current text of the label. `centerX` is also mentioned a few times... aha! This must be the constraint that horizontally centers the title within the menu bar. It's time to animate this bad boy.

Animating UILabel Constraints

Find the following line near the top of `actionToggleMenu(_:)`:

```
isMenuOpen = !isMenuOpen
```

Then add the following code *below* that line:

```
titleLabel.superview?.constraints.forEach { constraint in
  if constraint.firstItem === titleLabel &&
    constraint.firstAttribute == .centerX {
    constraint.constant = isMenuOpen ? -100.0 : 0.0
    return
  }
}
```

Here you loop over the list of constraints affecting the menu bar view, but this time you are looking for a certain constraint to adjust.

Do you recall the equation for the horizontal center constraint? It looked something like the following:

```
UILabel.CenterX = 1.0 * Superview.CenterX + 0.0
```

The `NSLayoutConstraint` properties map to the above equation in a very straightforward manner:

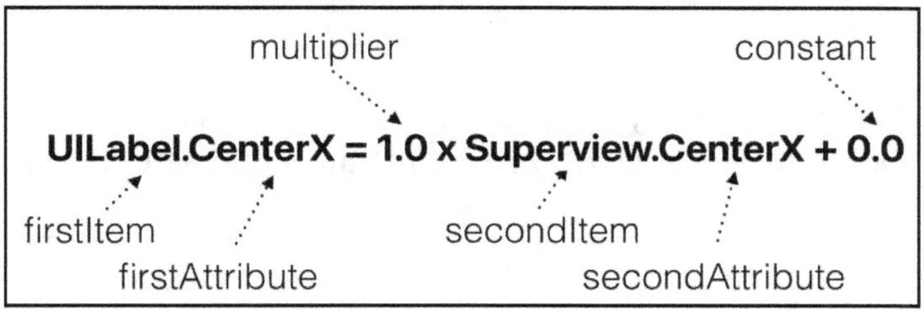

The `if` condition makes more sense now when you look back at the last piece of code you added: for each constraint, you check if the `firstItem` is the title label and the relevant attribute is the title's `.centerX`.

When you find the correct constraint, you adjust `constant` to 100 pt to push the title to the left when the menu opens.

> **Note**: There's a slightly easier way to dynamically find an existing constraint and work with it; you'll look into that next.

Build and run your project; tap the + button to see how your new constraint logic works:

Remember you're calling `layoutIfNeeded()` from within a spring animation API, so the title animation bounces a bit.

> **Note**: If by any chance your animation doesn't kick in, check out the Center Horizontally in Superview constraint on the label; make sure the label is the first item and the menu bar view is the second.

Your UI is starting to look really cool, but you know you can take this even further. The next section shows you how to *replace* constraints to create some neat animations.

Animating by Replacing Constraints

At this point in the chapter, you've only modified the `constant` property of your constraints. Ironically, the `constant` property is a *mutable* property in the `NSLayoutConstraint` class!

If you want to modify the multiplier, or change a constraint in any other way, you'll need to remove the constraint then add a new one in its place.

To learn how to do that, you'll animate the vertical alignment of the menu title to move it up a bit as the menu opens. This should leave enough empty space at the bottom of the menu to show some more content, which you'll add later in this chapter.

This time around, you'll use a different technique to make sure you've got the correct constraint.

In Interface Builder you can assign an identifier to each constraint, which can help you easily get hold of it at run time.

Open **Main.storyboard** and find the **Align Center Y** constraint of the title label:

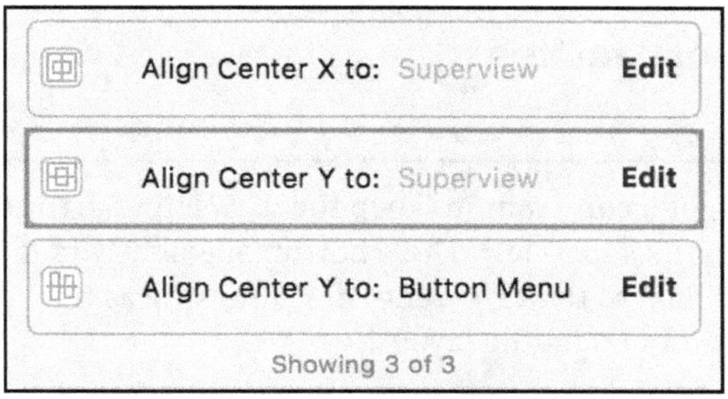

Double-click the constraint and in the **Identifier** text box enter **TitleCenterY**:

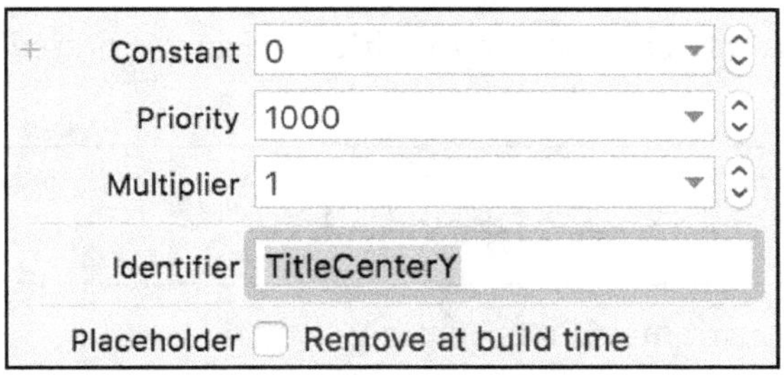

Back in **ViewController.swift** find the following spot in the code within `actionToggleMenu`, at the end of the `for` loop:

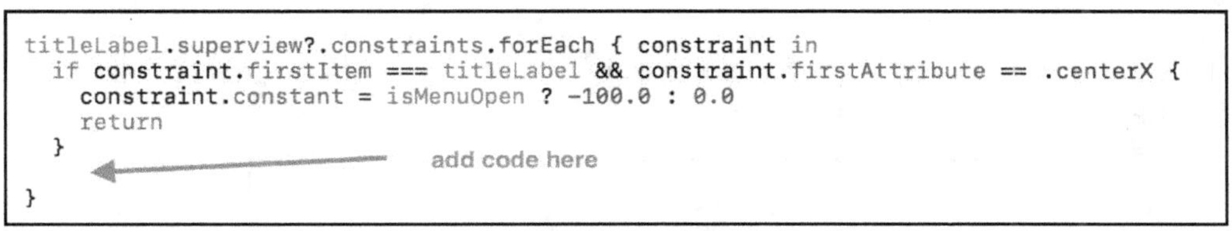

Insert the following code at the point indicated above:

```
if constraint.identifier == "TitleCenterY" {
  constraint.isActive = false
  //add new constraint
  return
}
```

You check if the identifier of the constraint is the same as the one you want to replace and if so, you remove the constraint. You do that by setting `isActive` to `false`; this causes the view hierarchy to remove the constraint. If you don't also have a reference to it, the constraint object will be deleted from memory.

Build and run your project; tap + and observe what happens:

Since there's no longer a constraint to keep the view aligned, the title simply bounces to the top of its superview. The + button obediently tags along because its own `CenterY` is attached to the title's `CenterY`. Amusing as the effect is, you'll need to add a new constraint and fix the layout.

Adding Constraints Programmatically

When the menu is retracted you want the title vertically centered within the menu view like so:

Or, to express the constraint via its equation:

```
Title.CenterY = Menu.CenterY * 1.0 + 0.0
```

But when the menu expands, you'd like to move the title a bit upwards to make space for the list of packing items later on:

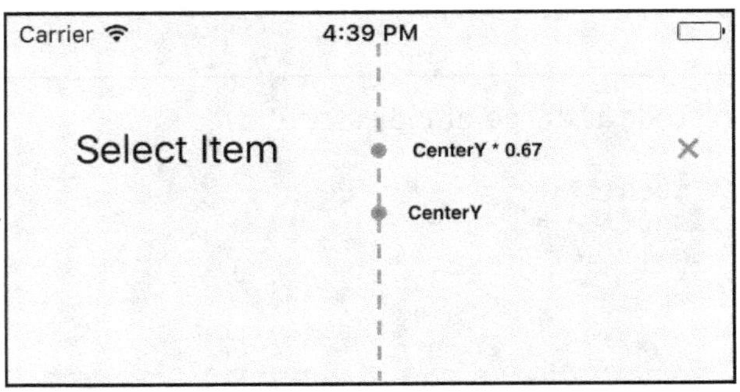

Here's the constraint's equation spelled out in detail:

```
Title.CenterY = Menu.CenterY * 0.67 + 0.0
```

Find the placeholder comment `//add new constraint` in the code you just added, and replace it with the following:

```
let newConstraint = NSLayoutConstraint(
  item: titleLabel,
  attribute: .centerY,
  relatedBy: .equal,
  toItem: titleSuperview,
  attribute: .centerY,
  multiplier: isMenuOpen ? 0.67 : 1.0,
  constant: 0
)
newConstraint.identifier = "TitleCenterY"
newConstraint.isActive = true
```

`NSLayoutConstraint`'s initializer takes a cartload of parameters, but happily they map exactly to all parts of the constraint's equation. The parameters are as follows:

- `item`: The first item in the equation; in this case, the title label.
- `attribute`: The attribute of the first item of the new constraint.
- `relatedBy`: A constraint can represent either a mathematical equality or an inequality. In this book, you'll only use equality expressions, so here you use `.equal` to represent this relationship.
- `toItem`: The second item in the constraint equation; in this case, it's your title's superview.
- `attribute`: The attribute of the second item of the new constraint.
- `multiplier`: The equation multiplier as discussed earlier.
- `constant`: The equation constant.

As an additional step you give the constraint the identifier **TitleCenterY**. You will use that identifier the next time the user toggles the menu to find and replace the constraint you just created.

Finally you need to set the active property on the constraint to `true` and that tells Auto Layout to apply it to the current layout.

Build and run your project; open the menu and the title should move up to a spot just above the vertical center of the menu bar as shown below:

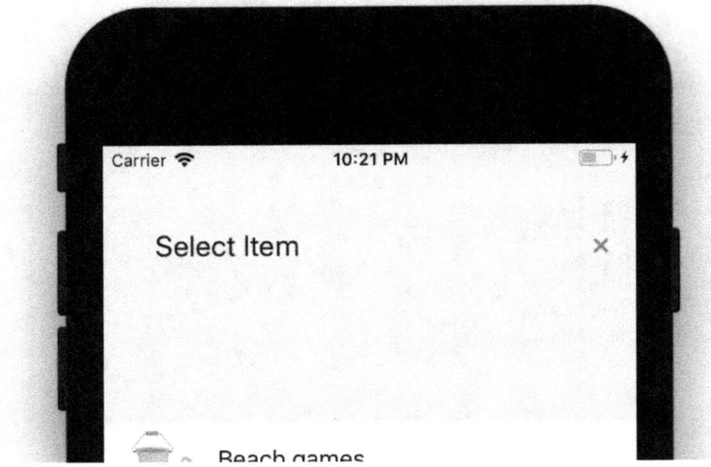

Adding Menu Content

Your next job is to show a list of items in the menu; these are all possible items you can add to your packing list.

The `HorizontalItemList` class that came with your starter project will assist you in displaying that list of items.

> **Note**: This chapter won't cover `HorizontalItemList` in detail; its implementation isn't relevant to creating animations. However, you're still welcome to peek into **HorizontalItemList.swift** if you want to see how it works!

Still in **ViewController.swift**, scroll to the bottom of `actionToggleMenu` and add the following code:

```
if isMenuOpen {
  slider = HorizontalItemList(inView: view)
  slider?.didSelectItem = {index in
    print("add \(index)")
    self.items.append(index)
    self.tableView.reloadData()
```

```
      self.actionToggleMenu(self)
    }
    if let superview = titleLabel.superview, let slider = slider {
      superview.addSubview(slider)
    }
  } else {
    slider?.removeFromSuperview()
  }
```

If the menu is about to open, you create a new instance of `HorizontalItemList` in `slider` to hold your new items, assign a closure expression to `didSelectItem` and then finally add slider to the menu bar.

`didSelectItem` runs when the user taps an image in the list; in this event, you add the image index to the list of selected items and reload the table view.

In the else branch, when the menu is about to close, you simply remove the image list from its parent view.

Build and run your project; add a few items to see what the list of images looks like:

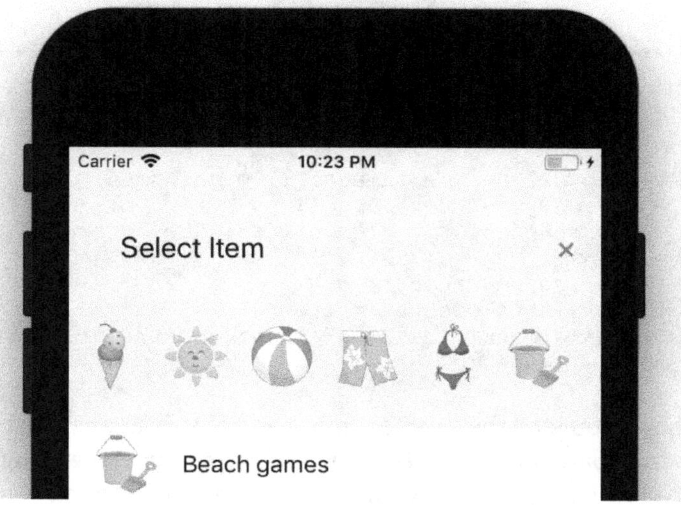

You're nearly done; the final section of this chapter will walk you through dynamically creating and animating views in code.

Animating Dynamically Created Views

Your ultimate task, which will use everything you've learned up to this point and close out the chapter nicely, will be to create a new view, add some constraints to the view and animate it on the screen.

`showItem(_:)` in `ViewController` is called when you tap a table row.

Your task is to create an image view with the tapped image index and display it at the bottom of the screen as shown below:

Add the following code to `showItem(_:)` to create an image view out of the selected image:

```
let imageView = UIImageView(image: UIImage(named:
"summericons_100px_0\(index).png"))
imageView.backgroundColor = UIColor(red: 0.0, green: 0.0, blue:
0.0, alpha: 0.5)
imageView.layer.cornerRadius = 5.0
imageView.layer.masksToBounds = true
imageView.translatesAutoresizingMaskIntoConstraints = false
view.addSubview(imageView)
```

In the code above, you load the selected image and create an image view from it. You give it a semi-transparent black background and round the corners slightly. Notice that you *don't* set the position of the image view in its parent view.

Next you'll create the constraints for the image view, one by one. Add the following code directly below the code you just added:

```
let conX = imageView.centerXAnchor.constraint(equalTo:
view.centerXAnchor)
```

This method uses the new `NSLayoutAnchor` class, which makes creating common constraints really easy. Here, you're creating a constraint between the center x anchor of the image view and the view controller's view.

Next, add the code below to give the image view a bottom constraint:

```
let conBottom = imageView.bottomAnchor.constraint(equalTo:
view.bottomAnchor, constant: imageView.frame.height)
```

This constraint sets the bottom of the image view to match the bottom of the view controller's view, plus the image height; this positions the image just off the bottom edge of the screen, which will serve as the starting point of the animation.

Next you are going to fix up the image width. Add the following code:

```
let conWidth = imageView.widthAnchor.constraint(equalTo:
view.widthAnchor, multiplier: 0.33, constant: -50.0)
```

This sets the image width to 1/3 of the screen width less 50 pt. The target size is 1/3 of the screen; you'll animate away the 50 pt difference to make the image "grow" into place later.

Finally, you just need to set the height of the image. Since the images are square you can just set the height as equal to the image width.

Add one final bit of code for the last constraint, then activate them all in a group:

```
let conHeight = imageView.heightAnchor.constraint(equalTo:
imageView.widthAnchor)

NSLayoutConstraint.activate([conX, conBottom, conWidth,
conHeight])
```

This last constraint is a little different from the rest, as it's the first time you've created a relationship between two properties of the same view. Don't worry — this will still work out just fine.

Build and run your project; tap a table row and you'll see your new image view appear like so:

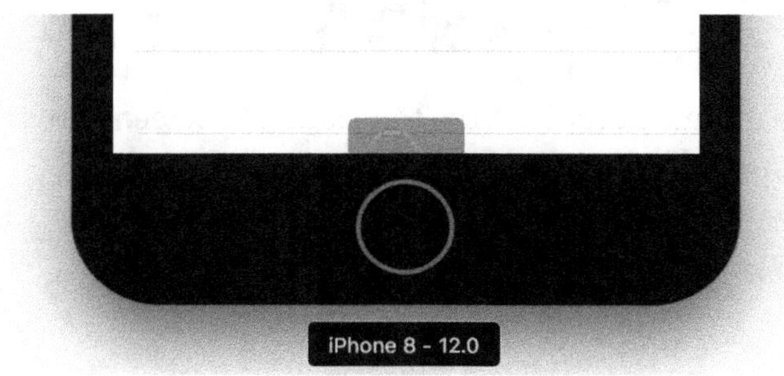

This is, of course, just the starting position of your animation. Your job now is to make the image pop up from the bottom.

Adding Additional Dynamic Animations

Add the following code to showItem(_:):

```
UIView.animate(withDuration: 0.8, delay: 0.0,
  usingSpringWithDamping: 0.4, initialSpringVelocity: 0.0,
  animations: {
    conBottom.constant = -imageView.frame.size.height/2
    conWidth.constant = 0.0
    self.view.layoutIfNeeded()
  },
  completion: nil
)
```

Changing constant on conBottom moves the image up, and the adjustment to conWidth grows the image width by 50 pt to make the image return to its original size. You don't need to set the height as it's automatically constrained to the image width.

Finally you call layoutIfNeeded(), which kicks off the animations. Build and run your project; tap a few table rows to see your image animate:

Hang on! The image view starts from the top left of the screen then flies into the middle! What happened?

Think about it for a moment: you added a view, set some constraints, then altered those constraints and animated a layout change.

However, the view never got the chance to perform its initial layout, so your image started from its default position at `(0, 0)` in the top left. Ah — that's why it's flying in like that.

To fix this, you need to make sure your initial layout happens before the animation starts. Add the following code *before* the animation call:

```
view.layoutIfNeeded()
```

This will immediately set your initial layout before anything else happens. All constraint changes you make between the call to `layoutIfNeeded()` and the next one will be part of your animation.

Build and run your project now and the animations should work as intended.

It's a little annoying that the images keep piling up on top of each other; you'll fix this in the challenge at the end of this chapter.

Don't forget to try the project in different simulators and orientations; your constraint animations should look good in all of them:

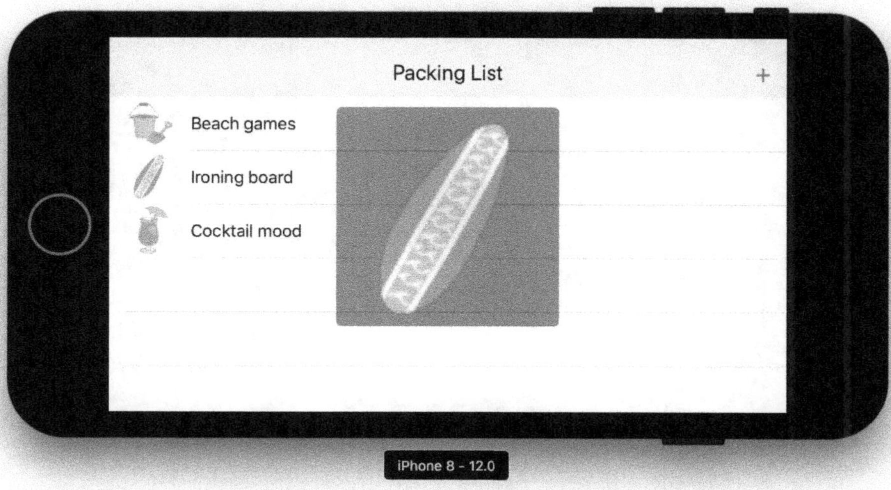

Challenges

Challenge 1: Animate the Image out of the Screen

OK — now you get to fix those pesky image views that stay stuck on the screen.

In `showItem(_:)`, keep the image visible for 1 second and then animate it back out of the screen.

Use the animation method that lets you set a delay for the animation, animate the image back out of the screen, and finally remove the image view from the view hierarchy in the animation completion closure.

That's all you need to know to complete the challenge. Good luck!

You now have a good understanding of how to create view animations in Auto Layout projects. Although not all projects in this book make use of Auto Layout, try to use it when you can to keep your skillset fresh!

Section IV: Layer Animations

In this section of the book, you'll learn about animating layers instead of views and how to use special layers. A layer is a simple model class that exposes a number of properties to represent some image-based content. Every UIView is backed by a layer, so you can think of layers as the lower-level behind-the-scenes class behind your content.

By the end of this section, you will know how — and when! — to animate your views, and when it's appropriate to use layers.

Chapter 10: Getting Started With Layer Animations

Layer animations work much like view animations; you simply animate a property between a start and an end value over a defined period of time and let Core Animation take care of the rendering in between.

However, layers have a bigger number of animatable properties than views; this gives you a lot of choice and flexibility when it comes to designing your effects; many specialized `CALayer` subclasses add other properties that you can use in your animations.

This chapter will introduce you to the basics of `CALayer` and Core Animation. You'll get a feel for working with animations in layers; you'll learn how to move layers around, fade them in and out and create animations comparable to the ones you created using UIKit.

Animatable Properties

Some of the animatable properties in `CALayer` correspond directly to the view properties you worked with in previous chapters, such as frame, position and opacity. You'll see both the familiar and the new animatable properties used in layer animation in this chapter. You'll re-create some of the earlier view animations but with layers, so you can draw the parallels and see for yourself where the similarities end — and where the new possibilities begin.

Position and Size

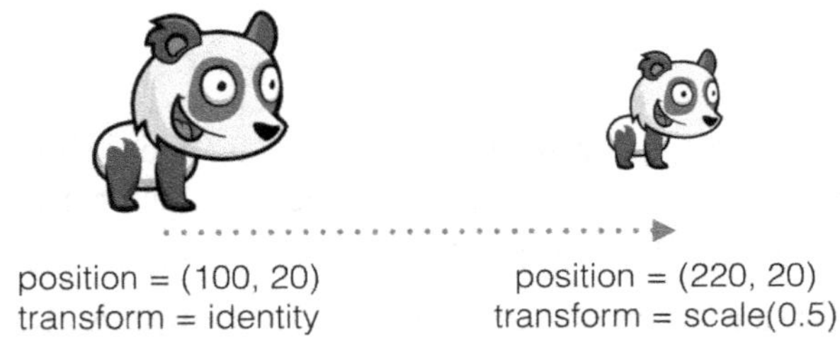

Animating the position, size, or transform of a layer equally affects any view contained within that layer, just as if you had directly animated the view itself.

- `bounds`: modify this to animate the bounding frame of the layer.
- `position`: modify this to animate the position of the layer within its parent layer. You can animate `position.x` or `position.y` separately if you want to control movement on only one axis.
- `transform`: modify this to move, scale, and rotate the layer. You can even animate layers in 3D space, which you can't do with views alone. You'll learn about 3D layer transforms in Section VII, "3D Animations".

Border

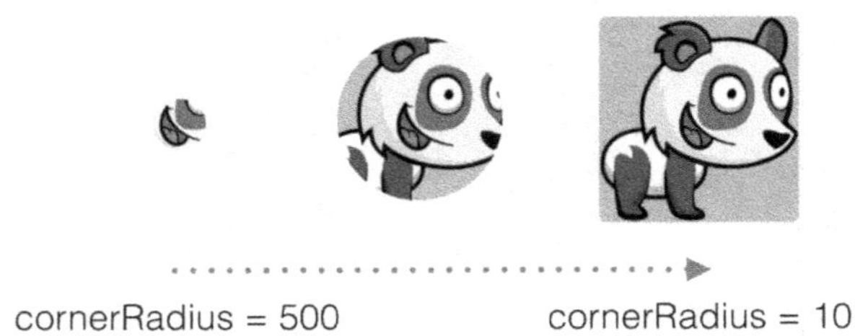

You can easily animate a layer's border to change its color, width and corner radius:

- `borderColor`: modify this to change the border tint.
- `borderWidth`: modify this to grow or shrink the width of the border.
- `cornerRadius`: modify this to change the radius of the layer's rounded corners.

Shadow

You can animate all aspects of the layer's shadow:

- `shadowOffset`: Modify this to make the shadow appear closer to or further away from the layer.
- `shadowOpacity`: Modify this to make the shadow fade in or out.
- `shadowPath`: Modify this to change the shape of the layer's shadow. You can create different 3D effects to make your layer look like it's floating with different shadow shapes and positions.
- `shadowRadius`: Modify this to control the blur of the shadow; this is especially useful when simulating movement of the view towards or away from the surface where the shadow is cast.

Contents

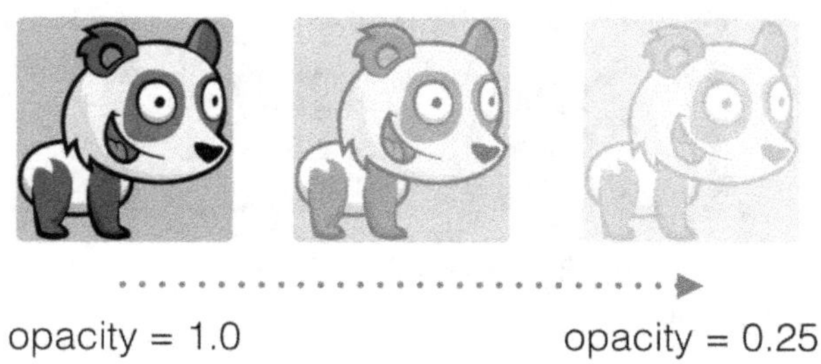

Finally, there are a few properties that control how the layer's contents are rendered:

- `contents`: Modify this to assign raw TIFF or PNG data as the layer contents.
- `mask`: Modify this to establish the shape or image you'll use to mask the visible contents of the layer; you'll use this property to create some very cool effects in Chapter 15, "Shapes & Masks".
- `opacity`: Modify this to animate the transparency of the layer contents.

Keep in mind that this is only a *partial* list of properties you can animate; subclasses of `CALayer` usually have other properties that you can animate as well.

The properties listed above are enough to get you started; it's time to get to work on your first animation with layer properties.

Your First Layer Animation

You'll begin with the completed Bahama Air login screen project from the end of Chapter 5, "Transitions". As always, you can build on your previous work or open the starter project included with this chapter.

Build and run your project to see the familiar sight of the Bahama Air login screen:

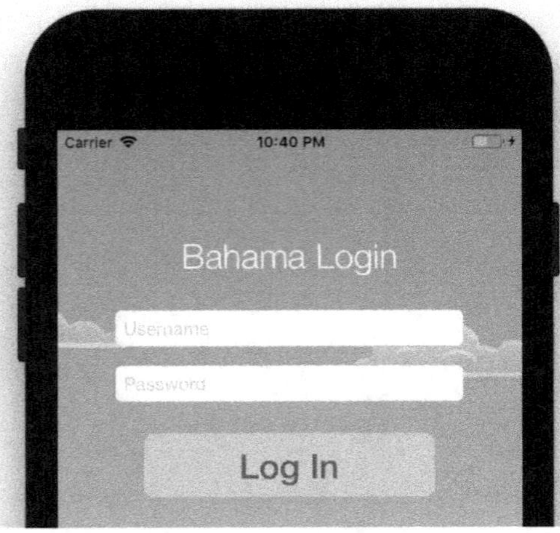

Your job is to remove the existing view animations and replace them one-by-one with layer-based animations.

Open **ViewController.swift** and find `viewWillAppear()`.

Remove the line below that moves the heading out of the screen bounds:

```
heading.center.x -= view.bounds.width
```

There's no need to perform this action anymore since you can specify *both* the start and end values in your layer animation.

Next, scroll down to `viewDidAppear()` and remove the animation call that moves `heading` as shown below:

```
UIView.animate(withDuration: 0.5) {
  self.heading.center.x += self.view.bounds.width
}
```

Build and run your project; watch the animation screen and check that the form title is no longer animated:

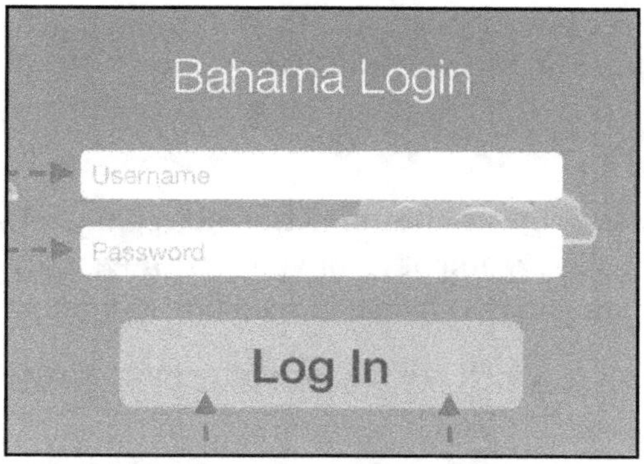

Now that you've stripped out the old view animation code, it's time to add some layer animations! Find `viewWillAppear()` and add the following code at the top of the method, underneath the call to `super`:

```
let flyRight = CABasicAnimation(keyPath: "position.x")
flyRight.fromValue = -view.bounds.size.width / 2
flyRight.toValue = view.bounds.size.width / 2
flyRight.duration = 0.5
```

Animation objects in Core Animation are simply data models; you create an instance of the model and set its data properties accordingly.

An instance of `CABasicAnimation` describes a *potential* layer animation: one that you might choose to run now, at a later time, or not at all. Since the animation isn't bound to a specific layer, you can re-use the animation on other layers and each layer will run a copy of the animation independently.

In an animation model you can specify the property to animate as the `keypath` argument; that's convenient, as you'll always be animating *something* in the layer.

Here, you're animating only the `x` component of the position. Core Animation conveniently exposes the individual members of position, bounds, and transform so you can animate them each separately.

Next, you set the `fromValue` and `toValue` for the property you've specified on `keypath`. In this case, you want it to start offscreen to the left and end up in the center of the screen.

Finally, the concept of the animation duration hasn't changed; here you set the duration to `0.5` seconds. Now that your animation is all set up, you can add it to a layer in your app and see how it looks. Add the following line below the code you just added to add your animation to your title layer:

```
heading.layer.add(flyRight, forKey: nil)
```

`add(_:forKey:)` makes a copy of the animation object and tells Core Animation to run it on the layer. The key argument is for your use only; it lets you identify the animation later on if you need to change or stop the animation.

Build and run your project; you'll see the form title move to the center of the screen as shown below:

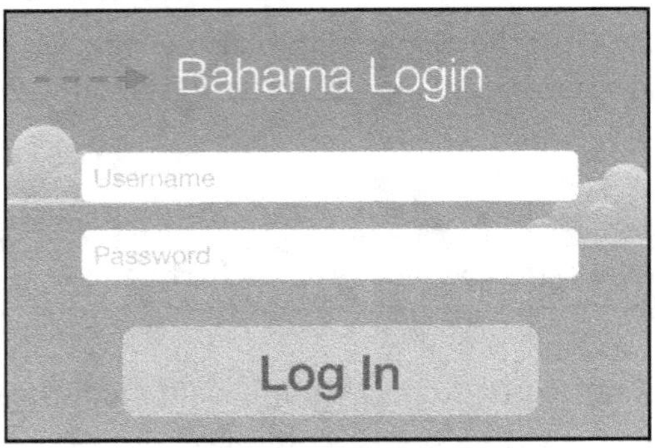

As expected, the layer — and its contained view — animate smoothly into position. This shows you how closely a view and its backing layer are bound.

> **Note:** Animating structs such as `CGRect` or `CATransform3D` isn't as straightforward as it is with object values, like you did above. You'll see how to animate structs in Chapter 14, "Layer Keyframe Animations & Struct Properties".

Now that you have the basics nailed down, things are only going to get more interesting!

More Elaborate Layer Animations

You've handled the title layer on your login screen; your next task is to take care of the username field.

Scroll to `viewWillAppear()` and **remove** the following line:

```
username.center.x -= view.bounds.width
```

Then **remove** the following view animation from the `username` field in `viewDidAppear()`:

```
UIView.animateWithDuration(0.5, delay: 0.3,
  usingSpringWithDamping: 0.6, initialSpringVelocity: 0,
  animations: {
    self.username.center.x += self.view.bounds.width
  },
  completion: nil
)
```

Before you rush through and blindly copy and paste the code to create a `CABasicAnimation` for the username field, consider the following two facts:

- A `CABasicAnimation` object is just a data model, which is *not* bound to any particular layer.
- `add(_:forKey:)` makes a *copy* of the animation object.

It turns out that you can simply take the animation from your heading layer, adjust the animation a bit if needed and reuse it to animate your username field onto the screen.

Add the following code in the same spot where you deleted the code above in `viewWillAppear()`:

```
username.layer.add(flyRight, forKey: nil)
```

Build and run your project to see the resulting effect of re-using your layer animation:

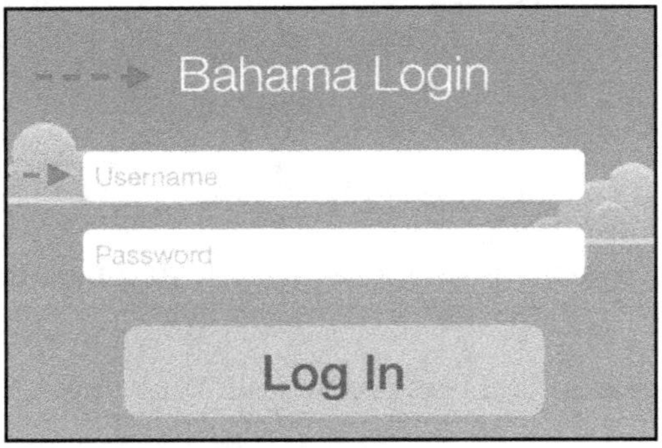

Well, the animation runs, but the title and username field slide onto the screen like those oh-so-unpopular synchronized kill-bots. You'll need to recreate the timing offset you had in the original animation.

Add the following line just **before** the line where you add the `flyRight` animation to your `username` layer:

```
flyRight.beginTime = CACurrentMediaTime() + 0.3
```

The `beginTime` property of your animation sets the absolute time the animation should start; in this case you get the current time with `CACurrentMediaTime()` and add to it the desired delay in seconds.

Build and run your app again to see how things look; it appears in the center of the screen, as it was designed in Interface Builder, and starts animating `0.3` seconds later. What gives?

It's time to learn about another layer animation property called `fillMode`; below are a few examples of how this property works.

Using fillMode

The `fillMode` property lets you control the behavior of your animation at the beginning and end of its sequence.

The constant `CAMediaTimingFillMode.removed` is the default value of `fillMode`. This starts the animation at the defined `beginTime` — or instantly, if you haven't set `beginTime` — and removes the changes made during the animation when the animation completes:

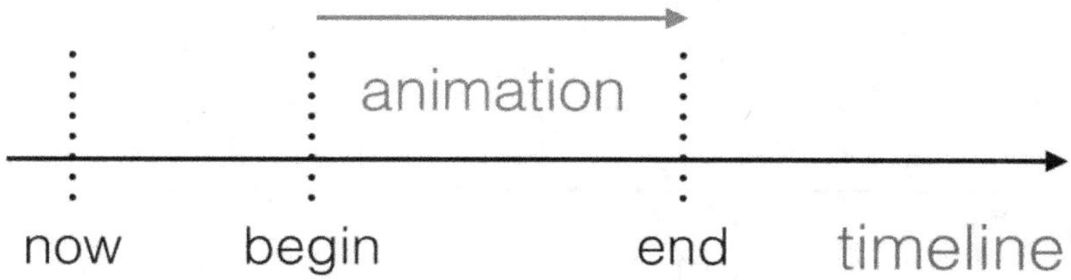

This is the approach you've used so far in this chapter. There are three other options in addition to `removed` that you can use in your animations:

backwards

`CAMediaTimingFillMode.backwards` displays the first frame of your animation instantly on the screen, regardless of the actual start time of the animation, and starts the animation at a later time.

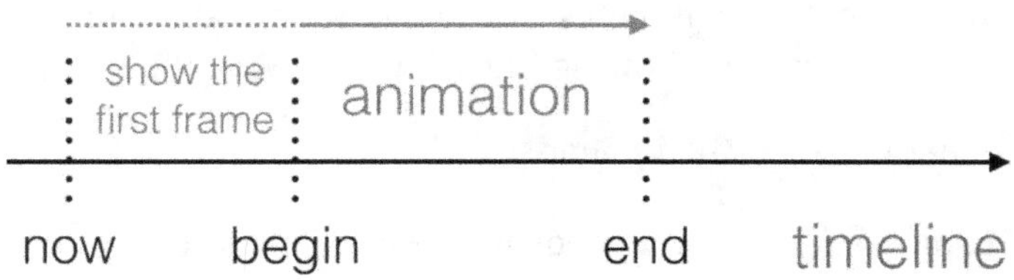

forwards

`CAMediaTimingFillMode.forwards` plays the animation as usual, but retains the final frame of the animation on the screen until you remove the animation:

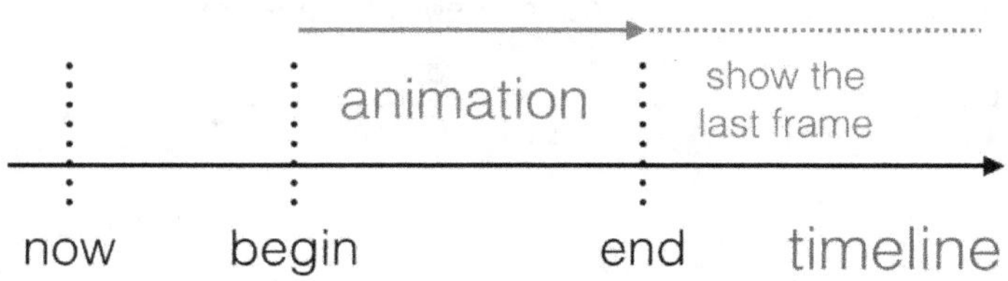

In addition to setting `CAMediaTimingFillMode.forwards`, you'll need to make some other changes to the layer to get the last frame to "stick". You'll learn about this a little later in the chapter.

both

`CAMediaTimingFillMode.both` is a combination of `forwards` and `backwards`; as you'd expect, this makes the first frame of the animation appear on the screen immediately and retains the final frame on the screen when the animation is finished:

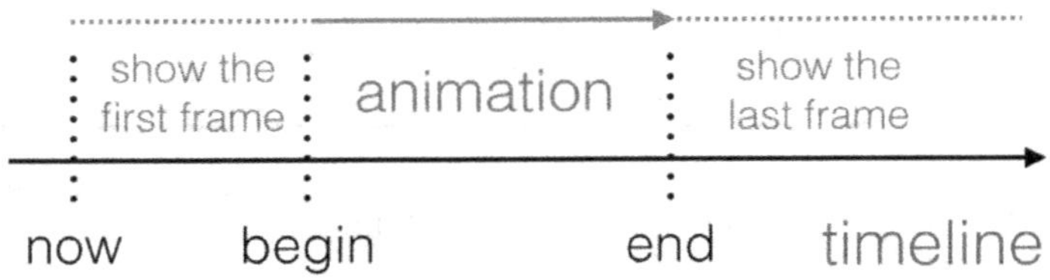

To fix the issue you discovered earlier, you'll use `both`.

Add the following line of code to where you set up `flyRight` (`fromValue`, `toValue`, `duration`, etc.) and before you add it to a layer:

```
flyRight.fillMode = .both
```

Build and run your project; you'll see that the `username` field doesn't appear at first and the animation only starts after a 0.3-second delay. Also, the fields remain in position when the animation completes. You can now animate your password field in a similar fashion. **Remove** the following line from `viewWillAppear()`:

```
password.center.x -= view.bounds.width
```

Then find and **remove** the following code in `viewDidAppear()`:

```
UIView.animate(withDuration: 0.5, delay: 0.4,
options: .curveEaseOut, animations: {
  self.password.center.x += self.view.bounds.width
}, completion: nil)
```

...and replace it with the following code in `viewWillAppear()`:

```
flyRight.beginTime = CACurrentMediaTime() + 0.4
password.layer.add(flyRight, forKey: nil)
```

Build and run your project; you'll see all three layers flying in, with the password field arriving just a tenth of a second behind the username field:

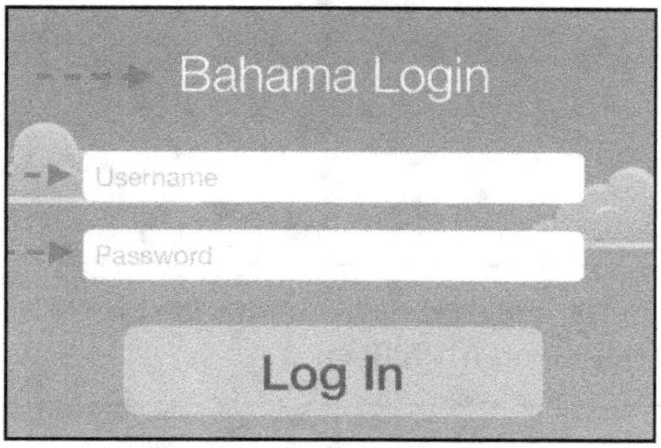

So far, your animations have happened to end at the exact position where the form elements were originally positioned in Interface Builder. Many times, this won't be the case. In the next section of this chapter, you'll discover how to handle the situation where layers end at a different position!

Animations vs. real content

First, you'll put the text fields off screen at the start of the animation. For testing purposes, add the following code to the start of `viewWillAppear()`:

```
username.layer.position.x -= view.bounds.width
password.layer.position.x -= view.bounds.width
```

Because the fields are now starting offscreen, add this line before you add the animation to the username layer:

```
flyRight.fromValue = nil
```

Build and run the project and the animation happens like it did before, but the text fields disappear at the end! What's going on? Well, the animation has finished, so the layers have returned to its original value. If you used the view hierarchy debugger you'd see them hovering off to the left of the main screen.

When you animate a layer, you're not actually seeing the layer itself animated; instead, you're seeing a cached version of it known as the **presentation layer**. The presentation layer is removed from the screen once the animation completes and the original layer shows itself again.

To start, remember you're setting the text fields to be positioned offscreen in `viewWillAppear(_:)`:

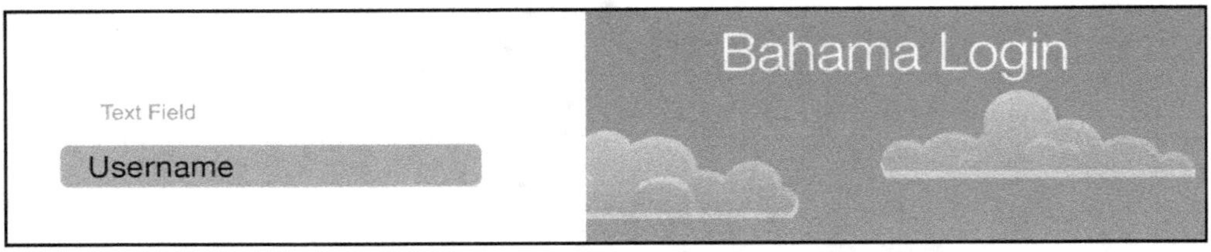

When the animation starts, a pre-rendered animation object replaces the field and the original text field is temporarily hidden:

You can't tap the animated field, enter any text or engage any other specific text field functionality, because it's *not* the real text field, just a "phantom" visible representation.

As soon as the animation completes, it disappears from the screen and the original text field is un-hidden. The text field is right where you left it: offscreen to the left!

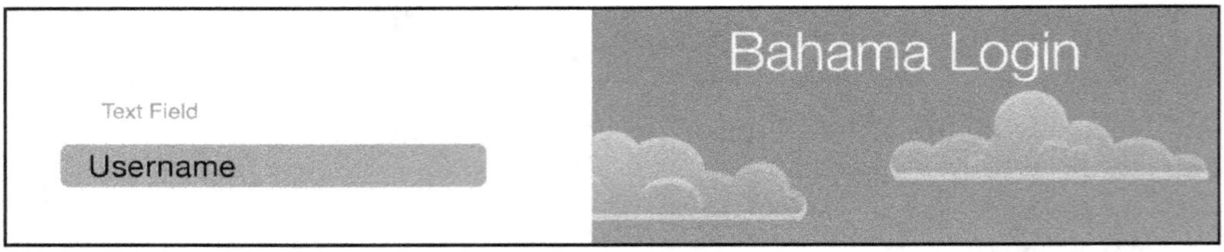

To solve this conundrum, you'll need to use another `CABasicAnimation` property: `isRemovedOnCompletion`.

Setting `fillMode` to `both` instructs the animation to remain on screen after it completes and also show the animation's first frame before its start. To complete the effect, you'll need to set `removedOnCompletion` accordingly; the combination of the two will leave the animation visible on the screen.

Add the following line to `viewWillAppear()`, just after you set the `fillMode`:

```
flyRight.isRemovedOnCompletion = false
```

`isRemovedOnCompletion` is true by default, so the animation disappears as soon as it completes. Setting it to false and combining it with the proper `fillMode` keeps the animation on the screen — and visible as well.

Build and run your project now; you should see that all elements remain on the screen as expected once the animation completes:

Success! Now tap on the username field to enter your username — oh, wait. Remember the earlier note about the difference between the actual text field and the presentation layer? You can't do anything with this pre-rendered image of a text field.

To complete the desired effect, you'll need to remove the animation and show the real text field in its place.

Updating the Layer Model

Once you remove a layer animation from the screen, the layer falls back to its current values for position and other properties. This means that you'll usually need to update the properties of your layer to reflect the final values of your animation.

Remove the line below from your project:

```
flyRight.isRemovedOnCompletion = false
```

Although you know how `isRemovedOnCompletion` works when set to `false`, try to avoid it whenever possible. Leaving animations on the screen affects performance, so you'll let them be removed automatically and update the original layer's position instead.

Next, find the line of code that adds the animation to `username` in `viewWillAppear()` and add the following line after it:

```
username.layer.position.x = view.bounds.size.width / 2
```

Next, add the code for the password field. Find the line that adds the animation to password and add the following line after it:

```
password.layer.position.x = view.bounds.size.width / 2
```

This will set the actual layers to be positioned in the middle of the screen where they belong.

Build and run your project; Uh oh. The fields have stopped animating altogether! What's going on?

You set the animation's `fromValue` to nil some time ago, but the code above updates the main layer's position; this causes the animation to start from the center of the screen. To fix this, remove the following line:

```
flyRight.fromValue = nil
```

Build and run your project again, and this time you'll see the fields animate as expected.

> **Note**: If the keyboard doesn't appear when you tap on a text field in the Simulator, you can activate it manually by navigating the menu to Hardware\Keyboard\Toggle Software Keyboard.

When possible, design your layers in Interface Builder with their final values, and use `fromValue` for the starting and in-between values. This reduces the complexity of keeping your model and presentation layers in sync.

Best Practices

Whoa — this was a long chapter! You tried out a ton of different layer animation techniques, and that's just the start!

At this point you might be feeling a bit overwhelmed and asking yourself "Should I use `fillMode`? Should I be removing my animations? And how do I update my layer to have smooth animation completion?"

As a rule of thumb: Remove your animations and consider never using `fillMode`, except if the effect you want to achieve is not possible otherwise. `fillMode` makes your UI elements lose their interactivity and also makes the screen not reflect the actual values in your layer object.

In some rare cases when you animate non-interactive visual elements fillMode will save your bacon; you'll read more about this in Chapter 18, "Replicating Animations."

As for updating your layer properties: consider always doing that immediately after you add the animation to your layer. Sometimes you might get the odd flash between the initial and final animation values.

In this case, try updating your layer property to the final animation value even before adding the animation.

Key Points

- Layer animations give you more options when it comes to creating UI animations. Unlike view animations, you can animate many additional treats such as corner radius, shadow, border width and color, border style, and more.
- `CABasicAnimation` is a basic animation model class you use to *describe* the desired animation, which you hand off for rendering by calling `CALayer.add(_, forKey:)`.
- Since layer animations are data models that are copied by Core Animation when added to a layer, you can reuse the same model instance to create a number of similar animations and even adjust some of its properties in between adding it to different layers.

Challenges

You covered a lot of ground in this chapter; if you want to really test that you've retained all of the concepts covered in each section, feel free to take on the challenges below.

Refer back to the various sections if you need some assistance, but if you've followed along with the exercises in this chapter, you're more than capable of working through each of the three challenges in this chapter!

Challenge 1: Fade in the Clouds With Layer Animations

In this challenge, you'll replace the UIKit cloud animations from Chapter 3, "Getting Started With View Animations" with layer animations instead.

If you need a recipe to follow, the steps below should give you a good starting point:

1. Remove the four UIKit animations that fade in `cloud1`, `cloud2`, `cloud3`, and `cloud4` from `viewDidAppear()`.
2. Remove the four lines from `viewWillAppear()` that set the clouds' `alpha` property to `0.0`.

3. At the bottom of `viewWillAppear()`, create a `CABasicAnimation` with `opacity` as the `keypath`.
4. Set `fromValue` to `0.0`, `toValue` to `1.0`, and `duration` to `0.5`. You'll need to set `fillMode` to `.backwards` to hide the clouds when the app starts.
5. Set the animation's `beginTime` to `CACurrentMediaTime() + 0.5` and add the animation to `cloud1`.
6. Set the animation's `beginTime` to `CACurrentMediaTime() + 0.7` and add the animation to `cloud2`.
7. Set the animation's `beginTime` to `CACurrentMediaTime() + 0.9` and add the animation to `cloud3`.
8. Set the animation's `beginTime` to `CACurrentMediaTime() + 1.1` and add the animation to `cloud4`.

The end result should recreate the initial cloud transition with layer animations as shown below:

Challenge 2: Animating Colors

In this challenge you'll re-create the Log In button tint animation.

First, **remove** your old UIKit code as shown below:

```
self.loginButton.backgroundColor = UIColor(red: 0.85, green:
0.83, blue: 0.45, alpha: 1.0)
```

Then scroll down to resetForm() and **remove** the following line:

```
self.loginButton.backgroundColor = UIColor(red: 0.63, green:
0.84, blue: 0.35, alpha: 1.0)
```

Create a new top-level function in **ViewController.swift** (e.g. a top-level function will be located outside the class body; add it below the delay function):

```
func tintBackgroundColor(layer: CALayer, toColor: UIColor)
```

In this new method, create a basic animation and run it on the layer parameter, keeping in mind these key requirements:

- Animate the backgroundColor property.
- Set fromValue to the current background color: layer.backgroundColor.
- Set toValue to toColor.CGColor; Core Animation uses CGColor values for colors.
- Set the animation duration for 1.0 second.
- Add the animation to layer.
- Don't forget to set the backgroundColor property on the layer itself so it retains the final animation color.

Now that tintBackgroundColor is complete, you can use it on your Log In button. To do that add, the following code to the very bottom of login():

```
let tintColor = UIColor(red: 0.85, green: 0.83, blue: 0.45,
alpha: 1.0)

tintBackgroundColor(layer: loginButton.layer, toColor:
tintColor)
```

Build and run your project; you'll see the button change its tint as soon as you tap it:

Now find the call to `animate(...)` within `resetForm()` and replace `completion: nil` with the following code:

```
completion: { _ in
  let tintColor = UIColor(red: 0.63, green: 0.84, blue: 0.35,
alpha: 1.0)
  tintBackgroundColor(layer: self.loginButton.layer, toColor:
tintColor)
}
```

This will tint the button back to green when the animation is complete. As an added bonus, since your new function `tintBackgroundColor` is a top-level function, you can re-use it anywhere you like in your project!

Challenge 3: Animating Corner Radius

In this challenge you won't recreate one of your existing view animations; instead, you'll animate the layer specific property `cornerRadius`. Just like you did in Challenge 2 above, create the following new top-level function in **ViewController.swift**:

```
func roundCorners(layer: CALayer, toRadius: CGFloat)
```

This method will take a layer parameter and run a basic animation on it that animates the corner radius from its current value to the supplied `toRadius`.

Simply repeat the routine from Challenge 2, but follow these requirements instead:

- Animate the `cornerRadius` property.
- Set `toValue` to `toRadius`.
- Set the animation `duration` to `0.33` seconds.
- Add the animation to `layer`.
- Don't forget to set the `cornerRadius` on the layer.

Once you've completed roundCorners(), add the following line to the bottom of login():

```
roundCorners(layer: loginButton.layer, toRadius: 25.0)
```

This should round the button when you tap it. To reverse the effect when the authentication process is done, add the following code to resetForm() after the call to tintBackgroundColor:

```
roundCorners(layer: self.loginButton.layer, toRadius: 10.0)
```

Build and run your project; you'll see the button appear with its initial color and corner radius:

Now tap the button to see it change in shape and color:

Once all animations complete, the button will return to its initial color and corner radius.

That's it for this chapter; by now you have a solid understanding of how to create basic layer animations, which is the perfect starting point to tackle the animation keys and delegate methods in the next chapter!

Chapter 11: Animation Keys & Delegates

One of the tricky parts about UIKit animations and the corresponding closure syntax is that, if you aren't using some of the new APIs like `UIViewPropertyAnimator` (which you will look into in later chapters), once you create and run a view animation you can't pause it, stop it or access it in any way.

With Core Animation, however, you can easily inspect animations that are running on a layer and stop them if you need to. Furthermore, you can even set a delegate object on your animations and react to animation events. In contrast to the completion block you've seen in view animations, you can receive delegate callbacks for when an animation begins and ends (or is interrupted).

In this chapter you'll continue to work with the Bahama Air login project and use animation delegates to make your animations more interactive.

Introducing Animation Delegates

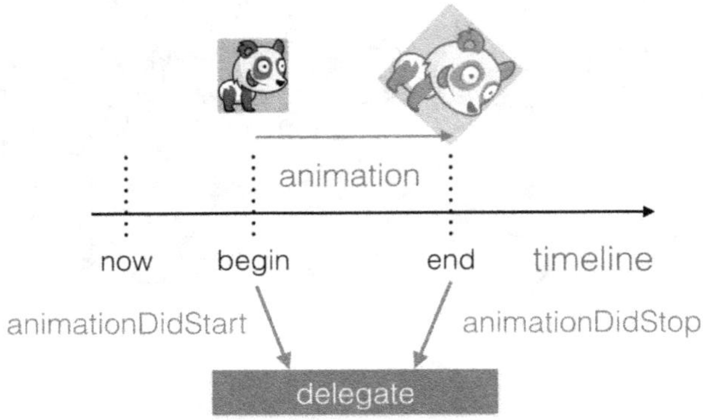

`CAAnimation` and its subclass `CABasicAnimation` implement the delegate pattern and let you respond to animation events.

`CAAnimationDelegate` features two methods that you can implement if you need either or both of them:

```
func animationDidStart(_ anim: CAAnimation)
func animationDidStop(_ anim: CAAnimation, finished flag: Bool)
```

You can either open the starter project for this chapter, or carry on with your own project if you've completed the previous chapter and its challenges.

Your first task is to make each form element pulse once when it reaches its final position on the screen using `animationDidStop()`.

Open **ViewController.swift** and add the following code to `viewWillAppear()`, just before the line where you add the animation to your `heading` layer:

```
flyRight.delegate = self
```

Then add the delegate method to the class in an extension to your view controller:

```
extension ViewController: CAAnimationDelegate {
  func animationDidStop(_ anim: CAAnimation,
    finished flag: Bool) {
    print("animation did finish")
  }
}
```

This simply prints out a line to the console to show that you are, in fact, calling your delegate method.

Build and run your project; you should see the following output in the Xcode console:

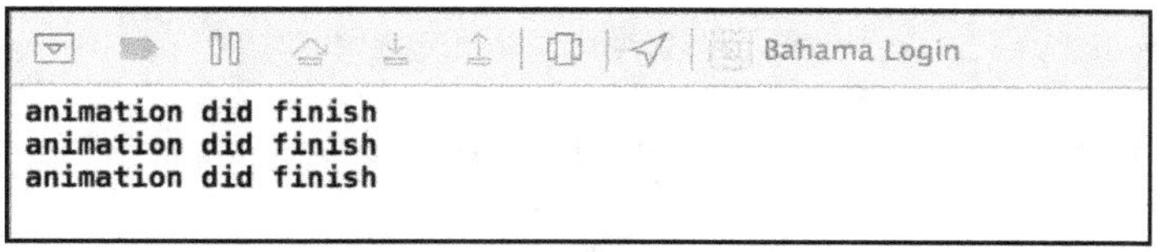

Okay, so your delegates are being called — but how do you discern *which* animation stopped in the code above? Remember, you added the same animation to three different layers! The following section shows you how to manage this with key-value pairs.

Key-value Coding Compliance

The `CAAnimation` class and its subclasses are written in Objective-C and are key-value coding compliant, which means you can treat them like dictionaries and add new properties to them at run time.

You'll use this mechanism to assign a name to the `flyRight` animation so that you can identify it out of the pack of other active animations.

Scroll back to `viewWillAppear()` and add the following code just after the line where you set `flyRight`'s delegate:

```
flyRight.setValue("form", forKey: "name")
flyRight.setValue(heading.layer, forKey: "layer")
```

In the code above, you create the key name on the `flyRight` animation and set it to `form`. Now you can check for this name key from your delegate callbacks to identify the animation as belonging to one of your form controls.

You also assign `heading.layer` to the layer key so you have a reference back to the layer the animation belongs to.

You can leave the name unchanged, but you should update the layer key each time you add the animation to a layer.

Find the line where you add the animation to the `username` layer, and add the following just before it:

```
flyRight.setValue(username.layer, forKey: "layer")
```

Similarly, find the line where you add the animation to the `password` layer, and add the following just before it:

```
flyRight.setValue(password.layer, forKey: "layer")
```

Now each copy of `flyRight` carries a reference to the layer on which it runs.

Switching on Key Values

Now that you have the keys set on your animation, you can check for them in the animation delegate methods.

Add the following code to the bottom of `animationDidStop`:

```
guard let name = anim.value(forKey: "name") as? String else {
  return
}

if name == "form" {
  //form field found
}
```

In the code above you use `value(forKey:)` to get the value of name from the animation and attempt to cast the value to String. The `guard` is used simply because `value(forKey:)` returns an optional in the case there is no value assigned for the provided key, or if the downcast fails. The optional binding statement takes care of these checks for you. If you can unwrap the value, then you have a value you can test for. If not, then your code carries on.

Now you have a spot to run some code when the form animation completes. Replace the comments `//form field found` with the following:

```
let layer = anim.value(forKey: "layer") as? CALayer
anim.setValue(nil, forKey: "layer")

let pulse = CABasicAnimation(keyPath: "transform.scale")
pulse.fromValue = 1.25
pulse.toValue = 1.0
pulse.duration = 0.25
layer?.add(pulse, forKey: nil)
```

Once that's done, you set the value of `layer` to `nil` to remove the reference to the original layer.

> **Note**: Remember that `value(forKey:)` always returns an `AnyObject?`; therefore you must cast the result to your desired type. Don't forget that the cast operation can fail, so you must use optionals in the example above to handle error conditions, such as when the name key exists but the layer key does not.

Finally, you create an animation that bumps the scale of the layer by a tiny bit (a factor of `1.25`), then animates the layer back to its original size (a factor of `1.0`).

Note that you're using optional chaining here with `layer?` — that means the `add(_:forKey:)` call will be skipped if there isn't a layer stored in the animation. And since you set the layer to `nil` earlier, this pulse animation will only happen the first time the form field flies in from the right. Build and run your project; you should see that any time a `flyRight` animation completes, the element will pulse once before it comes to rest:

This gives the animations a nice edge and draws the user's attention to these controls. That takes care of animations that have already stopped; but how can you work with animations that are *still running*? That's where **animation keys** come in.

Animation Keys

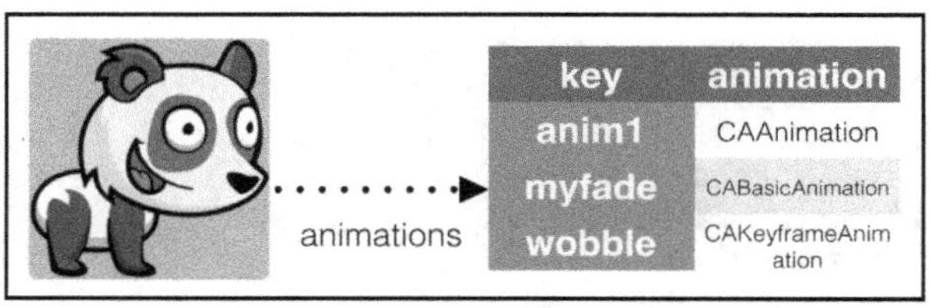

You've probably noticed that `add(_:key:)` has two parameters; so far, you've only been using the first to pass in the animation object itself.

The key parameter is a string identifier that lets you access and control the animation after it's been started.

In this part you'll create another layer animation, learn how to run more than one animation at a time, and discover how to use animation keys to control running animations. You're going to add a new animated label to your form that gives some basic instructions to the user, as shown below:

Your new label will animate slowly from right to left. As soon as the user starts to enter their username or password, this label will stop moving and jump directly to its final position. There's no need to continue the animation once the user knows what to do.

First you'll need to add some code that sets up the label to animate. Add the following property to the end of the property declarations at the top of ViewController:

```
let info = UILabel()
```

This is the label that will be used to display instructions to the user.

Next, add the following code to the bottom of viewDidLoad to set up the various properties of your label:

```
info.frame = CGRect(x: 0.0, y: loginButton.center.y + 60.0,
width: view.frame.size.width, height: 30)
info.backgroundColor = .clear
info.font = UIFont(name: "HelveticaNeue", size: 12.0)
info.textAlignment = .center
info.textColor = .white
info.text = "Tap on a field and enter username and password"
view.insertSubview(info, belowSubview: loginButton)
```

This adds the label just underneath the login button. When the user taps the login button, it will move down and cover the instructions, since the user won't need them anymore.

Now you need to slide the instructions in from the right when the app first opens. Find `viewDidAppear()` and add the following code to the end of that method:

```
let flyLeft = CABasicAnimation(keyPath: "position.x")
flyLeft.fromValue = info.layer.position.x +
view.frame.size.width
flyLeft.toValue = info.layer.position.x
flyLeft.duration = 5.0
info.layer.add(flyLeft, forKey: "infoappear")
```

This animates your label much like your form fields, only your label will slide in from the right side of the screen and fly to the left. Note that you set the animation's key to `infoappear`; you'll use this value to find and then stop the animation when the user starts to enter text in either the username or password field.

Adding a Second Layer Animation

You'll now add a second animation to the label that will fade in the instructions while the label slides in. Add the following code to the end of `viewDidAppear`:

```
let fadeLabelIn = CABasicAnimation(keyPath: "opacity")
fadeLabelIn.fromValue = 0.2
fadeLabelIn.toValue = 1.0
fadeLabelIn.duration = 4.5
info.layer.add(fadeLabelIn, forKey: "fadein")
```

The code fades in the label from a barely visible opacity of `0.2` to a fully visible opacity of `1.0`. The above animation runs on a different property — `opacity` — than in the previous animation — `position` — and has an entirely different duration. This shows you it's possible to run multiple animations independently of each other on the same layer.

> **Note**: If you need to synchronize animations on a layer, then you'll need to use **animation groups** to achieve this. This technique is covered in the next chapter.

Run the project to see the combined animations in action:

So far, so good. Now comes the tricky part: Cancelling the animation if the user starts to enter their username or password.

Identifying Running Animations

You'll need to know when the user taps on either the username or password field. Add the following extension to the very bottom of **ViewController.swift**:

```
extension ViewController: UITextFieldDelegate {
  func textFieldDidBeginEditing(_ textField: UITextField) {
    guard let runningAnimations = info.layer.animationKeys()
else {
      return
    }
    print(runningAnimations)
  }
}
```

This will add a class extension to say `ViewController` conforms to the `UITextFieldDelegate` protocol. Separating protocols into their own extensions like this helps keep the file organized.

The one method you need to implement, `textFieldDidBeginEditing`, will be called when the user starts editing a text field. For now, you'll just print out a list of all the active animations running on the label.

Next, add the following code to the bottom of `viewDidAppear`:

```
username.delegate = self
password.delegate = self
```

This will make the class a delegate of both text fields.

Build and run your project; tap either the username or password field before the label animation completes and you should see the following output in your Xcode console:

Success! Once you know which animations are running, you can do several things with them:

1. Call `removeAllAnimations()` on the layer to stop all running animations or `removeAnimation(forKey:)` to remove just one.

2. Enumerate over the list of animations returned by `animationKeys()`. The animation objects are immutable, so you can't modify the animation while they're in progress.

3. Fetch an animation by key using `animationForKey(_:)`. As before, the returned animation object will be immutable.

To finish your "stop animation" effect, you'll cancel the animation that moves the label, but leave the fade animation running as it would look weird for the opacity of the label to jump directly to `1.0`.

Add the following code to `textFieldDidBeginEditing`:

```
info.layer.removeAnimation(forKey: "infoappear")
```

This removes the slide-in animation and causes the info label to jump straight to the center of the screen — without affecting the fade-in animation.Build and run your project one final time; tap either of the text fields and you'll see the instructions jump straight to the center of the screen and continue to fade in:

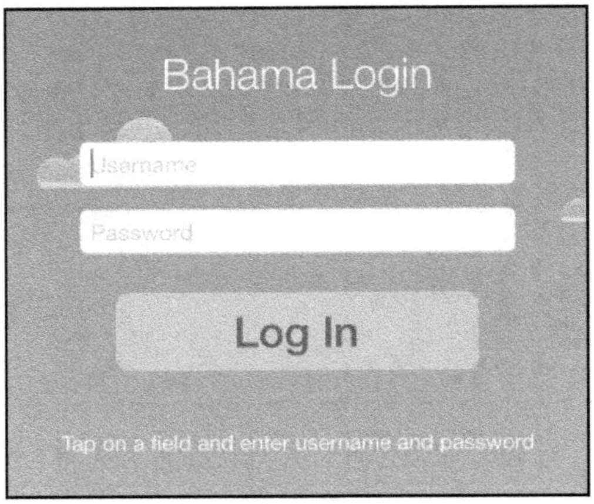

That's a wrap! You've learned about delegate methods, accessing animations by keys, and created your first composite layer animation as an added bonus! Why not test your knowledge with the following challenge?

Key Points

- You can set a delegate for your layer animations and be notified whenever the animations starts or finishes.
- Animations are key-value coding compliant so you can attach arbitrary pieces of data to give you more information about the animation's context.
- The `add(_, forKey:)` API allows you to optionally specify a `forKey` string parameter to give the particular animation a name.

Challenges

Challenge 1

In this challenge, you'll strengthen your knowledge of animation delegates and key-value coding by replacing the existing cloud animation with layer animations.

Replace the `animate(cloud: UIImageView)` method with the following:

```
func animateCloud(layer: CALayer) {

  //1
  let cloudSpeed = 60.0 / Double(view.layer.frame.size.width)
  let duration: TimeInterval = Double(
    view.layer.frame.size.width - layer.frame.origin.x)
    * cloudSpeed

  //2
  let cloudMove = CABasicAnimation(keyPath: "position.x")
  cloudMove.duration = duration
  cloudMove.toValue = self.view.bounds.width +
    layer.bounds.width / 2
  cloudMove.delegate = self
  cloudMove.setValue("cloud", forKey: "name")
  cloudMove.setValue(layer, forKey: "layer")
  layer.add(cloudMove, forKey: nil)
}
```

This method has a similar implementation to the one that animates the clouds using UIKit. In fact, the first few lines of part `//1` above are almost identical to the UIKit implementation.

In the second part of the above method, you create an instance of `CABasicAnimation` for the layer movement and set a name and layer on the animation.

Next, replace the calls in `viewDidAppear()` to `animateCloud()` with the following:

```
animateCloud(layer: cloud1.layer)
animateCloud(layer: cloud2.layer)
animateCloud(layer: cloud3.layer)
animateCloud(layer: cloud4.layer)
```

Your task now is to complete the animation by implementing the delegate code to reset each of the clouds.

You already know how to do this through `animationDidStop(_: finished:)`. Just follow these key points:

- Check if the animation name is `"cloud"`.
- If so, fetch the animation's layer from the `"layer"` key.
- Set the layer's `position.x` to `-layer.bounds.width/2`.
- Wait for half a second (use the `delay(seconds:)` function) and call `self.animateCloud()`, passing in the current layer.

Build and run your project; check that the clouds reappear once they've left the screen:

Congratulations — you've learned the basic layer animation techniques and are ready to move on to creating more complex animations. You'll learn about animation groups next in Chapter 12, "Groups & Advanced Timing."

Chapter 12: Groups & Advanced Timing

In the previous chapter you learned how to add multiple, independent animations to a single layer. But what if you want your animations to work synchronously and stay in step with each other? It's no fun having to fiddle with the math and timings of all the animations separately. That's where **animation groups** come in.

This chapter shows you how to group animations using `CAAnimationGroup`, which lets you add several animations to a group and adjust properties such as duration, delegate, and `timingFunction` all at once.

Grouping animations results in simplified code, and ensures that all your animations will synchronize as one, solid unit.

CAAnimationGroup

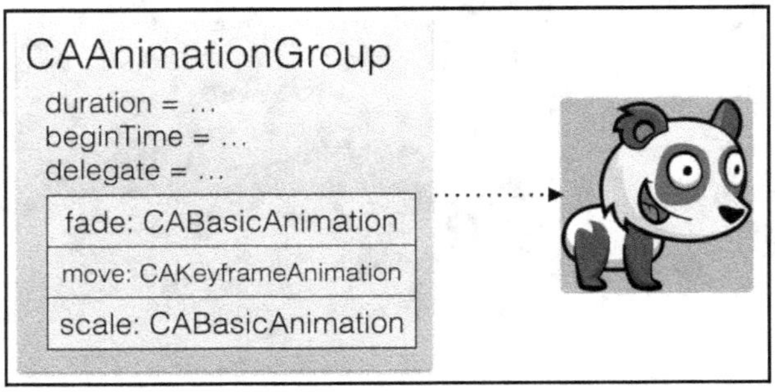

To start off, you'll extend your Bahama Air login screen using animation groups to add some new animation to the login button.

Open the starter project for this chapter, or carry on with your project from the previous chapter and challenge.

Open **ViewController.swift** and **remove** the following code from `viewWillAppear()`:

```
loginButton.center.y += 30.0
loginButton.alpha = 0.0
```

Then **remove** the following code from `viewDidAppear()`:

```
UIView.animate(withDuration: 0.5, delay: 0.5,
  usingSpringWithDamping: 0.5, initialSpringVelocity: 0,
  animations: {
    self.loginButton.center.y -= 30.0
    self.loginButton.alpha = 1.0
  },
  completion: nil
)
```

...and in its place add the following code:

```
let groupAnimation = CAAnimationGroup()
groupAnimation.beginTime = CACurrentMediaTime() + 0.5
groupAnimation.duration = 0.5
groupAnimation.fillMode = .backwards
```

This code creates a new animation group for your use. `CAAnimationGroup` inherits from `CAAnimation`, so you can work with the same properties you already know and love such as `beginTime`, `duration`, `fillMode`, `delegate`, and `isRemovedOnCompletion`.

You'll add one final animation to the login button to scale, rotate, and fade it in with the end effect that the button falls neatly into place on the screen.

Add the first animation by adding the following code directly below the group animation code you just added:

```
let scaleDown = CABasicAnimation(keyPath: "transform.scale")
scaleDown.fromValue = 3.5
scaleDown.toValue = 1.0
```

In the code above you start with a very large version of the button and, over the course of the animation, shrink it to its normal size.

Here you specify only the `fromValue` and `toValue`, but you don't say what the duration of the animation should be nor do you set the `fillMode` of the animation. Where will those values come from?

You might have already guessed that since these values will be the same for all animations in the group, you'll set them on the group as a whole instead of on each animation separately.

Now add code for the next animation below the code you just added:

```
let rotate = CABasicAnimation(keyPath: "transform.rotation")
rotate.fromValue = .pi / 4.0
rotate.toValue = 0.0
```

This animation is similar to the previous one, but it animates the rotation component of the layer transform instead of the scale component. The animation starts with the layer rotated at a 45-degree angle and moves it to its normal orientation of zero degrees.

All that's left to add is the fade-in animation. Add the following code again below the lines you just added:

```
let fade = CABasicAnimation(keyPath: "opacity")
fade.fromValue = 0.0
fade.toValue = 1.0
```

This is the basic fade-in animation you've seen multiple times in this book.

Now add the code below to combine all animations and add them to the button:

```
groupAnimation.animations = [scaleDown, rotate, fade]
loginButton.layer.add(groupAnimation, forKey: nil)
```

To group animations, you simply add them to an array and assign that array as the value of the animations property of the group, just as you would with an ordinary `CABasicAnimation`.

Build and run your project to see the end result:

The button flies in and rotates as expected, but the animation looks stiff. In real life, objects tend to accelerate as they fall through space.

Fortunately, it's easy to add some realism to your animation. This is a great opportunity to learn about using easing with Core Animation.

Animation Easing

You've already seen easing in action in the first chapters of this book that dealt with UIKit animations. Easing in layer animations is conceptually the same thing — only the syntax is different.

`CAMediaTimingFunction` has a few pre-defined easing modes, and `CAMediaTimingFunctionName` contains the names of these predefined functions:

- `.linear` runs the animation with an equal pace throughout its whole duration.

- `.easeIn` alters the animation so it starts slower and finishes at a faster pace.

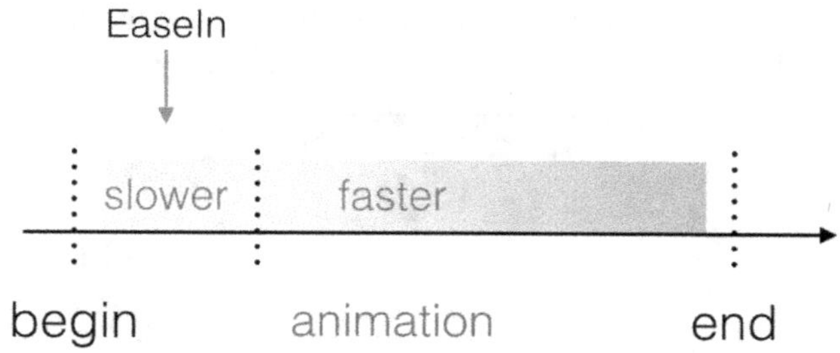

- `.easeOut` produces the opposite effect of `.easeIn`: the animations starts out faster and slows down as it finishes.

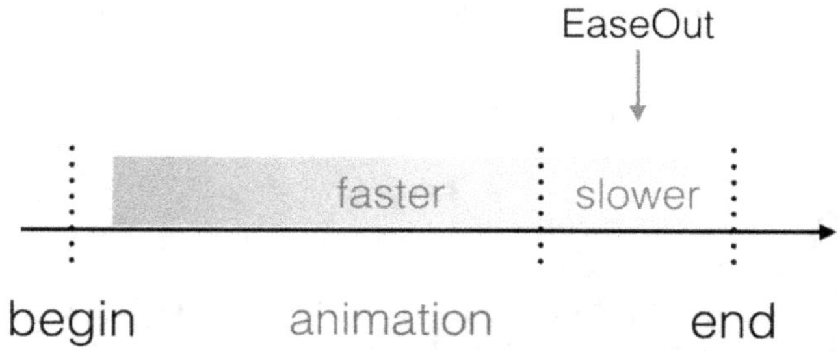

- `.easeInEaseOut` slows the animation in the beginning and at the end, but increases the pace during the middle section.

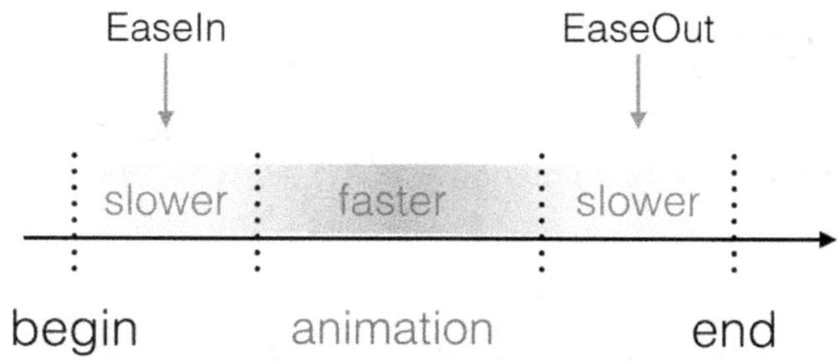

If you think about how objects accelerate as they fall through space, you'll see that you should use an ease-in animation that speeds up towards the end.

Find the piece of code in `viewDidAppear()` where you initialize `groupAnimation` and add the following line after that:

```
groupAnimation.timingFunction = CAMediaTimingFunction(
name: .easeIn)
```

This will set the animation easing on your animation group as a whole.

Build and run your project; the change is subtle, but the animation looks more realistic and snappier:

> **Note**: Although it's beyond the scope of this chapter, you can build your own custom easing function.
>
> Read up on the convenience initializer `CAMediaTimingFunction(controlPoints: _: _: _:)` in the Apple documentation or elsewhere on the web; this lets you define your easing function based on the control points of a cubic Bézier curve.

More Timing Options

The final section of this chapter explores four more animation properties that let you control the timing of your animation.

Repeating Animations

`repeatCount` lets you repeat your animation a specified number of times.

To show how this works, you'll make the instructions fly onto the screen repeatedly instead of just once. Find the code in `viewDidAppear()` where you set the properties of the `flyLeft` animation such as duration, and set the number of animation repeats to 4:

```
flyLeft.repeatCount = 4
```

Build and run your project; you'll see the instructions fly in a total of four times, after which the label remains centered under the login button.

If you want to set the total repeat time in seconds, instead of setting the number of repeats, use the `repeatDuration` property instead of `repeatCount`. However, the fact that the label flies off the screen each time it repeats looks a little weird. How could you create a fluid, reversing animation to make the label fly off the screen in the exact manner in which it entered? It's far easier than you might think. Add the following code just after you set the `repeatCount`:

```
flyLeft.autoreverses = true
```

This will run your animation in reverse each time it completes, then run it in forward motion again.

Build and run your project; you'll see the label fly in, then out, then in again, and so forth:

That was easy and cool-looking, but there's still a little imperfection in your animation. The instructions animate four times, but the label then jumps straight to the center of the screen.

This is because a single animation cycle moves the label to the screen center and then out again. So when you run the animation four times, the final cycle ends with the label off the screen. This is why the label appears to jump to the center of the screen. You can't run *half* an animation cycle — or can you?

Change the `repeatCount` from `4` to `2.5` as shown below:

```
flyLeft.repeatCount = 2.5
```

Build and run your project now; you should see the animation finishes smoothly at the precise location you intended:

Changing the Animation Speed

Although they look nice, some of these animations feel a bit slow. You can control the speed of the animation independently of the duration by setting the `speed` property.

Still in the properties for `flyLeft`, add the following code after the line that sets the `autoreverses` property:

```
flyLeft.speed = 2.0
```

Even though the animation group duration is set to `5` seconds, the animation will complete in just `2.5` seconds since it runs at **double** the speed.

You can set the speed of an animation on its own, but you can also set the speed of a layer as well. The layer conforms to the same timing protocol as an animation: you simply set the speed of the layer to affect all animations you run on that layer.

Add the following code after the `flyLeft.speed` line you just added:

```
info.layer.speed = 2.0
```

Build and run your project; the `flyLeft` animation runs at double speed as before — but wait! The animation that moves the info label runs at *quadruple speed*! What's going on?

Lesson learned: speeds multiply hierarchically. First you set a speed of `2.0` on the info layer, and *then* you set the speed of `flyLeft` to `2.0` as well! You end up with the info layer running at `2.0 x 2.0 = 4.0` times the normal speed.

Just for fun, you can make everything on the screen run super fast by adjusting the speed property of the top-level view controller's layer. Add the following line underneath the line you just added:

```
view.layer.speed = 2.0
```

Build and run your project; you'll see that the form title, the text fields and even the clouds in the sky are double-stepping their way around the screen.

Due to the multiplication factor of animations, the fade animation on the info label runs at 4x speed, and the animation moving the info label across the screen runs at 8x speed! Wheeeee!

Now that you've had some fun with your project, **remove** all the repeating and speed adjustments as shown below:

```
flyLeft.repeatCount = 2.5
flyLeft.autoreverses = true
flyLeft.speed = 2.0
info.layer.speed = 2.0
view.layer.speed = 2.0
```

Playing with animation speeds, reversing and repeating was fun, but your user will likely not appreciate UI elements zipping around the screen like that!

But if you do need to adjust animation speeds locally, you can now do so on the animation level as well as for an entire layer.

Key Points

- You can group animations via `CAAnimationGroup` and easily set common properties that all animations in the group share.
- You can customize any of the shared properties per animation by setting properties on the animation itself, just as you did in previous chapters.
- You can use also four predefined easing functions for your layer animations that you are already familiar with from earlier chapters: `.linear`, `.easeIn`, `.easeOut`, `.easeInOut`.

Challenges

You learned quite a lot of new stuff in this chapter; so instead of having to solve a challenge on your own I'm giving you a free pass and walking you through a few more examples of what you learned above.

The challenge below is optional, but by working through it you'll get some more experience with animation groups — which is never a bad thing!

Challenge 1: Group animations for all Form Elements

In this challenge, you'll create a group of animations and run it on your form elements. Since this code will replace the existing form animations, the first thing you need to do is remove some existing code.

Delete the code that sets up the initial positions of the form heading and form fields, and then remove the code that animates the fields into the center of the screen.

In `viewWillAppear(_:)` create an animation group just like the one shown in this chapter that combines the following two animations:

- Fade from `0.25` to `1.0` opacity
- Move from the layer `position.x` from `-view.bounds.size.width / 2` to `flyRight.toValue = view.bounds.size.width / 2`

Add the two animations to an animation group and run that group on the form heading label and the two text field views.

Since you want your animation delegate method to kick in when the group animation completes, you'll need to set the delegate and keys on the animation group object rather than on the individual animations.

Don't forget to use `setValue(_:forKey:)` to set the **name** and **layer** keys on your animation before adding it to each of the text fields so your delegate methods get called correctly.

Further, you will need to adjust the `beginTime` parameter of your animation group object to give the correct delay to the different layers being animated as you did before.

Working through this challenge gave you some more valuable experience in working with groups and delegates. At this point you're ready to move on to the next chapter and add some bounciness to your layer animations.

Chapter 13: Layer Springs

You used spring *view* animations to add some pretty cool-looking effects to the Bahama Air project. Now it's time to learn how to create spring animations for layers! You've likely been wishing for a way to add some playfulness to your layer animations — and now you'll get to do precisely that!

Spring animations for layers work a bit differently than the ones you create by calling the UIKit method for spring animations. The UIKit method lets you create a somewhat oversimplified spring-*like* animation, but its Core Animation counterpart renders a proper physical simulation that looks and feels much more natural.

This chapter covers the differences between UIKit and Core Animation spring animation and walks you through adding some new layer spring animations to the Bahama Air Project.

First though, you're going to *bounce* through a bit of theory!

Damped Harmonic Oscillators

Damped Harmonic What?

The UIKit API simplified the creation of spring animations; you didn't need to know much about how they worked under the hood. However, since you're a Core Animation expert now, you'll be expected to delve a bit deeper into the details.

Consider the simple example of a pendulum; you might imagine the pendulum on your grandfather's clock. It's too tall for the shelf, so has stood 90 years on the floor.

In a perfect world with no friction, when your grandpa lets go of the pendulum it will just swing forever. Tick, tock, tick, tock, tick, tock...:

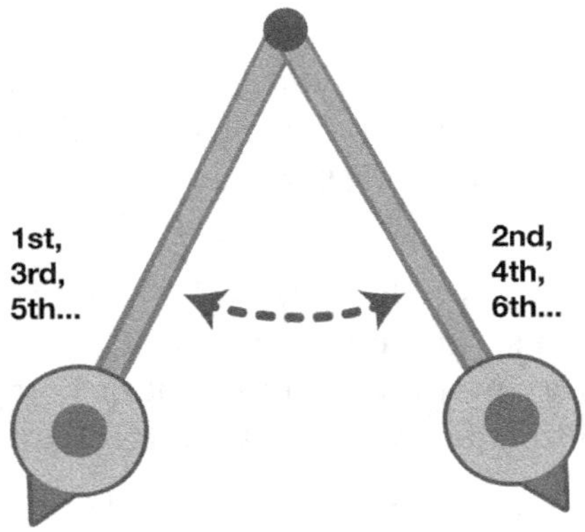

If grandpa were to attach a frictionless pen to the pendulum and slowly slide a sheet of paper underneath, he'd see a graph similar to the following:

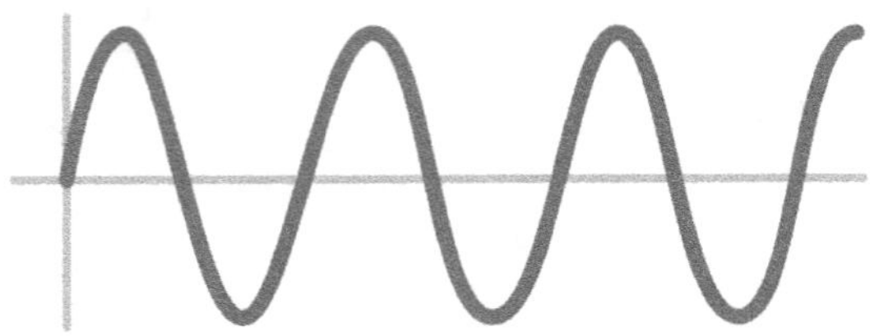

This is an example of a **harmonic oscillator**: the pendulum moves back and forth (or *oscillates*) by equal amounts about its equilibrium point (the point where the pendulum sits when it's at rest). Without friction, the pendulum would keep swinging forever.

In the real world, however, the system loses energy due to friction and ultimately settles at its equilibrium point:

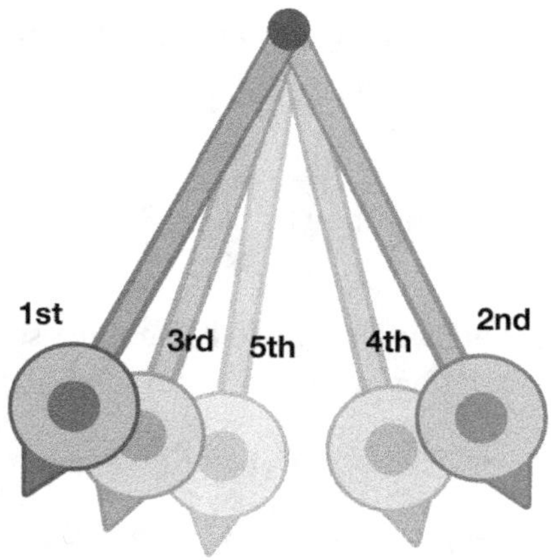

If grandpa slid a piece of paper underneath the pendulum now, the graph would look much like this:

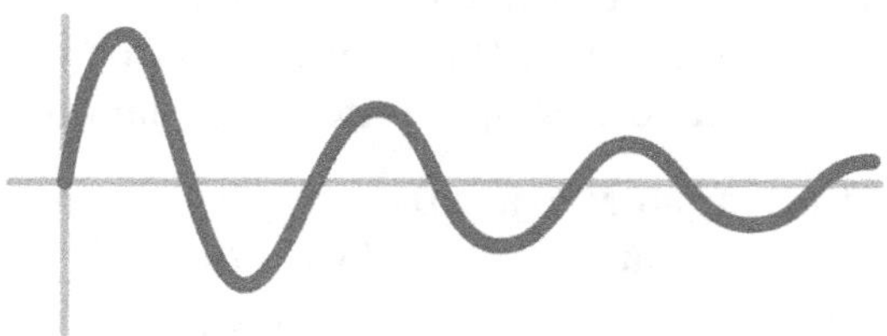

This is a **damped** harmonic oscillator — there are forces acting against (or *damping*) the oscillation, so it slows down by a little bit each time until it comes to rest.

That wasn't so bad, was it?

The length of time it takes the pendulum to settle down, and ultimately the way the graph of the oscillator looks, depends on the following parameters of the oscillating system:

- **damping**: This is due to air friction, mechanical friction and other external slowing forces acting on the system.
- **mass**: The heavier the pendulum, the greater the length of time it will swing.

- **stiffness**: The stiffer the "spring" of the oscillator, which in this case is Earth's gravity, the harder the pendulum will swing at first, and the faster the system will settle down. Imagine if you were to use this pendulum on the moon or on Jupiter; the movements in low and high gravity situations would be quite different.
- **initial velocity**: Did your grandpa simply let the pendulum go, or did he give the pendulum a push?

"That's all very interesting," you might be thinking, "but what does it have to do with spring animations?"

A great question, with a great answer! Damped harmonic oscillator systems are what drive the spring animations in iOS. The next section talks about this in more detail.

UIKit vs. Core Animation Springs

You've likely noticed that a damped harmonic oscillator involves many more variables than does a simple UIKit spring animation.

When you use the spring-damping `animate` methods (with the `usingSpringWithDamping` and `initialSpringVelocity` parameters), the only spring-relevant parameters are the damping and the initial velocity.

UIKit adjusts all the other variables in a dynamic manner to make the system settle down in the given **duration**. That's why the UIKit spring animations sometimes feel a bit — well, *forced*. UIKit animations are just a bit too jumpy, and to a trained eye, a tad unnatural.

Luckily, Core Animation lets you create proper spring animations for your layer properties via the **CASpringAnimation** class. `CASpringAnimation` creates the spring animations for UIKit behind the scenes, but when you call it directly you can set the various variables of the system and let the animation settle down by itself. The drawback to this approach is that you can't tell the animation what its duration *should be*; that's determined by the system itself, given the variables you provide.

Since you know how damped harmonic oscillators work, it's no surprise that `CASpringAnimation` exposes the following properties:

- `damping`: The damping applied to the system
- `mass`: The mass of the weight in the system

- `stiffness`: The stiffness of the spring attached to the weight
- `initialVelocity`: The initial *push* applied to the weight.

If at any time you're wondering which variables you need to adjust to get your animation working the way you want, simply think back to the grandfather clock example, and that should get you straightened around.

That's enough prep for now — it's time to open up Xcode and lay down some spring animation code.

Creating Your First Layer Spring Animation

Open the starter project for this chapter, or alternatively if you worked through the project from the previous chapter you can pick up where you left off.

Run the project and watch for the scaling animation applied to the text fields when they reach their final destination:

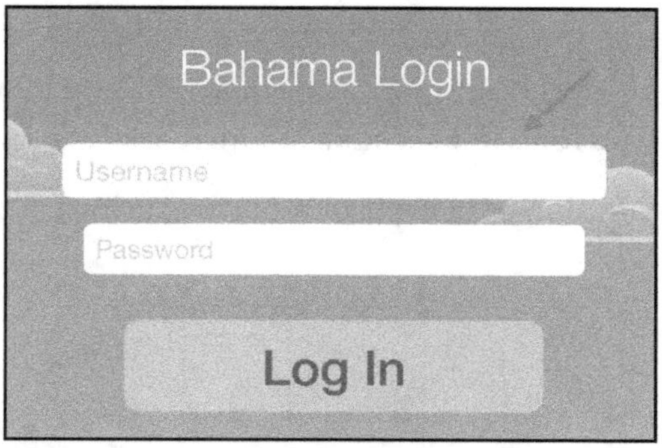

This little scaling animation lets the user know the field is active and ready to be used. However, the animation ends somewhat abruptly. You can make it look much nicer by replacing the existing animation with a proper spring animation.

Open **ViewController.swift** and find `animationDidStop(_:finished:)`. The piece of code that creates the scale animation is as follows:

```
let pulse = CABasicAnimation(keyPath: "transform.scale")
pulse.fromValue = 1.25
pulse.toValue = 1.0
pulse.duration = 0.25
layer?.addAnimation(pulse, forKey: nil)
```

Since `CASpringAnimation` descends from `CABasicAnimation`, you only need to replace the class name and set the spring damping.

To do that, find the following line:

```
let pulse = CABasicAnimation(keyPath: "transform.scale")
```

Replace it with the following:

```
let pulse = CASpringAnimation(keyPath: "transform.scale")
pulse.damping = 2.0
```

Run your project and enjoy your new spring animation!

Hold on — something's wrong with that animation. Run the project few more times and watch the animation closely; you'll notice the animation cuts off and jumps to its final frame at about `0.25` seconds in.

This is a case of your code doing precisely what you told it to do:

- You created a spring animation using a custom damping value and the defaults for all other system variables
- But you *also* told it to run for `0.25` seconds by setting its duration property.

The spring system can't settle within `0.25` seconds; the variables you provided mean the animation should run for a few seconds before it settles down.

Here's a visual demonstration of how you cut off the spring animation:

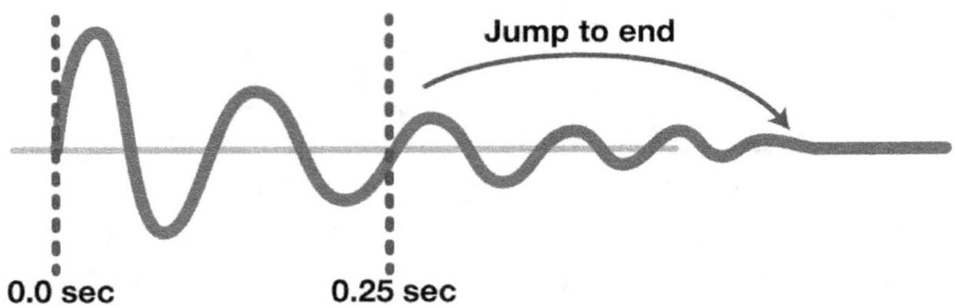

Fortunately, this is an easy fix. Once you set all system variables such as stiffness and damping, ask your `CASpringAnimation` how much time it will take to settle down and set that as the duration of the animation.

Replace `pulse.duration = 0.25` with the following:

```
pulse.duration = pulse.settlingDuration
```

`settlingDuration` estimates the time required for the system to settle; you can use that value to let Core Animation know how long the animation should remain on the screen.

Run your project again to enjoy smooth wobbly-bobbly animations:

It looks better, but *boy* does it run a long time. With the given parameters, the animation will take `1.93` seconds to settle down — that's way too long for an effect that's only meant to close off the preceding transition animation.

Think back to the pendulum example from the chapter's introduction: do you need *more* or *less* damping to decrease the animation's duration?

You're right — a greater damping value means the pendulum will settle faster. Change your animation's damping to `7.5` for a more subtle effect:

```
pulse.damping = 7.5
```

Run the project again; this time, the scaling effect is as *smooth as silk.*

Spring Animation Properties

That takes care of your first spring animation; all you had to do was adjust the damping and everything worked itself out.

But what about `stiffness`, `initialVelocity`, and `mass`?

CASpringAnimation comes with pre-defined values for all its springy properties:

- damping: 10.0
- mass: 1.0
- stiffness: 100.0
- initialVelocity: 0.0

In this section, you'll add input validation to the text fields and make the fields jump if the user enters too few characters. You'll use all four properties of CASpringAnimation to produce the precise effect you want.

Scroll to the very bottom of **ViewController.swift** and find the class extension that makes ViewController conform to the UITextFieldDelegate protocol.

Add to the extension body the following callback method:

```
func textFieldDidEndEditing(_ textField: UITextField) {
  guard let text = textField.text else { return }

  if text.count < 5 {
    // add animations here
  }
}
```

The delegate method textFieldDidEndEditing(_ textField:) receives as a parameter the text field that just lost focus. In the code above you check whether the text value of that field is shorter than 5 characters; if so, you play an animation to attract the user's attention to that field.

Add the following code below the comment // add animations here:

```
let jump = CASpringAnimation(keyPath: "position.y")
jump.fromValue = textField.layer.position.y + 1.0
jump.toValue = textField.layer.position.y
jump.duration = jump.settlingDuration
textField.layer.add(jump, forKey: nil)
```

Run your project; click (or tap if on a device) inside the username text field, then immediately click (or tap) inside the password field. This triggers textFieldDidEndEditing(_ textField:), and since you didn't enter any text, the validation failure animation plays.

At present, the animation simply moves the field one point down and animates it one up back to its original location. That's not much fun — but you can easily fix that with your animation ninja skills!

Initial Velocity

This property lets you specify the starting speed of the animation. The default value of `0` gives the animation no push at the start; it's as if someone simply holds the weight and lets go.

A positive value gives the animation a push in the direction of the equilibrium point, while a negative value starts the animation moving away from the equilibrium point.

Your jump animation should be quite visible, so give it a good push of `100.0` at the start. Add the following line just after the point where you initialize the animation object (the important thing is to add it **before** you calculate and set the `duration`):

```
jump.initialVelocity = 100.0
```

Check out your spring animation again:

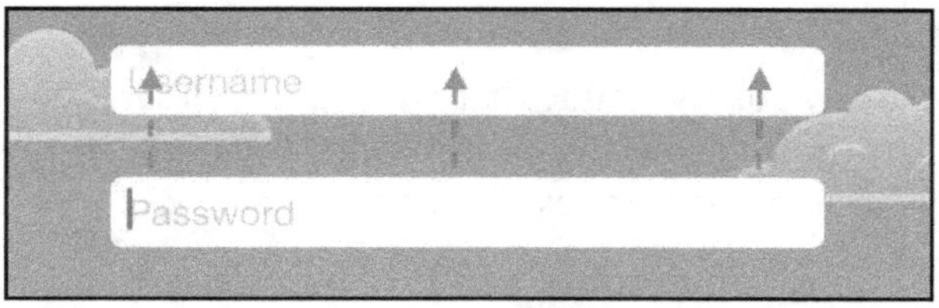

Even with a position delta of just `1` point, the field jumps much higher due to the extra push at the start. The field then oscillates a bit before settling down.

Mass

It looks better, but the jump animation settles a *bit* too fast. Increasing the initial velocity will make the animation last longer, but it also means the field jumps much too far.

What if you increase the *mass* of the attached weight instead, for an animation that lasts longer? Sounds good!

The default mass value is `1.0` (in your mind, you can choose pounds, kilograms, or any other measurement unit you fancy) and you can use any positive value that helps you achieve the desired effect.

For your current animation increase the mass to `10.0` like so:

```
let jump = CASpringAnimation(keyPath: "position.y")
jump.initialVelocity = 100.0
jump.mass = 10.0
```

Run your project; the change above increases the duration of your animation — but the extra mass means the text field jumps a little higher than planned.

No worries — you are still on the right path. Just couple more adjustments and you'll have this effect licked!

> **Note**: Adjusting the spring variables might not feel intuitive at the moment, but as you experiment further with these values you'll start to understand how to best achieve your desired effect.

Stiffness

The spring animation overshoots the target due to its high initial velocity and its extra mass. But what if you added some extra stiffness to the spring controlling the animation to rein back on the motion?

`stiffness` can take any positive value that you fancy: `0` creates a a very soft spring (bouncy bouncy), `100` is the default value (bouncy), and every increment above `100` makes the spring stiffer and stiffer (less bouncy bouncy).

In your animation, increase the stiffness to `1500` to restrain the jump to a sensible size; the new line of code is underlined below:

```
let jump = CASpringAnimation(keyPath: "position.y")
jump.initialVelocity = 100.0
jump.mass = 10.0
jump.stiffness = 1500.0
```

Run your project; the animation now jumps just the right distance and feels *tight*; this should definitely grab the attention of the user.

Damping

The animation looks great, but it does seem to go on a bit too long. You'll increase the system damping to make the animation settle faster.

The damping coefficient applied to the system can be any positive value; zero will make your animation oscillate forever. Increase the damping of your animation to `50.0`:

```
let jump = CASpringAnimation(keyPath: "position.y")
jump.initialVelocity = 100.0
```

```
jump.mass = 10.0
jump.stiffness = 1500.0
jump.damping = 50.0
```

Run the project now and enjoy a fine, subtle animation that attracts the user's attention without annoying them:

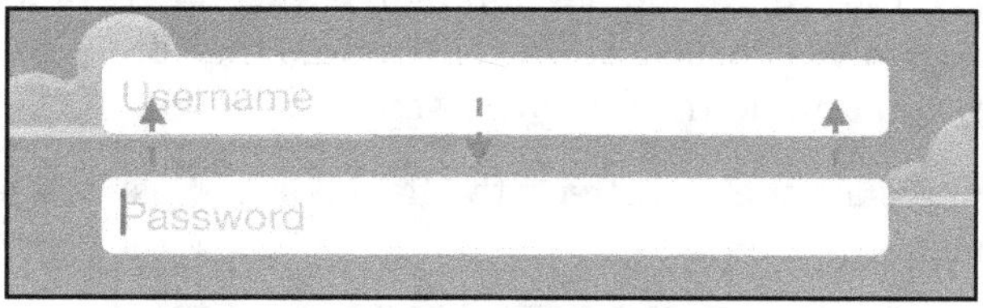

Specific Layer Properties

So far in this chapter you've created layer spring animations for the transform and position properties. Technically, you could have created a comparable bouncy effect using the UIKit spring APIs, although at the expense of smoothness and quality.

To wrap up with `CASpringAnimation`, you'll create a spring animation on a layer property that you *can't* create with view animations alone.

The validation animation is maybe a bit too subtle and smooth right now. You'll add a not-so-subtle flashing red border around the text field that contains invalid input.

In `textFieldDidEndEditing(_ textField:)`, inside the `if` statement and just after you add the `jump` animation to the text field, add the following code to set a border on your text field:

```
textField.layer.borderWidth = 3.0
textField.layer.borderColor = UIColor.clear.cgColor
```

This code adds a transparent border around your text field. Next, you'll animate that border color.

Add the following code just below the line that sets a transparent color on the border:

```
let flash = CASpringAnimation(keyPath: "borderColor")
flash.damping = 7.0
flash.stiffness = 200.0
flash.fromValue = UIColor(red: 1.0, green: 0.27, blue: 0.0,
alpha: 1.0).cgColor
flash.toValue = UIColor.white.cgColor
```

```
flash.duration = flash.settlingDuration
textField.layer.add(flash, forKey: nil)
```

Here you create a spring animation with damping and stiffness values that flash the border in sync with the text field jumping.

A simple `CABasicAnimation` would have animated the border color from red to white. But because you've chosen a spring animation, the border color starts from red and oscillates a bit around the final white color.

Run the app to appreciate the end effect; the field border flashes a few times before it settles down and disappears:

And that ends your crash course on layer spring animations!

> **Note**: In some iOS versions Core Animation removes the rounded corners of the text fields. If that's the case when you work through this chapter add this line after the last piece of code you wrote: `textField.layer.cornerRadius = 5`. This will *re-confirm* to Core Animation that you do want to keep the fields' rounded corners no matter what.

Key Points

- You can describe a spring animation's properties with a practical pendulum example that helps you understand the motivation behind the various spring animation properties.
- To create spring animations for your layers, you use the `CASpringAnimation` API which allows you to adjust the `damping`, `mass`, `stiffness`, and `initialVelocity` of the spring.

Challenges

You have a pretty solid understanding of layer spring animations by now, so I'll leave you to figure out the solution to this challenge on your own.

Challenge 1: Convert Corner Radius and Background Animations to Springs

Your task is to revisit the code in both `tintBackgroundColor(layer:, toColor:)` and `roundCorners(layer:, toRadius:)`, replace the existing code with spring animations and configure the animations so that you can clearly see the rounded corners bounce without overdoing it.

Working through this challenge on your own will give you some time to experiment with the properties of `CASpringAnimation` and give you a feeling for what values work well.

When you've finished, you'll be ready to move on to the next chapter and tackle layer keyframe animations.

Chapter 14: Layer Keyframe Animations & Struct Properties

Keyframe animations on layers are a bit different than keyframe animations on a `UIView`. View keyframe animations are a simple way to combine independent simple animations together; they can animate different views and properties, and the animations can overlap or have gaps in between.

In contrast, `CAKeyframeAnimation` lets you animate a single property on a given layer. You can define different key points of the animation, but you can't have any gaps or overlaps in your animation. Even though that sounds restrictive at first, you can create some very compelling effects with `CAKeyframeAnimation`.

In this chapter, you'll create a number of layer keyframe animations, from the very basic to more advanced animations that simulate real-world collisions. In Chapter 17, "Stroke & Path Animations", you'll learn how to take layer animations even further and animate your layers along a given path.

For now, you'll walk before you run and create a funky wobbly effect for your first layer keyframe animation.

Introducing Keyframe Animations

Think for a moment how a basic animation works. Using `fromValue` and `toValue`, Core Animation progressively modifies a particular layer property between those values over a specified duration.For instance, when you rotate a layer between 45° and -45° (or π/4 and -π/4 for you math types out there) you only need to specify those two values and the layer renders all intermediate values to complete the animation:

Instead of `fromValue` and `toValue`, `CAKeyframeAnimation` uses an array of values to animate through, named `values`. The elements of `values` are the measured milestones of your animation. You'll also need to supply the time that the animation should reach each value's key point.

Take a look at the following simple layer keyframe animation example:

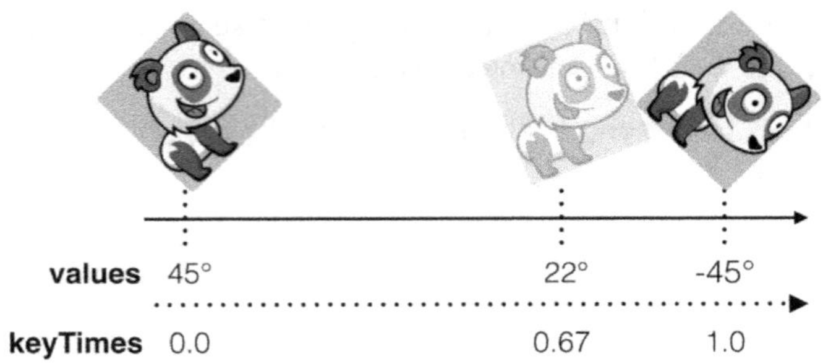

In the above animation, the layer rotates from 45° to -45°, but this time it has two separate stages: first, it rotates from 45° to 22° during the first two-thirds of the animation duration, and then it rotates all the way to -45° in the time remaining.

In essence, animating layers with keyframes requires you to provide key values for the property you're animating, along with a corresponding number of number of relative key times that progress between `0.0` and `1.0`.

Creating a Layer Keyframe Animation

Open the starter project for this chapter, or alternatively if you worked through the project from the previous chapter you can pick up where you left off.

Open **ViewController.swift** and find `resetForm()`; this method executes when you finish animating the different login status messages from "Connecting" to "Authorizing" and so on. You'll animate the form title slightly on the faux failed authentication attempt to tell the user that that an error has occurred.

Add the following code to the end of `resetForm()`:

```
let wobble = CAKeyframeAnimation(keyPath: "transform.rotation")
wobble.duration = 0.25
wobble.repeatCount = 4
wobble.values = [0.0, -.pi / 4.0, 0.0, .pi / 4.0, 0.0]
wobble.keyTimes = [0.0, 0.25, 0.5, 0.75, 1.0]
heading.layer.add(wobble, forKey: nil)
```

Here you create a new `CAKeyframeAnimation` in the same way you usually do for a `CABasicAnimation`: you specify a `keyPath`, set the animation's total duration and indicate how many times you want it to repeat.

Then you set up your animation values in the values array: you rotate the layer from `0`° to −45° (equal to π/4), back to `0`°, all the way to 45° and finally back to `0`°. The animation starts and ends on the same value, which makes repeating it an easy task.

Finally, you set the key times for the values of the animation, making sure to set the start and end times to `0.0` and `1.0` respectively to avoid any jumps in your animation.

Build and run your project; tap on the login button, wait until the end of the sequence and you'll see the title wobble to alert the user that their login attempt failed:

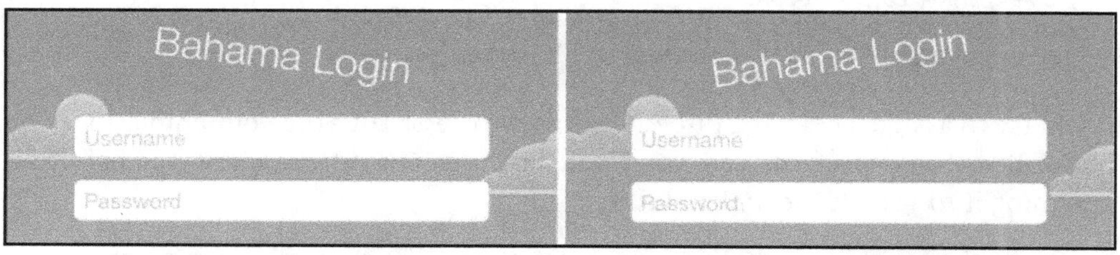

Keen-eyed readers have probably noticed that I haven't yet covered animations on `struct` properties.

Most of the time, you can get away with animating a single component of a struct, such as the `x` component of a `CGPoint`, or the `rotation` component of a `CATransformation3D`, but you'll find out next that there's more to animating struct values than you might think at first.

Animating Struct Values

Struct instances are first-class citizens in Swift. In fact, there's very little difference syntactically between working with classes and structs.

However, Core Animation is an Objective-C framework built on C, which means that structs are handled *very* differently. Objective-C APIs like to deal with objects, so structs need some special handling.

This is why it's relatively easy to animate a layer property such as a color or a number, but it's not quite as easy to animate a struct property such as a `CGPoint`.

There are many animatable properties of `CALayer` that hold struct values, including position of type `CGPoint`, transform of type `CATransform3D`, and bounds of type `CGRect`. To help manage this, Cocoa includes the `NSValue` class, which "boxes in" or "wraps" a struct value as an object. `NSValue` comes with a number of convenience initializers you can use for each struct you need to box, including the following:

```
init(cgPoint: CGPoint)
init(cgSize: CGSize)
init(cgRect rect: CGRect)
init(caTransform3D: CATransform3D)
```

How would you use these initializers to box your values? Here's what a sample position animation using `CGPoint` would look like:

```
let move = CABasicAnimation(keyPath: "position")
move.duration = 1.0
move.fromValue = NSValue(cgPoint: CGPoint(x: 100.0, y: 100.0))
move.toValue = NSValue(cgPoint: CGPoint(x: 200.0, y: 200.0))
```

If you try to assign a `CGPoint` directly to `fromValue` or `toValue` your animations will not work as you expect. Instead, you would box the `CGPoint` in an `NSValue` before assigning it to `fromValue` and `toValue`.

The same thing happens with keyframe animations: if you try to assign an array of `CGPoint` instances as the values of your animations the animations will not work since you have to use an array of boxed `CGPoint` `NSValues` instead.

The final section of this chapter will walk you through boxing your struct properties as you add the final layer keyframe animation involving, of all things, a hot-air balloon!

Intermediate Keyframe Animations

First you need to add the balloon image on screen. Open **ViewController.swift,** then add the following code to the bottom of `login()`:

```
let balloon = CALayer()
balloon.contents = UIImage(named: "balloon")?.cgImage
balloon.frame = CGRect(x: -50.0, y: 0.0, width:
50.0, height: 65.0)
view.layer.insertSublayer(balloon, below: username.layer)
```

In the code above, you create a new layer with the balloon image as its contents. If you need to show an image on screen but don't need all the benefits of using a `UIView` (such as Auto Layout constraints, attaching gesture recognizers and so forth), you can simply use a `CALayer` like in the code example above. You position the layer near the top left corner, just outside of the visible area of the screen. Finally, you insert the layer below the username field so the balloon appears behind all the other elements in your form.

Now you can create the animation in few familiar steps. Add the following code underneath the previous code:

```
let flight = CAKeyframeAnimation(keyPath: "position")
flight.duration = 12.0
```

Here you create a keyframe animation and set its duration to `12.0`, the approximate duration of the faux authentication process.

Next, add the following key value points and times:

```
flight.values = [
  CGPoint(x: -50.0, y: 0.0),
  CGPoint(x: view.frame.width + 50.0, y: 160.0),
  CGPoint(x: -50.0, y: loginButton.center.y)
].map { NSValue(cgPoint: $0) }

flight.keyTimes = [0.0, 0.5, 1.0]
```

Note how you use map to neatly convert an array of points into an array of points boxed as `NSValues`. Ain't Swift great?

This animates the balloon along the path that connects the three points you assigned to values, like so:

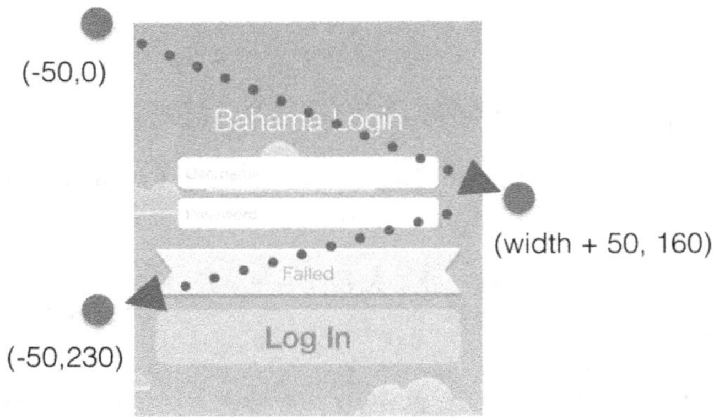

Add the final few following lines to run the animation and to set the final position of the balloon layer:

```
balloon.add(flight, forKey: nil)
balloon.position = CGPoint(x: -50.0, y: loginButton.center.y)
```

Build and run your project; watch as the balloon flies across the screen as soon as you tap the **Log In** button:

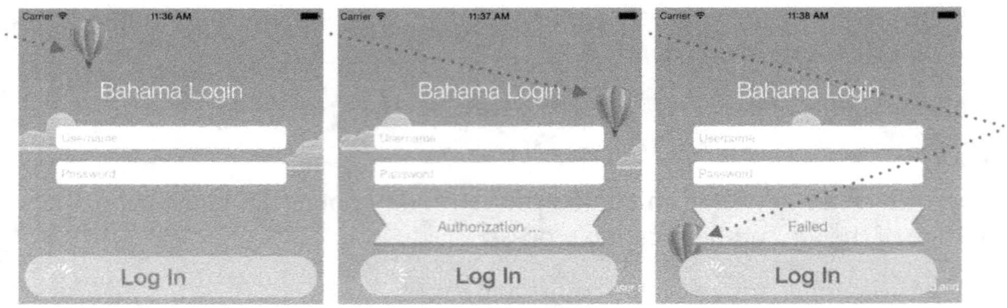

You can use the same technique to animate other struct properties such as `bounds`, `position`, and `transform`.

If you want to animate the balloon over a more complex set of points, such as a smooth curved path, stay tuned for Chapter 17, "Stroke & Path Animations" where you'll learn how to animate a layer over an arbitrary path using a special case of keyframe animation. You've covered all of the chapters in this book that deal with basic layer animations; the next chapters will introduce you to some of the cool animations you can create using specialized layers.

Key Points

- You can easily create layer keyframe animations by using the `CAKeyframeAnimation` class.
- Unlike views, layer keyframe animations animate a single property in a continuous animation over several possible key-points.
- You can animate complex property data types by wrapping them as an `NSValue` type.

Chapter 15: Shapes & Masks

This chapter marks a bit of a shift in this section of the book: not only are you going to start working with a different sample project, but you'll work with multi-layer effects, create layer animations that appear to interact physically with each other and morph between shapes as the animation runs.

If that sounds like a lot to take in, just think back to the great-looking animations you created in previous chapters with a relatively small bit of code!

The shapes in this chapter will be handled by `CAShapeLayer`, which is a `CALayer` sub-class that lets you draw various shapes on the screen, from the very simple to the very complex:

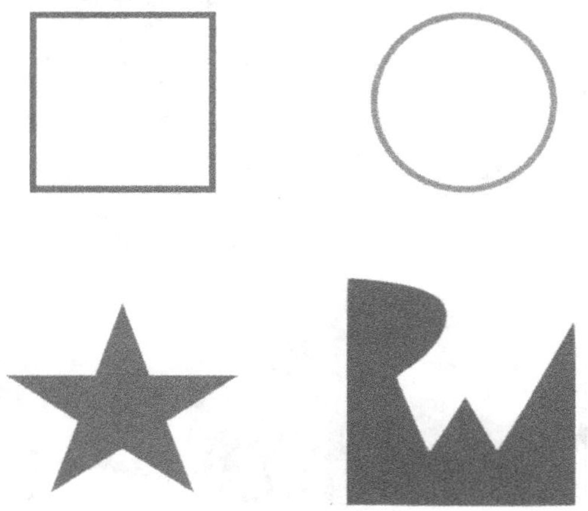

Instead of taking in drawing instructions, you give a the `CALayer` a `CGPath` to draw on screen. This comes in handy since Core Graphics already defines a very extensive API of drawing instructions for building `CGPath` shapes.

If you're more familiar with `UIBezierPath`, you can use that to define a shape and then use its `cgPath` property to get its Core Graphics representation. You will give that a try later in this very chapter.

After you create your desired shape you can set such properties on as the stroke color, fill color and stroke dash pattern.

Of course, by now you're likely asking "...but can I *animate* these properties?" Yes, you can:

- `path`: Morph the layer's shape into a different shape.
- `fillColor`: Change the fill tint of shape to a different color.
- `lineDashPhase`: Create a marquee or "marching ants" effect around your shape.
- `lineWidth`: Grow or shrink the size of the stroke line of your shape.

There are two more animatable properties that you can use when drawing shapes; you'll learn about these in Chapter 17: "Stroke & Path Animations."

The project for this chapter simulates the starting screen of a combat game that is searching for an online opponent. You'll simulate some online communication and add animations to show the communication state.

By the end of this chapter the project will look much like the screen below:

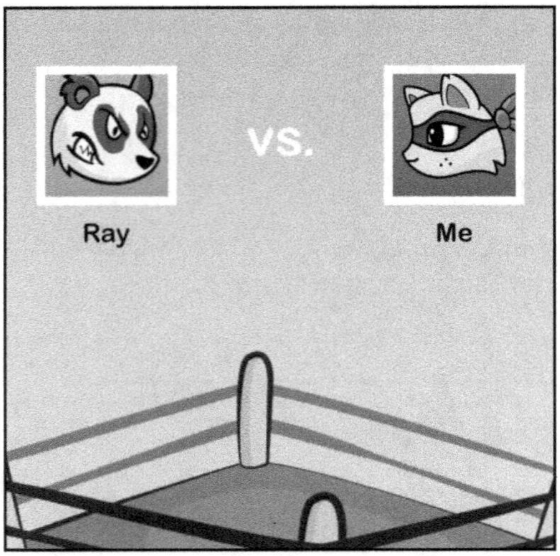

This chapter is designed to show you how to animate the new properties discussed above in the context of a common project you'd work on in real life. This will require a *bit* of extra work, but I know you'll enjoy the ride!

Finishing up the Avatar View

Open the starter project for this chapter, select **Main.storyboard** and take a look at the user interface you'll be working with in this chapter:

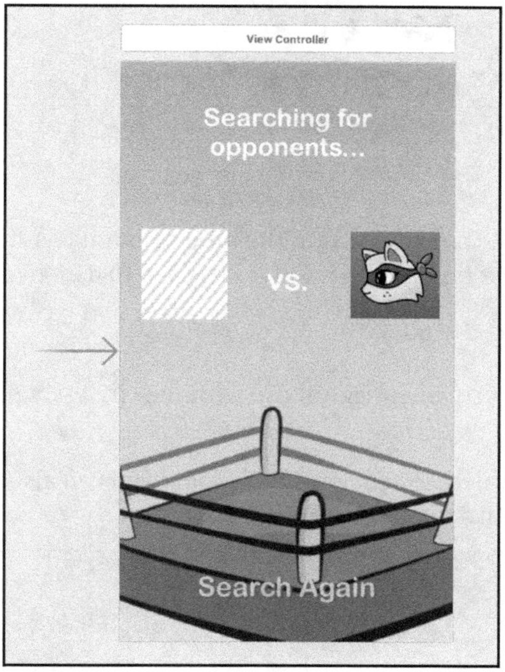

The project setup is fairly straightforward: a single view controller to display a nice background image, some labels, a "Search Again" button, and two avatar images, one of which will be empty until the app "finds" an opponent.

The two avatars are each an instance of the class `AvatarView`. In this section of the chapter, you'll quickly finish writing the class code while you learn how `AvatarView` works.

Open **AvatarView.swift** and have a look at `didMoveToWindow()`, where you'll build up the following elements of the avatar view:

- `photoLayer`: The avatar's image layer.
- `circleLayer`: A shape layer for drawing a circle.
- `maskLayer`: Another shape layer for drawing a mask.
- `label`: A label to show the player's name.

You'll layer these on top of each other to build the composite avatar view as follows:

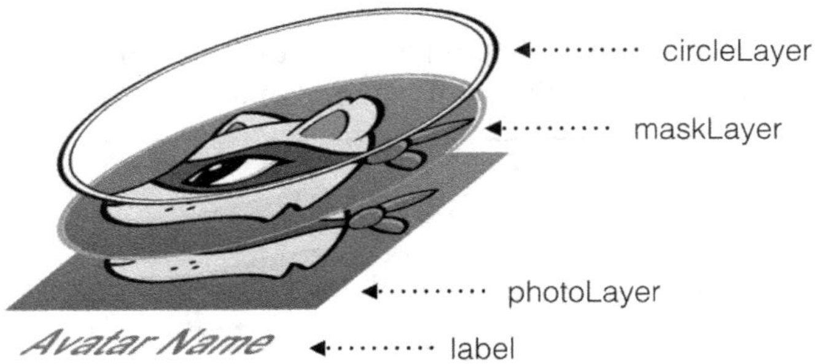

The above components already exist in the project, but haven't been added to the view — that's your first task. Add the following code to `didMoveToWindow()`:

```
photoLayer.mask = maskLayer
```

This simply masks the square image above with the circle-shaped mask in `maskLayer`.

Build and run your project to see how things look; you can also see the change right in the storyboard thanks to `@IBDesignable`:

Now add the border layer to the avatar view's layer in `didMoveToWindow()`:

```
layer.addSublayer(circleLayer)
```

This adds the circular-shaped layer to the avatar, which frames it in nicely:

Both the mask layer and the frame layer are instances of `CAShapeLayer`; you'll make use of this fact when you animate them in the next section.

There's one more piece to add — the player name label. Add the following code to `didMoveToWindow()`:

```
addSubview(label)
```

This wraps up the avatar view like so:

Now you're ready to add some animations!

Creating the Bounce-Off Animation

The first animation you'll create will make it appear as if the two avatars are bouncing off each other while your project "searches" for an opponent.

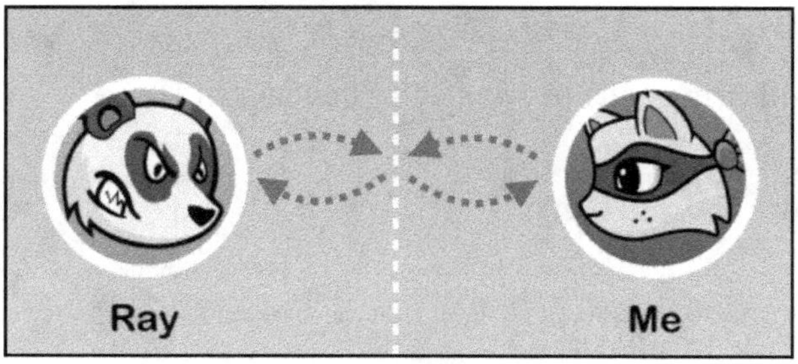

Open **ViewController.swift** and add the following line to `viewDidAppear()`:

```
searchForOpponent()
```

This method kicks off your searching-for-opponent animation.

Add the code below to `ViewController` to create the first iteration of this method:

```
func searchForOpponent() {
  let avatarSize = myAvatar.frame.size
  let bounceXOffset: CGFloat = avatarSize.width / 1.9
  let morphSize = CGSize(
    width: avatarSize.width * 0.85,
    height: avatarSize.height * 1.1)
}
```

A bit of math is involved in this animation — but not too much! First, you calculate the horizontal distance the avatars should move when they bounce towards each other and save that value in `bounceXOffset`. You'll use the morph size later to add an extra effect when the two avatars collide.

Now that you know the x-offset, you can calculate the locations to which the avatars should move. Add the following code to `searchForOpponent()`:

```
let rightBouncePoint = CGPoint(
  x: view.frame.size.width / 2.0 + bounceXOffset,
  y: myAvatar.center.y)

let leftBouncePoint = CGPoint(
  x: view.frame.size.width / 2.0 - bounceXOffset,
  y: myAvatar.center.y)
```

When the avatars reach the right and left bounce points, respectively, they will just barely touch each other, at which point you'll animate them away from each other again.

Finally, add the following code to `searchForOpponent()`:

```
myAvatar.bounceOff(
  point: rightBouncePoint,
  morphSize: morphSize)

opponentAvatar.bounceOff(
  point: leftBouncePoint,
  morphSize: morphSize)
```

`bounceOff(point: morphSize:)` doesn't yet exist; you'll add it in just a moment. It takes two parameters: the point to where the avatar should move and the size to which it should morph. That's all you need to create your animation.

Open **AvatarView.swift** and add the bounce method below:

```
func bounceOff(point: CGPoint, morphSize: CGSize) {
  let originalCenter = center

  UIView.animate(
    withDuration: animationDuration,
    delay: 0.0,
    usingSpringWithDamping: 0.8,
    initialSpringVelocity: 0.0,
    animations: {
      self.center = point
    },
    completion: { _ in
      //complete bounce to
    })
}
```

In the above method, you first store the center coordinate of the avatar view; you'll need this later to animate the view back to its original location. Next, you use a spring animation to move the avatar view to the bouncePoint coordinate.

Now you need something to animate the avatar to its starting location. Add the following code to the end of `bounceOff(point: morphSize:)`:

```
UIView.animate(
  withDuration: animationDuration,
  delay: animationDuration,
  usingSpringWithDamping: 0.7,
  initialSpringVelocity: 1.0,
  animations: {
    self.center = originalCenter
  },
  completion: { _ in
    delay(seconds: 0.1) {
      self.bounceOff(point: point, morphSize: morphSize)
    }
  })
```

The above code uses another spring animation to move the avatar back to its original location. After a slight delay, you re-start the animation again from the completion closure.

Build and run your project to see how the bounce animation looks.

Note that when the avatars views touch they stay together for a short period, as if there's tension building between them. This short period is where you'll add the "squishing" effect using shape morphing techniques.

Morphing Shapes

When the two avatars collide, they should squish a little in this perfectly-elastic collision. The view controller will pass in a morph size that makes the avatar image slightly taller and narrower for this effect:

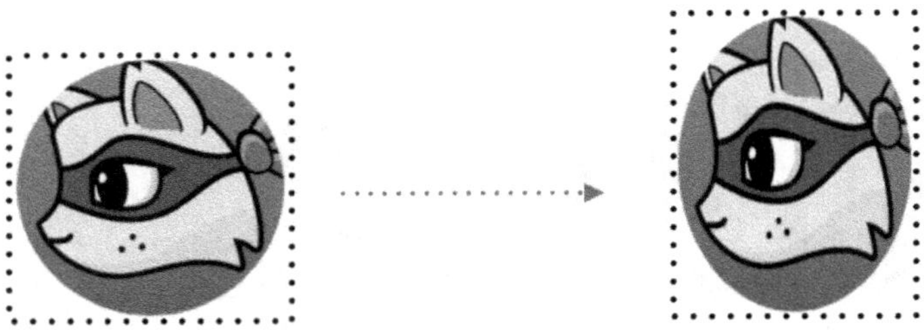

This will make it look like the avatars are pressing against each other when they meet in the middle of the screen. The first thing to take care of is the frame to use for the morphing effect. And just to complicate things a little, the frame will be different for each avatar, depending on whether it animates from the left or the right.

Add the following code to the bottom of `bounceOff(point: morphSize:)`:

```
let morphedFrame = (originalCenter.x > point.x) ?

  CGRect(
    x: 0.0,
    y: bounds.height - morphSize.height,
    width: morphSize.width,
    height: morphSize.height) :

  CGRect(
```

```
    x: bounds.width - morphSize.width,
    y: bounds.height - morphSize.height,
    width: morphSize.width,
    height: morphSize.height)
```

If the avatar animates from left to right, then the final position of the morphed avatar will touch the right edge of the original frame. It's the exact opposite for the avatar animating from right to left, as it will end up on the left edge of the original frame.

This means the avatar images end up touching slightly in the center of the screen, like so:

Finally, you can add the shape-shifting animation code to the bottom of `bounceOff(point: morphSize:)`:

```
let morphAnimation = CABasicAnimation(keyPath: "path")
morphAnimation.duration = animationDuration
morphAnimation.toValue = UIBezierPath(ovalIn:
morphedFrame).cgPath

morphAnimation.timingFunction =
CAMediaTimingFunction(name: .easeOut)
```

Here, you create a `CABasicAnimation` and set its `keyPath` as the path property. As with any other property layer animation, you only need to set the end value and Core Animation will render the intermediate states for you.

You then set the duration and use the class `UIBezierPath` to create an oval path for the effect. `UIBezierPath` is quite handy as it features a number of convenience initializer methods, including the one you used above which takes a `CGRect` and creates an oval path that fits into the rect.

Finally, you set the animation to ease-out which helps build the tension before the avatars bounce off.

That was a long haul, but all that's left is to add the animation to the avatar before you can see your crazy shape shifting in action!

Add the following line of code to the bottom of `bounceOff(point: morphSize:)`:

```
circleLayer.add(morphAnimation, forKey: nil)
```

Build and run your project to see the end result:

The avatar frames squish neatly against each other and then bounce off, like two angry battling amebae floating in the pre-historic sea!

The effect isn't quite complete, as only the frames morph, leaving the images underneath unchanged. Recall that you set the mask of the avatar image to be a `CAShapeLayer` — that's the same class as the avatar frame. So *theoretically* you could re-use the animation object on your frame for your mask.

Will theory work in practice? Give it a try, and add the following line to the bottom of `bounceOff(point: morphSize:)`:

```
maskLayer.add(morphAnimation, forKey: nil)
```

Build and run your project again; this time you should see both the frame and mask morph in perfect sync:

Awesome — you've just created a really nice-looking animation with only a bit of math and a few well-designed chunks of code! In the space of this chapter, you've learned how to create and animate shapes and how to use and animate shape layers as masks.

Key points

- You can draw dynamic shapes on screen by using the `CAShapeLayer` class and setting its stroke and fill colors and set setting the path of the shape.
- You can animate the shape rendered by `CAShapeLayer` by animating its `path` property.
- `CAShapeLayer` is a great way to clip the contents of another layer by *cutting out* and displaying on screen a circle, square, or a star of the underlaying content.

Challenges

The challenges in this chapter are optional, but I encourage you to work through them to practice your skills and add some real polish to your project. However if you're eager to start with gradient animations, then you can head straight on to the next chapter.

Challenge 1: Finish the Communication State Animations

For this challenge, you get a bit of a breather as you can simply follow along with the instructions below. Your task in this challenge is to add some status messages to show to the user as your faux "searching for an opponent" task progresses.

Open **ViewController.swift** and add the following code to the bottom of `searchForOpponent()`:

```
delay(seconds: 4.0, completion: foundOpponent)
```

The app will continue to "search" for four seconds before calling `foundOpponent()`, which will indicate to the player that the app has found an opponent.

Add the following method to the `ViewController` class:

```
func foundOpponent() {
  status.text = "Connecting..."

  opponentAvatar.image = UIImage(named: "avatar-2")
  opponentAvatar.name = "Ray"
}
```

Build and run your project and after about four seconds, you'll see the opponent's avatar appear:

Now that the app has found an opponent, it will start "connecting" the two players. All of this, of course, is just a simulation so you get to build a nice animation.

Add the following code to the bottom of `foundOpponent()`:

```
delay(seconds: 4.0, completion: connectedToOpponent)
```

This inserts another four-second delay after the app displays the opponent's avatar, after which you'll call the "connected state" method in the next code block.

Add the following new method to the class:

```
func connectedToOpponent() {
  myAvatar.shouldTransitionToFinishedState = true
  opponentAvatar.shouldTransitionToFinishedState = true
}
```

The above method sets `shouldTransitionToFinishedState` to true on both avatar views. This triggers a new animation that you will create in the next challenge, so for now nothing will happen.

Finally, you need to adjust the UI for the final state. Add the following code to the bottom of `connectedToOpponent()`:

```
delay(seconds: 1.0, completion: completed)
```

This code gives the animation a second to wrap up and then calls the final step in the sequence: `completed()`.

Add the final method to the `ViewController` class:

```
func completed() {
  status.text = "Ready to play"
  UIView.animate(withDuration: 0.2) {
    self.vs.alpha = 1.0
```

```
      self.searchAgain.alpha = 1.0
    }
  }
```

completed() sets the status message at the top of the screen to "Ready to play", then fades in the "vs." label and the "Search Again" button to restart the animation sequence. The button is already connected to actionSearchAgain() so you can tap it to restart the animations.

Build and run to see the entire sequence of animations:

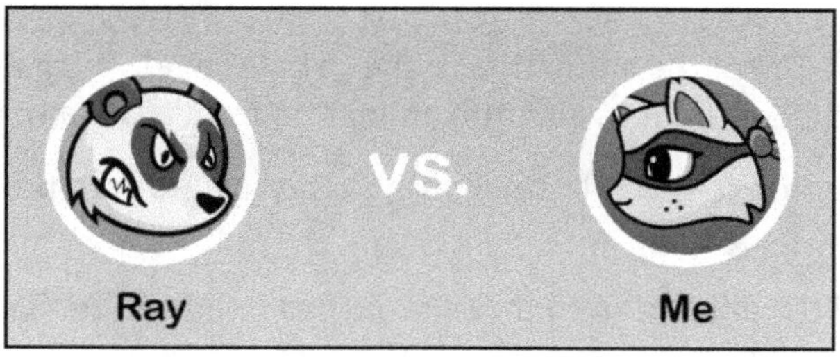

Challenge 2: Morph the Avatars to Squares

At this point the avatars just keep bouncing forever. Once the game is connected to an opponent, you'd like to stop the animation and reflect the state change in the UI.

In this challenge you are going to make use of the shouldTransitionToFinishedState property of the avatar class; when it's set to true you'll break the bounce animation and morph the avatars into a square shape.

Open **AvatarView.swift** and add a new variable called isSquare and set its initial value to false. Scroll to bounceOff(point: morphSize:) and find the animation completion block where there's a recursive call to bounceOff(point: morphSize:).

You'll need to wrap that call in a conditional so it only runs when isSquare is still false.

Next you'll run an extra animation while the avatars bounce off each other one last time.

Find the //complete bounce to comment and replace it with the following:

```
  if self.shouldTransitionToFinishedState {
    self.animateToSquare()
  }
```

Finally, add the `animateToSquare()` method to `AvatarView` and write the code to do the following:

1. Set `isSquare` to `true`.
2. Create a Bezier path with `UIBezierPath(rect:)` by using the avatar's bounds rectangle, and store the `CGPath` of this bezier path in a constant called `squarePath`.
3. Create a new layer animation with a `keypath` of path and set its `duration` to `0.25` seconds.
4. Set the `fromValue` of the animation to the `circleLayer.path` and the `toValue` to `squarePath`. This defines a morph animation from a circle to a square shape.
5. Add the animation to the `circleLayer` and then set its path property to the `squarePath`.
6. Similarly, add the animation to the `mask` layer as well and set its `path` property to `squarePath`.

Build and run your project; the final bounce will look much fancier. While the avatars touch for the last time they'll still look like this:

They bounce back to their starting point, morphing into squares for a *wow* effect:

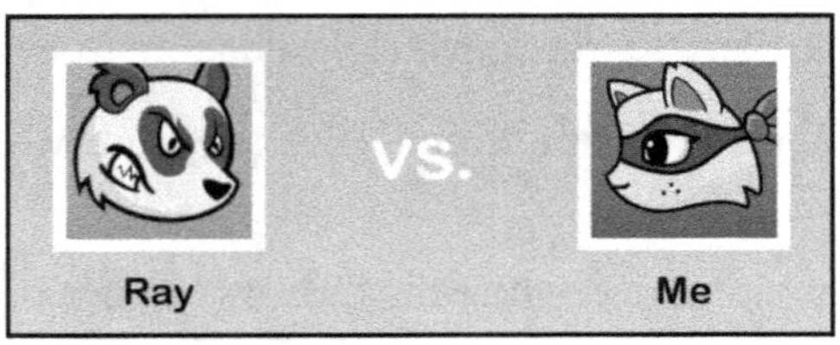

By now you know the basic animation techniques to work with shape layers and masks. You've likely already thought up many ways to apply shape animations in your own applications.

You continue to work with shapes and `CAShapeLayer` animations in Chapter 17, "Stroke & Path Animations." Head on to Chapter 16, "Gradient Animations," to learn how to add some really neat effects to your animations using animated gradients.

Chapter 16: Gradient Animations

A lot of the look and feel of iOS comes from very subtle animations in the UI.

While it is no longer a part of iOS, one of the nicest was a simple little animation: the “slide to unlock” label on the lock screen.

In this chapter you’ll learn how to mimic this effect with a moving gradient and how to animate the colors and layout of those gradients:

You’ll animate the gradient for a “Slide to reveal” label and then reveal a cool mystery effect when the user swipes over the label. You’ll have to work through this chapter, however, to see what this cool effect is!

As an extra bonus, you’ll learn how to create a layer mask out of a piece of text and use it to mask a gradient.

Drawing Your First Gradient

Open the starter project for this chapter and select **Main.storyboard** to see how the UI looks at present:

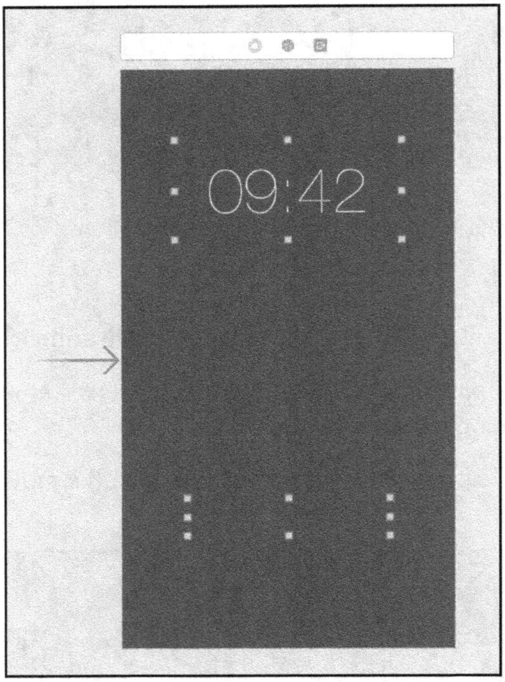

There's a static label on top that mimics the iPhone clock on the lock screen and another view near the bottom.

The bottom view is an instance of `AnimatedMaskLabel` that's included with the starter project. You'll work with this class throughout this chapter to add gradient animations.

Build and run your project; you'll see just the faux clock appear at the top of the screen:

You'll first draw the base gradient of `AnimatedMaskLabel`. Add the following code to **AnimatedMaskLabel.swift** inside the `gradientLayer` property code after the comment shown below:

```
// Configure the gradient here
gradientLayer.startPoint = CGPoint(x: 0.0, y: 0.5)
gradientLayer.endPoint = CGPoint(x: 1.0, y: 0.5)
```

This defines the orientation of the gradient and its start and end points.

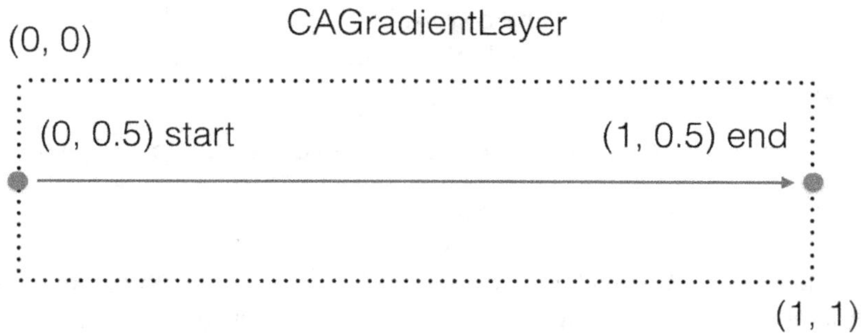

Now add the following code to define the colors that build up the gradient after the code you just added:

```
let colors = [
  UIColor.black.cgColor,
  UIColor.white.cgColor,
  UIColor.black.cgColor
]
gradientLayer.colors = colors
```

The gradient above starts with a black color, blends to white, and finally blends back to black.

You can also specify where exactly in the gradient's frame these colors should appear. Add the following code below:

```
let locations: [NSNumber] = [
  0.25,
  0.5,
  0.75
]
gradientLayer.locations = locations
```

This sets up the gradient color milestones as follows:

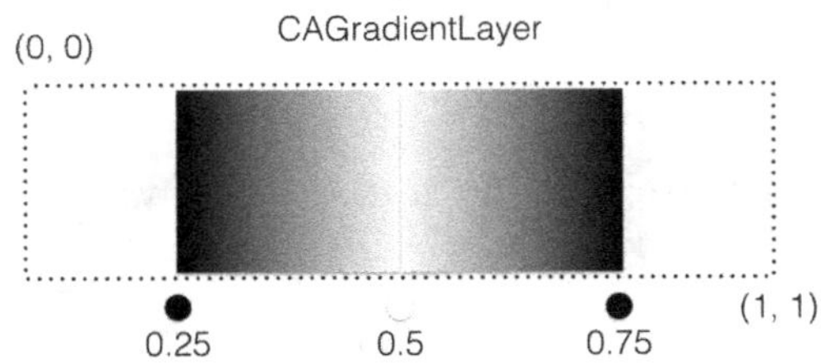

You can have as many key points and color milestones as you like, but the text gradient animation in this chapter only needs the simple black-white-black gradient shown above.

Add the following code to `layoutSubviews()` to give the gradient a frame:

```
gradientLayer.frame = bounds
```

All that you need to do now is add the gradient to the view's layer to see it in action. Add the line of code below to the end of `didMoveToWindow()`:

```
layer.addSublayer(gradientLayer)
```

Build and run your project; you should see the app display the exact gradient you're looking for:

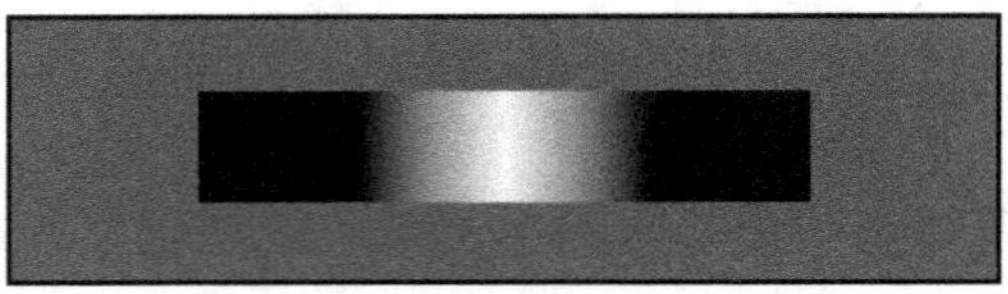

That's a great start! Now you need to figure out how to animate this gradient.

Animating Gradients

`CAGradientLayer` offers you four animatable properties along with the ones inherited from `CALayer`:

- `colors`: Animate the gradient's colors to give it a tint.
- `locations`: Animate the color milestone locations to make the colors move around inside the gradient.
- `startPoint` and `endPoint`: Animate the extents of the layout of the gradient.

In this section you'll animate locations to make the gradient "move". Add the following code to the end of `didMoveToWindow()`:

```
let gradientAnimation = CABasicAnimation(keyPath: "locations")
gradientAnimation.fromValue = [0.0, 0.0, 0.25]
gradientAnimation.toValue = [0.75, 1.0, 1.0]
gradientAnimation.duration = 3.0
gradientAnimation.repeatCount = Float.infinity
```

In this layer animation, you begin by pushing the three color milestones to the left edge of the gradient's frame and end the animation with all three pushed towards the right edge:

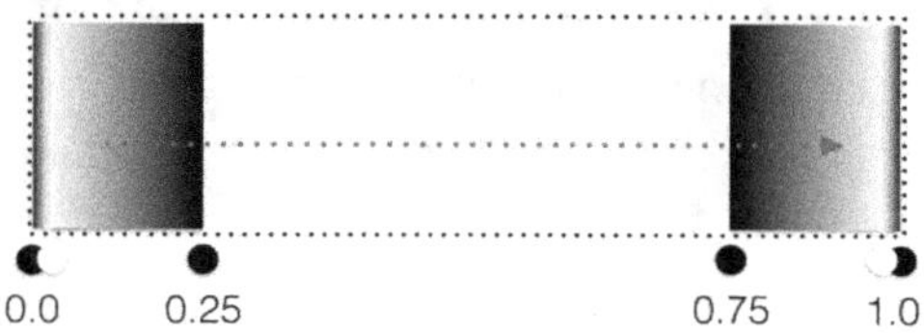

The animation lasts `3` seconds and will repeat forever since you set `repeatCount` to `infinity`.

Finally, add the following line to the end of `didMoveToWindow()`:

```
gradientLayer.add(gradientAnimation, forKey: nil)
```

This will add the animation to the gradient layer. Build and run your project and you'll see the animation take shape:

This looks pretty nice, but the gradient is quite harsh, especially near the middle. No problem: just enlarge the gradient bounds and you'll get a much gentler gradient.

Find the line `gradientLayer.frame = bounds` in `layoutSubviews()` and replace it with the following code that sets a much larger frame for the gradient layer:

```
gradientLayer.frame = CGRect(
  x: -bounds.size.width,
  y: bounds.origin.y,
  width: 3 * bounds.size.width,
  height: bounds.size.height)
```

This sets the gradient frame to three times the width of the visible area. The animation enters the view, passes right through it, and exits out the right hand side:

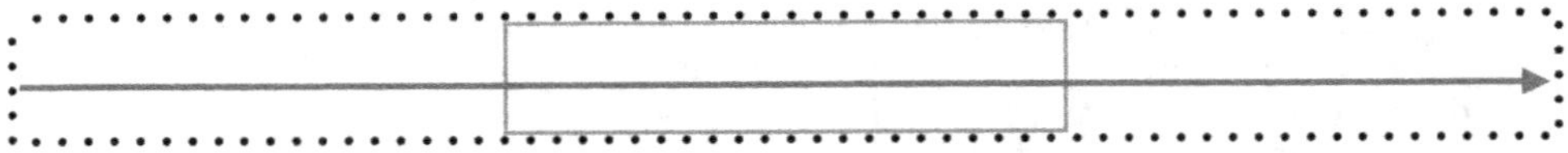

Build and run your project to see what your changes look like:

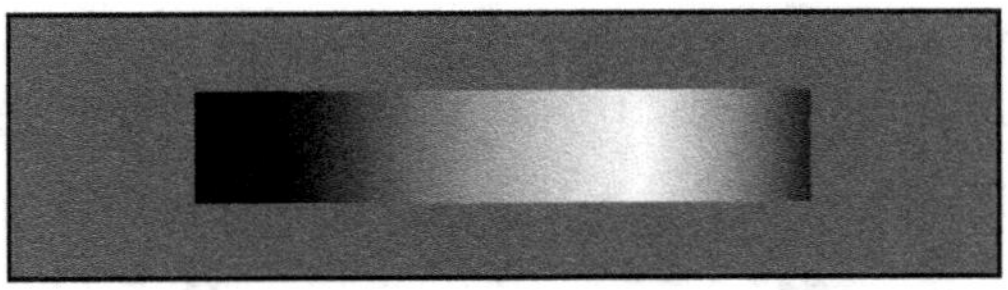

That looks more like the smooth gradient you're going for. Now that you have the gradient, you'll need to create the text layers to use as a mask.

Creating a Text Mask

In this section you'll render the string stored in the text property of `AnimatedMaskLabel` and use that to mask the gradient layer. Create a new constant property inside the `AnimatedMaskLabel` class to hold the text attributes as follows:

```
let textAttributes: [NSAttributedString.Key: Any] = {
  let style = NSMutableParagraphStyle()
  style.alignment = .center
  return [
    .font: UIFont.systemFont(
      ofSize: 28,
      weight: .thin),
    .paragraphStyle: style
  ]
}()
```

Next you need to render the text as an image. A natural place to do this is in the property observer for the text property. Add the following code after the `setNeedsDisplay()` call:

```
let image = UIGraphicsImageRenderer(size: bounds.size)
  .image { _ in
    text.draw(in: bounds, withAttributes: textAttributes)
}
```

Here you use an image renderer to set up a context, draw to it, and get the results out as a UIImage. Now you can use that image to create a mask on your gradient layer.

To do that, first create a layer out of the image as follows:

```
let maskLayer = CALayer()
maskLayer.backgroundColor = UIColor.clear.cgColor
maskLayer.frame = bounds.offsetBy(dx: bounds.size.width, dy: 0)
maskLayer.contents = image.cgImage
```

You create maskLayer as an empty layer simply by using the default initializer of CALayer. You then set a fully transparent layer background since you're going to use the layer as a mask. Then you offset the layer frame by the width of the view; this way, the mask will show up in the center of the gradient. This is necessary as your "stretched" gradient is currently three times as wide as the visible view. Finally, you assign the image object directly to the contents property of the layer.

Add one more line to set the new layer as a mask for the gradient:

```
gradientLayer.mask = maskLayer
```

Build and run your project to see the fully developed animation in action:

Hey — that looks really slick! But you haven't yet discovered what's revealed when the user swipes across the label — and are you limited to a monochrome palette for your gradient? All will be revealed — as you work through the challenges below!

Key Points

- You can draw gradients on screen by using the `CAGradientLayer` and setting the gradient colors.
- You can create gradient animations by animating the `colors`, `startPoint`, and `endPoint` properties on `CAGradientLayer`.
- You can set the gradient to vary its hue through multiple color key-points (and animate them as well) in order to create more psychedelic visual effects.

Challenges

I know the suspense is killing you; these two challenges will add a slide gesture recognizer to the label and add one additional color effect to the gradient animation.

Challenge 1: Slide to Reveal Gesture Recognizer

Open **ViewController.swift** and add the following code to `viewDidLoad()`:

```
let swipe = UISwipeGestureRecognizer(
  target: self,
  action: #selector(ViewController.didSlide))
swipe.direction = .right
slideView.addGestureRecognizer(swipe)
```

This creates a slide-to-right gesture recognizer and attaches it to `slideView`. The recognizer will call `didSlide()` on `ViewController`.

`didSlide()` is already implemented for you, so all you need to do now is fire up the application and slide your finger over the animating label to reveal what lies beneath.

Challenge 2: Psychedelic Gradient Animations

In the final challenge of this chapter you'll experiment with adding more colors to the gradient and observe the effects.

If you'd like something to guide your exploration, try using the following list of colors for your gradient:

```
UIColor.yellow
UIColor.green
UIColor.orange
UIColor.cyan
UIColor.red
UIColor.yellow
```

You'll need to adjust the locations values as well to keep all of your colors in order. Start your animation with the following locations: `0.0, 0.0, 0.0, 0.0, 0.0` and `0.25`. Then animate the locations to: `0.65, 0.8, 0.85, 0.9, 0.95` and `1.0`.

Build and run your project; play around with the animation and the various parameters until you have it tuned it to your own design preferences:

This brings the chapter to a close; you've seen how easy it is to animate gradients as well as how to implement some advanced layer masking tricks with text layers.

The next chapter covers stroke animations for shapes, which is the final topic you'll cover in this section of the book on layer animations; you'll learn how to draw shapes interactively, and as a bonus, you'll cover advanced keyframe animations.

Chapter 17: Stroke & Path Animations

In this chapter you'll learn about stroke and path animations as you add a cool pull-to-refresh animation to your existing Pack List project that entertains the user while the app pretends to fetch new data from the Internet:

Along the way, you'll learn how to animate the drawing of shapes, and as a bonus, you'll look at a special kind of keyframe animation that you can use to move an object along any arbitrary path.

Creating Interactive Stroke Animations

Open the starter project for this chapter, then build and run it to see how the UI looks:

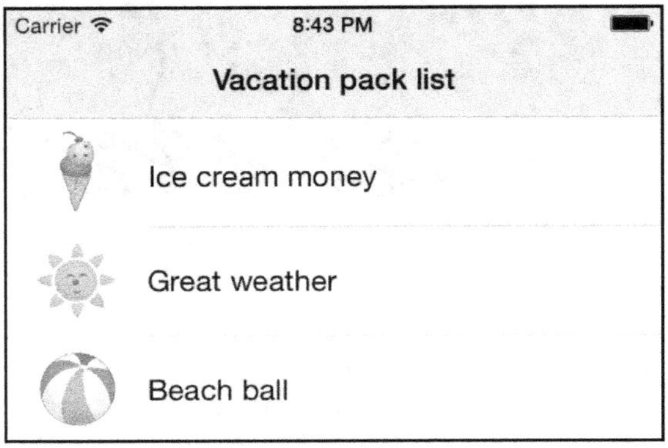

There's existing code in **ViewController.swift** to populate the table for you with a number of vacation items. Pull down the table and you'll see a refresh view appear at the top of the screen:

The refresh view stays visible for four seconds, then retracts. Your job here is to add an amusing animation to entertain users while they wait.

The refresh view already contains all the code for the pulling and releasing actions; you just need to worry about adding the animations.

> **Note**: The pull down to refresh code is based on one of our video tutorials. If you would like to know more about how it works check out the *Scroll View School* video series at the following link: https://www.raywenderlich.com/9223-scroll-view-school.

The first step in building your animation is to create a circle shape. Open **RefreshView.swift** and add the following code to `init(frame:scrollView:)`:

```
ovalShapeLayer.strokeColor = UIColor.white.cgColor
ovalShapeLayer.fillColor = UIColor.clear.cgColor
ovalShapeLayer.lineWidth = 4.0
ovalShapeLayer.lineDashPattern = [2, 3]

let refreshRadius = frame.size.height/2 * 0.8

ovalShapeLayer.path = UIBezierPath(ovalIn: CGRect(
  x: frame.size.width / 2 - refreshRadius,
  y: frame.size.height / 2 - refreshRadius,
  width: 2 * refreshRadius,
  height: 2 * refreshRadius)
  ).cgPath

layer.addSublayer(ovalShapeLayer)
```

`ovalShapeLayer` is a property on `RefreshView` of type `CAShapeLayer`. You're already quite familiar with shape layers; here you simply set the stroke and fill colors and set the circle diameter to be `80%` of the view height, which ensures a comfortable margin around the shape.

There's one property in the code above that you haven't encountered yet: `lineDashPattern`. This property lets you set a dash pattern for the shape stroke; you simply you provide an array with the length of the dash and the length of the gap in pixels.

Build and run your project to see how the circle looks:

That looks really nice — and it was easy to create. This will serve you well as a circular progress bar.

In `RefreshView`, `redrawFromProgress()` is called whenever the user scrolls via `scrollViewDidScroll(_ scrollView:)`; this makes it a convenient place to update the visuals of the progress bar.

Add the following code to `redrawFromProgress()`:

```
ovalShapeLayer.strokeEnd = progress
```

As progress increases from `0.0` to `1.0`, the stroke end of the shape moves forward towards the starting point of the stroke.

This is how the shape looks when progress is `0.25`:

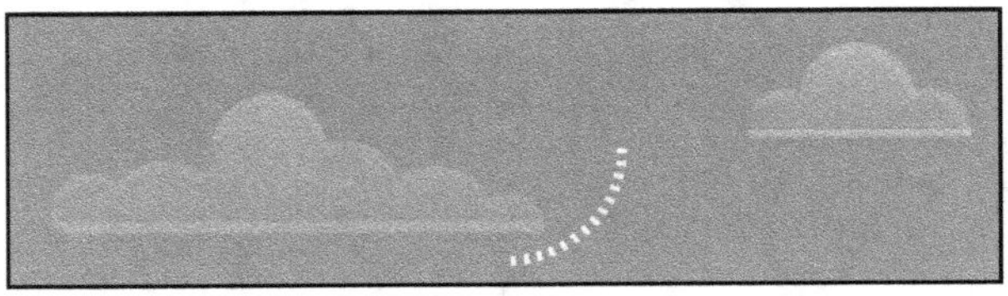

Here it is halfway around, at `0.5`:

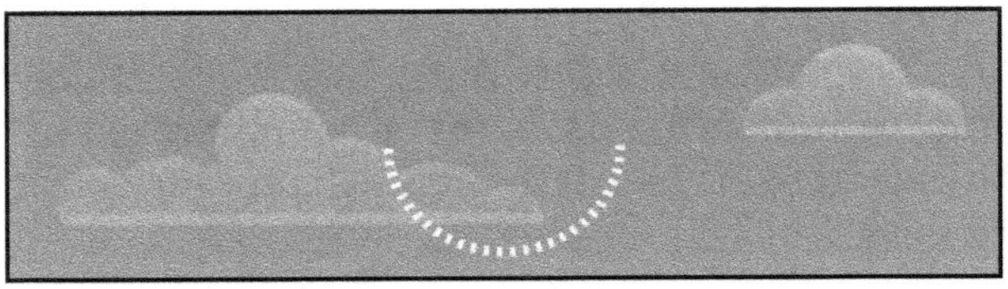

Build and run your project; drag the table view up and down to see the stroke length change.

Now you'll add a cool-looking airplane to the refresh control.

Scroll back to `init(frame:scrollView:)` and add the following code to the bottom of the initializer:

```
let airplaneImage = UIImage(named: "airplane.png")!
airplaneLayer.contents = airplaneImage.cgImage
airplaneLayer.bounds = CGRect(
  x: 0.0,
  y: 0.0,
  width: airplaneImage.size.width,
  height: airplaneImage.size.height)

airplaneLayer.position = CGPoint(
  x: frame.size.width / 2 + frame.size.height / 2 * 0.8,
  y: frame.size.height / 2)

layer.addSublayer(airplaneLayer)
```

The code should look familiar. You've already done this a few times in previous chapters. You simply load **airplane.png** and assign it as the contents of a layer on the screen, then position the airplane layer at the location where the circle starts drawing.

Build and run your project to see the airplane appear when you pull the table view down:

The plane should fade in as the user pulls the table down.

Add the following code to `init(frame:scrollView:)`:

```
airplaneLayer.opacity = 0.0
```

This makes the airplane completely transparent to start.

Now add the following code to `redrawFromProgress()` to progressively change the opacity of the airplane layer as the user pulls down:

```
airplaneLayer.opacity = Float(progress)
```

`opacity` is of type `Float` so you need to convert `progress` from a `CGFloat`.

Build and run your project; pull down the table and you should see the airplane appear gradually:

This wraps up the interactive animation part of this chapter. The next section walks you through animating a progress indicator to keep the users engaged while they wait for the faux refreshed data.

Animating Both Stroke Ends

In this section, you'll animate *both* the strokeStart and strokeEnd properties to make the shape "run around".

You'll start the animation when the app starts to fetch the faux data. Add the following code to the end of beginRefreshing():

```
let strokeStartAnimation = CABasicAnimation(
  keyPath: "strokeStart")
strokeStartAnimation.fromValue = -0.5
strokeStartAnimation.toValue = 1.0

let strokeEndAnimation = CABasicAnimation(
  keyPath: "strokeEnd")
strokeEndAnimation.fromValue = 0.0
strokeEndAnimation.toValue = 1.0
```

This code creates two animations: the first one animates strokeStart from -0.5 to 1.0. This is a simple and cheap animation trick; while the value animates from -0.5 to 0.0 nothing happens, as all negative values for these properties simply mean no part of the shape is visible.

This gives the second animation — the one on strokeEnd — a bit of a head start. This draws a small bit of the shape on the screen, until strokeStart catches up with strokeEnd at the end of the animation.

Add the following code the end of beginRefreshing() to run the two animations simultaneously:

```
let strokeAnimationGroup = CAAnimationGroup()
strokeAnimationGroup.duration = 1.5
strokeAnimationGroup.repeatDuration = 5.0
strokeAnimationGroup.animations =
  [strokeStartAnimation, strokeEndAnimation]
ovalShapeLayer.add(strokeAnimationGroup, forKey: nil)
```

In the code above, you create an animation group and repeat the animation five times. This should be long enough to keep the animation running while the refresh view is visible. Then you add both animations to the group and add the group to the progress bar.

Build and run your project; pull and release the table to see your animation in action:

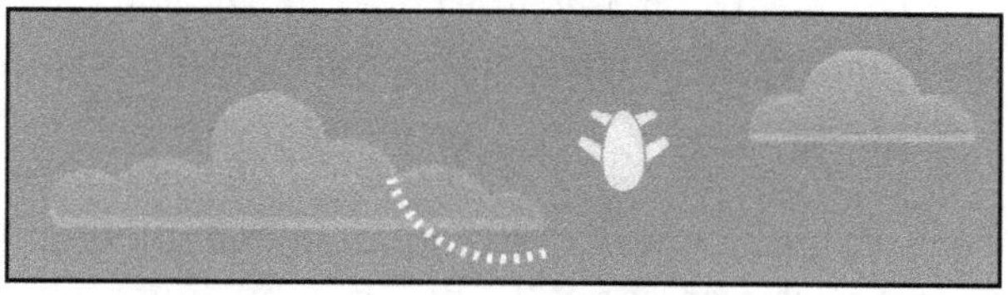

You've just created your own custom spinner! Although it looks pretty neat, you can make it even cooler with just a little effort - and some help from layer path animations!

Creating Path Keyframe Animations

You saw how to animate a layer using a keyframe animation and the values property in 4, "Keyframe Animations & Struct Properties". to animate a layer along a path you do much the same thing but you assign a `CGPath` to the animation's path property instead.

Core Animation will then calculate the intermediate positions of the layer along the `CGPath` and animate it nicely over the animation's duration.

Add the following code to `beginRefreshing()`:

```
let flightAnimation = CAKeyframeAnimation(keyPath: "position")
flightAnimation.path = ovalShapeLayer.path
flightAnimation.calculationMode = .paced
```

Here you create a `CAKeyframeAnimation` and, much like before, set the animated property to position. But this time you assign a value to path. In this case you can re-use the circular path of `ovalShapeLayer`.

Finally you set the animation `calculationMode` to a paced mode — this will make sure that the layer animates smoothly along the path.

`calculationMode` is yet another way you can control the timing of your animation. When you set that property to `.paced` Core Animation animates your layer with a constant pace ignoring any key times you've set. This is very useful for producing smooth animations across an arbitrary path.

The CAAnimationCalculationMode structure offers a few more constants. One interesting one is .discrete. This calculation mode makes Core Animation jump from key value to key value without any interpolation. Yes you got it right — Core Animation has a special mode to produce animations that don't animate anything.

Enough calculation mode fun — back to the task at hand.

Now you need to create a group out of this animation and run it on the airplane layer. You need the group later on as you'll add a second animation to complement the first.

Add the following code to beginRefreshing():

```
let flightAnimationGroup = CAAnimationGroup()
flightAnimationGroup.duration = 1.5
flightAnimationGroup.repeatDuration = 5.0
flightAnimationGroup.animations = [flightAnimation]
airplaneLayer.add(flightAnimationGroup, forKey: nil)
```

In the code above, you create the group and give it the same duration and repeat count as the progress bar stroke animation. You then add flightAnimation as the only item in the group and add the group to the airplane layer.

Run the animation and check out the pilot's skills:

You've never seen an airshow like this one: the airplane performs loops in the sky and stays perfectly vertical! As amusing as this is, you should probably make the plane fly more naturally.

> **Note**: CAKeyframeAnimation has a property called rotationMode of type CAAnimationRotationMode, which when set to .rotateAuto will automatically orient your layer in the direction it's moving. However, you'll create this effect manually in this chapter, as it's an easy task for simple, circular paths.

Insert the following new animation code **above** the line where you create `flightAnimationGroup`:

```
let airplaneOrientationAnimation = CABasicAnimation(
  keyPath: "transform.rotation")
airplaneOrientationAnimation.fromValue = 0
airplaneOrientationAnimation.toValue = 2.0 * .pi
```

`airplaneOrientationAnimation` rotates the layer a full `360` degrees — from `0` to `2π` — via its `transform`. In other words, the airplane image will rotate in a full circle around its center, and since you move the airplane layer along the circular path at the same time, the flight will end up looking natural.

Now you just need to add `airplaneOrientationAnimation` to the animation group.

Add the new animation to the array as shown below:

```
flightAnimationGroup.animations = [
  flightAnimation,
  airplaneOrientationAnimation
]
```

Build and run your project and enjoy your completed pull-down-to-refresh control:

If you'd like to experiment with air acrobatics, you can try setting the rotation animation to go from `0` to `4π` — good fun!

Keep in mind that you're not limited to simple paths such as squares or circles. You can feed just about any `CGPath` to your keyframe animation and send your layer along some extremely complicated paths.

If you're going to create more complex path animations and want to stay sane, you'd do well to keep in mind the note about `rotationMode` earlier in this chapter.

Key Points

- You can animate the very process of *drawing* a shape on screen by animating the `strokeStart` and `strokeEnd` properties of a `CAShapeLayer`.
- You can animate a layer along a path on screen by using a keyframe animation and animating the layer's `position` property with a given `CGPath`.

Chapter 18: Replicating Animations

In this chapter you're going to try something completely new: using a container layer that lets you **replicate** animations.

Let me introduce you to my favorite layer class: `CAReplicatorLayer`.

The idea behind `CAReplicatorLayer` is simple. You create some content — it could be a shape, an image or anything else you can draw with layers — and `CAReplicatorLayer` makes copies of it on the screen, like so:

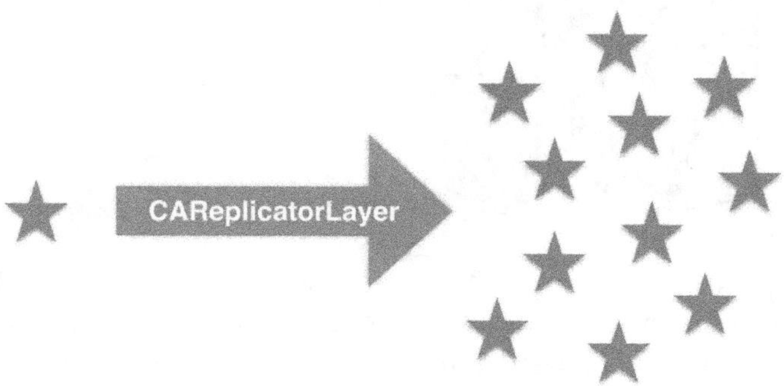

"Why would I need to clone shapes or images?" you would ask. And you would be right to ask that; it's not often you'd need the exact appearance of anything cloned a number of times.

`CAReplicatorLayer`'s superpowers come from the fact you can easily instruct it to make each clone slightly different from its ancestor.

For example, you could progressively change the tint of each copy. Your original layer could be magenta, while you progress the tint towards cyan as you create each copy.

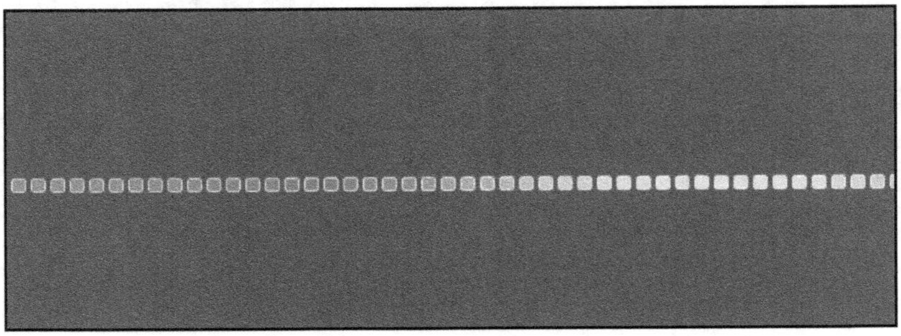

Furthermore, you can apply a transform between copies; for example, you can apply a simple rotation transform between each copy to draw them in a circle, as shown below:

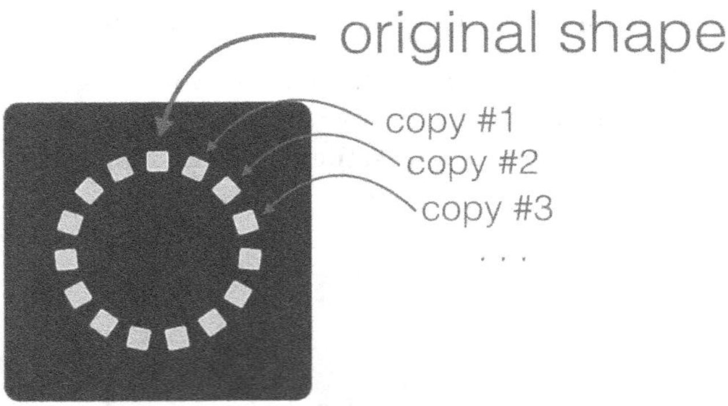

But the best feature of all is the ability to set an animation delay to follow each copy. When you set an `instanceDelay` of `0.2` seconds and add an animation to your original content, the first copy will animate with a delay of `0.2` seconds, the second copy will animate in `0.4` seconds, the third one in `0.6` seconds and so forth.

You can use this to create engaging and complex animations where you animate multiple elements in a synchronous manner.

In this chapter, you're going to work on a personal assistant app that will "listen" to your questions and answer back. As a wink to Apple's own personal assistant Siri, your project has been named Iris.

You're going to create two different replications. First, you'll create the visual feedback animation that plays while Iris talks, which will look much like a psychedelic sine wave:

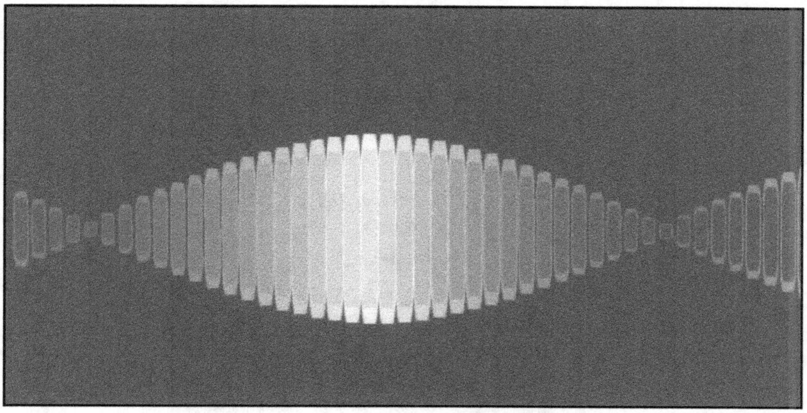

Then you'll use `CAReplicatorLayer` to create an interactive microphone-driven audio wave, which will provide visual feedback while the user speaks:

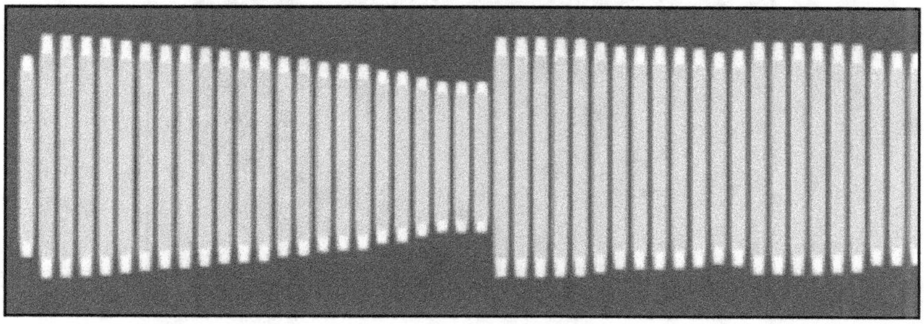

These two animations will introduce you to many features of `CAReplicatorLayer`. To cover every feature this layer offers would fill an entire book on its own!

But you don't need to listen to me yammer on about how much I like creating animations with `CAReplicatorLayer`; it's time to experience the magic for yourself.

Replicating Like Rabbits

Starter Project Overview

Launch the starter project for this chapter and open **Main.storyboard**. You'll notice that the project setup is quite straightforward:

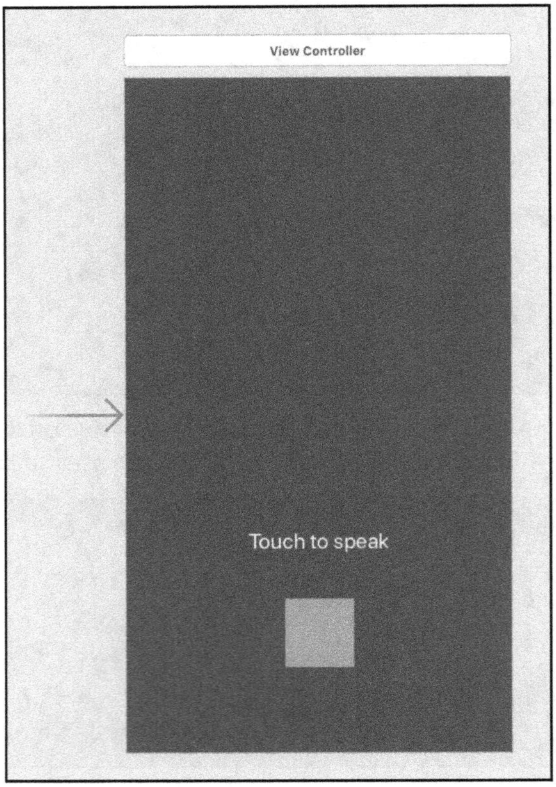

There is only a single view controller, which features a button and a label. The user asks their question while they hold down the button; when they release the button Iris will speak in response. The label will display the mic input levels and Iris' answer.

Open **ViewController.swift**; note the button events are already connected to actions. When the user touches down on the button, `actionStartMonitoring()` fires; when the user lifts their finger, `actionEndMonitoring()` fires.

Right now `ViewController` doesn't do much and simply calls `startSpeaking()` from within `actionEndMonitoring()` when the user lifts their finger.

The project features two more classes that are beyond the scope of this chapter, but they'll help you develop a fun and functional app while letting you focus on the animation parts.

- `Assistant`: The artificial intelligence assistant. It has a list of predefined amusing answers and speaks them in response to the user's questions.
- `MicMonitor`: Monitors the input levels on your iPhone's microphone and repeatedly calls a closure expression that you provide. This is where you have the chance to update the display.

Everything is ready for you to jump in and add some cool animations! First, run the project - it will ask you for microphone permissions:

Simply tap OK on the system alert:

This will get you set up for what's coming next.

Setting up the Replicator Layer

Open **ViewController.swift** and add the following two properties:

```
let replicator = CAReplicatorLayer()
let dot = CALayer()
```

`dot` will be a simple shape drawn using the `CALayer` basic properties such as background and border color. `replicator` will help you get multiple dot copies on screen.

Next, add the following constants you'll need to create your animation:

```
let dotLength: CGFloat = 6.0
let dotOffset: CGFloat = 8.0
```

You'll use the first constant as the width and height of the `dot` layer, while the second constant holds the offset between each dot replication.

To finish off the setup, you'll have to add the replicator layer to the view controller's view. Add the following to `viewDidLoad()`:

```
replicator.frame = view.bounds
view.layer.addSublayer(replicator)
```

Here, you make the replicator layer the same size as the view controller's view and add it as a sub-layer. If you were to run the project at this point, nothing would appear to have changed; that's because you didn't add any visible content to replicate.

The next step is to dress up the dot layer and add it to `replicator` in order to display the replications. Append the following to `viewDidLoad()`:

```
dot.frame = CGRect(
  x: replicator.frame.size.width - dotLength,
  y: replicator.position.y,
  width: dotLength,
  height: dotLength)

dot.backgroundColor = UIColor.lightGray.cgColor
dot.borderColor = UIColor(white: 1.0, alpha: 1.0).cgColor
dot.borderWidth = 0.5
dot.cornerRadius = 1.5
```

You first position the `dot` layer towards the right edge of the replicator and therefore, the right edge of the screen. Then you set the layer's background color and add a border. At this point the layer will look like the following:

To see it displayed on the screen, add the following:

```
replicator.addSublayer(dot)
```

This adds `dot` to `replicator`. Run your project and you'll see it show up:

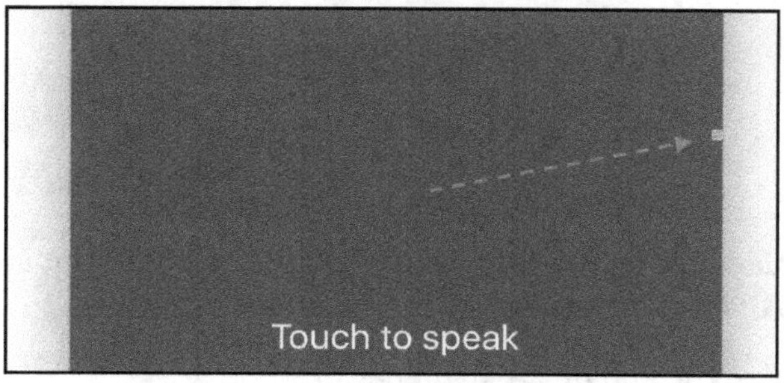

So far so good. What you see is what you would expect from adding just about any layer to any other layer.

"But where's the magic you promised us?" you're asking. Hang tight — you're almost there!

You're going to work with three `CAReplicatorLayer` properties that will help you access that replication magic:

- `instanceCount`: Sets the number of copies you want
- `instanceTransform`: Sets the transform to apply between copies
- `instanceDelay`: Sets the animation delay between copies

You want the replication to fill the screen, so you'll have to divide the screen width by the offset between copies (`dotOffset`) to get the number of dots needed to fill up the width. This will give you more replications on an Plus-sized iPhone and fewer on an iPhone SE.

Add the following line to `viewDidLoad()` to set the number of copies (including the original copy):

```
replicator.instanceCount = Int(view.frame.size.width /
dotOffset)
```

On an 5.5 inch screen instanceCount ends up as `51`; on a 4.7 inch screen `46`, and on a 4 inch screen, `40`.

Run the project again; hey, where are all the copies?

No, the photocopier isn't on the fritz again. All your copies of dot are there, but they're all on top of each other. You'll need to apply a transform to show them all.

Add the following to the end of `viewDidLoad()`:

```
replicator.instanceTransform = CATransform3DMakeTranslation(
  -dotOffset, 0.0, 0.0)
```

In the code above, you first set a translation transform between each replication. You then take the negative value of `dotOffset` for the translation on the X axis because you want the copies to progress from right to left.

`replicator` will consider dot and subtract 8 points from its position; the first copy will appear at this point. The second copy will appear at another 8 points to the left and so forth.

Run your project; you'll see all copies line up in the middle of the screen, each replication translated 8 points from the previous one:

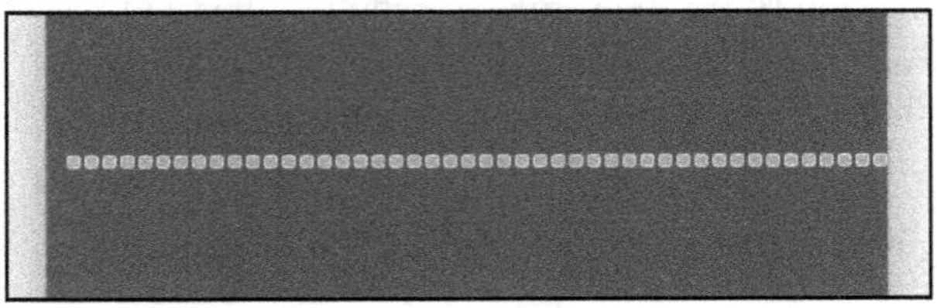

Your First Replicated Animation

To understand what `instanceDelay` does, you'll add a little test animation to `dot`. Add the following to the end of `viewDidLoad()`:

```
// This is a test animation, you're going to delete it
let move = CABasicAnimation(keyPath: "position.y")
```

```
move.fromValue = dot.position.y
move.toValue = dot.position.y - 50.0
move.duration = 1.0
move.repeatCount = 10
dot.add(move, forKey: nil)
// This is the end of the code you're going to delete
```

This animation simply moves `dot` up `50` points and repeats that action `10` times. Run the project and you'll see all clones obediently moving across the screen like so many synchronized kill-bots.

Next you'll add a bit of delay to the animation. Insert the following line of code:

```
replicator.instanceDelay = 0.02
```

Run your project once more and observe how all copies follow the original dot animation, but only after an ever-increasing delay:

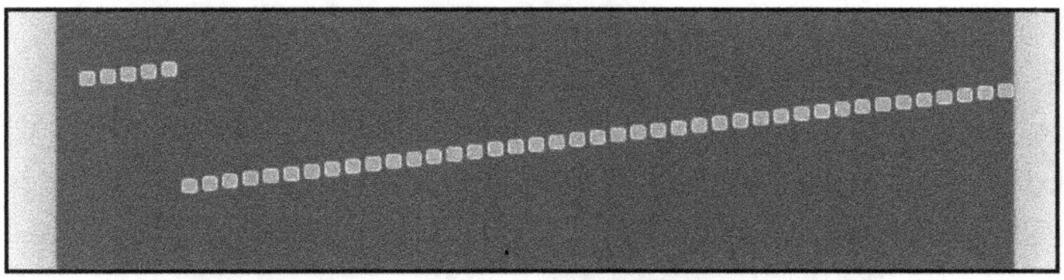

Now that you have the basics covered, it's time to move on to cooler animations.

Before you go on, **delete** the test animation you just added (use the comments above as a guide); you're going to create much better animations in its place.

> **Note**: Make sure you leave the line of code where you set the `instanceDelay` property - you'll need it for the effects you are going to build shortly.

Replicating Multiple Animations

`CAReplicatorLayer` replicates the content and animations you create in the manner you instruct. But it's up to you to come up with some cool animations that would look even *cooler* when replicated.

In this section, you'll work on the animation that plays while Iris speaks. To do this, you'll combine a number of simple animations with different delays to produce the final effect.

Scale Animation

First you'll continuously scale the dot layer up and down to produce a wave of dots.

Find `startSpeaking()` and add the following scale animation:

```
let scale = CABasicAnimation(keyPath: "transform")
scale.fromValue = NSValue(caTransform3D: CATransform3DIdentity)
scale.toValue = NSValue(caTransform3D:
  CATransform3DMakeScale(1.4, 15, 1.0))
scale.duration = 0.33
scale.repeatCount = .infinity
scale.autoreverses = true
scale.timingFunction = CAMediaTimingFunction(name: .easeOut)
dot.add(scale, forKey: "dotScale")
```

This is a simple layer animation like the many others in this section of the book. You scale the dot layer vertically 15-fold and run the animation continuously back and forth.

Run the project and tap the gray button; this calls `actionStartMonitoring()`, `actionEndMonitoring()` and finally your code in `startSpeaking()`. You should see your original dot layer animate and all copies follow with their respective delays:

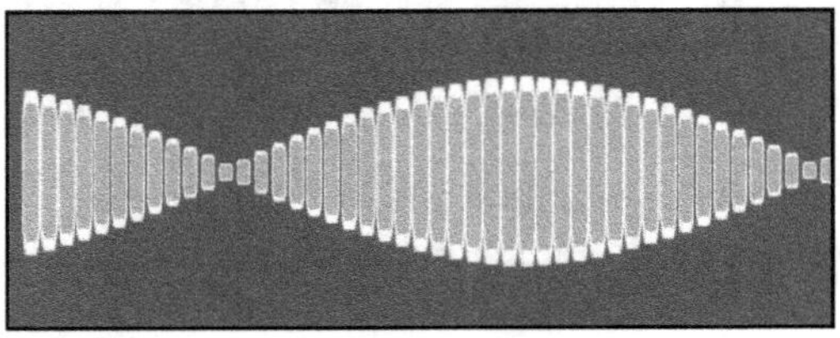

Congrats — you're off to a great start with `CAReplicatorLayer`!

if you want to get some extra kicks out of this animation, try changing the timing function of the animation to see what other cool waveforms you can create. For example here's how an ease-in timing shapes the resulting effect:

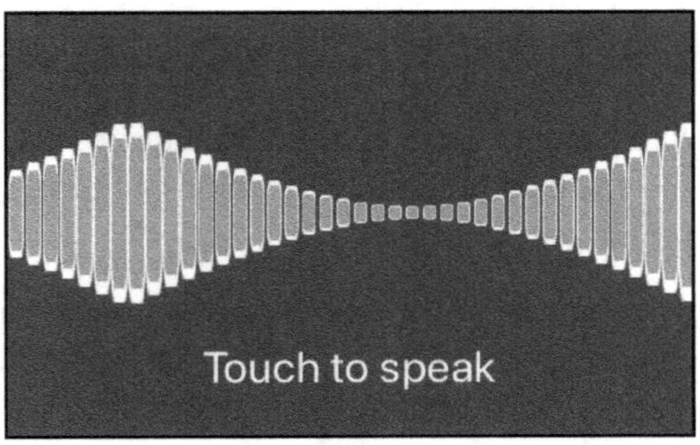

Opacity Animation

Next you'll make the original dot layer fade in and out. This will make the wave some dimension and change the alpha as it grows and shrinks to simulate light conditions. It will look much like a spinning twisty ribbon candy:

Add the following fade animation to startSpeaking():

```
let fade = CABasicAnimation(keyPath: "opacity")
fade.fromValue = 1.0
fade.toValue = 0.2
fade.duration = 0.33
fade.beginTime = CACurrentMediaTime() + 0.33
fade.repeatCount = .infinity
fade.autoreverses = true
fade.timingFunction = CAMediaTimingFunction(name: .easeOut)
dot.add(fade, forKey: "dotOpacity")
```

You fade the dot layer from opacity 1.0 to 0.2 over the duration of the scale animation. This time around, you start the animation with a delay of 0.33 seconds; this starts the fade-out effect when the wave it at its fullest.

Run your project and enjoy the new effect as the two animations run simultaneously:

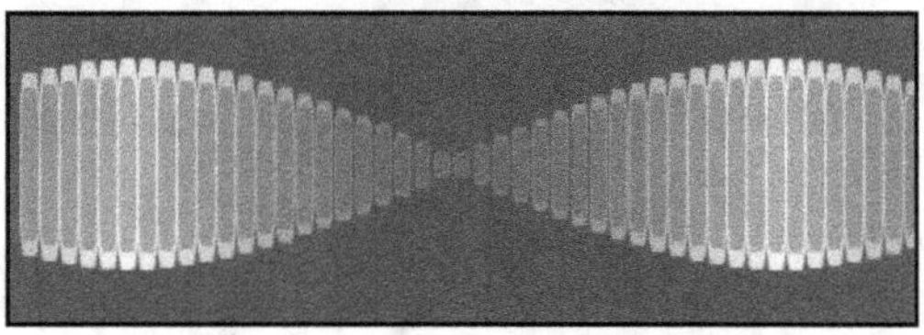

Tint Animation

If you push your imagination (and squint a little) you can imagine the wave twisting around and around on your screen. That impression would be a lot more clear if you animated its tint, as if the wave had a different color on each side.

This should be an easy enough task – all you have to do is animate the background color of dot.

Add a third animation to startSpeaking():

```
let tint = CABasicAnimation(keyPath: "backgroundColor")
tint.fromValue = UIColor.magenta.cgColor
```

```
tint.toValue = UIColor.cyan.cgColor
tint.duration = 0.66
tint.beginTime = CACurrentMediaTime() + 0.28
tint.fillMode = .backwards
tint.repeatCount = .infinity
tint.autoreverses = true
tint.timingFunction =
CAMediaTimingFunction(name: .easeInEaseOut)
dot.add(tint, forKey: "dotColor")
```

This animation changes the dot's tint from magenta to cyan and back. You use a duration of `0.66` seconds; this is twice the frequency of the scaling animation and gives the impression that the color changes every time the wave "twists".

You also give the animation a delay of `0.28` seconds; this makes the color tint animation start just before the "twist" occurs in the wave. This subtle effect provides a hint of the next color just before the wave "twists" as if there's a bit of reflection going on.

Run the project to check out the new effect:

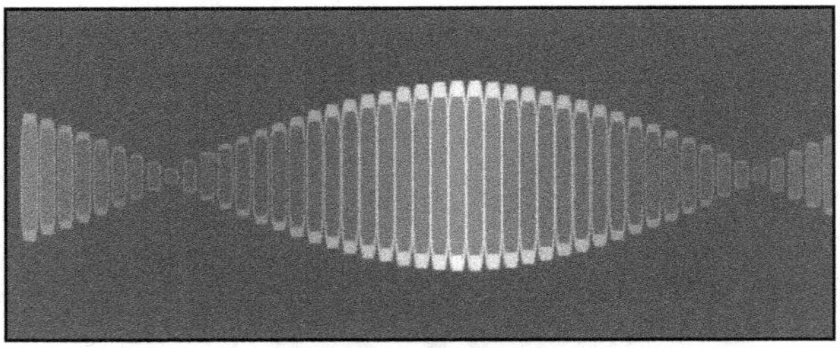

Animating CAReplicatorLayer Properties

So far you've created a pretty dazzling effect by animating the content in your replicator layer. But since `CAReplicatorLayer` is a layer itself, you can animate a number of its own properties too. You can animate `CAReplicatorLayer`'s basic properties like `position`, `backgroundColor` or `cornerRadius` but, you can create some interesting effects by animating some of the special properties in this layer that aren't present in other layers.

The animatable properties unique to `CAReplicatorLayer` include the following:

- `instanceDelay`: Animate the amount of delay between instances
- `instanceTransform`: Change the transform between replications on the fly

- `instanceColor`: Change the blend color used for all instances
- `instanceRedOffset`, `instanceGreenOffset`, `instanceBlueOffset`: Apply a delta to apply to each instance color component
- `instanceAlphaOffset`: Change the opacity delta applied to each instance

In this section, you'll animate the instance transform to make the speech wave even *more* psychedelic! Add one more animation to the end of `startSpeaking()`:

```
let initialRotation = CABasicAnimation(keyPath:
  "instanceTransform.rotation")
initialRotation.fromValue = 0.0
initialRotation.toValue   = 0.01
initialRotation.duration = 0.33
initialRotation.isRemovedOnCompletion = false
initialRotation.fillMode = .forwards
initialRotation.timingFunction =
CAMediaTimingFunction(name: .easeOut)
replicator.add(initialRotation, forKey: "initialRotation")
```

This animation affects just the rotation component of the instance transform; that is, it preserves the translation component you set for the instances in `viewDidLoad()` and only animates the rotation.

You animate the rotation between instances from `0.0` radians to `0.01` radians. Each replication will appear slightly rotated compared to its neighbor.

Run your project; enjoy your replicating animations on a totally new level — or should I say *curve*?

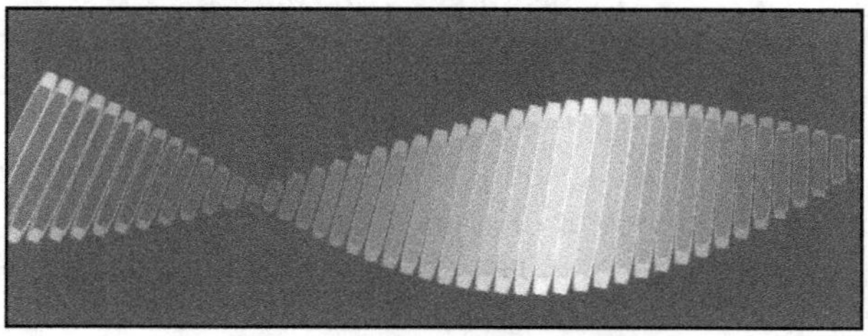

The instanceRotation animation above looks nice — but when I say *psychedelic*, I mean *PSYCHEDELIC*! What if you were to combine the effect of all running replication animations AND twist and spin the wave at the same time?

Add the animation below to complete the effect:

```
let rotation = CABasicAnimation(keyPath:
"instanceTransform.rotation")
rotation.fromValue = 0.01
```

```
rotation.toValue    = -0.01
rotation.duration = 0.99
rotation.beginTime = CACurrentMediaTime() + 0.33
rotation.repeatCount = .infinity
rotation.autoreverses = true
rotation.timingFunction =
CAMediaTimingFunction(name:  .easeInEaseOut)
replicator.add(rotation, forKey: "replicatorRotation")
```

Here, you run a second animation on `instanceTransform.rotation` that starts once the first animation has finished. You then animate the transform rotation from `0.01` radians (the final value of the first animation) to `-0.01` radians and back. This gives the speech animation a final, crazy boost:

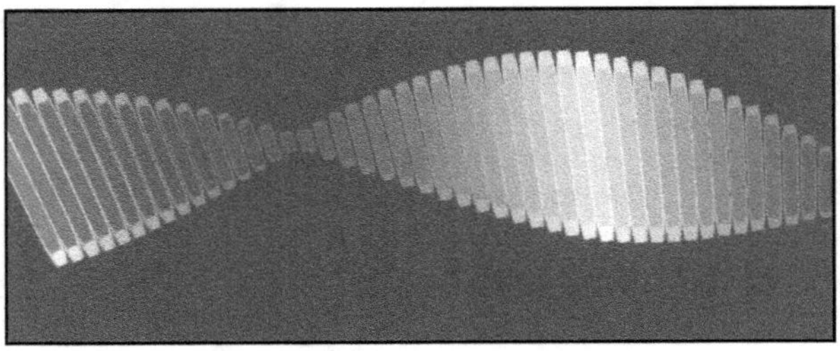

This is an outstanding (if not hypnosis-inducing) animation, and you created it by combining just a few select animations. The trick is to know which properties to animate and how to select the correct delays and durations to get the effect you're looking for.

> **Note**: Personally, I think the effect looks best if I rotate my head 45 degrees right. But be careful not to watch it too long - it could make you dizzy!

All that's left is to give your not-so-helpful assistant, Iris, the ability to listen and to respond. First you'll give the power of speech to Iris. The starter project class named `Assistant` will help you do that. Add the following to the top of `startSpeaking()`:

```
let answer = assistant.randomAnswer()
meterLabel.text = answer
assistant.speak(answer, completion: endSpeaking)
speakButton.isHidden = true
```

You first get a random answer from the `Assistant` class and visualize it via the `meterLabel`. Then you call `speak(_:completion:)` on assistant; passing in `endSpeaking()` as the `completion` parameter to be called when speaking is finished.

Next you'll add the code in `endSpeaking()` that removes all running animations and gracefully returns the wave to its initial state.

Insert the following into `endSpeaking()`:

```
replicator.removeAllAnimations()
```

This removes the animations on `instanceTransform` of `replicator`.

Next you need to animate the `dot` layer back to its original scale. Add:

```
let scale = CABasicAnimation(keyPath: "transform")
scale.toValue = NSValue(caTransform3D: CATransform3DIdentity)
scale.duration = 0.33
scale.isRemovedOnCompletion = false
scale.fillMode = .forwards
dot.add(scale, forKey: nil)
```

For this animation you don't specify a `fromValue`; this means that Core Animation will start the animation from the current value and animate the transform to `CATransform3DIdentiy`. This is necessary because at any given time each of the replicated instances has a different transform. Omitting `fromValue` animates each replication from its current scale to the animation's final value.

Finally, add the following code to remove the rest of the currently running animations from `dot` and reset the speak button state:

```
dot.removeAnimation(forKey: "dotColor")
dot.removeAnimation(forKey: "dotOpacity")
dot.backgroundColor = UIColor.lightGray.cgColor
speakButton.isHidden = false
```

Run the project again; this time, Iris will speak a random answer right back at you!

When Iris is done speaking, the wave will gracefully animate back to its initial state:

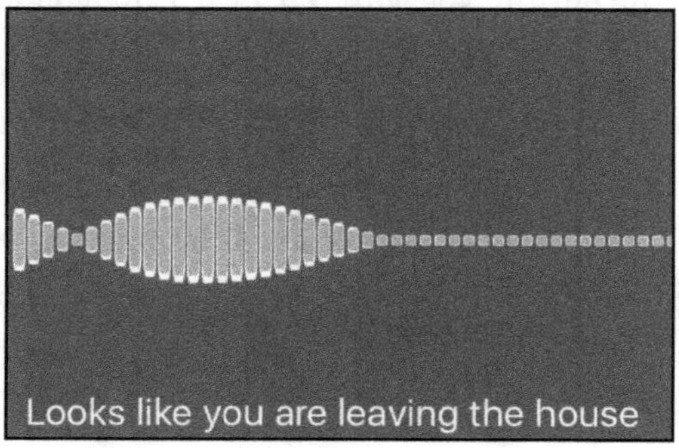

Interactive Replication Animations

Right now you need to press the speak button each time to see and hear Iris' answer. But you don't get to actually *ask* her anything, which, to be honest, is the really fun part.

In this final section you'll create an animation that displays the microphone input while you ask Iris your questions.

> **Note**: In case the microphone in the iOS simulator does not work for you use a physical device to test your app in this part of the chapter.

Add the following to `actionStartMonitoring()`:

```
dot.backgroundColor = UIColor.green.cgColor
monitor.startMonitoringWithHandler { level in
  self.meterLabel.text = String(format: "%.2f db", level)
}
```

The above method fires when the user presses on the speak button. To indicate the app is "listening", you change the dot layer color to green. Then you call `startMonitoringWithHandler()` on the monitor instance.

> **Note**: The `MicMonitor` class is pretty simple – peek inside **MicMonitor.swift** if you're interested to see how it gets the microphone levels.

The closure block you provide as a parameter executes repeatedly and gets the current microphone level as a parameter.

Run the app and hold the button; speak to the device and you'll see the current mic levels displayed.

So far so good; all you need now is to use the level variable to animate the replicator content accordingly.

First of all, you'll need to normalize the mic level to something you can use for your animations. level has a value in the rage of `-160.0` db to `0.0` db, `-160.0` db being the quietest and `0.0` db meaning extremely loud sound.

Add an extra line of code to the handler block to convert the level value to something useful and store it in `scaleFactor` so that the complete block looks like this:

```
monitor.startMonitoringWithHandler { level in
  self.meterLabel.text = String(format: "%.2f db", level)
  let scaleFactor = max(0.2, CGFloat(level) + 50) / 2
}
```

`scaleFactor` will store values between `0.1` and `25.0`. You can use this to scale dot to a reasonable size to represent the microphone input levels.

Add the following instance property to the `ViewController` class:

```
var lastTransformScale: CGFloat = 0.0
```

For the scaling animation, you'll need to save the last scaled value to this property. Since you'll constantly overwrite the running scale animation, you need to keep track of the last value the layer was supposed to scale to.

Now jump back to the microphone handler closure and add to it the following code, which animates from the last transform to the new one you calculated from the current microphone levels:

```
let scale = CABasicAnimation(keyPath: "transform.scale.y")
scale.fromValue = self.lastTransformScale
scale.toValue = scaleFactor
scale.duration = 0.1
scale.isRemovedOnCompletion = false
scale.fillMode = .forwards
self.dot.add(scale, forKey: nil)
```

This layer animation runs only on the y-axis of the scale component of the dot layer `transform`. You animate the scale from the last value used to the current `scaleFactor`.

Finally, still inside the handler, add the following code to save the current `scaleFactor` value for the next handler call:

```
self.lastTransformScale = scaleFactor
```

This code ought to bring the replicator layer to life. Run the project, hold the button and speak.

You'll see an actual audio wave show up on screen, all handled by the replicator layer while you simply animate the original dot layer:

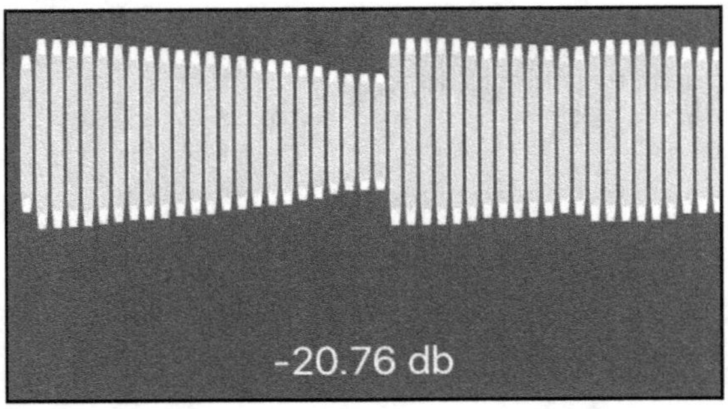

But when you let go of the speak button, the result is somewhat baffling:

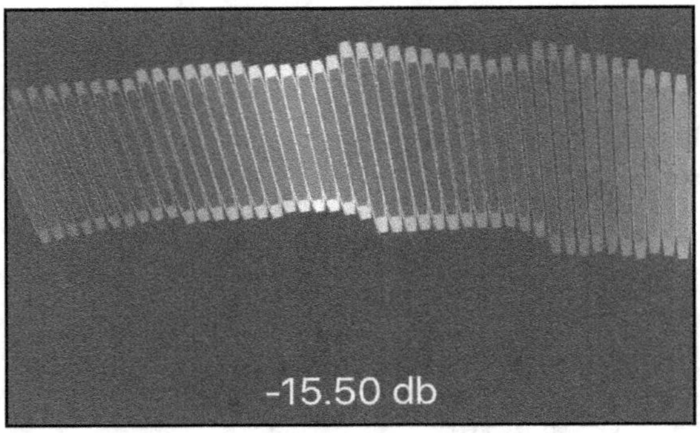

Aha — you need to reset the animations and stop monitoring the microphone. You can take care of that in `actionEndMonitoring()`.

Insert the following at the top of that method:

```
monitor.stopMonitoring()
dot.removeAllAnimations()
```

Here you disable the microphone monitor by calling `stopMonitoring()` and removing all animations running on the `dot`layer. This way the app can move on and display the Iris animation.

Give the app a try. Isn't talking to Iris a lot of fun?

The microphone input animation ends somewhat abruptly, but you'll get to fix that in the challenges below.

Key Points

- You can easily create compound animation effects via `CAReplicatorLayer` to combine multiple copies of the same animation.
- You set number and variations between the animation replications via the `instanceCount`, `instanceTransform` and `instanceDelay` properties on `CAReplicatorLayer`.
- Besides animating properties on the original animation, you can animate also properties on the replicator layer itself.

Challenges

Challenge 1: Smooth the Transition Between Microphone Input and Iris Animations

Your first challenge is to not just remove the two animations running on the `dot` layer by calling `dot.removeAllAnimations()`, but to animate the wave back to a state suitable for the next animation to be run.

Take this challenge in three steps:

- First, delete the line where you remove the running animations on dot from `actionEndMonitoring()`.
- Then, in its place, animate the scale of dot back to a value of `1.0` on the y-axis. Leave the animation on the screen to wait for the Iris animation to start — don't remove it when it's done.
- Finally, add another animation that changes the dot tint from green to magenta. For this animation, use a `fillMode` of `.backwards` — without it, the replicator layer will reset the tint to the final value retroactively.

Mind the durations of these two new animations. They should finish before the Iris animation starts.

When you've completed this challenge, the two animations should blend nicely into each other like so:

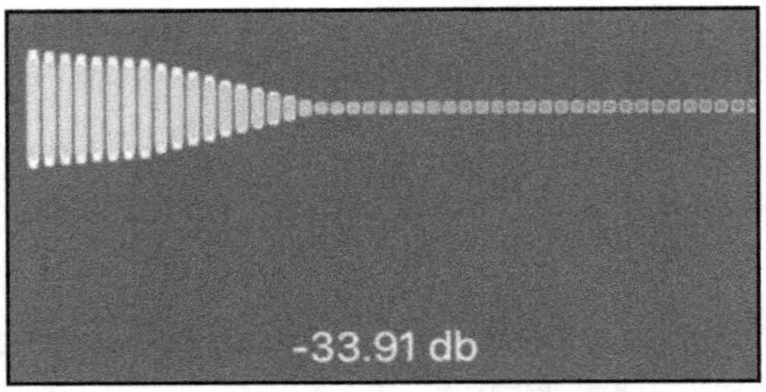

Section Conclusion

This wraps up the basic layer animations section. You've been through a lot — and learned a ton of things along the way!

In this section of the book you covered:

- Basic movement, fading, rotation, and scaling animations
- Groups and keyframe animations
- Shapes, masks, and gradient animations
- Stroke and path animations
- Replicating animations

Section V: View Controller Transition Animations

It’s time to learn how to use UIKit and Auto Layout animation techniques in the broader context of app navigation and layout. You’ve animated multiple views and layers already, but now you’ll take a bigger-picture perspective and think about animating entire view controllers!

Implementing custom view controller transitions takes some coding, but the results are lots of fun to look at and use. No matter which API you use, custom transitions are an important animation technique that really make an app stand out!

Chapter 19: Presentation Controller & Orientation Animations

Presenting view controllers is the common way to "move" the user focus modally from one contained piece of UI to another. When the user has finished making use of the presented UI they will choose to save their work, cancel the pending changes, or otherwise actively dismiss the UI. Whether you're presenting the camera view controller, the address book, or one of your own custom-designed modal screens, you call the same UIKit method every time: `present(_:animated:completion:)`. This method "gives up" the current screen to another view controller. The default presentation animation simply slides the new view up to cover the current one.

The illustration below shows a "New Contact" view controller sliding up over the list of contacts:

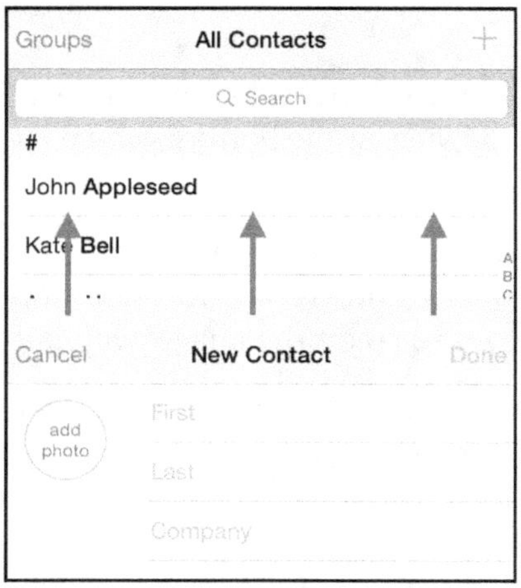

In this chapter, you'll create your own custom presentation controller animations to replace the default one and liven up this chapter's project.

Looking Through the Starter Project

Open the starter project for this chapter, an app called Beginner Cook. Select **Main.storyboard** to begin the tour:

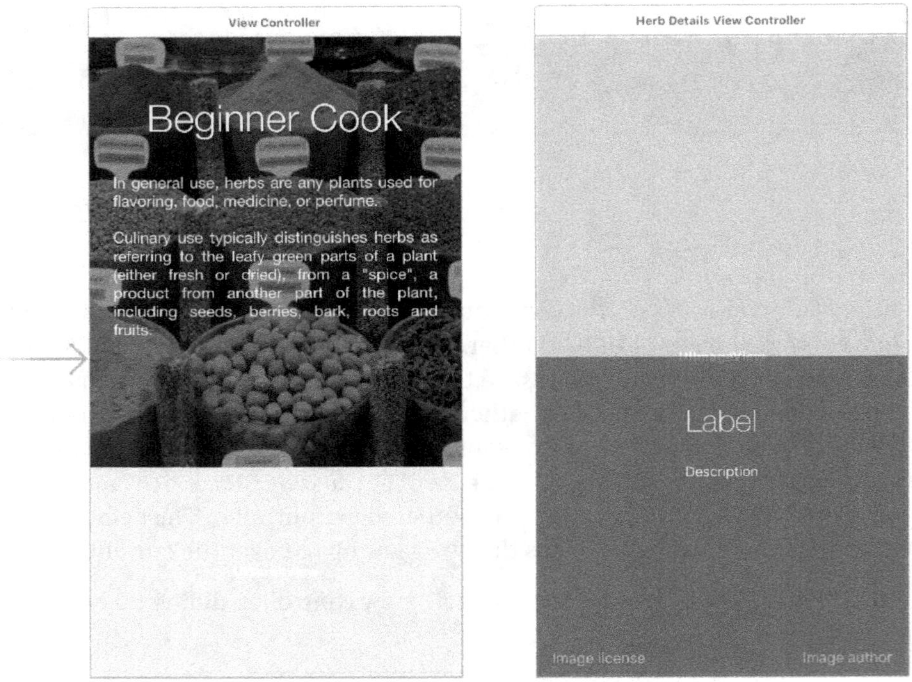

The first view controller (`ViewController`) contains the app's title and main description as well as a scroll view at the bottom, which shows the list of available herbs.

The main view controller presents `HerbDetailsViewController` whenever the user taps one of the images in the list; this view controller sports a background, a title, a description and some buttons to credit the image owner.

There's already enough code in **ViewController.swift** and **HerbDetailsViewController.swift** to support the basic application.

Build and run the project to see how the app looks and feels:

Tap on one of the herb images, and the details screen comes up via the standard vertical cover transition. That might be OK for your garden-variety app, but your herbs deserve better!

Your job is to add some custom presentation controller animations to your app to make it blossom! You'll replace the current stock animation with one that expands the tapped herb image to a full-screen view like so:

Roll up your sleeves, put your developer apron on and get ready for the inner workings of custom presentation controllers!

Behind the Scenes of Custom Transitions

UIKit lets you customize your view controller's presentation via the delegate pattern; you simply make your main view controller (or another class you create specifically for that purpose) adopt `UIViewControllerTransitioningDelegate`.

Every time you present a new view controller, UIKit asks its delegate whether or not it should use a custom transition. Here's what the first step of the custom transitioning dance looks like:

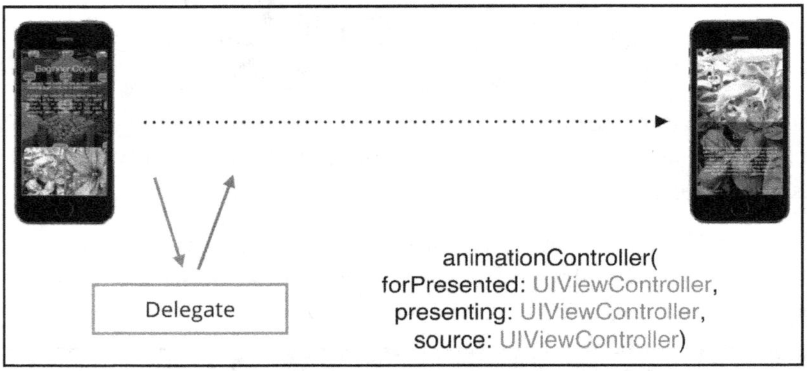

UIKit calls `animationController(forPresented:presenting:source:)` to see if a `UIViewControllerAnimatedTransitioning` is returned. If that method returns `nil`, UIKit uses the built-in transition. If UIKit receives a `UIViewControllerAnimatedTransitioning` object instead, then UIKit uses that object as the animation controller for the transition.

There are a few more steps in the dance before UIKit can use the custom animation controller:

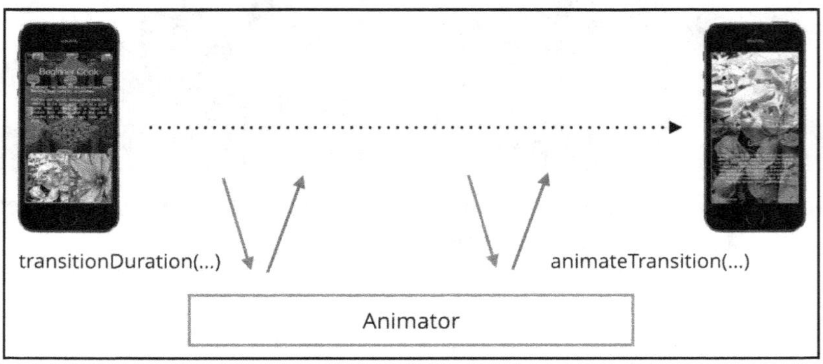

UIKit first asks your animation controller (simply known as the **animator**) for the transition duration in seconds, then calls `animateTransition(using:)` on it. This is when your custom animation gets to take center stage.

In `animateTransition(using:)`, you have access to both the current view controller on the screen as well as the new view controller to be presented. You can fade, scale, rotate and manipulate the existing view and the new view however you like.

Now that you've learned a bit about how custom presentation controllers work, you can start to create your own.

Implementing Transition Delegates

Since the delegate's task is to manage the animator object that performs the actual animations, you'll first have to create a stub for the animator class before you can write the delegate code.

From Xcode's main menu select **File\New\File...** and choose the template **iOS\Source\Cocoa Touch Class**.

Set the new class name to **PopAnimator**, make sure Swift is selected, and make it a subclass of **NSObject**.

Open **PopAnimator.swift** and update the class definition to make it conform to the `UIViewControllerAnimatedTransitioning` protocol as follows:

```
class PopAnimator: NSObject,
UIViewControllerAnimatedTransitioning {

}
```

You'll see some complaints from Xcode since you haven't implemented the required delegate methods yet, so you'll stub those out next.

Add the following method to the class:

```
func transitionDuration(using transitionContext:
UIViewControllerContextTransitioning?) -> TimeInterval {
  return 0
}
```

The `0` value above is just a placeholder value for the duration; you'll replace this later with a real value as you work through the project.

Now add the following method stub to the class:

```
func animateTransition(using transitionContext:
UIViewControllerContextTransitioning) {

}
```

The above stub will hold your animation code; adding it should have cleared the remaining errors in Xcode.

Now that you have the basic animator class, you can move on to implementing the delegate methods on the view controller side. Open **ViewController.swift** and add the following extension to the end of the file:

```
extension ViewController: UIViewControllerTransitioningDelegate
{

}
```

This code indicates the view controller conforms to the transitioning delegate protocol. You'll add some methods here in a moment.

Find `didTapImageView(_:)` in the main body of the class. Near the bottom of that method you'll see the code that presents the details view controller. `herbDetails` is the instance of the new view controller; you'll need to set its transitioning delegate to the main controller.

Add the following code right before the line where you call `present(...)` to present the details view controller:

```
// ...
herbDetails.transitioningDelegate = self // <-- Add this line
present(herbDetails, animated: true, completion: nil)
```

Now UIKit will ask `ViewController` for an animator object every time you present the details view controller on the screen. However, you still haven't implemented any of the `UIViewControllerTransitioningDelegate` methods, so UIKit will still use the default transition.

The next step is to actually create your animator object and return it to UIKit when requested. Add the following new property to `ViewController`:

```
let transition = PopAnimator()
```

This is the instance of `PopAnimator` that will drive your animated view controller transitions. You only need one instance of `PopAnimator` since you can use the same object each time you present a view controller, as the transitions are the same every time.

Now add the first delegate method to the extension in `ViewController`:

```
func animationController(
  forPresented presented: UIViewController,
  presenting: UIViewController,
  source: UIViewController
) -> UIViewControllerAnimatedTransitioning? {
  guard let selectedImage = selectedImage else {
   return nil
  }
  return transition
}
```

This method takes a few parameters that let you make an informed decision whether or not you want to return a custom animation. In this chapter you'll always return your single instance of `PopAnimator` since you have only one presentation transition.

You've already added the delegate method for presenting view controllers, but how will you deal with dismissing one?

Add the following delegate method to handle this:

```
func animationController(forDismissed dismissed:
UIViewController) -> UIViewControllerAnimatedTransitioning? {
  return nil
}
```

The above method does essentially the same thing as the previous one: you check which view controller was dismissed and decide whether to return `nil` and use the default animation, or return a custom transition animator and use that instead.

At the moment you return `nil`, as you aren't going to implement the dismissal animation until later.

You finally have a custom animator to take care of your custom transitions. But does it work?

Build and run your project and tap one of the herb images:

Nothing happens. Why? You have a custom animator to drive the transition, but... oh, wait, you haven't added any code to the animator class! You'll take care of that in the next section.

Creating your Transition Animator

Open **PopAnimator.swift;** this is where you'll add the code to transition between the two view controllers.

First, add the following properties to this class:

```
let duration = 1.0
var presenting = true
var originFrame = CGRect.zero
```

You'll use `duration` in several places, such as when you tell UIKit how long the transition will take and when you create the constituent animations.

You also define `presenting` to tell the animator class whether you are presenting or dismissing a view controller. You want to keep track of this because typically, you'll run the animation forward to present and in reverse to dismiss.

Finally, you will use `originFrame` to store the original frame rect of the image the user taps — you will need that to animate from the original frame to a full screen image and vice versa. Keep an eye out for `originFrame` later on when you fetch the currently selected image and pass its frame to the animator instance.

Now you can move on to the `UIViewControllerAnimatedTransitioning` methods.

Replace the code inside `transitionDuration()` with the following:

```
return duration
```

Reusing the `duration` property lets you easily experiment with the transition animation. You can simply modify the value of the property to make the transition run faster or slower.

Setting your Transition's Context

It's time to add some magic to `animateTransition`. This method has one parameter of type `UIViewControllerContextTransitioning`, which gives you access to the parameters and view controllers of the transition. Before you start working on the code itself, it's important to understand what the animation context actually *is*.

When the transition between the two view controllers begins, the existing view is added to a transition container view and the new view controller's view is created but not yet visible, as illustrated below:

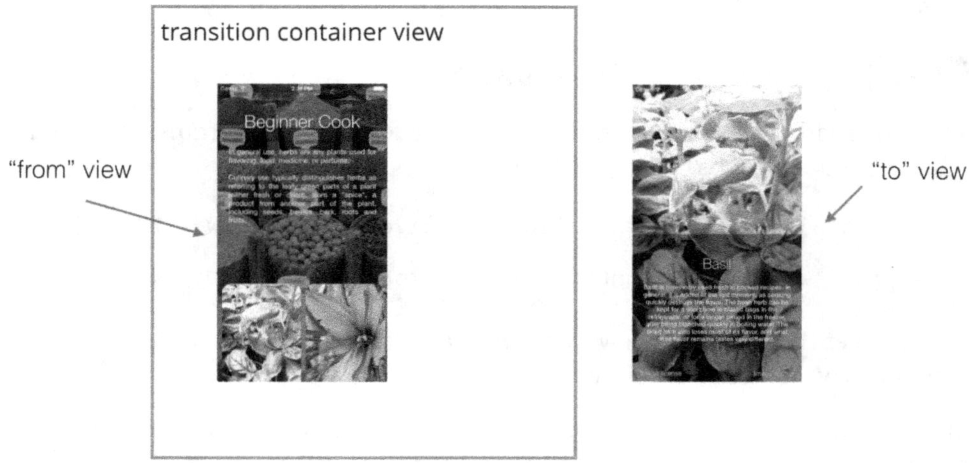

Therefore your task is to add the new view to the transition container within `animateTransition()`, "animate in" its appearance, and "animate out" the old view if required.

By default, the old view is removed from the transition container when the transition animation is done.

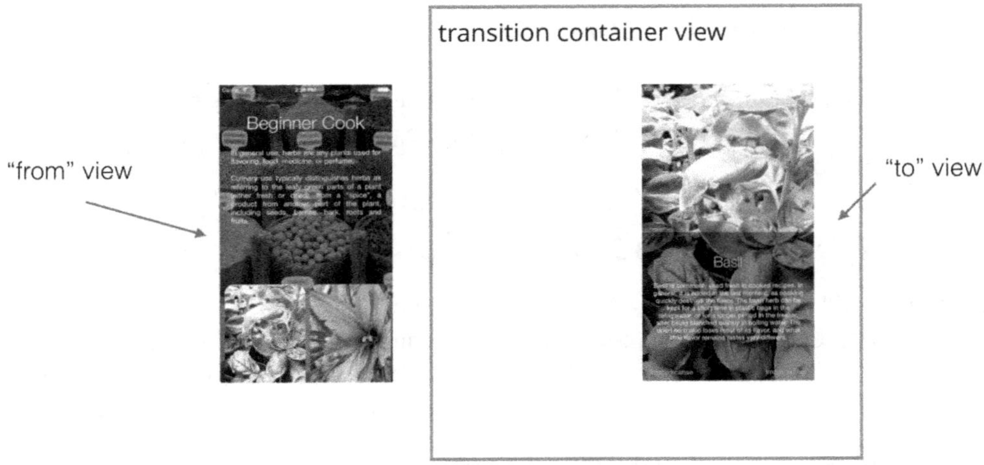

Before you get too many cooks in this kitchen, you'll create a simple transition animation to see how it works before implementing a much cooler, albeit more complicated, transition.

Adding a Fade Transition

You'll start with a simple fade transition to get a feel for custom transitions. Add the following code to `animateTransition()`:

```
let containerView = transitionContext.containerView
let toView = transitionContext.view(forKey: .to)!
```

First, you get the container view where your animations will take place, and then you fetch the new view and store it in toView.

The transition context object has two very handy methods that give you access to the transition players:

- `view(forKey:)`: This lets you access the views of the "old" and "new" view controllers via the arguments `UITransitionContextViewKey.from` or `UITransitionContextViewKey.to` respectively.
- `viewController(forKey:)`: This lets you access the "old and "new" view controllers via the arguments `UITransitionContextViewControllerKey.from` or `UITransitionContextViewControllerKey.to` respectively.

At this point, you have both the container view and the view to be presented. Next you need to add the view to be presented as a child to the container view and animate it in some way.

Add the following to `animateTransition()`:

```
containerView.addSubview(toView)
toView.alpha = 0.0
UIView.animate(withDuration: duration,
  animations: {
    toView.alpha = 1.0
  },
  completion: { _ in
    transitionContext.completeTransition(true)
  }
)
```

Note that you call `completeTransition()` on the transition context in the animation completion block; this tells UIKit that your transition animations are done and that UIKit is free to wrap up the view controller transition.

Build and run your project; tap one of the herbs in the list and you'll see the herb overview fade in over the main view controller:

The transition is acceptable and you've seen what to do in `animateTransition` — but you're going to add something even better!

Adding a Pop Transition

You're going to structure the code for the new transition slightly differently, so replace all the code in `animateTransition()` with the following:

```
let containerView = transitionContext.containerView
let herbView = presenting ?
  transitionContext.view(forKey: .to) :
  transitionContext.view(forKey: .from)
guard let herbView = herbView else {
  transitionContext.completeTransition(false)
  return
}
```

`containerView` is where your animations will live. If you're presenting, `herbView` is fetched from the context using the appropriate key, depending if you're presenting or dismissing. For both presenting and dismissing, `herbView` will always be the view that you animate. When you present the details controller view, it will grow to take up the entire screen. When dismissed, it will shrink to the image's original frame.

Add the following to `animateTransition()`:

```
let initialFrame = presenting ? originFrame : herbView.frame
let finalFrame = presenting ? herbView.frame : originFrame

let xScaleFactor = presenting ?
  initialFrame.width / finalFrame.width :
  finalFrame.width / initialFrame.width

let yScaleFactor = presenting ?
  initialFrame.height / finalFrame.height :
  finalFrame.height / initialFrame.height
```

In the code above, you detect the initial and final animation frames and then calculate the scale factor you need to apply on each axis as you animate between each view.

Now you need to carefully position the new view so it appears exactly above the tapped image; this will make it look like the tapped image expands to fill the screen.

Add the following to `animateTransition()`:

```
let scaleTransform = CGAffineTransform(
  scaleX: xScaleFactor,
  y: yScaleFactor)

if presenting {
  herbView.transform = scaleTransform
```

```
    herbView.center = CGPoint(
      x: initialFrame.midX,
      y: initialFrame.midY)
    herbView.clipsToBounds = true
  }
```

When presenting the new view, you set its scale and position so it exactly matches the size and location of the initial frame.

Now add the final bits of code to `animateTransition()`:

```
  if let toView = transitionContext.view(forKey: .to) {
    containerView.addSubview(toView)
  }
  containerView.bringSubviewToFront(herbView)

  UIView.animate(
    withDuration: duration,
    delay:0.0,
    usingSpringWithDamping: 0.4,
    initialSpringVelocity: 0.0,
    animations: {
      herbView.transform = self.presenting ?
        CGAffineTransform.identity : scaleTransform
      herbView.center = CGPoint(x: finalFrame.midX, y:
  finalFrame.midY)
    },
    completion: { _ in
      transitionContext.completeTransition(true)
    })
```

This will first add `toView` to the container. Next, you need to make sure the `herbView` is on top since that's the only view you're animating. Remember that when dismissing, `toView` is the original view so in the first line, you'll be adding it *on top* of everything else, and your animation will be hidden away unless you bring herbView to the front.

Then, you can kick off the animations. Using a spring animation here will give it a bit of bounce. Inside the `animations` expression, you change the transform and position of `herbView`. When presenting, you're going from the small size at the bottom to the full screen so the target transform is just the identity transform. When dismissing, you animate it to scale down to match the original image size.

At this point, you've set the stage by positioning the new view controller over the tapped image, you've animated between the initial and final frames, and finally, you've called `completeTransition()` to hand things back to UIKit. It's time to see your code in action!

Build and run your project; tap the first herb image to see your view controller transition in action.

Well, it's not perfect, but once you take care of a few rough edges your animation will be exactly what you wanted!

Currently your animation starts from the top-left corner; that's because the default value of `originFrame` has the origin at `(0, 0)` – and you never set it to any other value.

Open **ViewController.swift** and add the following code to the top of `animationController(forPresented:)`:

```
transition.originFrame =
selectedImage.convert(selectedImage.bounds, to: nil)

transition.presenting = true
selectedImage!.isHidden = true
```

This sets the `originFrame` of the transition to the frame of `selectedImage`, which is the image view you last tapped. Then you set `presenting` to `true` and hide the tapped image during the animation.

Build and run your project again; tap different herbs in the list and see how your transition looks for each.

Adding a Dismiss Transition

All that's left to do is dismiss the details controller. You've actually done most of the work in the animator already — the transition animation code does the logic juggling to set the proper initial and final frames, so you're most of the way to playing the animation both forwards and backwards. Sweet!

Open **ViewController.swift** and replace the body of `animationController(forDismissed:)` with the following:

```
transition.presenting = false
return transition
```

This tells your animator object that you're dismissing a view controller so the animation code will run in the correct direction.

Build and run the project to see the result. Tap on an herb and then tap anywhere on screen to dismiss it.

The transition animation looks great, but notice the herb you picked has disappeared from the scroll view! You'll need to make sure the tapped image re-appears when you dismiss the details screen.

Open **PopAnimator.swift** and add a new closure property to the class:

```
var dismissCompletion: (() -> Void)?
```

This will let you pass in some code to run when the dismiss transition completes.

Next, find `animateTransition()` and add the following code to the completion handler in the call to `animateWithDuration(...)`, right before the call to `completeTransition()`:

```
if !self.presenting {
  self.dismissCompletion?()
}
```

This code executes `dismissCompletion` once the dismiss animation has finished — which is the perfect spot to show the original image.

Open **ViewController.swift** and add the following code to `viewDidLoad()`:

```
transition.dismissCompletion = {
  self.selectedImage?.isHidden = false
}
```

This code displays the original image to replace the herb details view controller once the transition animation completes. Build and run your app to enjoy the transition animations both ways, now that the herbs aren't getting lost along the way!

The transition animation still looks a bit rough around the edges but you'll finish it on your own in this chapter's challenges.

Before you get to the challenges though, there's one more animation topic to deal with: view transitions for managing changes to device orientation.

Device Orientation Transition

> **Note**: This section of the chapter is optional; if you're not interested in learning how to handle changes in device orientation in your view controllers, skip ahead directly to the challenges.

You can think of device orientation changes as a presentation transition from a view controller to itself, just at a different size.

`viewWillTransition(to size:coordinator:)`, introduced in iOS 8, gives you a simple and straightforward way to handle device orientation changes. You don't need to build separate portrait or landscape layouts; instead, you just need to react to the change to the view controller view's size.

Open **ViewController.swift** and add the following stub for `viewWillTransition(to:with:)`:

```
override func viewWillTransition(to size: CGSize, with
coordinator: UIViewControllerTransitionCoordinator) {
  super.viewWillTransition(to: size, with: coordinator)

}
```

The first parameter (`size`) tells you what size your view controller is transitioning to. The second parameter (`coordinator`) is the transition coordinator object, which gives you access to a number of the transition's properties.

All you need to do in this app is reduce the alpha of the app's background image to improve the readability of the text when the device is in landscape mode.

Add the following code to `viewWillTransitionToSize`:

```
coordinator.animate(
  alongsideTransition: { context in
    self.bgImage.alpha = (size.width>size.height) ? 0.25 : 0.55
  },
  completion: nil
)
```

`animate(alongsideTransition:)` lets you specify your own custom animations to execute in parallel with the rotation animation that UIKit performs by default when you change the orientation.

Your animation closure will receive a transitioning context, just like the one you used when presenting a view controller. In this case, you don't have "from" and "to" view controllers since they're the same, but instead you can fetch properties such as the transition duration.

Inside the animation closure you check if the width of the target size is bigger than the height; if so, you reduce the alpha value of the background image to `0.25`. This makes the background fade out when transitioning to landscape mode and fade in to `0.55` alpha when transitioning to portrait orientation.

Build and run your app; rotate the device (or press Cmd + left arrow if testing in the iPhone Simulator) to see your alpha animation in action.

You can clearly see the background dim when you rotate the screen to a landscape mode. This makes the longer lines of text easier to read.

However if you tap on a herb image you will notice that animation is somewhat messy.

This happens because the screen has a landscape orientation, but the images still have portrait dimensions. Therefore the transition between the original image and the image stretched to fill up the screen is not fluid.

Not to fear — you can use your new friend `viewWillTransition(to:with:)` to fix this problem too.

There is an instance method on `ViewController` called `positionListItems()` that sizes and positions the herb images. This method is called from `viewDidLoad()` when your app first starts.

Add a call to this method inside the `animate(alongsideTransition:)` animation block you added last, just after you set the `alpha`:

```
self.positionListItems()
```

This will animate the size and position of the herb images while the device rotates. As soon as the screen finishes re-orientating the herb images will also have resized:

And since those images will now have a landscape layout also your transition animation will work just fine. Give it a try!

That's it for this chapter; take a look at the challenges below where you'll polish some of the remaining rough edges of your transition animations.

Key Points

- You enable and configure a custom presentation transition by implementing the `UIViewControllerTransitioningDelegate` protocol in one of your types and making it the presentation delegate.
- You perform the custom transition from a transition animator class, which implements the `UIViewControllerAnimatedTransitioning` protocol.
- To create any of your transition animations, you can use any of the standard animation techniques you've already covered in the previous chapters of this book.

Challenges

There are two tiny imperfections in your presentation animation: you can see the detail view text up to the very last moment when it just disappears; in addition, the initial herb images have rounded corners, which makes the animation look jumpy at the end.

Challenge 1: Smooth the Transition Animation

Your first task is to fade the contents of the herb details view in or out as appropriate while transitioning. This corrects that awkward moment when the text of the detail view just disappears as it's dismissed.

Take a look at the storyboard file; you'll see the details controller already has all of its text views added to a main view connected to the `containerView` outlet. All you need to do is fade `containerView` in or out while the transition animation takes place.

There are three steps in the solution to this challenge:

- Get a reference to the `HerbDetailsViewController` using the transition context's `viewController(forKey:)` method. Remember that the key will be different depending on whether you are presenting or dismissing and that you'll need to cast the result as `HerbViewController`. The two keys to choose from are `UITransitionContextViewControllerKey.to` and `UITransitionContextViewControllerKey.from`.

- Before you start the animation (the one animation already in `animateTranstion`), set the `alpha` of `containerView` to zero; it's an outlet property of `HerbDetailsViewController`. You only need to do this when you're presenting the view controller, not when dismissing it since it will be visible already when dismissing.
- Set the alpha of `containerView` in your animation closure — where you animate `herbView` – to fully opaque (`1.0`) when you're presenting and fully transparent (`0.0`) when you're dismissing.

To check the result of your changes more closely, you can increase the transition duration to `10` seconds and observe the animation in detail (or use **Debug/Toggle Slow Animations in Frontmost App** from the iOS Simulator main menu).

Challenge 2: Animate the Corner Radius

Finally you'll animate the corner radius of the details view so that it matches the rounded corners of the herb images in the main view controller.

At the end of `animateTransition()` create and run a layer animation to change the corner radius of `herbView`'s layer. Animate `herbView.layer.cornerRadius` from `20.0 / xScaleFactor` to `0.0` if presenting, and vice versa if dismissing. You need to take the scale factor into account because you're also transforming the view. Set the duration of the animation to `duration / 2` so that it has finished before the springing starts, otherwise it will look quite strange!

Here's a little trick you might want to use. `cornerRadius` is one of the few special layer properties that the UIKit animation APIs can animate. You can just change the corner radius from within an `animation` block and it'll just work - give it a try!

That wraps up presentation controller animations. Next up, navigation controller animations. You'll notice a lot of similarities between the two, so put the herbs aside and dive right in!

Chapter 20: UINavigationController Custom Transition Animations

Using a navigation stack via a `UINavigationController` is a common way to let your app's users navigate through your app's UI. Pushing a new view controller onto the navigation stack or popping one off gives you a sleek animation with no work on your part. A new screen comes from the right and pushes away the old one with a slight lag:

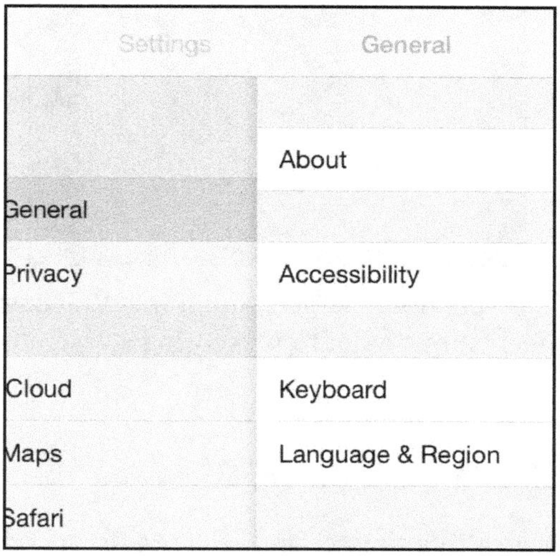

The above screenshot shows how iOS pushes a new view controller onto the navigation stack in the Settings app: The new view slides in from the right to cover the old view and the new title fades in while the old title titles fades from view.

The navigation paradigm in iOS has become old hat to users, as the same animations have been used for many years. This frees you to embellish your navigation controller transitions without throwing the user off.

In much the same way you built custom presenting view controllers in the previous chapter, you can build custom transitions to push and pop new view controllers.

You'll be working with the Logo Reveal project. In this chapter, you'll add a custom transparent view that gives the user a glimpse of the content hidden behind:

If you worked through the previous chapter, you'll find that custom navigation controller transitions feel quite similar to presenting view controllers.

Introducing Logo Reveal

Open the starter project for this chapter and select **Main.storyboard**. You'll see the project features a navigation controller, main view controller, and a detail view controller.

It will look like this:

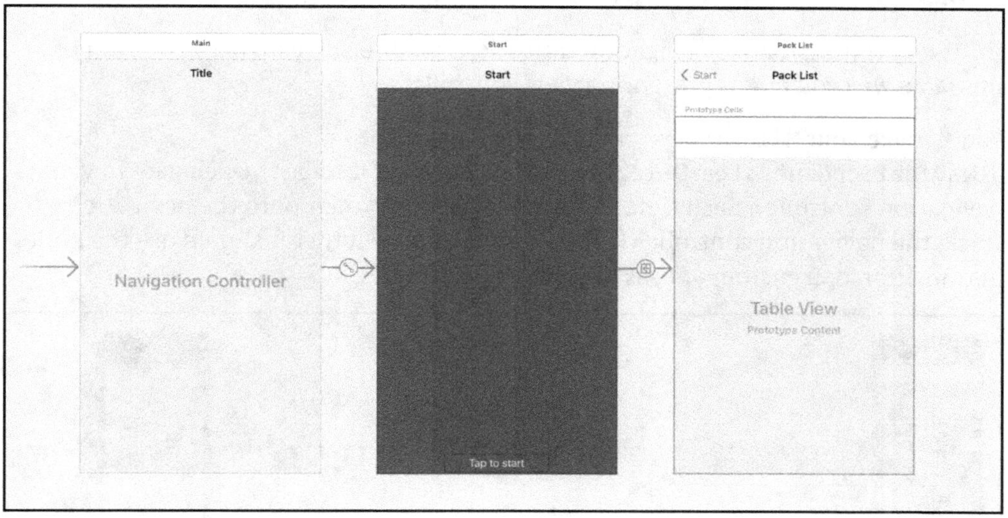

The navigation's already been hooked up for you so you can focus on customizing your navigation controllers.

Build and run your project; tap anywhere on the default screen (`MainViewController`) to present the vacation packing list (`DetailViewController`):

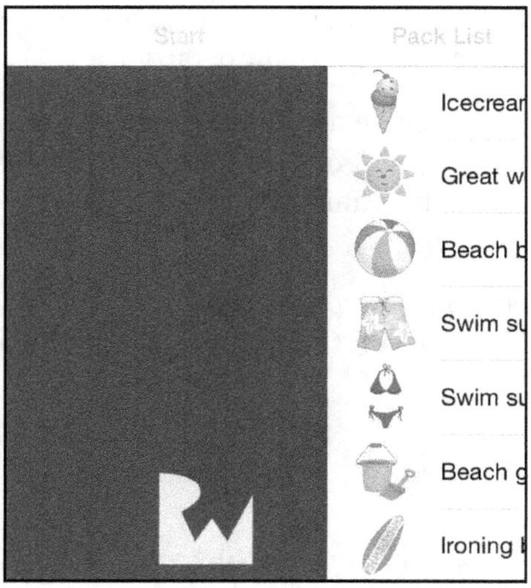

Custom Navigation Transitions

UIKit lets you customize navigation transitions via the delegate pattern in almost the same way you do for presenting view controllers.

You'll make your `MainViewController` class adopt the `UINavigationControllerDelegate` protocol and set it to be the delegate to your navigation controller. Each time you push a view controller onto the navigation stack, the navigation controller will ask its delegate whether it should use the built-in transition or a custom one, as illustrated below:

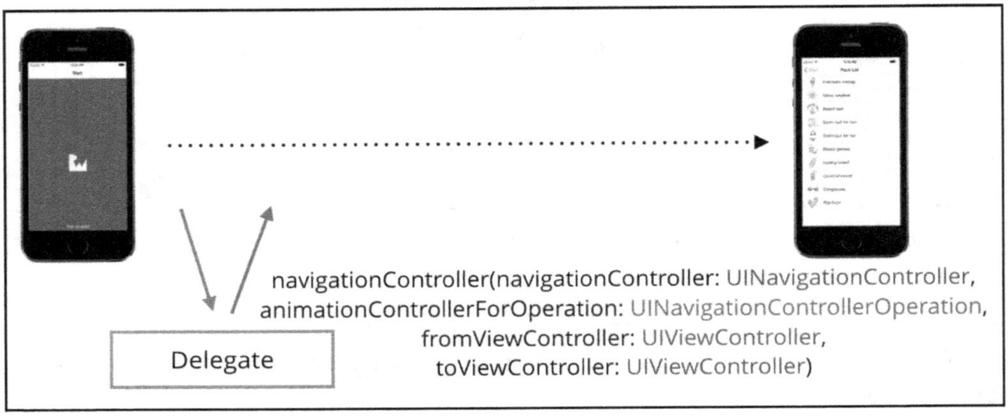

When you push or pop a view controller, the navigation controller asks its delegate to provide an animation controller for that operation.

If you return `nil` from that delegate method, the navigation controller will use the default transition. However, if you return an object, the navigation controller will use this instead as a custom transition animation controller. Yup — this sounds a *lot* like the previous chapter, doesn't it?

The animation controller should adopt the same `UIViewControllerAnimatedTransitioning` protocol you worked with in the previous chapter.

Once you provide an animation controller object (or animator), the navigation controller will call the following methods on it:

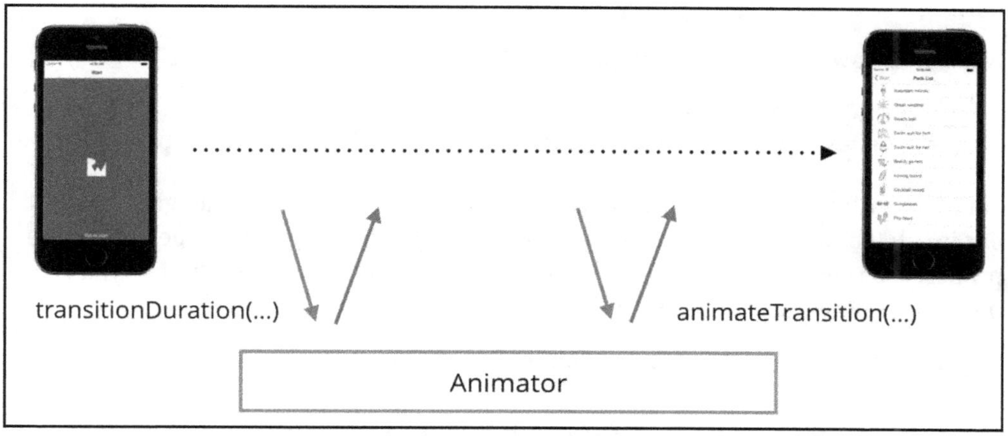

First, the navigation controller calls `transitionDuration()` to find out how long the transition will last; it then calls `animateTransition()`, which is where your custom transition animation code will live.

The Navigation Controller Delegate

Before you can implement the delegate methods, you'll need to create the basic skeleton of the animator class.

From Xcode's main menu select **File\New\File...** and choose the template **iOS\Source\Cocoa Touch Class.**

Set the new class name to **RevealAnimator** and make it a subclass of **NSObject**.

Make the new class comply with the `UIViewControllerAnimatedTransitioning` protocol like so:

```
class RevealAnimator: NSObject,
UIViewControllerAnimatedTransitioning {

}
```

Now you need to implement the two required `UIViewControllerAnimatedTransitioning` methods to resolve Xcode's error messages.

Add the following properties to the class:

```
let animationDuration = 2.0
var operation: UINavigationController.Operation = .push
```

Your animation will last two seconds. That's a long time in the UI navigation world, but it will let you see your animation in minute, excruciating detail. `operation` is a property of type `UINavigationController.Operation` that tells whether you're pushing or popping a view controller.

Now add the following two `UIViewControllerAnimatedTransitioning` methods to the class:

```
func transitionDuration(using transitionContext:
UIViewControllerContextTransitioning?) -> TimeInterval {
  return animationDuration
}

func animateTransition(using transitionContext:
UIViewControllerContextTransitioning) {

}
```

`transitionDuration()` returns the animation duration in seconds, while `animateTransition()` is the future home for your custom animations. You'll populate `animateTransition()` once you finish setting up your navigation controller delegate.

All your Xcode errors should have resolved by this point. Open **MainViewController.swift**, which will serve as your navigation controller delegate.

Add the code below to the bottom of the file, outside of the class definition:

```
extension MainViewController: UINavigationControllerDelegate {

}
```

This adopts the `UIViewNavigationControllerDelegate` protocol in a new extension; this view controller can now serve as the navigation controller delegate.

You'll need to set the navigation controller's delegate early in the view controller lifecycle, before you invoke any segues or push something onto the stack.

Add the following code to `viewDidLoad()`:

```
navigationController?.delegate = self
```

Your next task is to create an instance of `RevealAnimator` and pass it to the navigation controller when asked for an animation controller.

Add the following property to `MainViewController`:

```
let transition = RevealAnimator()
```

This is the animator you'll use for pushing and popping view controllers.

Now that you have your animator, add the following method to the class extension:

```
func navigationController(_
  navigationController: UINavigationController,
  animationControllerFor
  operation: UINavigationController.Operation,
  from fromVC: UIViewController,
  to toVC: UIViewController) ->
  UIViewControllerAnimatedTransitioning? {
  transition.operation = operation
  return transition
}
```

That's one monster of a method name, but if you cut through the noise you'll see that it boils down to the following parameters:

- `navigationController`: This helps to distinguish between navigation controllers in the event your object is a delegate of more than one navigation controller; this isn't likely, but you still need to protect against the possibility.
- `operation`: This is a `UINavigationController.Operation` value, either `.push` or `.pop`.
- `fromVC`: This is the view controller currently visible on the screen; it's usually the last view controller in the navigation stack.
- `toVC`: This is the view controller you'll transition to.

If you support different transitions for different view controllers, this is where you'll choose what kind of animator object to return. To keep things simple in this project, you'll always return your `RevealAnimator` object after you set the animator's operation property to indicate either a push or pop transition.

Build and run your project; tap the first view controller and you'll see the navigation bar animate over two seconds.

Note that the update to the navigation bar lasts for the duration you specified in `RevealAnimator` – but at this point nothing else will happen. Your animator takes control of the transition, but since you didn't write any code in `animateTransition()`, no animation of the content takes place.

However, at least this indicates that the navigation controller is calling through to your custom transition properly. Now it's time to get animating!

Adding a Custom Reveal Animation

The plan for your custom transition animation is relatively simple. You'll simply animate a mask on `DetailViewController` to make it look like the transparent part of the RW logo reveals the contents of the underlying view controller. You'll have to juggle layers and some animation tasks, but it's nothing you haven't done so far in the book. Creating the transition animation will be an easy feat for an animation pro like you!

Open **RevealAnimator.swift** and add the following property:

```
weak var storedContext: UIViewControllerContextTransitioning?
```

Since you're going to create some layer animations for your transition, you'll need to store the animation context somewhere until the animation ends and the delegate method `animationDidStop(_:finished:)` executes. At that point, you'll call `completeTransition()` from within `animationDidStop()` to wrap up the transition.

Add the following code to `animateTransition()` to store the transition context for later use:

```
storedContext = transitionContext
```

> **Note**: If you skipped ahead, you can learn more detail on how you fetch transition view controllers from the context and animation container views in Chapter 19, "Presentation Controller & Orientation Animations".

Now add the following initial transition code to `animateTransition()`:

```
let fromVC = transitionContext.viewController(forKey:
  .from) as! MainViewController
let toVC = transitionContext.viewController(forKey:
  .to) as! DetailViewController

transitionContext.containerView.addSubview(toVC.view)
toVC.view.frame = transitionContext.finalFrame(for: toVC)
```

Since you'll work on the push transition initially, you can make an assumption about the identity of the "from" and "to" view controllers of the transition.

First, you fetch the "from" view controller (`fromVC`) and cast it to a `MainViewController`; you then fetch `toVC` as a `DetailViewController`.

Finally, you simply add `toVC.view` to the transition container view and set its `frame` to the "final" frame within the `transitionContext`. This places the vacation packing list in its final location over the main screen.

Now you're going to create the reveal animation. The secret to a reveal animation is to have an object — in your case, the RW logo — grow to cover the entire area of the screen.

This sounds like a job for a scale transformation! Add the following to `animateTransition()`:

```
let animation = CABasicAnimation(keyPath: "transform")
animation.fromValue =
  NSValue(caTransform3D: CATransform3DIdentity)
animation.toValue =
  NSValue(caTransform3D:
  CATransform3DConcat(
    CATransform3DMakeTranslation(0.0, -10.0, 0.0),
    CATransform3DMakeScale(150.0, 150.0, 1.0)
  )
)
```

This animation grows the logo `150` times in size and moves it up a little at the same time. Why? The logo is uneven in shape and you want the view controller behind to show through the "hole" of the RW shape.

Moving it up a little bit means the bottom of the zoomed image will cover the screen much faster.

The image below shows how your zoom animation will work:

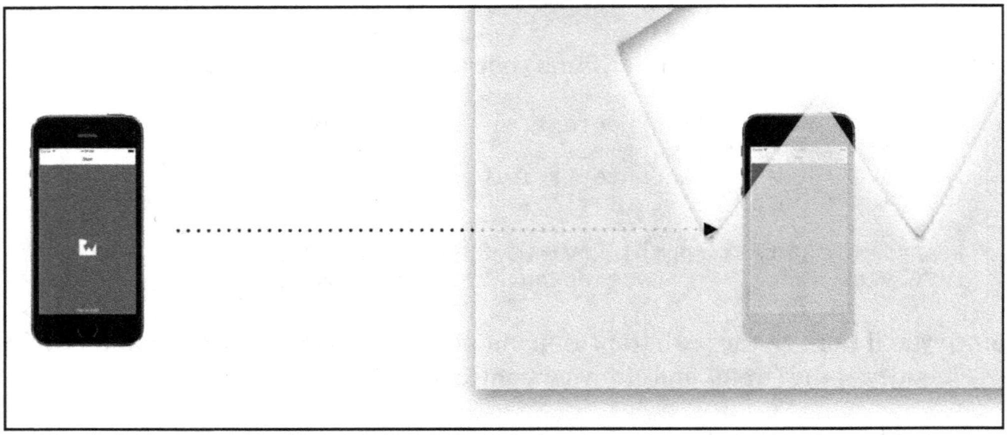

If you used a symmetrical shape like a circle or ellipse, you wouldn't have this problem, but your animation wouldn't be nearly as cool.

Now add the following lines to `animateTransition()` to refine the animation a bit:

```
animation.duration = animationDuration
animation.delegate = self
animation.fillMode = .forwards
animation.isRemovedOnCompletion = false
animation.timingFunction = CAMediaTimingFunction(name:
  .easeIn)
```

First, you set the duration of the animation to match the transition duration. You then set the animator as the delegate and configure the animation model to leave the animation on screen; this avoids glitches when the transition wraps up since the RW logo will be hidden away anyway. Finally, you add easing to make the reveal effect accelerate over time.

`RevealAnimator` is not currently an animation delegate, so jump to the top of the file and add the `CAAnimationDelegate` protocol to the class definition like so:

```
class RevealAnimator: NSObject,
UIViewControllerAnimatedTransitioning, CAAnimationDelegate {
...
}
```

This should clear the compiler error you currently have.

Your animation is complete — but to which layer should it be applied?

Add the following code to the end of `animateTransition(using:)`:

```
let maskLayer: CAShapeLayer = RWLogoLayer.logoLayer()
maskLayer.position = fromVC.logo.position
toVC.view.layer.mask = maskLayer
maskLayer.add(animation, forKey: nil)
```

This creates a `CAShapeLayer` to be applied to the `DestinationViewController`. The `maskLayer` is positioned in the same location as the "RW" logo on the `MainViewController`. Then you simply set `maskLayer` as the mask of the view controller's view.

You then add the animation to the mask layer — which means you can test out the current state of your transition.

Build and run your project to see how things look so far:

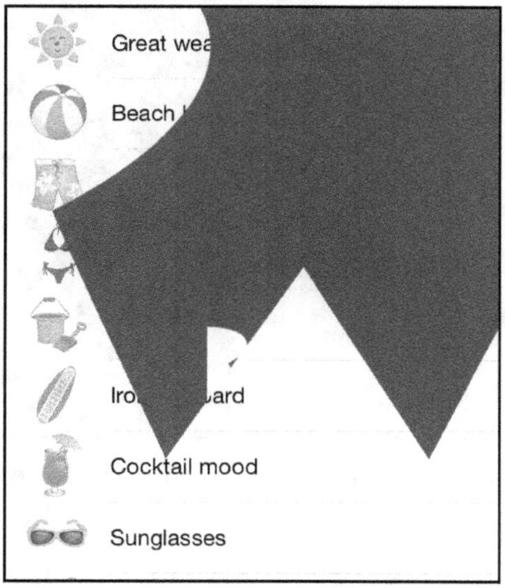

Not bad, not bad; your reveal is running, but the animation is somewhat clunky and you can't go back to the main screen once you push the pack list on top. Time to fix those issues!

Taking Care of the Rough Edges

You likely noticed you can still see the original logo behind the zooming reveal logo. The easiest way to handle this is to run the reveal animation on the original logo as well. You already have the animation, so it's no matter to reuse it. This will make the original logo grow with the mask, matching its shape exactly so it won't be in the way.

Add the following to `animateTransition()`:

```
fromVC.logo.add(animation, forKey: nil)
```

Build and run your project again to verify that the original logo is no longer hanging around.

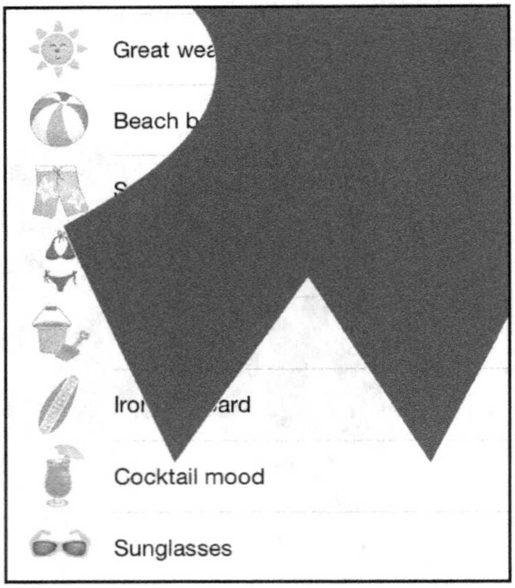

Now, a slightly harder problem: What's up with the navigation not working any more after the first push transition?

If you take a look at what you've done so far, you'll see that you never really wrap up the transition. You planned to call `completeTransition()` when the animation ended — but never got around to implementing that code.

RevealAnimator is set as the delegate of your reveal animation. Therefore, you need to override animationDidStop(_:finished:) and complete the transition within that method.

Add the following code to RevealAnimator:

```
func animationDidStop(_ anim: CAAnimation, finished flag: Bool)
{
  if let context = storedContext {
    context.completeTransition(!context.transitionWasCancelled)
    // reset logo
  }
  storedContext = nil
}
```

Here you check whether you have a stored transition context; if so, you call completeTransition() on it. This passes the ball back to the navigation controller to wrap up with the transition on UIKit's side.

At the end of the method, you simply set the reference to the transition context to nil.

Since the reveal animation won't be removed automagically upon completion, you'll need to handle things yourself.

Replace the // reset logo comment, located in animationDidStop(), with the following:

```
let fromVC = context.viewController(forKey: .from)
  as? MainViewController

fromVC?.logo.removeAllAnimations()
```

Since the only time you need to mask the contents of the view controller is during push transitions, you can safely remove the mask once the view controller finishes transitioning.

Add the following code below removeAllAnimations() in animationDidStop():

```
let toVC = context.viewController(forKey: .to)
  as? DetailViewController
toVC?.view.layer.mask = nil
```

This will remove the mask after the view has appeared and the transition is complete.

That should do it. Build and run your project; push the packing list view controller onto the screen, then tap **Start** to return to the original view. The proof that you're calling your custom transition is shown by the following crash:

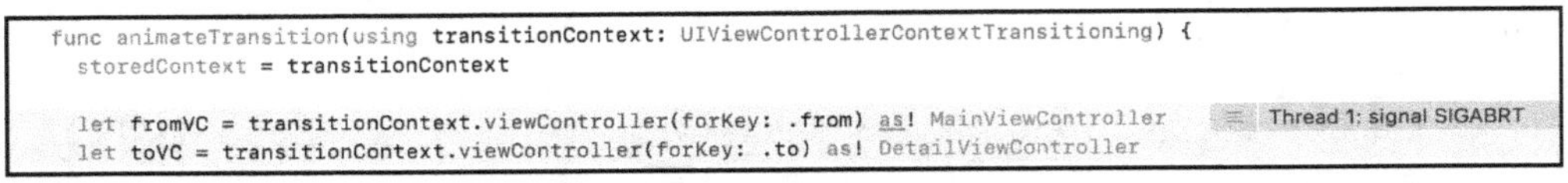

You're trying to cast the "from" view controller to a `MainViewController` instance – which is true only for the push transition, but not for the pop transition. Whoops.

Open **RevealAnimator.swift** and find `animateTransition()`. You'll need to wrap most of the code here in a conditional. Replace the two lines where you assign `toVC` and `fromVC` with the following:

```
if
  operation == .push,
  let fromVC = transitionContext
    .viewController(forKey: .from) as? MainViewController,
  let toVC = transitionContext
    .viewController(forKey: .to) as? DetailViewController {
```

Then, scroll all the way to the end of the method and add a closing brace for the `if` at the very end of the method.

The condition checks whether you're dealing with a push transition before you try to cast it, and that the view controllers are what you expect them to be. This should take care of that crashing piece of code.

Build and run to try it out again. Your push transition is working, but your pop transition won't do anything yet since you don't have any code in `animateTransition()` to handle it.

This is where you get to flex your ninja coding muscles; you'll create the pop transition on your own in the Challenges section below – and add a bit of elegance to the reveal animation along the way.

Key Points

- To enable and customize custom navigation transitions, you adopt the `UINavigationControllerDelegate` protocol in one of your types and make it your navigation delegate.
- To perform any custom navigation transition animations, you adopt the `UIViewControllerAnimatedTransitioning` protocol your transition's animator.
- As long as you wrap up your transition correctly and call into the neccessary UIKit methods at the end, you can successfully use layer animations for your custom transitions.
- To preserve the context of the navigation transition and access it asynchronously throughout the transition's duration, you can retain it in a `UIViewControllerContextTransitioning` property within your animator type.

Challenges

Challenge 1: Fade in the New View Controller

Right now the transition looks like a sharp cutout; the contents of the new view controller are visible instantly and make the whole animation look a bit clunky.

Your challenge is to fade in the new view controller as the reveal animation runs.

To do this, create a fade in `CABasicAnimation` and add it to the layer of `toVC.view`. Use the same transition duration for this new animation and set fromValue and `toValue` to animate from fully transparent to fully opaque.

Call your new animation just after the point where you add the reveal animation to both the logo and the mask layers.

When you are finished, your transition should look like the following:

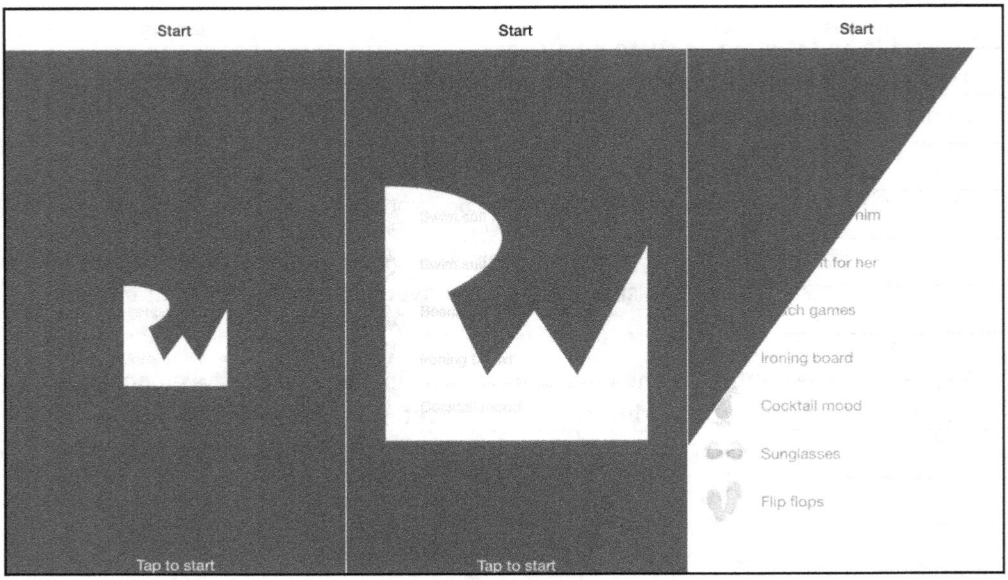

It appears as if your cutout becomes progressively more transparent as it grows; this gives the transition a mysterious effect.

Challenge 2: Add Pop Transition

To create a pop transition, you'll simply add a complementary else branch to the if statement inside `animateTransition()` of `RevealAnimator`. Inside the else branch you can add any animations you want, but don't forget to call `completeTransition()` when you're finished. Here's how to create a simple shrink transition:

- Add an else branch to the if inside `animateTransition()`.
- Fetch the "from" and "to" views using the `viewForKey` method on the context. Because you're not doing anything with the properties of the view controller this time, you can just fetch the views alone.

- Work with the transition `containerView` and insert the toView **below** fromView. Tip: use `insertSubview(_:belowSubview:_)`.
- Use an animation to scale `fromView` to `0.01`. Don't use `0.0` for scaling — this will confuse UIKit. For this animation you can use an ordinary view animation – there's no need to create a layer animation.
- When the animation finishes, call `completeTransition()` on the transition context just as you did before.

This will result in the following tasteful shrinking transition:

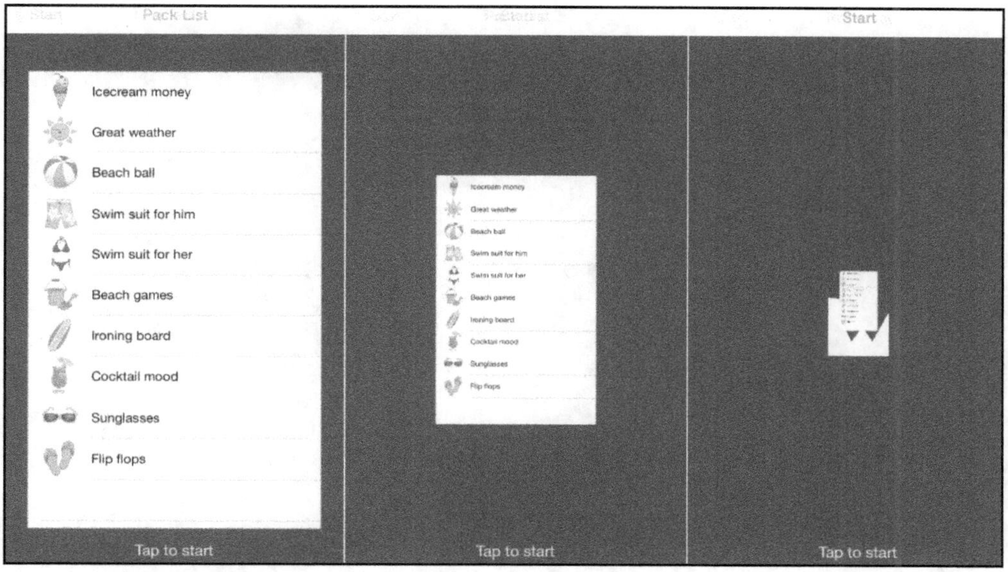

As you might have guessed, you can create custom transitions for `UITabBarController` too. You won't cover them here, but they work in a similar way to navigation controller transitions so you can easily figure them out based on what you've learned so far.

The next chapter takes transitions to the next level, and shows you how to let your user *interact* with the transitions themselves!

Chapter 21: Interactive UINavigationController Transitions

The reveal transition you created in the previous chapter looks pretty neat, but custom animations are only half the story. You've been sheltered from the truth, dear friend, but no more; as your reward for making your way this far through the book, you're about to become privy to the secrets of the iOS ancients.

Not only can you create a custom animation for your transition — you can also make it *interactive* and respond to the actions of the user.

Typically, you'd drive this action through a pan gesture, which is the approach you're going to take in this chapter.

When you're done, your users will be able to scrub back and forth through the reveal transition by sliding their finger across the screen. How cool would that be?

Yeah, I thought you'd be interested! Read on to see how it's done!

Creating an Interactive Transition

When your navigation controller asks its delegate for an animation controller, two things can happen. You can return `nil`, in which case the navigation controller runs the standard transition animation. You know that much already. However — if you *do* return an animation controller, then the navigation controller asks its delegate for an interaction controller like so:

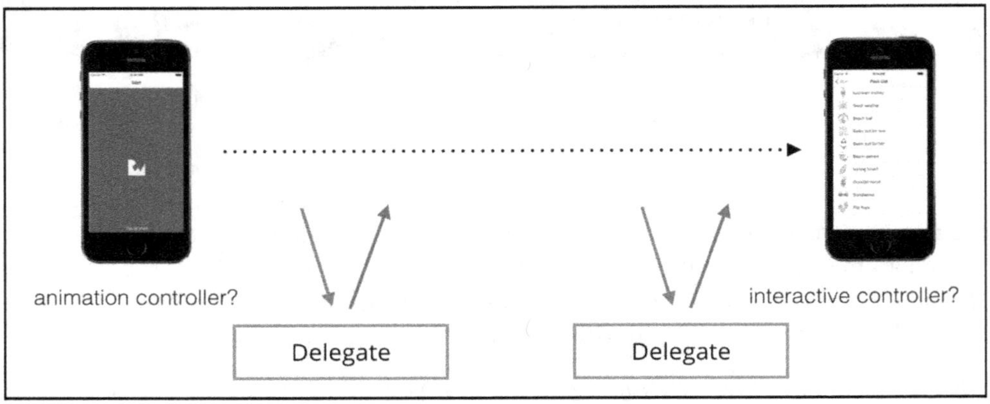

The interaction controller moves the transition along based on the user's actions, instead of simply animating the changes from start to finish.

The interaction controller does not necessarily need to be a separate class from the animation controller; in fact, performing some tasks is a little easier when both controllers are in the same class. You just need to make sure that said class conforms to both `UIViewControllerAnimatedTransitioning` and `UIViewControllerInteractiveTransitioning`.

`UIViewControllerInteractiveTransitioning` has only one required method — `startInteractiveTransition(_:)` — that takes a transitioning context as its parameter. The interaction controller then regularly calls `updateInteractiveTransition(_:)` to move the transition along. To begin, you'll need to change how you handle your user input.

Handling the Pan Gesture

First of all, the tap gesture recognizer in `MainViewController` just won't cut it anymore. A tap happens momentarily and then it's gone; you can't track its progress and use it to drive a transition. On the other hand, a pan gesture has clear states for the starting, progressing, and ending phases of the transition.

Open the starter project for this chapter; alternatively, you can use your completed project (including the challenges) from the previous chapter.

Open **Main.storyboard**; go to the main view controller and change the text of the label towards the bottom of the screen to "**Slide to start**" like so:

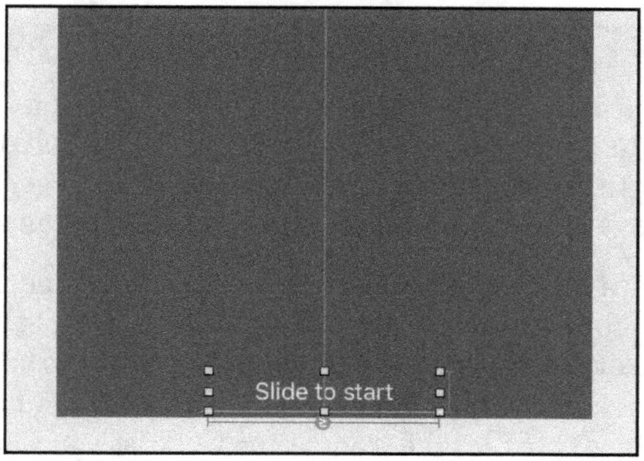

This will reflect the action you expect from the user.

Next, open **MainViewController.swift** and **remove** the following code from `viewDidAppear(_:)`:

```
let tap = UITapGestureRecognizer(target: self, action:
#selector(didTap))
view.addGestureRecognizer(tap)
```

In its place, insert the following pan recognizer code:

```
let pan = UIPanGestureRecognizer(target: self, action:
#selector(didPan(_:)))
view.addGestureRecognizer(pan)
```

As the user pans across the screen, the recognizer invokes `didPan(_:)` on your `MainViewController` class.

To get rid of the error, showing right now in Xcode, add an empty `didPan(_:)` method to `MainViewController`:

```
@objc func didPan(_ recognizer: UIPanGestureRecognizer) {
}
```

You'll need to modify your `RevealAnimator` class quite a bit to handle the new, interactive transition; you'll take care of this in the next section.

Using Interactive Animator Classes

To manage your transition, you'll use one of Apple's built-in interactive animator classes: `UIPercentDrivenInteractiveTransition`. This class conforms to `UIViewControllerInteractiveTransitioning` and lets you get and set your transition's progress as a value representing the percentage complete.

This makes your life a little easier, as you can use this class to adjust the `percentComplete` property accordingly and call `update()` to set the current visible progress of the transition. This will skip through the transition animation to the point that corresponds to the calculated transition progress. You'll learn more about how `UIPercentDrivenInteractiveTransition` works as you work through the rest of this chapter.

Open **RevealAnimator.swift** and update the class definition at the top of the file as follows:

```
class RevealAnimator: UIPercentDrivenInteractiveTransition,
  UIViewControllerAnimatedTransitioning, CAAnimationDelegate {
```

Note that `UIPercentDrivenInteractiveTransition` is a class and not a protocol like the rest so it needs to be in first position. Now `RevealAnimator` inherits from `UIPercentDrivenInteractiveTransition`.

Next, add the following property to tell the animator whether or not it should drive the transition in an interactive fashion:

```
var interactive = false
```

Now add the following method to `RevealAnimator`:

```
func handlePan(_ recognizer: UIPanGestureRecognizer) {

}
```

When the user pans across the screen, you'll pass the recognizer to `handlePan(_:)` in `RevealAnimator`, at which point you'll update the current progress of the transition. You'll populate `handlePan(_:)` in just a bit, but first you'll need to set up the gesture handling.

Open **MainViewController.swift** and add the following delegate method to provide an interaction controller to the `UINavigationControllerDelegate` extension in that file:

```
func navigationController(
  _ navigationController: UINavigationController,
  interactionControllerFor
  animationController: UIViewControllerAnimatedTransitioning
) -> UIViewControllerInteractiveTransitioning? {
  if !transition.interactive {
    return nil
  }
  return transition
}
```

You only return an interaction controller when you want the transition to be interactive. For example, in your Logo Reveal project the reveal transition is interactive, but the custom pop transition will remain as-is.

Now you need to hook up your pan gesture recognizer to the interaction controller. Find `didPan(_:)` in `MainViewController` and replace with:

```
@objc func didPan(_ recognizer: UIPanGestureRecognizer) {
  switch recognizer.state {
  case .began:
    transition.interactive = true
    performSegue(withIdentifier: "details", sender: nil)
  default:
    transition.handlePan(recognizer)
  }
}
```

As the pan gesture starts, you ensure `interactive` is set to `true` and then begin the segue to the next view controller. Performing the segue kicks off the transition as detailed in the previous chapter; the delegate methods you've added return transition for the animation controller *and* for the interaction controller.

In all cases, if the gesture has already started you simply hand things over to the interaction controller as illustrated below:

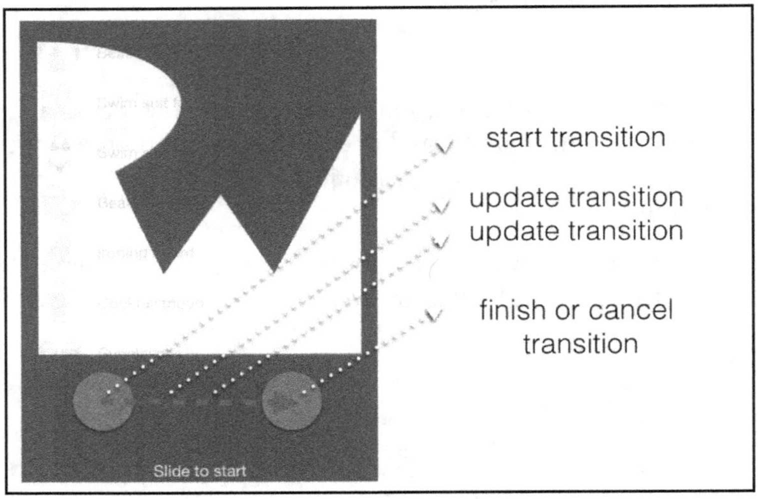

Calculating Your Animation's Progress

The most important bit of your pan gesture handler is to figure out how far along the transition should be.

Open **RevealAnimator.swift** and add the following code to `handlePan()`:

```
let translation = recognizer.translation(
  in: recognizer.view?.superview)
var progress: CGFloat = abs(translation.x / 200.0)
progress = min(max(progress, 0.01), 0.99)
```

First, you get the translation from the pan gesture recognizer; the translation lets you know how many points the user moved their finger/stylus/appendage/whatever on both the X and Y axes. Logically, the further the user pans from the initial location, the greater the progress of the transition.

To calculate the current progress, you take the translation on the X axis and divide it by `200` points. For example, if the user's finger is `100` points away from the initial pan location, the transition will be `50%` complete. `200` points is a bit of an arbitrary number, but it's a good starting point for the total distance the user needs to pan to complete the transition. You shouldn't care whether the user pans to the right or to the left - that's why you use `abs()` to get the absolute value of the pan distance.

Finally, you cap the progress variable between 0.01 and 0.99; my testing shows that interaction controllers behave better if you don't let the user finish or revert the transition from the pan gesture alone.

Now that you know the progress of the transition animation, you can update the transition animation as well.

Add the following code to handlePan():

```
switch recognizer.state {
case .changed:
  update(progress)
default:
  break
}
```

update() is a method from UIPercentDrivenInteractiveTransition which sets the current progress of the transition animation.

As the user pans across the screen, the gesture recognizer repeatedly calls didPan() in MainViewController, which in turn forwards the recognizer to handlePan() in RevealAnimator.

Unfortunately, if you were to build and run at this time, you'd see some of the animations appear to follow your gesture and the others just run along at their own pace. UIPercentDrivenInteractiveTransition doesn't play as nicely with layer animations as it does with view animations, so you have to do some extra work.

First, add this property and calculated variable to RevealAnimator:

```
private var pausedTime: CFTimeInterval = 0
private var isLayerBased: Bool {
  return operation == .push
}
```

Only the push transition uses layers, so you only need to do the following work when animating the push. Now, take control of the layer by adding the following code to the beginning of animateTransition(using:):

```
if interactive && isLayerBased {
  let transitionLayer = transitionContext.containerView.layer
  pausedTime = transitionLayer.convertTime(CACurrentMediaTime(),
from: nil)
  transitionLayer.speed = 0
  transitionLayer.timeOffset = pausedTime
}
```

What you're doing here is stopping the layer from running its own animations. This will freeze all sublayer animations as well. Now override `update(_:)` to move the layer along with the animation:

```
override func update(_ percentComplete: CGFloat) {
  super.update(percentComplete)
  if isLayerBased {
    let animationProgress = TimeInterval(animationDuration) *
TimeInterval(percentComplete)
    storedContext?.containerView.layer.timeOffset =
      pausedTime + animationProgress
  }
}
```

Here, you're calculating how far through the animation you are and setting the layer's `timeOffset` accordingly, which moves the animations along to the appropriate point in the timeline.

Build and run your project; pan across the screen to see what your transition looks like:

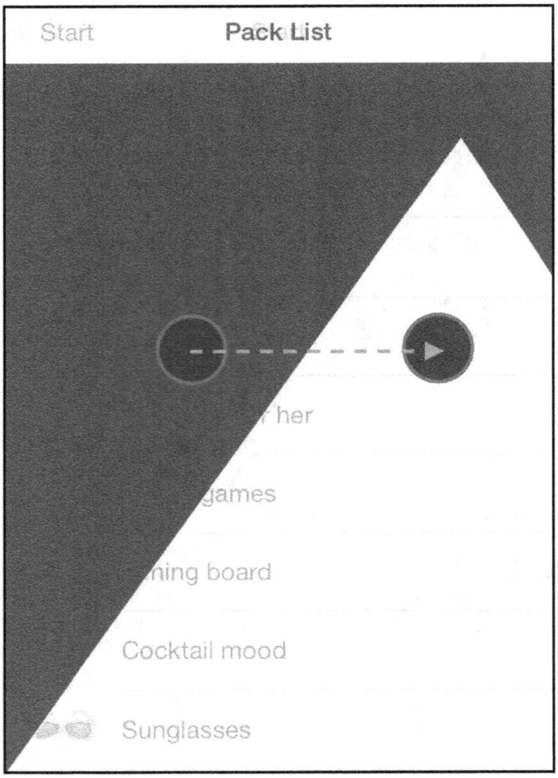

Since your transition isn't quite complete, the whole navigation breaks as soon as you lift your finger. However, you can see that the reveal animation followed your pan gesture – you're getting close to completing your interactive transition!

> **Note**: It feels like this extra work for layer animations is a UIKit bug; if you *don't* use layer animations in the transition, you don't have to do all this messing about, but under the hood the transition is doing the same sort of thing to make the view animations scrub back and forth.

All that's left is to handle the end state of your interactive transition.

Handling Early Termination

Here you face a totally new problem: the user might lift their finger before they've panned `200` points on the X axis. This leaves the transition in an unfinished state.

Luckily, `UIPercentDrivenInteractiveTransition` gives you a couple of methods for free that you can use to revert, or complete, the transition depending on the user's actions.

Add the following two cases inside the `switch` statement you added above, just before the default case:

```
case .cancelled, .ended:
  if progress < 0.5 {
    cancel()
  } else {
    finish()
  }
```

The `.cancelled` and `.ended` cases are effectively the same thing as far as your project is concerned. In either case, if the user panned far enough before they released, you fully present the new view controller; if not, you want to roll back the animation progress.

If the user pans through less than `50%` of the required distance, you call `cancel()` — an inherited method — to animate the transition back to its initial state. If the user pans through more than `50%` of the distance, you call `finish()`, which plays the animation the rest of the way through.

These two states are illustrated below:

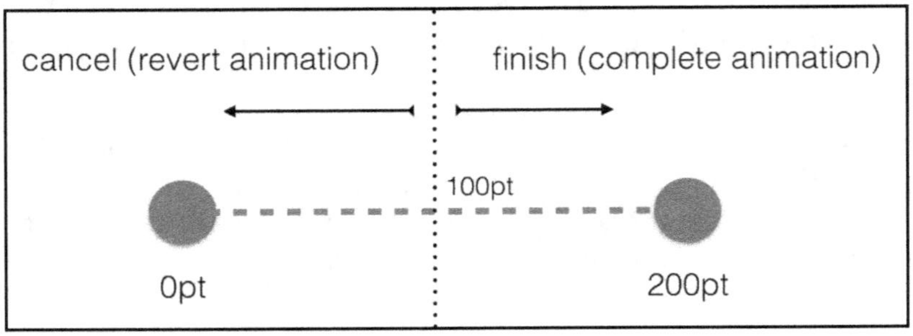

Because you're using layer animations, there is a little bit more work to do here. Remember you'd frozen the layer and were updating it manually; when you cancel or complete the transition you need to un-freeze it.

Override `cancel()` and `finish()` like so:

```
override func cancel() {
  if isLayerBased {
    restart(forFinishing: false)
  }
  super.cancel()
}

override func finish() {
  if isLayerBased {
    restart(forFinishing: true)
  }
  super.finish()
}

private func restart(forFinishing: Bool) {
  let transitionLayer = storedContext?.containerView.layer
  transitionLayer?.beginTime = CACurrentMediaTime()
  transitionLayer?.speed = forFinishing ? 1 : -1
}
```

When cancelling, you need to set the layer running backwards, so the speed is set to -1.

Build and run the app, and try panning part way and most of the way to see the difference.

Did you notice that when you panned through the reveal animation, you couldn't go *back* to the list? That's because you set interactive to true in `handlePan(_:)`, and you never reset it to false!

Therefore, when you pop the view controller, you return an interaction controller from the delegate method that's never updated — and your pop transition gets stuck at `0%` progress.

The correct spot to reset the interactive property is when the pan gesture ends.

Add the following code to the `.cancelled, .ended` case:

```
interactive = false
```

This should let you pop back to the initial screen. Build and run again, and you should be able to move back and forth.

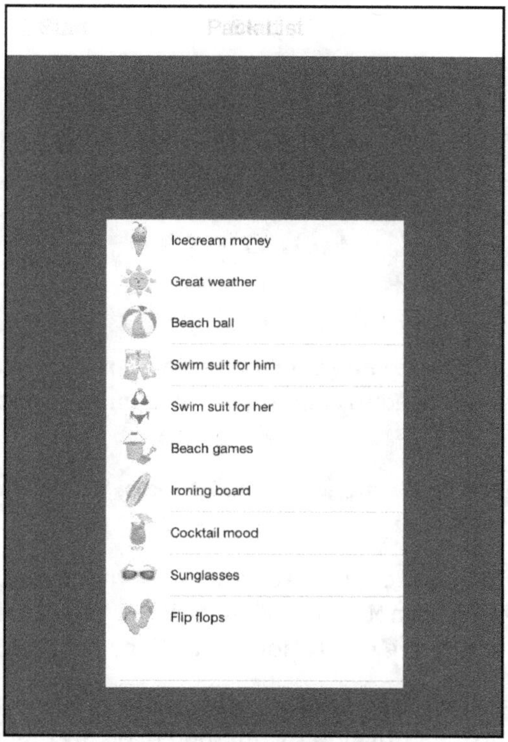

You've completed your Logo Reveal project. `RevealAnimator` is now performing two *different* transition animations, including one that's interactive! Great job! This wraps up the section on view controller transitions. Congratulations on working through this section; these transition APIs are not easy to learn, but all the effort has been worth it.

Key Points

- By adopting the `UIPercentDrivenInteractiveTransition` protocol in your transition animator, you can easily add interactivity to your custom transitions.
- Interactive transitions are usually driven by user gestures. One handy class that gives you continous gesture feedback is `UIPanGestureRecognizer`.
- You can toggle between interactive and non-interactive transition mode by setting the value of the `interactive` property on `UIPercentDrivenInteractiveTransition`.

Challenges

The final challenge is a bit more difficult than usual, but by now you're an animation ninja, and I know you can handle anything I throw at you!

Challenge 1: Make the Pop Transition Interactive

Your task in this challenge is to make the pop transition interactive. That's not as easy as it sounds, as you'll need to change code in a number of places throughout the project.

The challenge directions below are just broad strokes, so you'll need to plan your approach before you start coding.

First, in `DetailViewController`; make a weak property to hold the animator and fetch the animator object from `MainViewController`. You can access `MainViewController` from the navigation controller stack.

Once you do that, add a pan gesture handler to `DetailViewController`. Your handler should be almost identical to the method in `MainViewController` with one small difference: it should pop the current view controller rather than invoke a segue.

You'll end up with a cool interactive pop transition — and don't forget to make sure that tapping the **Back** button in the navigation bar still works!

Section VI: Animations With UIViewPropertyAnimator

`UIViewPropertyAnimator` is a class that helps developers create interactive, interruptible view animations.

You could do everything you learned so far in the book by using a combination of layer and view animations, but `UIViewPropertyAnimator` wraps a number of APIs together conveniently in the same class, which makes it a bit easier to use.

After working through this section, you'll definitely be at home with using `UIViewPropertyAnimator` for all kinds of animations in your apps!

Chapter 22: Getting Started With UIViewPropertyAnimator

`UIViewPropertyAnimator` was introduced in iOS 10 and addressed the need to be able to create easily interactive, interruptible, and/or reversible view animations.

Before iOS 10, the only option to create view-based animations was the `UIView.animate(withDuration:...)` set of APIs, which did not provide any means for developers to pause or stop already running animations. Further, to reverse, speed up, or slow an animation, developers had to use layer-based `CAAnimation` animations.

`UIViewPropertyAnimator` makes creating all of the above a bit easier since it's a class that lets you keep hold of running animations, lets you adjust the currently running ones and provides you with detailed information about the current state of an animation.

`UIViewPropertyAnimator` is a big step away from the pre-iOS 10 "fire-and-forget" animations. That being said, `UIView.animate(withDuration:...)` APIs still do play a big role in creating iOS animations; these APIs are simple and easy to use, and often times you really just want to start a short fade-out or a simple move and you really don't need to interrupt or reverse those. In these cases using `UIView.animate(withDuration:...)` is just fine.

Keep in mind that `UIViewPropertyAnimator` does not implement everything that `UIView.animate(withDuration:...)` has to offer, so sometimes you will still need to fall back on the *old* APIs.

Basic Animations

Open and run the starter project for this chapter. You should see a screen similar to the lock screen in iOS. The initial view controller displays a search bar, a single widget, and an edit button at the bottom:

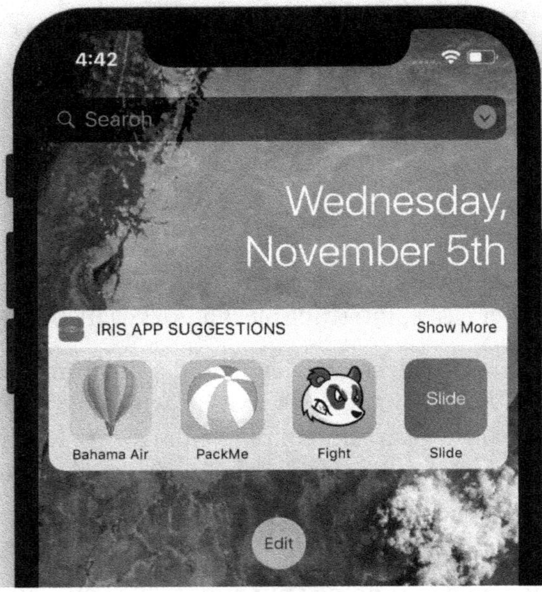

Some of the app's functionality that doesn't have to do with animations is already implemented for you. For example, if you tap on **Show More**, you will see the widget expand and show more items. If you tap on **Edit** you will see another view controller pop up for editing the widget list.

Of course, the app is just a simulation of the lock screen in iOS. It doesn't actually perform any actions, and is set up specially for you to play with some `UIViewPropertyAnimator` animations. Let's go!

First, you are going to create a very simple animation starting when the app initially opens up. Open **LockScreenViewController.swift** and add a new `viewWillAppear(_:)` method to that view controller:

```
override func viewWillAppear(_ animated: Bool) {
  super.viewWillAppear(animated)
  tableView.transform = CGAffineTransform(scaleX: 0.67, y: 0.67)
  tableView.alpha = 0
}
```

The table view in LockScreenViewController displays the widgets on that screen, so in order to create a simple scale and fade view animation transition, you first scale the whole table view down and make it transparent.

If you run the project right now you will see the date and some empty space below:

Next, create an animator when the view controller's view appears on screen. Add the following to LockScreenViewController:

```
override func viewDidAppear(_ animated: Bool) {
  super.viewDidAppear(animated)
  let scale = UIViewPropertyAnimator(duration: 0.33,
    curve: .easeIn)
}
```

Here, you use one of the convenience initializers of UIViewPropertyAnimator. You are going to try all of them, but you'll start with the simplest one: UIViewPropertyAnimator(duration:, curve:).

This initializer makes an animator instance and sets the animation's total duration and timing curve. The latter parameter is of type UIViewAnimationCurve, and this is an enum with the following curve-based options:

- easeInOut
- easeIn
- easeOut
- linear

These match the timing options that you've used with the UIView.animate(withDuration:...) APIs, and they produce similar results.

Now that you've created an animator object, let's have a look at what can you do with it.

Adding Animations

Add the animation code to `viewDidAppear(_:)`:

```
scale.addAnimations {
  self.tableView.alpha = 1.0
}
```

You use `addAnimations` to add blocks of code, which perform the desired animations just like you do with `UIView.animate(withDuration:...)`. The difference when using an animator is that you can add multiple animation blocks. For example, you can include logic to conditionally add more or fewer animations to the same animator.

Besides being able to conditionally build up complex animations, you can also add animations with different delays. There is a version of `addAnimations` which takes the following two parameters:

- `animation`, which is the block with animations to perform,
- and `delayFactor`, which is the delay before the animations start.

Notice that the latter parameter isn't called `delay`, but specifically: `delayFactor`. This is because you don't provide an absolute value in seconds, but rather a factor (between `0.0` and `1.0`) of the animator's **remaining** duration.

Add a second animation to the same animator with some delay:

```
scale.addAnimations({
  self.tableView.transform = .identity
}, delayFactor: 0.33)
```

To figure out the actual delay in seconds, take `delayFactor` and multiply it by the **remaining duration** of the animator. Since you haven't yet started the animations, the **remaining duration** is equal to the **total duration**.

So in the case above:

```
delayFactor(0.33) * remainingDuration(=duration 0.33) = delay of
0.11 seconds
```

Why isn't that second parameter just a simple value in seconds?

Well, imagine your animator is already running, and you decide to add some new animations to it mid-way. In this case the **remaining duration** will not be equal to the **total duration**, since some time has already passed since you starter the animations.

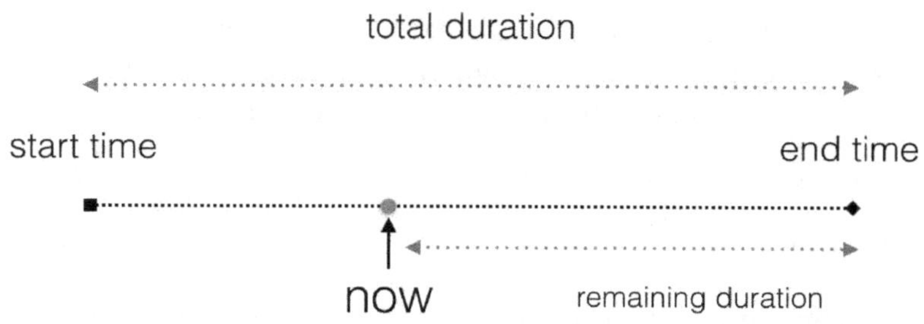

In this situation, `delayFactor` will let you schedule an animation with delay based on the remaining available time. Further, this ensures you cannot set a delay longer than the remaining running time.

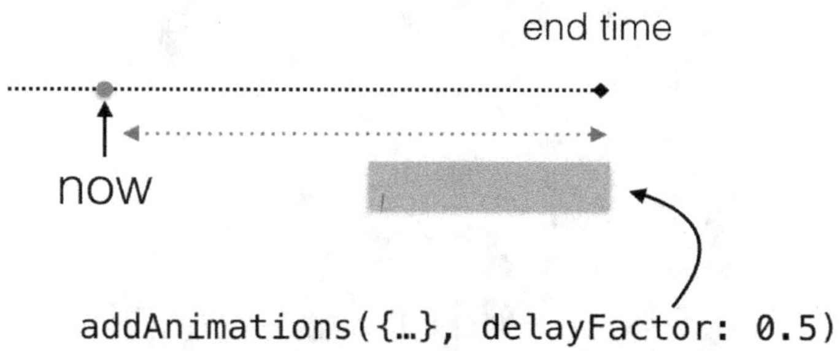

Adding Completions

Now add a completion block, just like you're used to with `UIView.animate(withDuration:...)`:

```
scale.addCompletion { _ in
  print("ready")
}
```

In this simple example, you are only printing to the console, but you can do literally anything you wish; clean up some temporary views, reset the position of visual elements you moved around, and so on.

As with `addAnimations(_:)`, you can call `addCompletion(_:)` several times to add more completion handlers. These will be executed one after another and in the order you added them to the animator.

Last but not least, you need to **start the animator**.

Before you call `startAnimations()`, nothing will happen on screen, so keep in mind while getting accustomed with `UIViewPropertyAnimator` that if you don't see your animations on screen, you probably have forgotten to start them.

Add at the end of `viewWillAppear(_:)`:

```
scale.startAnimation()
```

Run the project now and enjoy a smooth transition animation when the app pops up on the screen:

Abstracting Animations Away

You've probably already noticed that just like layer animations, animations with `UIViewPropertyAnimator` add quite a bit of code.

Working with an object that isn't "fire-and-forget" makes it really easy to extract some of your animation code into a separate file. Since you are going to create plenty of animations for the project in this section of the book, you'll extract most of them in a separate file.

Create a new file called **AnimatorFactory.swift** and replace its default contents with:

```
import UIKit

enum AnimatorFactory {
}
```

Then add a method, which includes the animation code you just wrote, but instead of running the animations by default, returns the animator as the result:

```
static func scaleUp(view: UIView) -> UIViewPropertyAnimator {
  let scale = UIViewPropertyAnimator(duration: 0.33,
    curve: .easeIn)
  scale.addAnimations {
    view.alpha = 1.0
  }
  scale.addAnimations({
    view.transform = CGAffineTransform.identity
  }, delayFactor: 0.33)
  scale.addCompletion { _ in
    print("ready")
  }
  return scale
}
```

That method takes a view as its parameter and creates all animations on that view. Finally it returns the ready-to-go animator.

Switch to **LockScreenViewController.swift** and replace `viewDidAppear(_:)` with:

```
override func viewDidAppear(_ animated: Bool) {
  AnimatorFactory.scaleUp(view: tableView)
    .startAnimation()
}
```

That's much nicer, shorter, and cleaner!

By the end of this section, you will really appreciate `AnimatorFactory` since it's going to remove a lot of code from your view controller.

> **Note**: We prefer a caseless enum to group together methods like this, to prevent accidentally instatiating a type that doesn't do anything.

Running Animators

At this point you might be asking yourself *"What's the point of creating an animator object if its only purpose is to be started right away?"* That is a good question!

Should you need a single block of animations that you run and don't need to alter anymore, go ahead and use `UIView.animate(withDuration:...)`. The tipping point in your decision on which API to use depends whether you want to simply run an animation — or run it and *eventually* interact with it later on.

What if you **do** want to use a `UIViewPropertyAnimator`, but you still have just one block of animations and completion, and want to run it right away? Isn't there a more streamlined way to create such animations? Why, yes there is! I'm glad you asked. This is the very reason this section of the chapter is called *running animators*. There's a class method on `UIViewPropertyAnimator` that creates an animator and starts it right away for you.

Next you will fade in a blur layer (`blurView`) while the user is using the search bar, and fade it out when the user is done searching. Open **LockScreenViewController.swift** and add a new method to the `LockScreenViewController` class:

```
func toggleBlur(_ blurred: Bool) {
  UIViewPropertyAnimator.runningPropertyAnimator(
    withDuration: 0.5, delay: 0.1, options: .curveEaseOut,
    animations: {
      self.blurView.alpha = blurred ? 1 : 0
    },
    completion: nil
  )
}
```

In `toggleBlur(_:)` you use `UIViewPropertyAnimator.runningPropertyAnimator(withDuration:delay:options:animations:completion )` to create an animator that is already running.

You have certainly noticed that `UIViewPropertyAnimator.runningPropertyAnimator(withDuration:...)` takes exactly the same parameters as `UIView.animate(withDuration:...)` to make it easier for you to use this new API.

Even though it looks like this might be a "fire-and-forget" kind of API, please note that it *does* return an animator instance. You can add more animations, more completion blocks, and generally interact with the animations that are currently running.

Now let's see what that fade animation looks like. `LockScreenViewController` is already set as the delegate of the search bar, so you simply need to implement the required methods to trigger the animation at the correct times.

Add a new `LockScreenViewController` extension:

```
extension LockScreenViewController: UISearchBarDelegate {

  func searchBarTextDidBeginEditing(_ searchBar: UISearchBar) {
    toggleBlur(true)
  }

  func searchBarTextDidEndEditing(_ searchBar: UISearchBar) {
    toggleBlur(false)
  }
}
```

When the users taps on the search field you fade in the blur, and fade it out when the user has finished using the search bar. To give the user more ways to cancel the search, add also these two methods:

```
func searchBarResultsListButtonClicked(_ searchBar: UISearchBar)
{
  searchBar.resignFirstResponder()
}

func searchBar(_ searchBar: UISearchBar, textDidChange
searchText: String) {
  if searchText.isEmpty {
    searchBar.resignFirstResponder()
  }
}
```

This will allow the user to dismiss the search by tapping on the right hand side button or by deleting their search query. Run the app now and tap in the search bar text field.

You'll see the widgets disappear under a blur effect view. When you tap the button on the right side of the search bar, the blur view fades back out.

Basic Keyframe Animations

Earlier you learned how to add more animation blocks to the same animator and make them start with a given delay factor. This is handy, but it doesn't do quite the same thing as you're used to with using view keyframe animations.

The `UIView.animateKeyframes` API is very powerful as it allows you to group animations in any way, with any kind of delay and duration.

Prepare for some good news!

You can actually use `UIView.animate` and `UIView.animateKeyframes` from within your `UIViewPropertyAnimator` animation blocks.

So in the event you would like to create a complex keyframe animation but still realize the benefits of creating an animator, like being able to pause or reverse, you can!

In this section of the chapter, you are going to create a simple jiggle keyframe animation. You'll play that animation on any icon the user taps to give them a little visual tap feedback:

Switch to **AnimatorFactory.swift** and add a new method:

```
static func jiggle(view: UIView) -> UIViewPropertyAnimator {
  return UIViewPropertyAnimator.runningPropertyAnimator(
    withDuration: 0.33, delay: 0, animations: {

    },
    completion: { _ in

    }
  )
}
```

Your jiggle animator will run for `0.33` seconds, but still doesn't really do much. Add the following **inside** the `animations` block:

```
UIView.animateKeyframes(withDuration: 1, delay: 0,
  animations: {

    UIView.addKeyframe(withRelativeStartTime: 0.0,
      relativeDuration: 0.25) {
      view.transform = CGAffineTransform(rotationAngle: -.pi /
8)
    }
    UIView.addKeyframe(withRelativeStartTime: 0.25,
      relativeDuration: 0.75) {
      view.transform = CGAffineTransform(rotationAngle: +.pi /
8)
    }
    UIView.addKeyframe(withRelativeStartTime: 0.75,
      relativeDuration: 1.0) {
      view.transform = CGAffineTransform.identity
    }
  },
  completion: nil
)
```

This code defines a view keyframe animation much like the ones you've created while working through Chapter 7, "Keyframe Animations".

The first keyframe rotates the given view to the left, the second rotates it to the right, and finally the third one brings it back home — er, I mean resets its `transform`.

To make sure the icon remains in its initial position even if the animation was interrupted, add this in the completion block:

```
view.transform = .identity
```

There isn't an obvious way to interrupt the animation, but since you are using an animator, there's always the possibility to add the code to pause or stop that particular animator later on.

There's quite a difference between how you think about your animations now, as compared to the `UIView.animate(withDuration:...)` family of APIs. When using an animator, your animation can always end up completing successfully or being stopped mid-way, or even completing not at its end state, but at its starting state if it was reversed during execution.

Next, since the animation is finalized, you can use the `jiggle(view:)` method to get the keyframes animator and run it on some views.

Open **IconCell.swift** (the file is located in the *Widget* sub-folder). This is the custom collection cell class that displays each of the icons in the widget view:

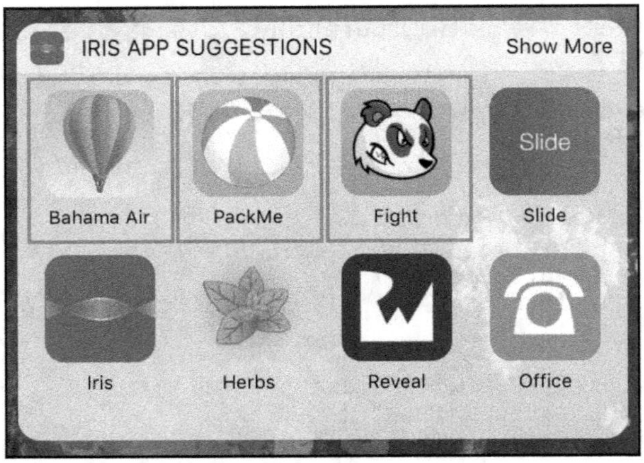

Whenever one of those cells is selected, you will run the jiggle animator on its image to give the user a bit of touch feedback.

Add a new convenience method on the cell to start an animator on its image:

```
func iconJiggle() {
  AnimatorFactory.jiggle(view: icon)
}
```

Now Xcode complains that your `AnimatorFactory.jiggle` method returns a result, but you don't use it in any way. Luckily that's an easy problem to fix.

Switch to **AnimatorFactory.swift** and add the following to the line before `static func jiggle(view: UIView) -> UIViewPropertyAnimator` a `@discardableResult` attribute, so that Xcode knows that you might choose to ignore the result of the method:

```
@discardableResult
static func jiggle(view: UIView) -> UIViewPropertyAnimator
```

Do not remove the return type altogether — you will use the result of that method later on.

To finally run the animation, open **WidgetView.swift** and find `collectionView(collectionView:didSelectItemAt:)`. This is the collection view delegate method called when the user taps on a collection view cell.

Append the following to it:

```
if let cell = collectionView.cellForItem(at: indexPath) as?
IconCell {
  cell.iconJiggle()
}
```

Run the app one more time and try tapping on some icons; you will see them shortly jump under your finger:

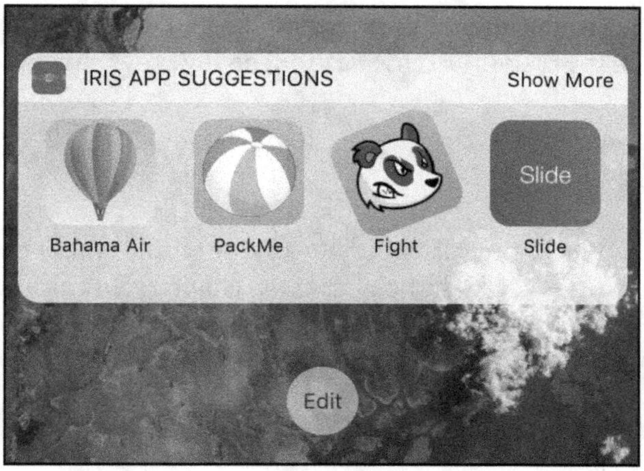

> **Note**: There currently isn't a streamlined way to make the animator animation repeat, if you happened to be wondering. If you want a repeating animation you will have to observe the animator's `running` property and once the animation completes, reset the animator's progress to `0%` and start it over. Or just use the `UIView.animate(withDuration:animations)` method.

With this animation, you've concluded the basics tour. Hopefully you've learned some of the benefits of using `UIViewPropertyAnimator` over the older APIs.

What you covered, however, is but a small fraction of what `UIViewPropertyAnimator` can do. In the next chapters, you will look into more interesting ways to set your animations' timing, interactivity, and power view controller transitions.

Key Points

- When using the `UIViewPropertyAnimator` type, you create an object, add animation and/or completion closures to it, and start the animations at your convenience.
- Containing animation closures within class instances provides a whole new approach to reusing animations via animation factories.
- To create view keyframe animations, you still need to use the *old* api `UIView.animateKeyframes(withDuration:delay:keyframes:)`.

Challenges

You already know some of the basics about working with `UIViewPropertyAnimator`, but there's much more to learn in the next three chapters. In this chapter's challenge section, take the time to reflect on what you've learned and experience your first encounter with property animator's state.

Challenge 1: Extract Blur Animation into Factory

To practice abstracting animations one more time, extract the blur animation from `toggleBlur(_:)` into a static method on `AnimatorFactory`.

This time, the static factory method should take two parameters: the view to animate and whether to animate to a fully transparent or fully opaque state.

In the end, you should be able to easily toggle the visibility of `blurView` by using this one-liner:

```
func toggleBlur(_ blurred: Bool) {
  AnimatorFactory.fade(view: blurView, visible: blurred)
}
```

Do you appreciate how easy it is to abstract and re-use animations with `UIViewPropertyAnimator`? I know I certainly do!

Challenge 2: Prevent Overlapping Animations

In this challenge, you will learn how to check if an animator is currently executing its animations.

If you tap repeatedly on the same icon, you will see that it jumps back to its initial state on each tap and the animations look choppy.

Right now, you simply ignore the result of `AnimatorFactory.jiggle` — but what if you didn't? If you actually get hold of the animator object and use it to check if there's a currently active jiggle animation, you can prevent further taps on that same icon.

First, add an optional property called `animator` to the `IconCell` class.

Next, instead of discarding the result of `AnimatorFactory.jiggle`, store it in `animator`. Now each time the user taps the icon, you can check if there's an animation already running on the icon.

At the beginning of `iconJiggle()` check if `animator` is set, and if so, check if its `isRunning` property is `true`. `isRunning` tells you if the animator is currently running its animations — i.e., it has been already started but it hasn't completed yet.

If there's a running animator, all that is left to do is return out of `iconJiggle()` without creating a new animation. This will fix your problem and the users can tap as many times on the icon as they wish.

Up next — even more complex animations with `UIViewPropertyAnimator`!

Chapter 23: Intermediate Animations With UIViewPropertyAnimator

You've already tried some animations with `UIViewPropertyAnimator`, and have started improving the Widgets project user experience by adding delightful animations to the interface. You've also looked into creating basic and keyframe animations and saw that using the `UIViewPropertyAnimator` class isn't difficult at all! More importantly you've tackled some issues that aren't as straightforward when using the `UIView.animate(withDuration:...)` set of APIs — for example, checking if an animation is currently running, conditionally adding animations and completions, and abstracting animations into standalone classes.

If you successfully completed the challenges from the previous chapter, just re-open the project and keep working on it. Otherwise, you can use the starter project provided for this chapter:

Let's see how you can give your animations this extra *something* by using custom timings!

Custom Animation Timing

Throughout this book, you've been using the four built-in curves: linear, ease in, ease out, and ease in out. By now there isn't much left to say about those that hasn't been said already, so through most of this chapter you are going to focus on custom curves. If by any chance, you skipped over the earlier chapters where built-in curves are explained, have a quick detour to Chapter 3, "Getting Started With View Animations" and search for the **Animation Easing** section.

Assuming you have a solid grasp of what the four built-in curves are, let's have a look at using one in an animation.

Built-in Timing Curves

Currently, when you activate the search bar you fade in a blur view on top of the widgets. In this example, you are going to remove that fade animation and animate the blur effect itself.

Open **LockScreenViewController.swift** and add a new method to the class:

```
func blurAnimations(_ blurred: Bool) -> () -> Void {
  return {

  }
}
```

This is a method that will return a prepared animations block, which you can add to an animator later on. Depending on the parameter value, the animations in the block will either remove or create the blur effect in `blurView`.

First let's add the code to create the animations. Insert in between the braces:

```
self.blurView.effect = blurred ?
  UIBlurEffect(style: .dark) : nil
self.tableView.transform = blurred ?
  CGAffineTransform(scaleX: 0.75, y: 0.75) : .identity
self.tableView.alpha = blurred ? 0.33 : 1.0
```

Setting the `effect` property on `blurView` to either `nil` or a blur effect will spawn an animation. Furthermore, you adjust the visibility and transform of the table view, that contains the widgets. Great! Now the completed method looks like this:

```
func blurAnimations(_ blurred: Bool) -> () -> Void {
  return {
    self.blurView.effect =
```

```
      blurred ? UIBlurEffect(style: .dark) : nil
    self.tableView.transform = blurred ?
      CGAffineTransform(scaleX: 0.75, y: 0.75) : .identity
    self.tableView.alpha = blurred ? 0.33 : 1.0
  }
}
```

You can use this to produce two different animations depending on the current state of the screen.

Next you will need to adjust the UI. Scroll to `viewDidLoad()` and **remove** these two lines:

```
blurView.effect = UIBlurEffect(style: .dark)
blurView.alpha = 0
```

These are the lines that set the effect up, but you don't need them anymore since you are going to use the new effect-based animations.

Speaking of which, replace the contents of `toggleBlur(_:)` with:

```
func toggleBlur(_ blurred: Bool) {
  UIViewPropertyAnimator(
    duration: 0.55,
    curve: .easeOut,
    animations: blurAnimations(blurred))
    .startAnimation()
}
```

Note that the `curve` parameter is of type `UIViewAnimationCurve`. This enumeration includes the four built-in curve types: `.linear`, `.easeIn`, `.easeOut`, and `easeInOut`.

Give the new animation a try; tap into the search bar and you will see the blur effect gradually appear on screen:

Notice how the blur doesn't simply fade in or out, but it actually interpolates the **amount** of blur in the effect view.

Now you can try different timing curves like `.easeIn` or `.linear` to see how they alter the animation.

> **Note**: Blur animations can be a bit jerky in the Simulator, to enjoy the power of iOS animations always enjoy the final effect on a device.

Custom Bézier Curves

Sometimes when you would like to be very specific about the timing of your animations, using these curves to simply "slow down at start" or "slow down about the end" isn't enough.

Earlier in the book you learned that you can create a custom `CAMediaTimingFunction` and give your layer animations custom timings. However, this was mentioned briefly in a note and you didn't have the chance to look more into that.

In this section, you are going to learn what Bézier curves are and how to use them to design your own custom animation timings. The good news is since `UIViewPropertyAnimator` uses layer animations behind the scenes, you can go back and apply what you master in this chapter to your layer animations as well.

But first — what *are* Bézier curves?

> **Note**: If you already have a solid understanding of Bézier curves, skip over this rather simple explanation of the mechanics behind them.

Let's start with something simple – a line. It's pretty neat, because all you need to draw a line on screen are the coordinates of the two points that define it; the start (A) and the end (B):

The handy aspect of being able to describe a shape on screen so precisely is that you can also apply transforms to it: you can scale the line up, you can move it, and rotate it too. All thanks to those two points in a coordinate system. Further, you can persist lines to disk and load them back, because you can describe them with numbers, and you know how to persist those!

Now let's look at curves. Curves are much more interesting than lines, because they can draw *anything* on screen. For example:

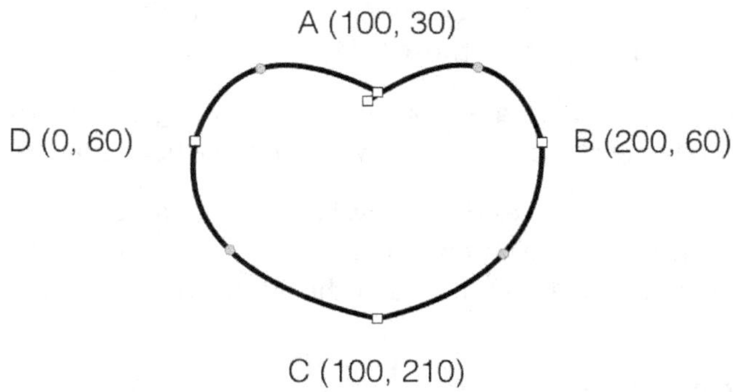

What you see above are four curves put together; their ends meet at the points where you see the little white squares. The interesting thing to note in the picture are the little green circles. After you look at the picture for a while you will notice that the circles "kind of define" where each one of the curves bends.

So curves are not random. They also have some specifics just like lines, which can help you define them via coordinates. You can then get all the benefits of coordinates like persisting them, transforming them, etc.

You define a curve by adding control points to lines. Let's add one control point to the line we had before:

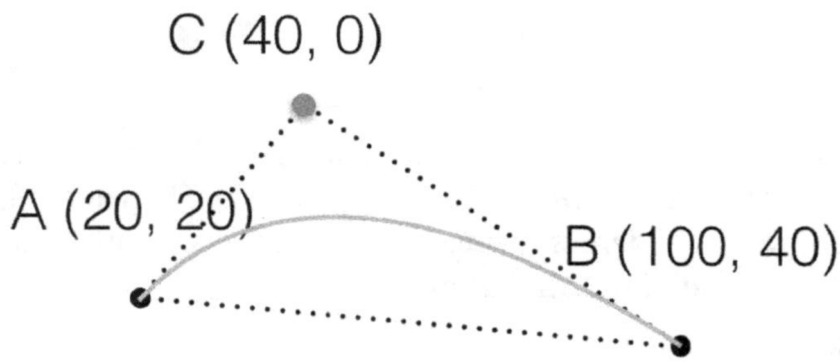

You can imagine the curve being drawn by a pencil attached to a line, whose start point moves along the line AC, and its end point moves along the line CB:

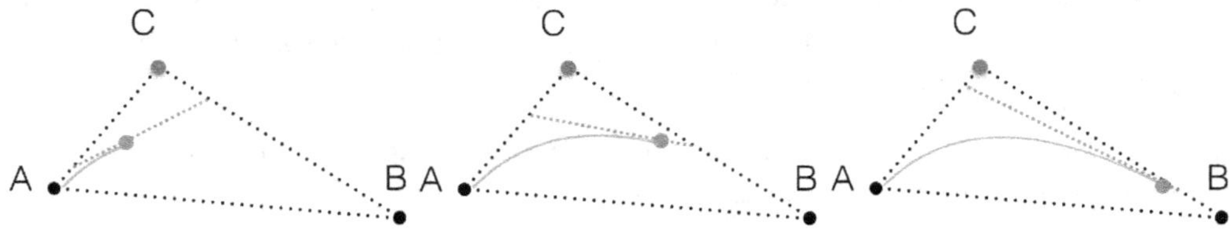

Bézier curves with one control point are called quadratic. You are, however, more interested in cubic Bézier curves — those have two control points.

You can also use cubic curves to describe animation timing. In fact, the built-in curves you've been using are also cubic curves that have been predefined for you.

Core Animation uses cubic curves that always start at coordinate `(0, 0)`, which represents the beginning of the animation duration. Naturally the end point of these timing curves is always `(1, 1)` — the end of the duration and progress of the animation.

Let's have a look at an ease-in curve:

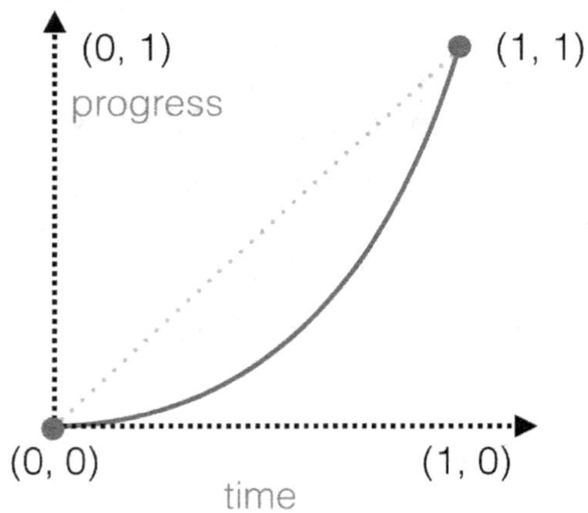

As the time passes (moving left-to-right horizontally across the coordinate space), the curve makes very little progress on the vertical axis, Then about half way through the animation duration, progress speeds up and catches up with time so they both reach `(1, 1)` by the end of the animation.

It all makes sense now, right?

Can you guess which one below is an ease-out and which one is an ease-in-out curve?

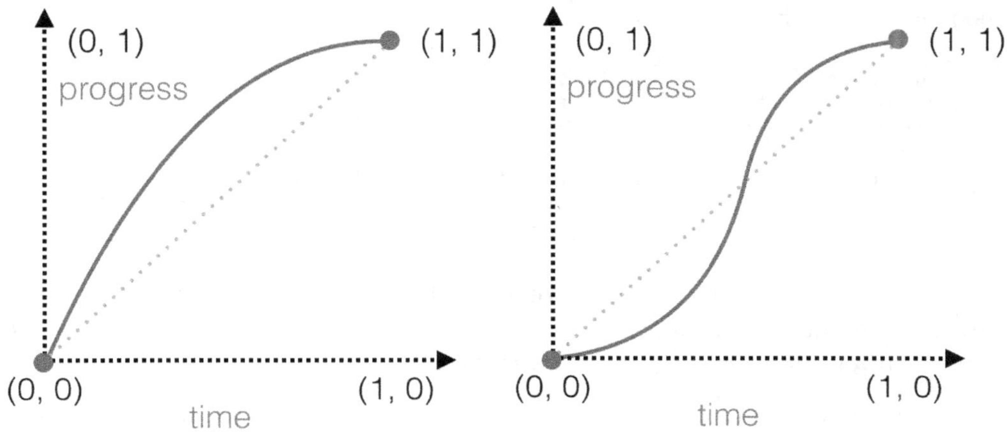

Now that you understand how Bézier curves work, the only remaining question is how to visually design some curves and get the control points' coordinates so you can use them for an iOS animation.

> **Note**: Open a web browser and visit **http://cubic-bezier.com**. This is a handy web site by computer science researcher and speaker Lea Verou. It allows you to drag around the two control points of a cubic Bézier and see an instant animation preview.

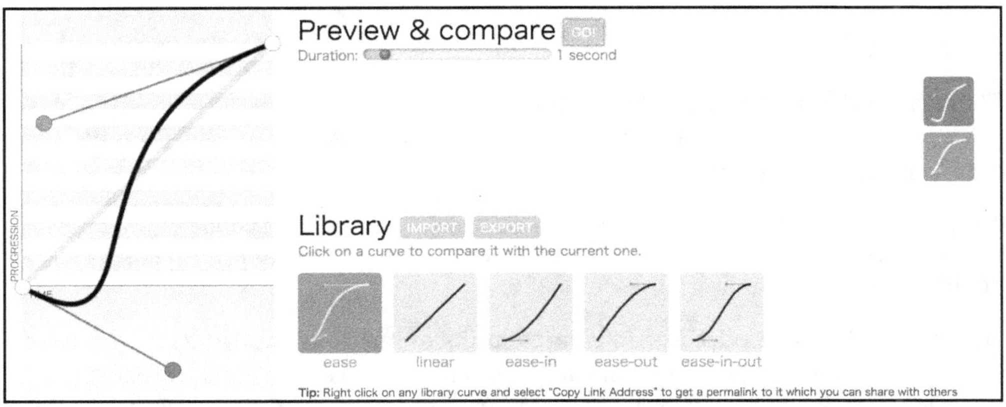

I encourage you to play around until you have a good idea how different timing curves affect animation timing.

Next, you'll move on to adding a custom timing animation to the Widgets project.

Open **LockScreenViewController.swift** and replace the existing animation in `toggleBlur()` with:

```
func toggleBlur(_ blurred: Bool) {
  UIViewPropertyAnimator(duration: 0.55,
    controlPoint1: CGPoint(x: 0.57, y: -0.4),
    controlPoint2: CGPoint(x: 0.96, y: 0.87),
    animations: blurAnimations(blurred))
    .startAnimation()
}
```

This is the second convenience initializer of the `UIViewPropertyAnimator` class. Besides the duration and animations block, it takes two control points as parameters. These help you define your custom cubic curve.

Wait a second! One of those points above has a negative coordinate! Indeed! Since you're anyways doing a custom timing curve, why not do something exotic?

You can drag the control points so they pull the curve into the space defining negative values for the progress axis. The effect is rather amusing: If you're moving a view in the right direction from point **A** to point **B**, it'll first take a "step back" leftwards, and then continue in the correct direction towards point **B**.

In the case of your blur and scale animations, the table view will actually first scale *up* a bit before scaling down. Doing this adds a bit of "elasticity" to your animation. Be careful though: If you overdo it, this will create a rather comical effect on your animation.

Spring Animations

There is another convenience initializer — `UIViewPropertyAnimator(duration:dampingRatio:animations:)` — for defining spring driven animations.

This will produce the same animation as UIView's `animate(withDuration: delay: usingSpringWithDamping: initialSpringVelocity: options: animations: completion:)` with an initial velocity of `0`.

Like the `UIView` method, this API creates spring animations *backwards* as discussed in Chapter 13. You provide the duration you'd like to have for your animation, and UIKit calculates all aspects of the spring that would give you that duration. You know that doesn't give as good a spring effect as doing the calculation properly. Luckily, there is a better way of creating spring animations with `UIViewPropertyAnimator`.

Custom Timing Providers

Meet the fourth and last initializer you're going to cover here: `UIViewPropertyAnimator(duration:timingParameters:)`.

This time, you can create a whole new object that could provide any timing data for your animations! You can use one of the UIKit objects that let you define custom cubic or spring based timings, but you can also roll out your own.

You'll see how to create a custom spring animation before moving on to the next section in this chapter where you'll create some spring animations in practice.

The second parameter named `timingParameters` is of type `UITimingCurveProvider` — a protocol defined by UIKit. There two classes in UIKit that conform to that protocol: `UICubicTimingParameters` and `UISpringTimingParameters`.

Let's look at `UISpringTimingParameters`.

Providing Damping and Velocity

Even if you're using a custom timing provider, you can still chose to go the easy way and provide just the damping ratio and initial velocity as you do when using the convenience initializer. The code would look like this:

```
let spring = UISpringTimingParameters(
  dampingRatio: 0.5,
  initialVelocity: CGVector(dx: 1.0, dy: 0.2))

let animator = UIViewPropertyAnimator(
  duration: 1.0,
  timingParameters: spring)
```

The `spring` parameter represents the configuration of your spring, and you provide it to your `animator` object to use for the timing of your animations. This would still calculate the spring "backwards" as discussed earlier.

Note how initial velocity is a vector type. UIKit will apply a two-dimensional initial velocity at the start, in case you are animating the position or size of any of your views. If you're animating `alpha` or a single axis of your view's location, UIKit will consider only the `dx` property of your initial velocity vector.

`initialVelocity` is also an optional parameter so if you don't need to set a velocity at all, simply provide a damping ratio.

Custom Springs

If you would like to be more specific about your spring, you can use a different initializer on `UISpringTimingParameters` that lets you specify the spring's mass, stiffness, and damping, much like you did for your layer animations earlier in the book.

The code to configure a custom spring is thus:

```
let spring = UISpringTimingParameters(
  mass: 10.0,
  stiffness: 5.0,
  damping: 30,
  initialVelocity: CGVector(dx: 1.0, dy: 0.2))

let animator = UIViewPropertyAnimator(
  duration: 1.0,
  timingParameters: spring)
```

If you need a quick refresher on how all those parameters work, take a quick detour to Chapter 13 "Layer Springs".

In the next section you will try some of those custom timing animations.

Auto Layout Animations

Phew! That was a rather lengthy theoretical part of the chapter, so I'm sure you're excited to write some code and give few animations a try.

You became proficient in Auto Layout animations in Chapter 9, "Animating Constraints", so it won't come as a surprise to you that in the next part you are going to be animating some constraints.

Layout constraint animations with `UIViewPropertyAnimator` are very similar to how you create them with `UIView.animate(withDuration:...)`. The trick was to update a constraint, and then call `layoutIfNeeded()` from within an animations block.

Let's try the same with `UIViewPropertyAnimator`.

Open **AnimatorFactory.swift** and add a new factory method:

```
@discardableResult
static func animateConstraint(
  view: UIView,
```

```
  constraint: NSLayoutConstraint,
  by amount: CGFloat
) -> UIViewPropertyAnimator {

}
```

In this method, you are going to animate a change to a constraint's `constant` and then call `layoutIfNeeded()` on the provided view.

What is this animation going to look like? No idea! It really depends what kind of constraint you provide to the method. If you give it a trailing space constraint, it will move the view horizontally; if you provide it with a height constraint, the view will scale up or down.

Inside the method create an animator:

```
let spring = UISpringTimingParameters(dampingRatio: 0.2)
let animator = UIViewPropertyAnimator(
  duration: 2.0,
  timingParameters: spring)

animator.addAnimations {
  constraint.constant += amount
  view.layoutIfNeeded()
}
return animator
```

You use the simple convenience spring initializer, then you simply change the constraint and trigger an AutoLayout pass.

Now switch to **LockScreenViewController.swift** and add to `viewWillAppear(_:)`:

```
dateTopConstraint.constant -= 100
view.layoutIfNeeded()
```

This will move the date label up by `100` points like so:

Next, trigger an animation to move the label (and all other views attached to it) down to its original location.

Append the following to viewDidAppear(_:):

```
AnimatorFactory.animateConstraint(
  view: view,
  constraint: dateTopConstraint,
  by: 100)
  .startAnimation()
```

Run the app and check out the resulting animation! Since you are moving down all views *and* scaling up your table view, this results in a rather complex yet smooth transition:

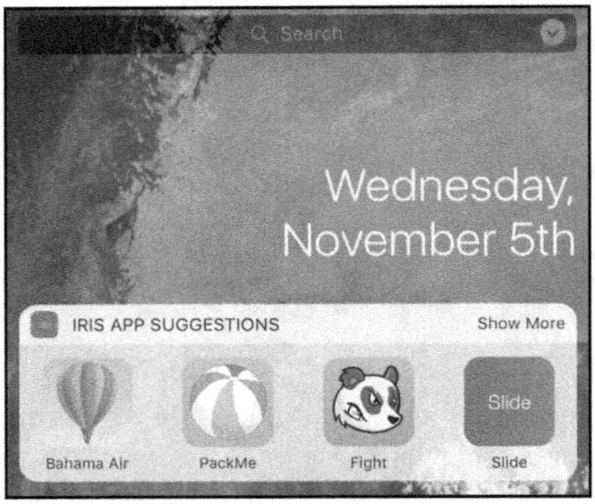

The animation looks a bit excessive though. The first couple of times, it looks nice, but if your users see this bouncy transition multiple times every day they are certainly going to hate your app.

This is a nice reminder that UI spring animations should be all about *moderation*.

Switch back to **AnimatorFactory.swift** and change the parameters of your spring animation. Set dampingRatio to **0.55**, and duration to **1.0**. This should make the animation more subtle yet still playful.

Next, you'll explore a different situation when you will animate constraints. Currently, when you tap on **Show More** the widget changes its Height constraint and reloads the top table view contents to resize the widget.

In the next animation, you are going to animate the cell height change.

Open the **WidgetCell.swift** file and find `toggleShowMore(_:)`. You can peek inside to see the current code that changes the cell height and reloads the parent table view.

You will completely rebuild this method. Remove all the code within `toggleShowMore(_:)` and replace it with:

```
self.showsMore.toggle()
```

First let's define the animations you'd like to run. Append to `toggleShowMore(_:)`:

```
let animations = {
  self.widgetHeight.constant = self.showsMore ? 230 : 130
  if let tableView = self.tableView {
    tableView.beginUpdates()
    tableView.endUpdates()
    tableView.layoutIfNeeded()
  }
}
```

In this piece of code, you perform a little trick. First you change the constraint as usual, but then you call `beginUpdates()` and `endUpdates()` on the table view. Doing this will ask all cells about their height and adjust the layout as needed. If any of your cells says it wants to be higher or shorter, UIKit will adjust its frame accordingly.

At the end of the block, you call `layoutIfNeeded()` to ensure the layout change will happen inside the animations block.

Now let's create the animator. Add to the end of `toggleShowMore(_:)`:

```
let spring = UISpringTimingParameters(
  mass: 30,
  stiffness: 1000,
  damping: 300,
  initialVelocity: CGVector(dx: 5, dy: 0))

toggleHeightAnimator = UIViewPropertyAnimator(duration: 0.0,
timingParameters: spring)
toggleHeightAnimator?.addAnimations(animations)
toggleHeightAnimator?.startAnimation()
```

The view already features a property called `toggleHeightAnimator`, so you simply create a spring configuration and store the new animator in that property. Note that in this case you define all of the spring properties, so the duration that you pass to the property animator is ignored. The spring itself determines how long the animation takes to run.

Run the app, tap Show More, and enjoy a smooth spring-driven animation:

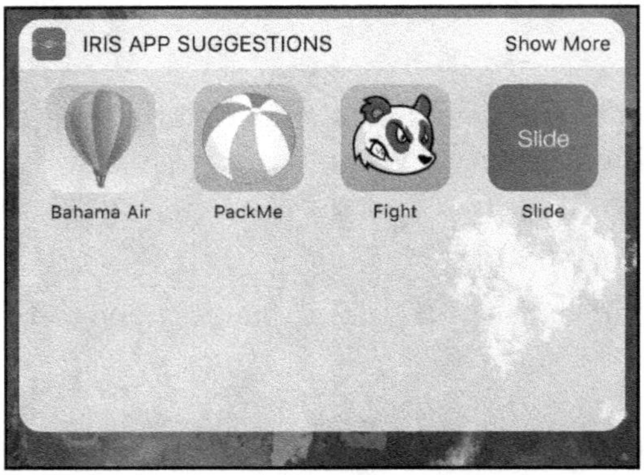

At the bottom of the method, add the following code that reloads the icons in the widget:

```
widgetView.expanded = showsMore
widgetView.reload()
```

This code triggers `reloadData()` on the collection view and that reloads all icons. Try the animation again and this time you see a different number of icons depending on the widget height:

Built-in View Transitions

To finish up this animation, you'll have a look at using the built-in view transitions with `UIViewPropertyAnimator`. In Chapter 5, "Transitions", you learned about the built-in view transitions you can use in iOS. Now you are going to use a cross-fade to change the title of the widget button from **Show More** to **Show Less** and vice versa.

Inside `toggleShowMore(_:)` add this code after you define your `animations` block (but before you define your animator):

```
let textTransition = {
  UIView.transition(
    with: sender,
    duration: 0.25,
    options: .transitionCrossDissolve,
    animations: {
      sender.setTitle(
        self.showsMore ? "Show Less" : "Show More",
        for: .normal)
    },
    completion: nil)
}
```

You define a view transition, and inside its `animations` block, you alter the button title depending whether the widget is currently expanded or not. So how do you add this transition to your animator? Just as you would with any other animations block!

Find the spot where you add `animations` to your animator and add `textTransition` as well with a `0.5` delay factor. The final code should look like this:

```
toggleHeightAnimator?.addAnimations(animations)
toggleHeightAnimator?.addAnimations(textTransition, delayFactor:
0.5)
toggleHeightAnimator?.startAnimation()
```

This will change the button title with a nice cross-fade effect:

In case you'd like to try other transitions go ahead and replace `.transitionCrossDissolve` with `.transitionFlipFromTop` - this is my personal favorite. This transition makes updating the button title look extra fancy.

You're starting to push `UIViewPropertyAnimator` to its limits! Before you move on to the next chapter and interactive animations, make sure to look into this chapter's challenge, which will introduce you to creative additive animations with `UIViewPropertyAnimator`.

Key Points

- With `UIViewPropertyAnimator`, you can animate `UIBlurEffect` values and create impressive blur animations.
- You can create your own custom animation timings and move away from the predefined easing constants by using two control point custom Bézier curves with `UIViewPropertyAnimator`.
- Last but not least, you can mix in the pre-defined UIKit transition APIs like `UIView.transition(with:duration:options:animations:completion)` with other `UIViewPropertyAnimator` animations and they'll "just work" together.

Challenges

Challenge 1: Additive Animations

When using `UIView.animate(withDuration:...)`, adding animations to the same view property happens additively.

For example, if you are moving a view across the screen from point **A** to **B**, and change your mind mid-way about the end point and decide to send the view over to point **C** instead, it will not just break off the movement at the current point and move directly towards the new end point.

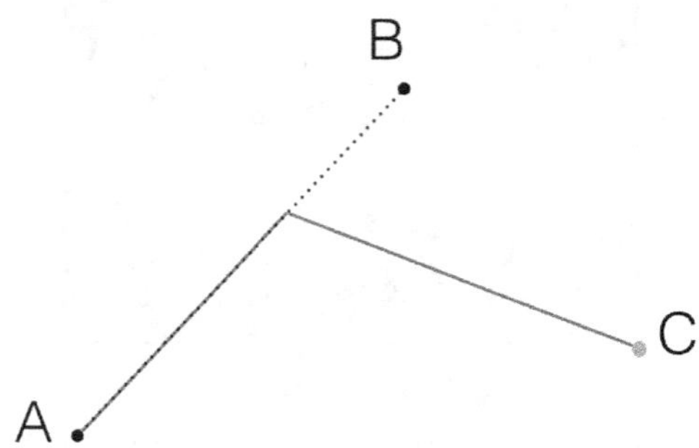

UIKit is smarter than that, so by default it will try to "ease" your view into its new trajectory. The actual movement will look something like this:

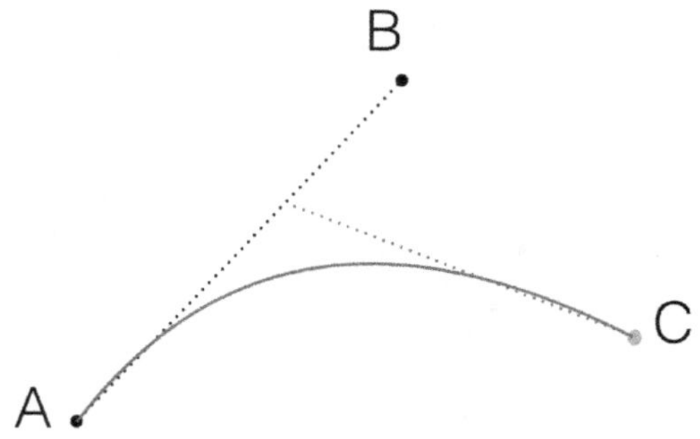

The animations aren't replaced at the time you add changes, but are combined so that the changes happen additively.

`UIViewPropertyAnimator` can handle these kinds of situations as well (with varying success for different timing providers).

For this challenge, if the menu state is switched again in `toggleShowMore(_:)` before the previous animation completes, then instead of creating a new animator you should "add" animations to the existing `toggleHeightAnimator`.

- Check if `toggleHeightAnimator` is currently running using `isRunning`.
- `isRunning` can be a little... unreliable, so also check that `fractionComplete` is less than 1.
- If the animator has already been created, pause it, add the new animation block, and continue the animation!
- I did mention that some timing parameters work better with this than others - try adjusting the initial spring velocity to zero or replacing the spring altogether if it isn't looking right.

When you're done with this challenge, move on to the next chapter to learn how to add interactivity to your property animator animations.

Chapter 24: Interactive Animations With UIViewPropertyAnimator

You've already covered a lot of the `UIViewPropertyAnimator` APIs such as basic animations, custom timings and springs, and abstracting of animations. But you haven't yet looked into what makes this class really interesting compared to the old style "fire-and-forget" APIs.

`UIView.animate(withDuration:...)` offers a way to animate views on screen, but once you've defined the desired end state, the animations are sent off for rendering and control is out of your hands.

But what if you wanted to interact with the animations? Or to create animations, which aren't static but are driven by user gestures or microphone input like you did in the part of the book covering layer animations?

This is where `UIViewPropertyAnimator` really comes through in regard to animating views. The animations created with this class are fully interactive: you can start, pause them, and alter their speed. Finally you can simply "scrub-through" the animation by directly setting the current progress.

Since `UIViewPropertyAnimator` can drive both preset animations and interactive animations, things get a bit complicated when it comes to telling what state an animator is currently. The next part of the chapter will teach you how to deal with animator state.

If you have completed the challenge in the previous chapter, just keep working on your Xcode project; if you skipped over the challenge, open the starter project provided for this chapter.

You should have the project featuring different animations which kick in when you enter text in the search bar, tap on an icon, or expand the widget view.

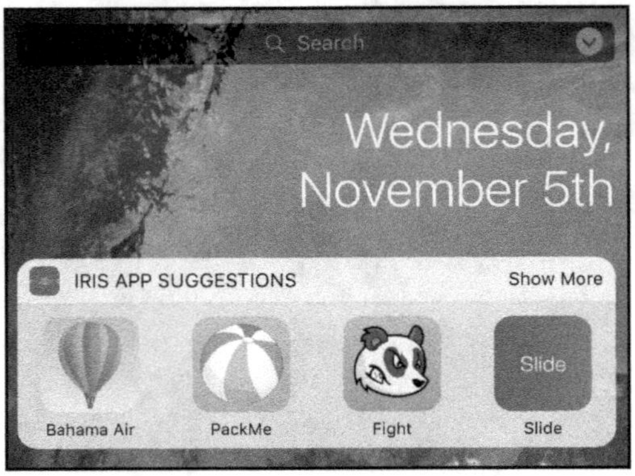

An Animation State Machine

Besides taking care of your animations, `UIViewPropertyAnimator` exhibits behaviors of a state machine, and can give you information about many different aspects of the current state of your animations.

You can check if an animation has started, if it has been paused or completely stopped, or whether the animation has been reversed. And finally, you can check where the animation "completed", such as at the desired end state, from the beginning, or somewhere in between.

There are three properties on `UIViewPropertyAnimator` that help you figure out the current state:

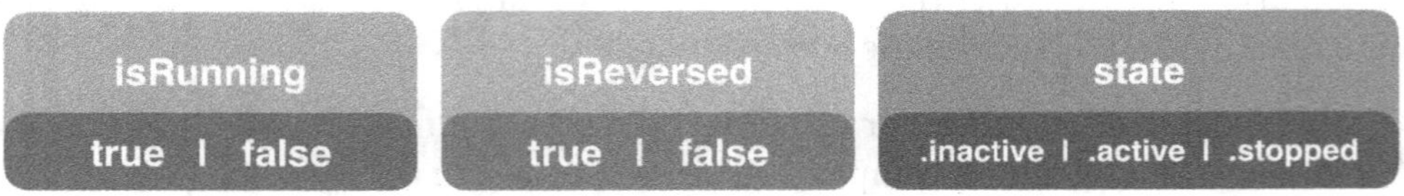

The `isRunning` property (read-only) tells you if the animator's animations are currently in motion. The property is `false` by default and becomes `true` when `startAnimation()` is called. It becomes `false` again if you pause or stop the animations, or your animations complete naturally.

The `isReversed` property is, by default, `false` since you always start your animations in forward direction, i.e. your animation plays from its start state to its end state. If you change this property to `true`, the animation will reverse direction and play back to its initial state.

The `state` property (read-only) determines whether the animator is active and currently animating, or in some other passive state.

By default, `state` is `inactive`. This usually means you've just created the animator and haven't called any methods on it yet. Please note that this is not the same as having `isRunning` set to `false`: `isRunning` is really only concerned with animations being played, while when `state` is `inactive` that really means that the animator hasn't done anything much yet.

`state` becomes `active` when you either:

- Call `startAnimation()` to start your animations
- Call `pauseAnimation()` without even starting your animations first,
- Set the `fractionComplete` property to "rewind" the animation to a certain position.

Once your animations complete naturally, `state` switches back to `inactive`.

If you call `stopAnimation()` on your animator, it will set its `state` property to `stopped`. In this state, the only thing you could do is either abandon the animator altogether or call `finishAnimation(at:)` to complete the animations and bring the animator back to the `inactive` state.

As you probably figured out, `UIViewPropertyAnimator` can only switch between states in a certain sequence. It can't go straight from `inactive` to `stopped`, nor from `stopped` to `active`.

There is one more option under your control: if you set the property called `pausesOnCompletion`, once the animator has finished running its animations instead of stopping itself it will pause. This will give you the opportunity to continue working with it from a paused state.

If you're in doubt, you can always come back to this part of the chapter and consult the state flow diagram below:

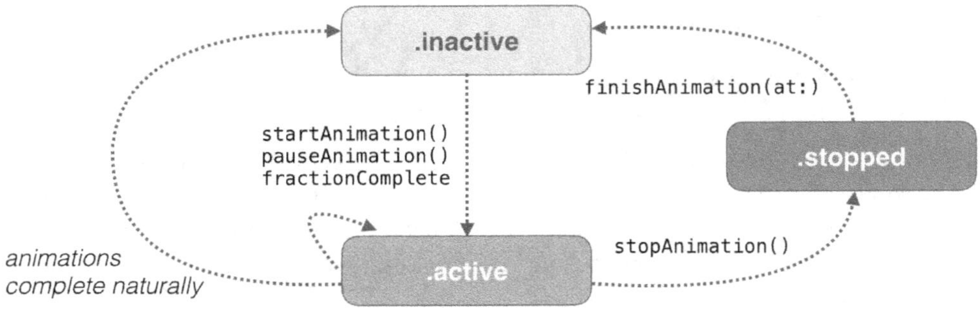

Don't worry if managing the state with `UIViewPropertyAnimator` sounds a bit complicated at first. Should you call a method you're not allowed to call in the current state, your app will immediately crash so you will have the chance to figure out where you went wrong.

Interactive 3D Touch Animation

In this part of the chapter, you are going to create an interactive animation similar to the 3D touch interaction on your iPhone home screen:

Note: For this section, you'll need either a 3D touch compatible iOS device, or a Force Touch trackpad for the simulator. A device is better as the 3D touch gives you finer control. Apple stopped building 3D touch into iPhones when the iPhone 11 was released. The iPhone 8 simulator in Xcode 13 supports the feature.

As you continue to press on a home screen icon, you'll see the animation interactively progress under your finger; the background gets more and more blurred, and there's a light blur frame growing out of the icon.

These two animations tell the user they are working through a gesture and gives them feedback about their progress through that animation. When you've pressed hard enough, the icon frame detaches from the icon and becomes a menu:

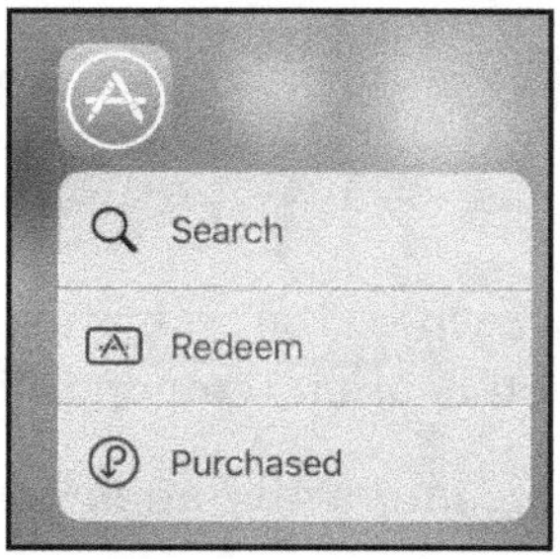

It's a neat little interactive animation, which you will get to reproduce in this chapter.

> **Note**: You are not going to learn the details about handling 3D touch with `UIPreviewInteractionDelegate`, since the chapter is about creating animations. If you want to learn more about `UIPreviewInteractionDelegate`, check out our *iOS 10 by Tutorials* book on raywenderlich.com.

Open **WidgetView.swift** and find the extension on `WidgetView` that conforms to `UIPreviewInteractionDelegate`. These are the delegate methods that UIKit calls when the user is pressing on your widget view.

In order to get you started developing the animation itself, the `UIPreviewInteractionDelegate` methods have already been wired to call relevant methods on `LockScreenViewController`.

What the code in `WidgetView` does is as follows:

- Call `LockScreenViewController.startPreview(for:)` when the 3D touch starts.
- Call `LockScreenViewController.updatePreview(percent:)` repeatedly while the user presses harder (or softer).
- Call `LockScreenViewController.finishPreview()` when the peek interaction has finished successfully.
- Finally, call `LockScreenViewController.cancelPreview()` if the user lifted their finger without completing the preview gesture.

Without further ado, let's get to coding!

Open **LockScreenViewController.swift** and add these three properties, which you will need in order to create the peek interaction:

```
var startFrame: CGRect?
var previewView: UIView?
var previewAnimator: UIViewPropertyAnimator?
```

You will use `startFrame` to track where the animation started. `previewView` will be a snapshot view of your icon; you'll use it temporarily during the animation.

The `previewAnimator` will be the interactive animator driving the preview animation.

Add one more property to hold the blur effect to display the icon frame (as in the screenshots above):

```
let previewEffectView = IconEffectView(blur: .extraLight)
```

`IconEffectView` is a custom class included with the starter project. It's a simple blur view which contains a single label. You're going to use it to mock the menu that pops out of the pressed icon like so:

Scroll down to `extension LockScreenViewController: WidgetsOwnerProtocol` and insert a new method inside:

```
func startPreview(for forView: UIView) {
  previewView?.removeFromSuperview()
  if let preview = forView.snapshotView(afterScreenUpdates:
false) {
    previewView = preview
    view.insertSubview(preview, aboveSubview: blurView)
  }
}
```

As you saw previously, `WidgetView` calls `startPreview(for:)` whenever the user starts pressing on an icon. The `forView` parameter is the collection cell image that the user began the gesture on.

First you remove any existing `previewView` view, just in case to make sure you don't leave artifacts on screen. Then you make a snapshot of the collection view icon and finally add it onscreen just above the blur effect view.

You can run the app right now and start pressing on an icon. You will see a copy of the icon popup at the top left corner!

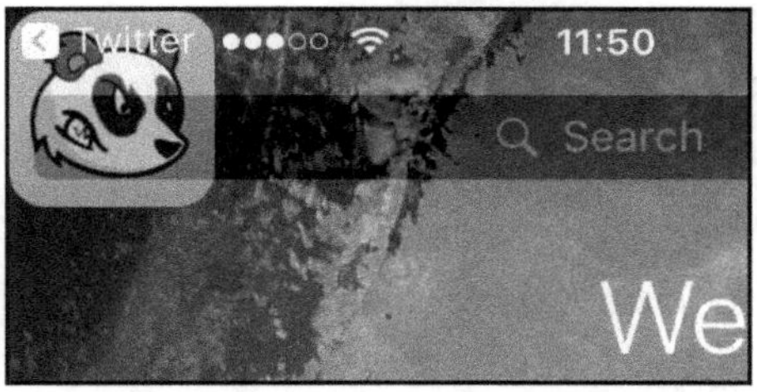

Of course the icon isn't covering the existing one because you haven't set its position. Let's keep on building the animation:

```
preview.frame = forView.convert(forView.bounds, to: view)
startFrame = preview.frame
addEffectView(below: preview)
```

You set the correct position on the icon copy so that it covers completely the existing icon. Then you store that start location and size for future reference in `startFrame`. Finally you call `addEffectView(below:)` to add the blur frame below the icon snapshot.

Add the implementation of `addEffectView(below:)` to `LockScreenViewController` using the snippet below to insert the effect below the icon snapshot:

```
func addEffectView(below forView: UIView) {
  previewEffectView.removeFromSuperview()
  previewEffectView.frame = forView.frame

  forView.superview?.insertSubview(
    previewEffectView,
    belowSubview: forView)
}
```

This completes the setup stage of the animation. Congrats for making it through!

Next switch to **AnimatorFactory.swift** to create the animation itself. Add the following method to `AnimatorFactory`:

```
static func grow(
  view: UIVisualEffectView,
  blurView: UIVisualEffectView
) -> UIViewPropertyAnimator {
  // 1
  view.contentView.alpha = 0
  view.transform = .identity

  // 2
  let animator = UIViewPropertyAnimator(
    duration: 0.5, curve: .easeIn)

  return animator
}
```

Your new factory method takes two parameters:

- `view`: The view to animate
- `blurView` The blur background that will animate alongside the primary animation.

It then performs the following actions:

1. First, it baselines the current state of the view by fading out the view contents — that's the label saying "Customize Actions..." — and resetting the transform on the view.
2. Then a new animator is created with `0.5` seconds duration and an ease-in timing curve.

Now, just before the line `return animator`, you can add the animations and completions for this animator. To do that, insert the following:

```
// 3
animator.addAnimations {
  blurView.effect = UIBlurEffect(style: .dark)
  view.transform = CGAffineTransform(scaleX: 1.5, y: 1.5)
}

// 4
animator.addCompletion { _ in
  blurView.effect = UIBlurEffect(style: .dark)
}
```

3. In the animation added here, setting the `effect` property on your blur view will create a nice blur transition. You've already done this in previous chapters, but this time the blur will happen interactively depending on how hard the user is pressing the screen. Finally, the blur is scaled up on the icon frame by simply adjusting its `transform` property.

4. The completion method explicitly sets the final state of the blur view. These interactive animations with `UIViewPropertyAnimator` are sometimes a bit buggy, so as soon as your animations complete, UIKit will call your completion and the code in it will make sure you're leaving the UI in the condition you want.

You're almost ready with your grow animation. You just need to scrub through it interactively as the user presses on the icon.

Go back to **LockScreenViewController.swift** and append the following to `startPreview()`:

```
previewAnimator = AnimatorFactory.grow(
  view: previewEffectView,
  blurView: blurView)
```

Note how this time, unlike in the previous chapters, you create and configure your animator — but you don't start the animations. This time, you'll drive the animation progress interactively based on the 3D touch input.

In order to progress through the animation, implement the `updatePreview(percent:)` method. This is the one `WidgetView` will repeatedly call with the current touch force:

```
func updatePreview(percent: CGFloat) {
  previewAnimator?.fractionComplete =
    max(0.01, min(0.99, percent))
}
```

The important aspect to understand is that you restrict `fractionComplete` in the range `0.01` and `0.99`. If you set the `fractionComplete` to `0.0` or `1.0`, the animator will complete and you don't want that to happen inside `updatePreview`. You will finish or cancel the animation from the designated methods.

You can give your interactive animation a try right now!

Run the app and start gently pressing on one of the icons. When you start pressing, you will see the blur frame starting to "grow out" of the icon. The blur effect appears subtly in the background:

When you press harder and harder, the frame keeps growing and the blur becomes more prominent:

As soon as you apply enough force to complete the preview gesture, you will feel the haptic feedback under your finger and the animation will stop in this state.

Why does the animation stop? No, it's not your fault — the peek gesture completes, and once it does that, it just stops sending updates; that is, it stops calling your `updatePreview(percent:)` method.

Next, you will implement the methods to cancel or complete the interaction.

You will (surprise!) need more animators. Open **AnimatorFactory.swift** and add an animator, which undoes everything your "grow" animator does.

One situation where you'll need this animator is when the user cancels the gesture. Another is at the very end of a successful interaction when you need to clean up the UI.

Add the new factory method:

```
static func reset(
  frame: CGRect,
  view: UIVisualEffectView,
  blurView: UIVisualEffectView
) -> UIViewPropertyAnimator {
  UIViewPropertyAnimator(
    duration: 0.5,
    dampingRatio: 0.7) {
    view.transform = .identity
    view.frame = frame
    view.contentView.alpha = 0
    blurView.effect = nil
  }
}
```

This method takes in the starting `frame` of the original animation, the `view` to animate, and the background `blurView`. The animation block resets all properties in the state before the interaction started.

Switch back to **LockScreenViewController.swift** and add a new method inside the `WidgetsOwnerProtocol` extension:

```
func cancelPreview() {
  if let previewAnimator = previewAnimator {
    previewAnimator.isReversed = true
    previewAnimator.startAnimation()
  }
}
```

This is the method that `WidgetView` will call if the user abruptly lifts their finger, or if a FaceTime calls pops on screen, and cancels the ongoing gesture.

So far you haven't started your animator at all. You have been repeatedly setting `fractionComplete` and this drove the animations interactively.

However, once the user cancels the interaction, you can't keep driving the animation interactively because you have no more input. Instead, you play back the animation to its initial state by setting `isReversed` to `true`, and calling `startAnimation()`. Now **this** is something you can't do with `UIView.animate(withDuration:...)`!

Give the interaction another try. Press through half of the animation and then let go to test `cancelPreview()`.

The animation correctly plays back when you lift your finger but in the end the dark blur reappears abruptly.

The issue is rooted in your grow animator's code. Switch back to **AnimatorFactory.swift** and look at the code in `grow(view: UIVisualEffectView, blurView: UIVisualEffectView)` — more specifically, this part:

```
animator.addCompletion { _ in
  blurView.effect = UIBlurEffect(style: .dark)
}
```

Now that the animation can play either forwards or backwards, you need to take care of this in your completion block.

The parameter that `addCompletion()`'s closure takes is of type `UIViewAnimatingPosition`. Its value can be either `.start`, `.end`, or `.current`.

If your animation completed naturally, or otherwise reached its end state, you will get the `.end` value in your completion closure. If you reversed the animation, it will complete at the `.start` position. Finally, if you stop your animation mid-way and finish it right there, your completion block will get the `.current` value.

So, to handle the possibility of completing or canceling the preview gesture, remove the existing completion block and replace it with this:

```
animator.addCompletion { position in
  switch position {
    case .start:
      blurView.effect = nil
    case .end:
      blurView.effect = UIBlurEffect(style: .dark)
    default:
```

```
      break
    }
  }
```

In case the animation was reversed, you remove the blur effect. If it completed successfully, you explicitly adjust the effect to a dark blur.

Give the adjusted animation a try few times; make sure everything goes as expected. It should mostly do that.

Now there's a new issue. If you cancel the press on a certain icon, you cannot press it anymore!

This is because the icon snapshot is still located just over the original icon, and it swallows all touches. To fix that issue, you need to remove the snapshot as soon as the reset animator has completed.

Let's add this code to `cancelPreview()` back in **LockScreenViewController.swift**, just below `previewAnimator.startAnimation()`:

```
previewAnimator.addCompletion { position in
  switch position {
  case .start:
    self.previewView?.removeFromSuperview()
    self.previewEffectView.removeFromSuperview()
  default: break
  }
}
```

Remember that this call to `addCompletion(_:)` does not replace the existing completion block, but rather adds a second one.

The goal is to check if the animation has been reversed; and if so, remove the snapshot and the icon frame from the view hierarchy. That's why the only case you're interested in is when `position` is `.start`.

Try the app again, and you will see that the icons are interactive again after a canceled gesture. Hooray! You're almost there.

Let's add one more animator to display the icon menu. Switch to **AnimatorFactory.swift** and add to it:

```
static func complete(view: UIVisualEffectView) ->
UIViewPropertyAnimator {
  return UIViewPropertyAnimator(
    duration: 0.3,
    dampingRatio: 0.7) {
```

```
      view.contentView.alpha = 1
      view.transform = .identity
      view.frame = CGRect(
        x: view.frame.minX - view.frame.minX / 2.5,
        y: view.frame.maxY - 140,
        width: view.frame.width + 120,
        height: 60
      )
    }
  }
```

This time you create a simple spring animator. For its animators you do the following:

- Fade in the "Customize Actions" menu item.
- Reset the transform.
- Animate the frame of the view directly to a location just above the icon.

The location of the menu changes depending on which icon the user pressed on.

You set the horizontal position to `view.frame.minX - view.frame.minX/2.5`, which shows the menu to the right if the icon is on the left side of the screen, and shows the menu to the left if the icon is on the right side of the screen. See the difference below:

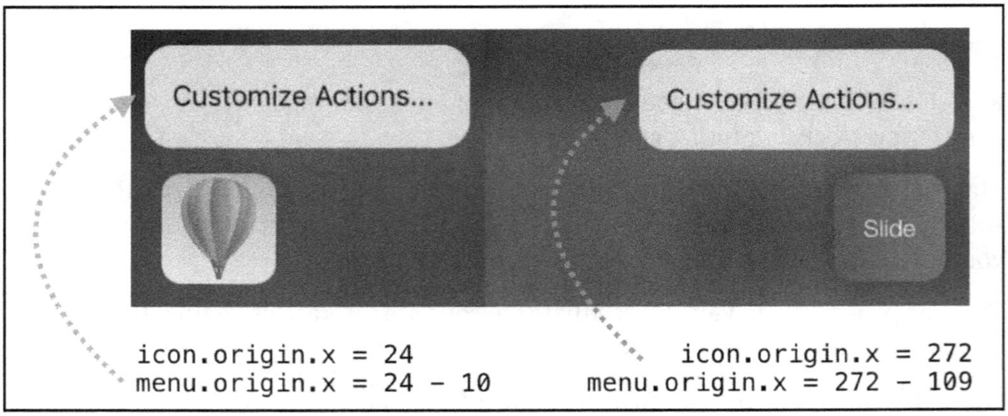

The animator is ready to go, so open **LockScreenViewController.swift** and add the last required method in the `WidgetsOwnerProtocol` extension:

```
func finishPreview() {
  // 1
  previewAnimator?.stopAnimation(false)

  // 2
  previewAnimator?.finishAnimation(at: .end)

  // 3
  previewAnimator = nil
}
```

`finishPreview()` is called when the user pushes through the 3D touch gesture, at about the time you feel the haptic feedback.

1. `stopAnimation(_:)` stops the animations currently running on screen and has two different behaviors depending on the boolean parameter you pass in.
2. When you call `stopAnimation(false)`, you put the animator in the `stopped` state. It will wait for you to call `finishAnimation(at:)` at some point later on. If you call `stopAnimations(true)`, this will clear all animations and put the animator in the `inactive` state without calling your completion blocks. Use this to completely cancel the current animations on an animator.

Once you put the animator in the `stopped` state, you have a few options. The one you pursue in `finishPreview()` is to tell the animator to complete at its end state. Thus you call `finishAnimation(at: .end)`; this will update all views with the target values of the scheduled animations and call your completion.

3. You won't need the `previewAnimator` anymore for this gesture, so you can remove it.

You can call `finishAnimation(at:)` with one of the following:

- `start`: To reset the animations to their initial state.
- `current`: To update your views' properties from the current progress of the animation and complete.

After you call `finishAnimation(at:)`, your animator is in the `inactive` state.

Back to the Widgets project. Since you got rid of the preview animator, you can run the complete animator to display the menu. Append the following to the end of `finishPreview()`:

```
AnimatorFactory.complete(view: previewEffectView)
  .startAnimation()
```

That will complete the effect. As soon as you run the app and press on an icon, you will see its menu pop up interactively:

And when the animation is finished, the menu will position itself nicely along the icon:

Congratulations — you deserve a pat on the shoulder. That was a complex effect to develop! But brace yourself — that's just the start! In the next chapter, you are going to work on interactive view controller transition animations!

Meanwhile, work through the challenges provided in this chapter so you can get a bit more experience with adding and re-using animators, and also with using interactive keyframe animations!

Key Points

- You can introspect the state of an animator by checking the combination of the values of `state`, `isRunning`, and `isReversed`.
- You can pause animators by toggling `isRunning` and reverse the execution of the animations by toggling `isReversed`.
- When you allow animations to be reversed, take care to correctly wrap up those animations in your completion closures. This is because they might be ending on their intended final state or their initial state, depending on which direction they were running when they completed.

Challenges

Challenge 1: Allow the Users to Dismiss the Menu

Once the user sees the complete animation which displays the menu, they can't do anything else with the app.

In this challenge, you are going to reset the UI if the user taps on the blur view or on the menu item. This will allow them to "dismiss" the menu and further interact with the app.

In `finishPreview()` add the following code to prepare the blur for being interactive:

```
blurView.effect = UIBlurEffect(style: .dark)
blurView.isUserInteractionEnabled = true
blurView.addGestureRecognizer(UITapGestureRecognizer(target:
self, action: #selector(dismissMenu)))
```

Above, you make sure that the blur effect is set to dark and you enable user interactivity on the blur view itself. This will allow the user to tap anywhere around the icon to dismiss the menu.

Finally, you add a touch recognizer and connect it to a method called `dismissMenu()`.

Next — add `dismissMenu()` on your own:

- Use the `AnimatorFactory.reset(frame:, view:, blurView:)` animator for the dismiss animation.
- Use the `startFrame` property for the `frame` parameter of `AnimatorFactory.reset(frame:, view:, blurView:)`.
- Before starting the animator, add one more completion block which remove `previewEffectView` and `previewView` from the screen. Also disable user interactivity on the blur view so it doesn't swallow any other touches.

Finally, in `viewDidLoad()`, add a tap recognizer on `previewEffectView`, connected to `dismissMenu()` as well. This will allow the users to tap on **Customize Actions...** to close the menu.

Run the app and try opening and dismissing the menu few times. Isn't that jolly old fun?

Challenge 2: Interactive Keyframe Animations

In chapter 22 you learned how easy it is to add keyframe animations to an animator. If you have an animator with keyframes, you can still use it to create interactive animations. Your users can scrub through the keyframes back and forth.

To give that a try, you will add an extra element to the grow animation — the one you scrub through interactively while the user presses on an icon.

Open **AnimatorFactory.swift** and find the place in `grow(view: UIVisualEffectView, blurView: UIVisualEffectView)` where you add animations to the animator:

```
animator.addAnimations {
  blurView.effect = UIBlurEffect(style: .dark)
  view.transform = CGAffineTransform(scaleX: 1.5, y: 1.5)
}
```

Delete this whole block of code and **replace** it with:

```
animator.addAnimations {
  UIView.animateKeyframes(withDuration: 0.5, delay: 0.0) {
    UIView.addKeyframe(withRelativeStartTime: 0.0,
relativeDuration: 1.0) {
      blurView.effect = UIBlurEffect(style: .dark)
      view.transform = CGAffineTransform(scaleX: 1.5, y: 1.5)
    }
```

```
      UIView.addKeyframe(withRelativeStartTime: 0.5,
relativeDuration: 0.5) {
        view.transform = view.transform.rotated(by: -.pi / 8)
      }
    }
  }
```

You create an animation with two keyframes:

- The first keyframe goes for the total duration of the animation, and runs the same animation you had previously.
- The second keyframe kicks in the second half of the total duration and rotates the view slightly.

The new element in the animation will help give the user feedback when they are about to complete the gesture. Just before they've pressed hard enough, they'll see the icon frame tilt:

This will also add a bit of playfulness to the complete animations that shows the menu:

With the complete interaction and all animations in place, you are now ready to proceed to the next chapter and dabble on creating view controller transitions with `UIViewPropertyAnimator`.

Chapter 25: UIViewPropertyAnimator View Controller Transitions

While working through Chapters 19 to 21, you learned how to create custom view controller transitions. You saw how flexible and powerful those can be, so naturally you are probably craving to know how to use `UIViewPropertyAnimator` to create them as well.

Good news — using an animator for your transitions is pretty easy, and there are almost no surprises there.

In this chapter, you are going to review building custom transition animations and create both static and interactive transitions for your Widgets project.

When you've finished working through the chapter, your users will be able to scrub through presenting the settings view controller by pulling down the widget table.

If you worked on the challenges from the last chapter, keep working on the same project; if you skipped over the challenges, open the starter project provided for this chapter.

Static View Controller Transitions

Currently, the experience is pretty stale when the user taps the "Edit" button. The button presents a new view controller on top of the current one, and as soon as you tap any of the available options in that second screen, it disappears.

Let's spice that up a notch!

Create a new file and name it **PresentTransition.swift**. Replace its default contents with:

```
import UIKit

class PresentTransition: NSObject,
  UIViewControllerAnimatedTransitioning {
  func transitionDuration(
    using transitionContext:
UIViewControllerContextTransitioning?
  ) -> TimeInterval {
    return 0.75
  }

  func animateTransition(
    using transitionContext:
UIViewControllerContextTransitioning
  ) {
  }
}
```

You are familiar with the `UIViewControllerAnimatedTransitioning` protocol, so you should hopefully be familiar with this piece of code.

> **Note**: In case you skipped the View Controller Transitions section of the book, I'd recommend taking a step back and working through at least Chapter 19, "Presentation Controller & Orientation Animations".

In this part of the chapter, you are going to create a transition animation that animates the blur layer and moves the new view controller on top of it.

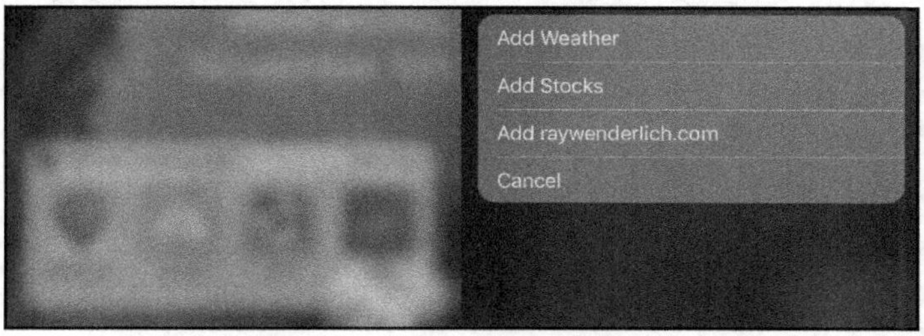

Add the following method, in the same file you have open, to create an animator for the transition:

```
func transitionAnimator(using transitionContext:
  UIViewControllerContextTransitioning) ->
UIViewImplicitlyAnimating {
  let duration = transitionDuration(using: transitionContext)

  let container = transitionContext.containerView
  guard let toView = transitionContext.view(forKey: .to) else {
    return UIViewPropertyAnimator()
  }

  container.addSubview(toView)
}
```

In the code above, you make all necessary preparations for the view controller transition. You begin by getting the animation duration, you then fetch the target view controller's view, and finally add this view to the transition container.

Next you can set up the animation and run it. Add this code to `transitionAnimator(using:)` to prepare the UI for the transition animation:

```
toView.transform = CGAffineTransform(scaleX: 1.33, y: 1.33)
  .concatenating(CGAffineTransform(translationX: 0.0, y: 200))
toView.alpha = 0
```

This scales up and moves down the target view controller's view and fades it out. Now it's ready to be animated onto the screen.

Add the animator after `toView.alpha = 0` to run the transition:

```
let animator = UIViewPropertyAnimator(duration: duration, curve:
.easeOut)

animator.addAnimations({
  toView.transform = CGAffineTransform(translationX: 0.0, y:
100)
}, delayFactor: 0.15)

animator.addAnimations({
  toView.alpha = 1.0
}, delayFactor: 0.5)
```

In this code, you create an animator with two animation blocks:

1. The first animation moves the target view controller's view to its final position.
2. The second animation fades the content in from an `alpha` of 0 to 1.

As in the previous chapters you should never forget to wrap up the transition. Add a completion to the animator:

```
animator.addCompletion { _ in
  transitionContext.completeTransition(
    !transitionContext.transitionWasCancelled
  )
}
```

Once your animations complete, you let UIKit know that you're finished transitioning. At the end of your method simply return the animator:

```
return animator
```

Now that you have your animator factory method, you have to also use it. Scroll up to `animateTransition(using:)` and insert this code:

```
transitionAnimator(using: transitionContext).startAnimation()
```

This will fetch a ready-to-go animator, and begin via `startAnimation()`. That should do it for the time being. Let's wire up the view controller to the transition animator and give the animation a try.

Open **LockScreenViewController** and define the following constant property:

```
let presentTransition = PresentTransition()
```

You will provide this object to UIKit when it asks you for a presentation animation and interaction controller. To do that, add a `UIViewControllerTransitioningDelegate` conformance to `LockScreenViewController`:

```
extension LockScreenViewController:
UIViewControllerTransitioningDelegate {
  func animationController(
    forPresented presented: UIViewController,
    presenting: UIViewController,
    source: UIViewController
  ) -> UIViewControllerAnimatedTransitioning? {
    return presentTransition
  }
}
```

The `animationController(forPresented:presenting:source:)` method is where you have your chance to tell UIKit that you're planning on spawning a new custom view controller transition. You return the `presentTransition` from that method and UIKit uses it for the animations to follow.

Now for the last step — you need to set `LockScreenViewController` as the presentation delegate. Scroll to `presentSettings(_:)`, and just before calling `present(_:animated:completion:)` set `self` as the transition delegate:

```
settings.transitioningDelegate = self
```

This should be it! Run the app and tap on the Edit button to try the transition.

The initial result isn't all that exciting (at least not yet!). The settings controller seems to be a bit off:

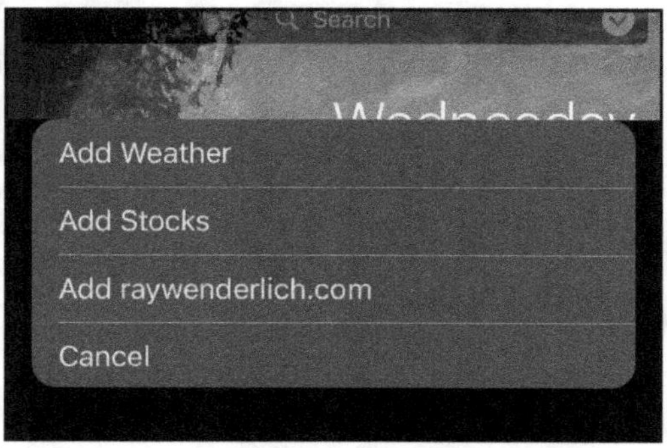

You'll want to take care of few rough edges, but your job here is almost finished. The first thing to correct is the target view controller doesn't need the solid background color.

Open **Main.storyboard** (it's in the Assets project folder) and select the settings view controller view.

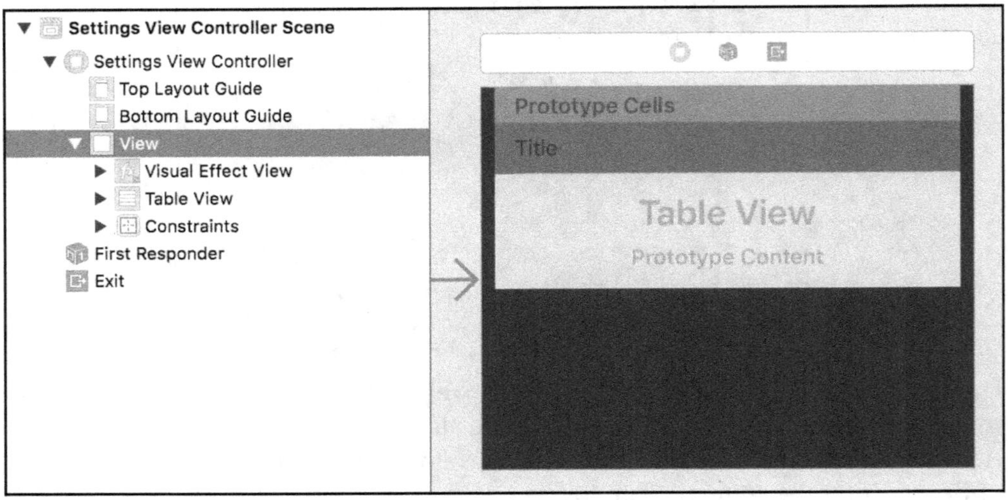

Change the view's Background to **Clear Color** and you should see the storyboard reflect that change like so:

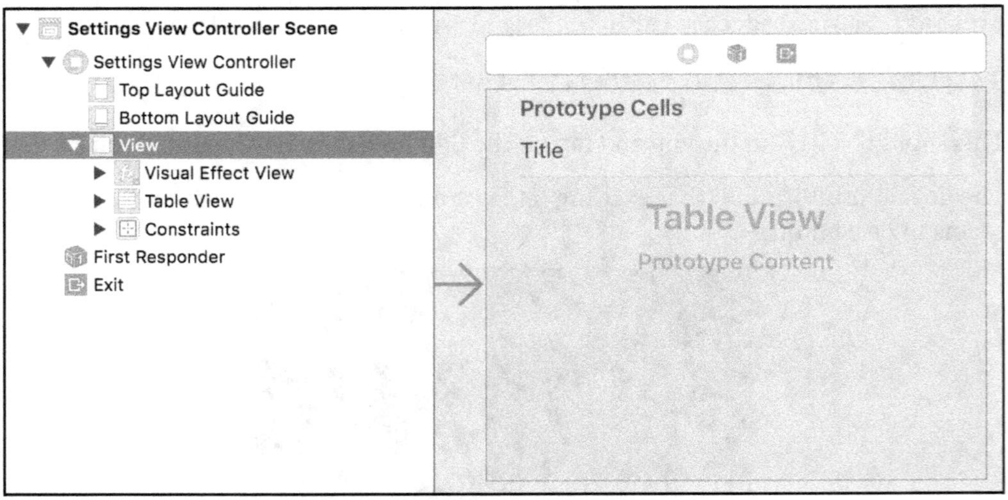

Give that transition another try. This time you should see the contents of the settings view controller appear directly over the lock screen:

It looks like this transition can do with a few more animations. Wouldn't it be nice, for example, to fade in the blur on top of the widget so that the user can see better the modal view controller on top?

Since you're a pro already, let's do something new — "*animation injection*"! (No need to look that term up — I just came up with it for this chapter).

You will add a new property to the animator that will allow you to inject any custom animation into the transition. This will allow you to use the same transition class to produce slightly different animations.

Switch to **PresentTransition.swift** and add a new property:

```
var auxAnimations: (() -> Void)?
```

Append this to the bottom of `transitionAnimator(using:)`, just before `return`:

```
if let auxAnimations = auxAnimations {
  animator.addAnimations(auxAnimations)
}
```

In case you've added any arbitrary block of animations to the object, they will be added to the rest of the animator's animations.

This allows you to, depending on the situation, add custom animations into the transition. For example, let's add a blur animation to the current transition.

Open **LockScreenViewController** and insert the following **at the top** of `presentSettings()`:

```
presentTransition.auxAnimations = blurAnimations(true)
```

This will add the blur animation you created many chapters ago to the view controller transition!

Give the transition another try and see how that one line changed it:

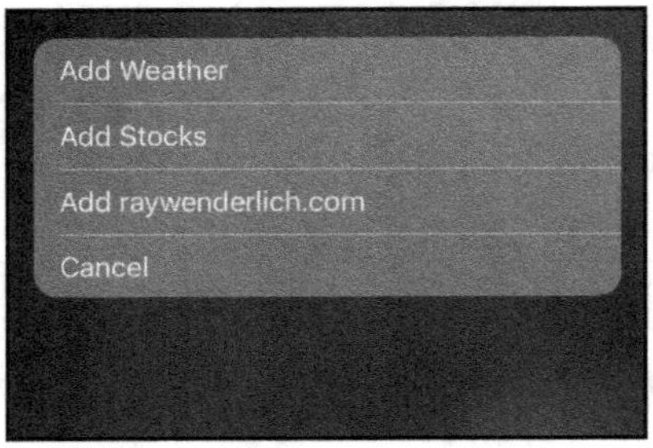

Isn't reusing animations simply amazing?

Now you also need to hide the blur when the user dismisses the presented controller. `SettingsViewController` already has a `didDismiss` property so you simply need to set that property to a block that animates the blur out.

In `presentSettings(_:)` on the second-to-last line before `settings` is presented, insert:

```
settings.didDismiss = { [unowned self] in
  self.toggleBlur(false)
}
```

Now tapping on one of the options in the settings screen will dismiss it. The blur will then disappear and the user will be successfully taken back to the first view controller:

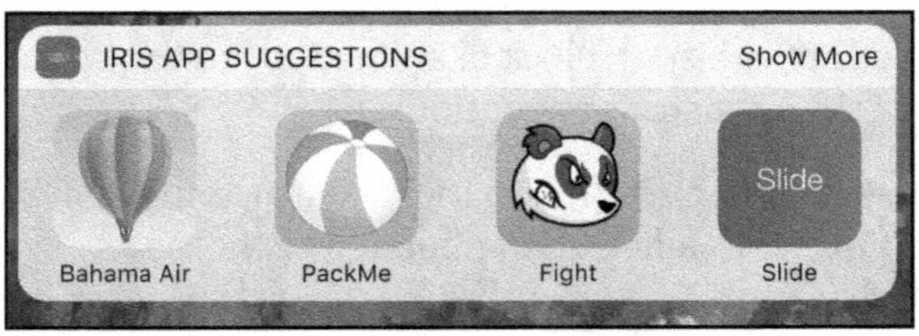

This concludes this part of the chapter. Your view controller transition is ready!

Interactive View Controller Transitions

As the final topic in the `UIViewPropertyAnimator` section of the book, you are going to create an interactive view controller transition. Your user will drive the transition by pulling down the widget table.

First and foremost, let's use the powerful `UIPercentDrivenInteractionTransition` class to enable interactivity for the view controller transition. Open **PresentTransition.swift** and replace:

```
class PresentTransition: NSObject,
  UIViewControllerAnimatedTransitioning {
```

With:

```
class PresentTransition: UIPercentDrivenInteractiveTransition,
  UIViewControllerAnimatedTransitioning {
```

`UIPercentDrivenInteractiveTransition` is a class that defines the "percent" based transition methods such as:

- `update(_:)` to rewind through the transition.
- `cancel()` to cancel the view controller transition.
- `finish()` to play the the transition until it completes.

You may remember these from Chapter 21, "Interactive UINavigationController Transitions", but you didn't look at some of the advanced APIs that accommodate using a `UIViewPropertyAnimator` specifically. Some of the new functionally built to make animator transitions easier include:

- `timingCurve`: In case your user drives the transition interactively and lets go at a point when you need to play the transition till the end, you can provide a custom timing curve for the animation by setting this property. This can be a cubic, spring, or another custom timing provider.
- `wantsInteractiveStart`: By default this is `true` since you are probably going to use this class mostly for interactive transitions. However, if you set the property to `false`, the transition will start non-interactively and you could pause it and go to interactive mode at a later point.
- `pause()`: Call this method to pause a non-interactive transition and switch to interactive mode.

For an interactive animation, you need to keep track of the animator object rather than keep making new ones. Add a new property to `PresentTransition`:

```
var animator: UIViewPropertyAnimator?
```

Then, in `transitionAnimator(using:)`, just before the return statement, add this code:

```
self.animator = animator

animator.addCompletion { [unowned self] _ in
  self.animator = nil
}
```

This line stores the animator object that you create for the non-interactive transition, and removes it once the animation is complete. Now, add a new method to `PresentTransition`:

```
func interruptibleAnimator(
  using transitionContext: UIViewControllerContextTransitioning
) -> UIViewImplicitlyAnimating {
  return animator ?? transitionAnimator(using:
transitionContext)
}
```

This is a method on the `UIViewControllerAnimatedTransitioning` protocol. It allows you to provide to UIKit an interruptible animator, which it will use for your transition animations. It can get called multiple times, and it's important that you return the same animator each time, so you only create a new animator object if one doesn't already exist.

Your transition animator class has now two different behaviors:

1. If it is used **non-interactively** (when the user presses the Edit button) UIKit will call `animateTransition(using:)` to animate the transition.
2. If it is used **interactively**, UIKit will call `interruptibleAnimator(using:)`, get your animator, and use it to drive the transition that way.

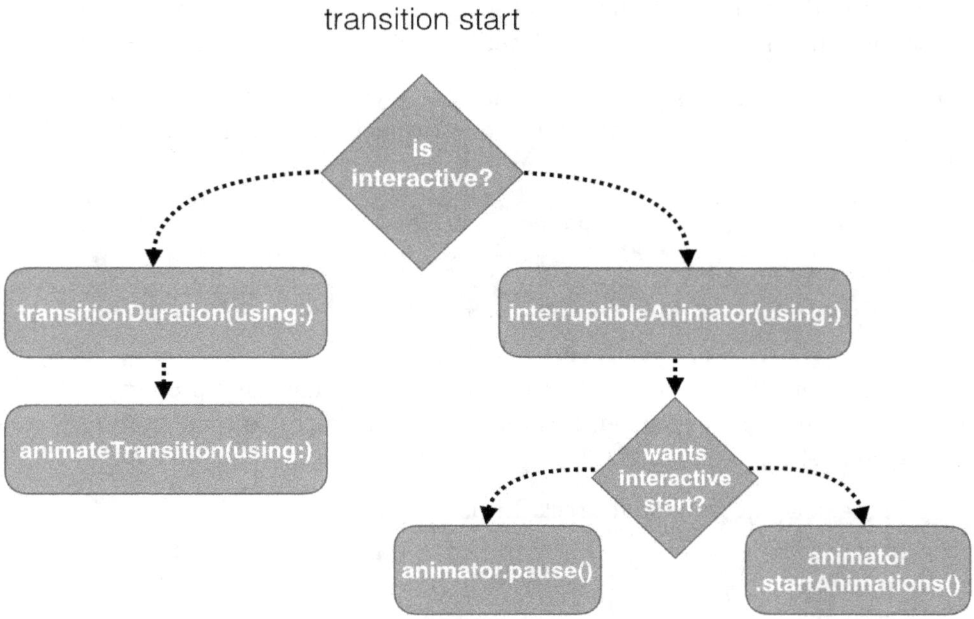

Switch to **LockScreenViewController.swift** and add this new method inside the `UIViewControllerTransitioningDelegate` extension:

```
func interactionControllerForPresentation(
  using animator: UIViewControllerAnimatedTransitioning
  ) -> UIViewControllerInteractiveTransitioning? {
  return presentTransition
}
```

This will let UIKit know you're planning some playful interactiveness during the view controller presentation.

Next, still in **LockScreenViewController.swift**, add two new properties; you will need them to keep track of the user's gesture:

```
var isDragging = false
var isPresentingSettings = false
```

As the user pulls the table down you will set the isDragging flag to true, and once the user has pulled far enough, you will set isPresentingSettings to true in turn.

To track how far has the user pulled the table view, you will need to implement some of its scroll view delegate methods. Add a new extension and insert the first of those methods:

```
extension LockScreenViewController: UIScrollViewDelegate {
  func scrollViewWillBeginDragging(_ scrollView: UIScrollView) {
    isDragging = true
  }
}
```

This might seem a bit redundant since UITableView already has a property to track if it's being currently dragged, but this time you are going to do some custom tracking yourself.

Next add the delegate method to track the user's progress:

```
func scrollViewDidScroll(_ scrollView: UIScrollView) {
  guard isDragging else {
    return
  }

  if !isPresentingSettings && scrollView.contentOffset.y < -30 {
    isPresentingSettings = true
    presentTransition.wantsInteractiveStart = true
    presentSettings()
    return
  }
}
```

First, you check if your isDragging flag is enabled; you are not interested in tracking the table view's offset otherwise. Then you check if the user has pulled far enough to start the transition.

If both conditions are true, you prepare the transition setup. You set isPresentingSettings to true, you set the transition animator to interactive mode, and finally you call presentSettings().

presentSettings() takes care to start the view controller transition in interactive mode because you set the wantsInteractiveStart to true in advance.

Next, you need to add the code to update it interactively. Append the following to the end of `scrollViewDidScroll(_:)`:

```
if isPresentingSettings {
  let progress = max(0.0, min(1.0, ((-
scrollView.contentOffset.y) - 30) / 90.0))
  presentTransition.update(progress)
}
```

You calculate a progress in the range `0.0` to `1.0` based on how far the user has pulled the table view and call `update(_:)` on the transition animator to position the animation at the current progress.

Give the transition a try right now, and you will see the table view blur progressively as you drag it down.

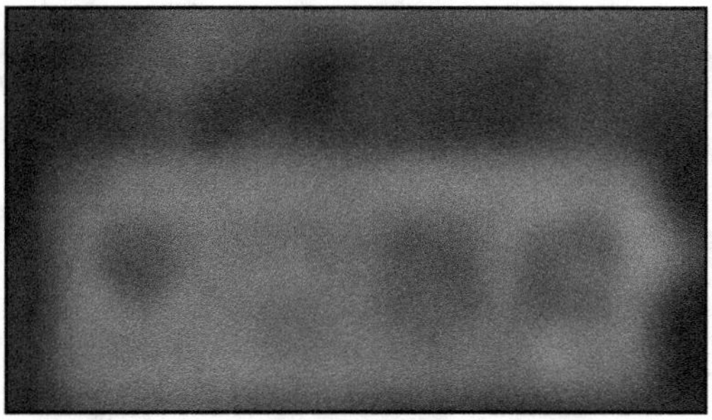

You also need to take care of completing and canceling the transition. Add to the same extension as before:

```
func scrollViewWillEndDragging(
  _ scrollView: UIScrollView,
  withVelocity velocity: CGPoint,
  targetContentOffset: UnsafeMutablePointer<CGPoint>
) {
  let progress = max(0.0, min(1.0, ((-
scrollView.contentOffset.y) - 30) / 90.0))

  if progress > 0.5 {
    presentTransition.finish()
  } else {
    presentTransition.cancel()
  }

  isPresentingSettings = false
  isDragging = false
}
```

This code should look similar; it's the same approach you employed in Chapter 21, "Interactive UINavigationController Transitions".

If the user has pulled through more than half of the distance (that you decided to be "far enough") you consider the transition successful and play the animation to the end. If the user hasn't dragged more than half the distance, you cancel the transition. Either way, you reset the values of the two flags and the interactive part of the transition is over.

The transition, however, is not complete just yet — there are few more things to polish before it's production ready.

Switch to **PresentTransition.swift** and find `transitionAnimator(using:)`. In the completion block, you ignore the parameter and always call `completeTransition(_:)` with the same value.

You can help UIKit by checking at which position the animator completed and provide the relevant value. Replace the existing call to `addCompletion(...)` where you complete the transition, with:

```
animator.addCompletion { position in
  switch position {
  case .end:
    transitionContext.completeTransition(
      !transitionContext.transitionWasCancelled)
  default:
    transitionContext.completeTransition(false)
  }
}
```

Indeed the view controller transition has succeeded only if the animator completes at its `.end` position. Any other case means the transition has been canceled, so you can call `completeTransition(false)` directly. Build and run and try wiggling the table up and down a bit - sweet!

But there's a problem. Think for a second about your non-interactive transition. Tap on Edit. Something is wrong!

You need to change your code to explicitly set the view controller transition to non-interactive whenever the user taps the button.

Switch back to **LockScreenViewController.swift** and find the widgets table data source method `tableView(_:cellForRowAt:)`.

You will see that the code assigns a closure to the Edit button, like so:

```
(cell as? FooterCell)?.didPressEdit = { [unowned self] in
  self.presentSettings()
}
```

Just before the `self.presentSettings()` line, insert:

```
self.presentTransition.wantsInteractiveStart = false
```

This ensures that you are presenting the settings view controller non-interactively. Run the app another time and give the transition a try.

Interruptible Transition Animations

Next you are going to look into switching between non-interactive and interactive modes during the transition. The integration of `UIViewPropertyAnimator` with view controller transitions aims to solve the issues around situations where the user starts the transition to another controller, but changes their mind mid-way.

In this part of the chapter, you will add code to start presenting the settings controller after a tap on Edit, but pause the transition if the user taps again on the screen during the animation.

Switch to **PresentTranstion.swift**. To allow touches during a non-interactive transition, you have to explicitly set the animator as able to handle user activity. In `transitionAnimator(using:)`, insert this line towards the bottom:

```
animator.isUserInteractionEnabled = true
```

You make sure the transition animation is interactive so that the user can continue interacting with the screen after they've paused it.

You will allow the user to scroll either up or down to complete or cancel the transition respectively. To do that, switch back to **LockScreenViewController.swift** and add a new property:

```
var touchesStartPointY: CGFloat?
```

In case the user touches the screen during a transition, you pause it and store the location of that first touch:

```
override func touchesBegan(
    _ touches: Set<UITouch>,
    with event: UIEvent?
) {
    guard presentTransition.wantsInteractiveStart == false,
      presentTransition.animator != nil else {
      return
    }

    touchesStartPointY = touches.first?.location(in: view).y
    presentTransition.pause()
}
```

You check if the touch happened during a non-interactive transition and the transition's animator is currently running.

In that case, you store the current touch location and then call `pause()` on the transition, which will pause the transition and leave it in an interactive mode.

Run the app, tap on Edit, and quickly tap again a second time. The transition will freeze onscreen like so:

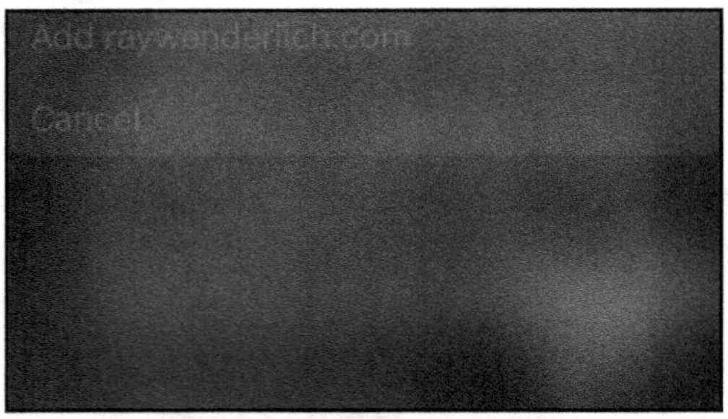

Now you need to track the user touches and see if the user pans up or down. Add the following:

```
override func touchesMoved(
    _ touches: Set<UITouch>,
    with event: UIEvent?
) {
    guard
      let startY = touchesStartPointY,
      let currentPoint = touches.first?.location(in: view).y
    else {
      return
    }
```

```
    if currentPoint < startY - 40 {
      touchesStartPointY = nil
      presentTransition.animator?.addCompletion { _ in
        self.blurView.effect = nil
      }
      presentTransition.cancel()
    } else if currentPoint > startY + 40 {
      touchesStartPointY = nil
      presentTransition.finish()
    }
  }
```

With this rather big chunk of code, your non-interactive-turned-interactive transition is complete!

You observe for two different cases. First, if the user moves their touch downwards more than `40` points, you cancel the transition and reset the blur effect. If the user moved their touch upwards more than 40 points, you complete the transition successfully. Give the app a try one last time. Tap on Edit, tap again to pause the transition, and either cancel or complete it depending on the direction you pan. And that's all for this section of the book!

You've learned plenty about `UIViewPropertyAnimator` and how to make the best of it. You've worked through a rather lengthy four chapters but you achieved a lot, and the project looks amazing:

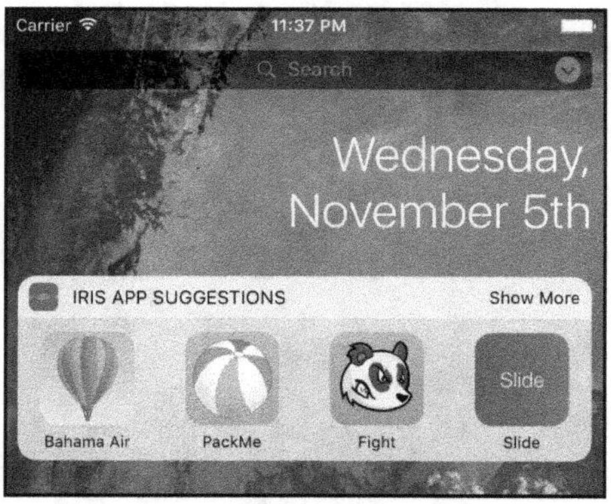

Key Points

- By combining your knowledge about custom transitions and creating interactive, interruptible animations with `UIViewPropertyAnimator`, you can create stunning transition effects.

Section VII: 3D Animations

Core Animation helps you float free from the two dimensional world of your app's UI. Although it isn't a true 3D framework, Core Animation has a lot of smart features to help you position two-dimensional objects in 3D space.

In the next two chapters, you'll learn how to set up your layers in 3D space, how to choose the distance from the camera to your layer and how to create animations in your 3D scene.

Chapter 26: Simple 3D Animations

In this chapter you'll get to try out your newfound knowledge about camera distance and perspective.

Once you set up your layer's perspective, you can work on the layer's transform as you usually would; but now you can rotate, translate and scale your layer in three dimensions.

The project for this chapter features a folding pull-out menu as popularized in many apps, such as Taasky:

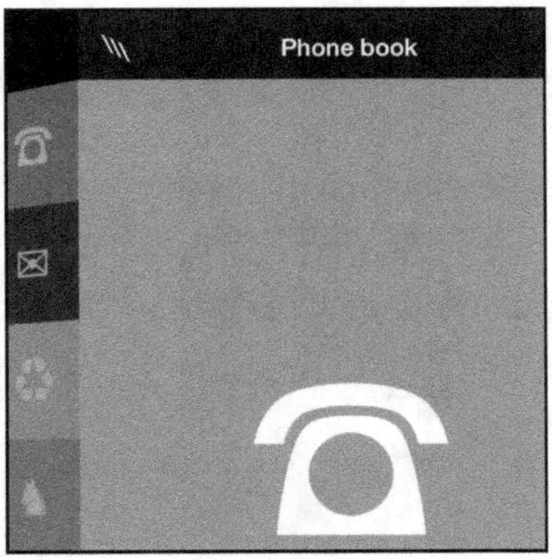

Office Buddy is an office helper app for employees to access categorized information about day-to-day company life.

The starter project already has all the code to make the menu functional, but it only works in 2D. Your task is to bring the menu into the third dimension and give it life!

Creating 3D Transformations

Open the starter project for this chapter and build and run it to see what the initial version of the Office Buddy app looks like:

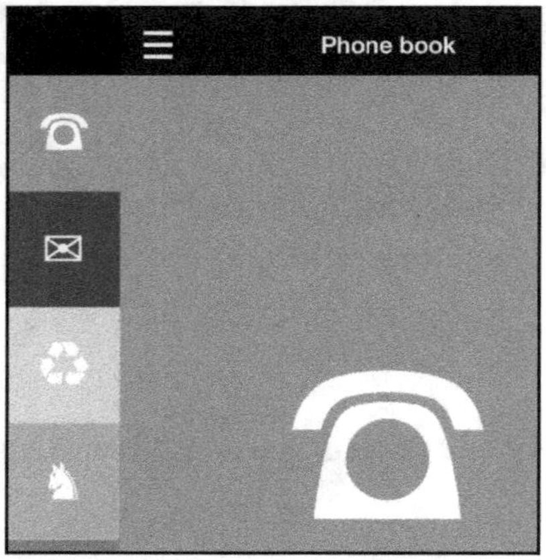

Tap the menu button to reveal the side menu; alternatively, you can swipe right to reveal the side menu.

As you can see, this app is as flat as they come. But armed with your new insight on 3D perspective, you're going to add some depth to the menu.

Open **ContainerViewController.swift**; this controller displays both the menu view controller and the content view controller on the screen. It also handles pan gestures so the user can open and close the menu.

Your first task is to build a class method that creates the corresponding 3D transform for a given percentage of "openness" of the side menu.

Add the following method declaration to **ContainerViewController.swift**:

```
func menuTransform(percent: CGFloat) -> CATransform3D {
}
```

The above method accepts a single parameter of the current progress of the menu, which was calculated by the code in `handleGesture(_:)`, and returns an instance of `CATransform3D`. You're going to assign the result of this method directly to the menu layer's transform property.

Add the following code to your new method:

```
var identity = CATransform3DIdentity
identity.m34 = -1.0 / 1000
```

This code might look a bit surprising; so far you've only used *functions* to create or modify transforms. This time, however, you're modifying one of the class' *properties*.

> **Note**: Why is this property called `m34`? View and layer transforms are expressed as two-dimensional math matrices. In the case of a layer transform matrix, the element in the `3rd` row at the `4th` column sets your z-axis perspective. You can set this element directly to apply the desired perspective transform.

So you create a new `CATransform3D` struct and you set its m34 property to `-1.0/1000`... why would you choose that value?

Okay, I'll back up a little. To enable 3D transforms on a layer you need to set `m34` to `-1.0 / [camera distance]`. Since you read through the introduction for this section (you *did* read it, right?), you have some understanding of how the camera distance affects the scene perspective.

But why are you using `1000` for the camera distance? The distance is expressed in points between the camera and the front of the scene. As to what value to use, the truth is that you need to try different values and see what looks good for your particular animation.

Working with Camera Distance

For UI elements in an average app you can consult the following reference for some guidelines on an appropriate camera distance:

- `0.1...500`: Very close, lots of perspective distortion.
- `750...2,000`: Nice perspective, content is clearly visible.
- `2,000` and up: Almost no perspective distortion.

For the Office Buddy app, a distance of `1000` points will give the menu a nice subtle perspective. You can see it in action once you finish working on the current method.

Add the following code to the bottom of menuTransform(percent:):

```
let remainingPercent = 1.0 - percent
let angle = remainingPercent * .pi * -0.5
```

In the above code you calculate the current angle of the menu based on its "openness" value.

Now add the following code to the bottom of menuTransform(percent:):

```
let rotationTransform = CATransform3DRotate(
  identity, angle, 0.0, 1.0, 0.0)

let translationTransform = CATransform3DMakeTranslation(
    menuWidth * percent, 0, 0)
return CATransform3DConcat(
  rotationTransform, translationTransform)
```

Here, you use rotationTransform to rotate the layer away from you around its y-axis.

The menu is moving in from the left, so you also create a translation transform to move it along the x-axis, eventually to menuWidth at **100%**.

Finally, you concatenate the two transforms and return the result.

Now you can use menuTransform(percent:) to update the menu transform as the user pans right or left.

Remove the following line from setMenu(toPercent:) that modifies the menu's origin:

```
menuViewController.view.frame.origin.x =
  menuWidth * CGFloat(percent) - menuWidth
```

You don't need the above line anymore because you will move the menu via its transform. Add the following code to setMenu(toPercent:):

```
menuViewController.view.layer.transform =
  menuTransform(percent: percent)
```

Build and run your project; pan right to see how the menu rotates around its y-axis:

The menu rotates in 3D, but it's rotating around its horizontal center, which separates the menu from the content view controller.

Moving the Layer's Anchor Point

By default, the anchor point of a layer has an x coordinate of `0.5`, meaning it is in the center. You need to set the x of the anchor point to `1.0` to make the menu rotate around its right edge like a hinge, as shown below:

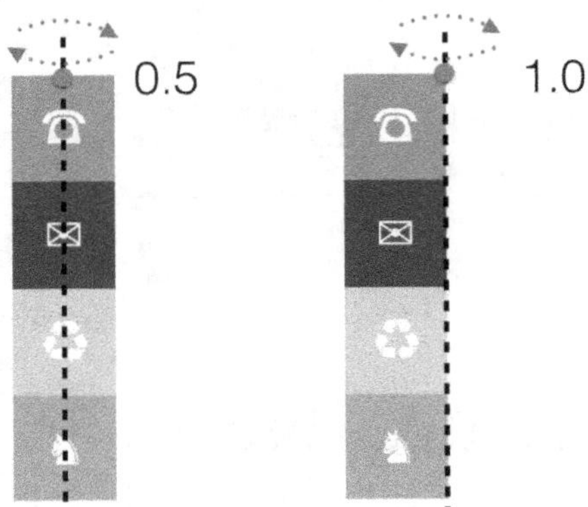

All transforms are calculated around the layer's anchor point. You also use the anchor point as your reference point when setting the position of the layer. This means it's best to change the layer's `anchorPoint` before you set its position on the screen.

Find the following line in `viewDidLoad()` where you set the menu frame:

```
menuViewController.view.frame = CGRect(
  x: -menuWidth, y: 0,
  width: menuWidth, height: view.frame.height)
```

Now insert the following code just **above** that line (it's important to insert the line before you set the view frame because otherwise setting the anchor point will offset the view — if you're curious to see the difference give both ways a try):

```
menuViewController.view.layer.anchorPoint.x = 1.0
```

This rotates the menu around its right edge.

Build and run your project again, then pan horizontally through the view and observe how the effect has changed:

That looks much better!

You're almost done — there's just a few more bits to take care of.

Creating Perspective Through Shading

Shading lends a lot of realism to 3D animations; to that end, you will rotate the menu out of the "shadow" of the left side of the content view controller.

You're not using any advanced shading techniques here; instead, you can simulate this by changing the alpha of the menu as it rotates.

Add the following code to `setMenu(toPercent:)`:

```
menuViewController.view.alpha = CGFloat(max(0.2, percent))
```

In the code above, you assign the percent value directly to the layer's alpha, but you limit it to `0.2` to ensure the menu remains visible when it's edge-on to the user and doesn't disappear completely.

Since the background of this app is black, lowering the alpha of the menu view makes the black color show through the menu and simulates a shadow effect.

Build and run your project and observe the effect:

It's a small detail, but it really makes your 3D animation "pop"! You might have noticed that when you tap the menu button the first time, the animation does not play in 3D. The effect only kicks in on the second and subsequent animations.

That's because you're not setting the 3D animation parameters and the layer transforms until *after* the first time you toggle the menu. This is easy to fix: As soon as the menu view controller loads, set the menu progress to 0.0 to set the proper menu layer transform.

Add the following to the bottom of `viewDidLoad()`:

```
setMenu(toPercent: 0.0)
```

This will get the starting frames and layer transforms in place from the start. Build and run your project again; tap the menu button and you'll see that the animation works properly the first time through.

Rasterizing for Efficiency

There's one last task to make your animation "perfect". If you stare at the menu long enough while you pan back and forth you'll notice the borders of the menu items look pixelated.

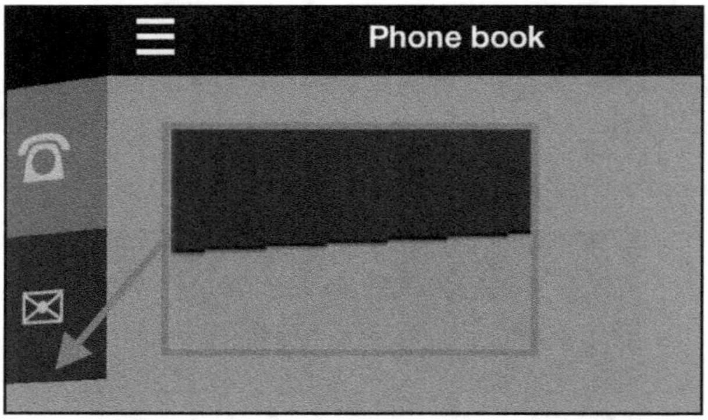

Core Animation continually redraws all contents of the menu view controller and recalculates the perspective distortion for all elements as it moves, which isn't terribly efficient — hence the jagged edges.

It's better to let Core Animation know that you won't change the menu contents during the animation so that it can render the menu once and simply rotate the rendered and cached image.

That sounds complicated at first, but you'll see it's quite easy to implement. Scroll to `handleGesture()` and find the `.began` case block; this code executes when the user starts the pan action. This is where you'll instruct Core Animation to cache the menu.

Add the following code to the end of the `.began` case block:

```
// Improve the look of the opening menu
menuViewController.view.layer.shouldRasterize = true
menuViewController.view.layer.rasterizationScale =
  UIScreen.main.scale
```

`shouldRasterize` instructs Core Animation to cache the layer contents as an image. You then set `rasterizationScale` to match the current screen scale and you're golden!

Build and run your project again to see how your graphics have improved:

Core Animation really shines in this instance. Working with 2D images is one of the things this framework really does well!

To avoid any unnecessary caching while using the app, you should turn off rasterization as soon as the animation is done.

Find the empty animation completion closure inside the `.ended, .cancelled, .failed` case and add the following code:

```
self.menuViewController.view.layer.shouldRasterize = false
```

Now you're only activating rasterization during the animation. How efficient of you!

In only a few pages, you learned about camera distance, perspective, and how to set up your 3D scene and apply animations to it.

There's one more chapter in this section, which contains some more 3D fun — but before you go, take a look at this chapter's challenge first.

Key Points

- The `.m34` value of a `CATransform3D` is important as it gives perspective to your 3D transforms.
- The **anchor point** of a layer sets the point around which your transforms take place.

Challenges

Challenge 1: Create Your Own 3D Animation

For this challenge you are going to create a 3D rotation animation for the menu button. As the user pans the button will rotate alongside the menu view controller.

Specifically, you will create a rotation around both the x- and y-axes to make the menu button flip on its diagonal.

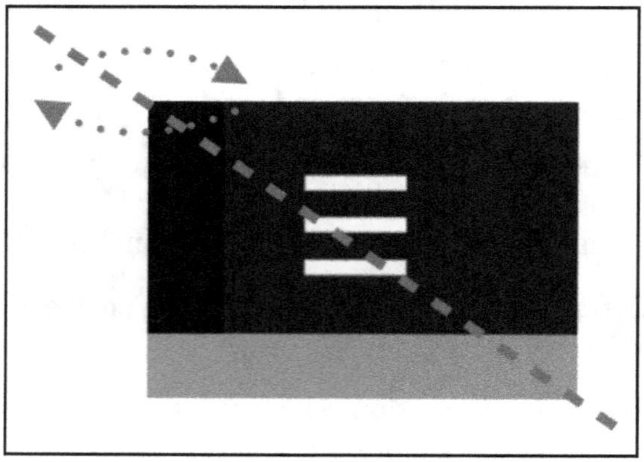

Add the following code to `setMenu(toPercent:)` in **ContainerViewController.swift**:

```
let centerVC = centerViewController.viewControllers.first as?
CenterViewController
```

This fetches the current content view controller so you can work with it.

The menu button is accessible via the `menuButton` property of `CenterViewController`. For this challenge, adjust the 3D transform of the button's `imageView`.

If you directly rotate the button rather than use the 3D transform, it will clash with the navigation bar views underneath and might get partially obscured by the navigation bar.

In contrast, the button's own 2D space is already positioned on top of all navigation bar views before you rotate it — so if you rotate `menuButton.imageView`, it rotates within the button's own plane, which is on top of the navigation bar at all times.

Another gotcha is that the first time the code runs `menuButton` will be `nil`, so you should treat it like an optional, even though it is implicitly unwrapped.

For the rotation, create a transform just like you did earlier in this chapter, but this time rotate the view around the x- and y-axes. If necessary, have a look at the documentation for `CATransform3DRotate()`.

This time you don't need to calculate the remaining percentage; to get the rotation angle, simply multiply the progress by `.pi`.

When you are finished with your solution the button image should flip around while you pan through the screen like so:

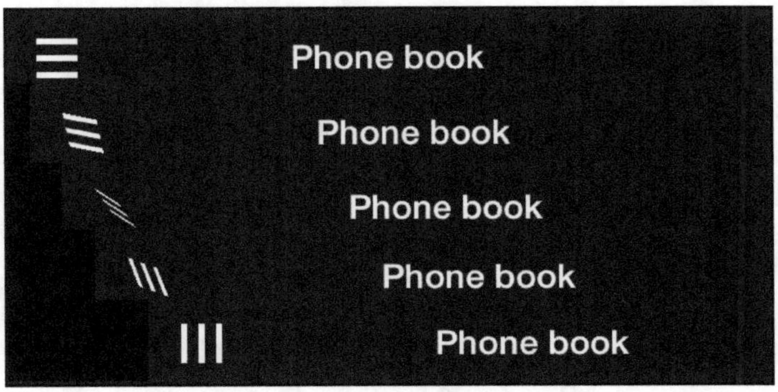

That's it! Head on in to the next chapter for more awesome animations in 3D!

Chapter 27: Intermediate 3D Animations

In the previous chapter, you learned that applying perspective to a single view isn't a complicated task; in fact, once you know the secret of `m34` and camera distance you can create all kinds of 3D animations.

This chapter builds on what you've already learned and shows you how to create convincing 3D animations with more than one view.

The starter project for this chapter is a simple hurricane image gallery. By the end of this chapter, you'll have a 3D effect to get an overall view of the images in the gallery:

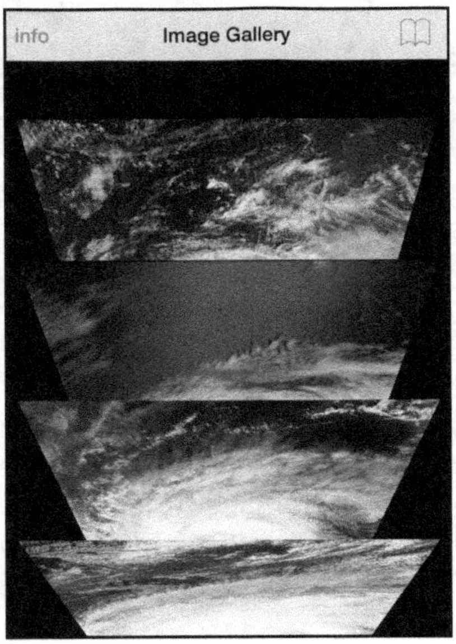

You'll be able to tap on a photo to bring it full screen, and tapping the top right button fans all the images open again — with a cool animation to take you between the two states, of course!

Ready to get started? Hang on to your hat and prepare to get blown away by this "stormy" project!

Exploring the Starter Project

Open the starter project from the Resources folder for this chapter; build and run it to see what you have to start with:

All you have is a blank screen with two bar buttons on top: the left one shows the NASA image credits and the right one invokes the method that shows or hides the gallery as appropriate.

First, you'll need to display all images on the screen and set them up so they're ready for your "fan" animation.

Open **ViewController.swift** and inspect the class code. You'll see an array called `images`; this array contains some slightly customized image views. The `ImageViewCard` class inherits from `UIImageView` and adds a string property `title` to hold the hurricane title, and a property called `didSelect` so you can easily set a tap handler on the image.

Your first task is to add all images to the view controller's view. Add the following code to the end of viewDidAppear(_:):

```
for image in images {
  image.layer.anchorPoint.y = 0.0
  image.frame = view.bounds

  view.addSubview(image)
}
```

In the code above, you loop over all images, set each image's anchor point to 0.0 on the y-axis and resize each image so it takes up the full screen. When that's done, you add each image to view.

Setting the anchor point lets the images rotate around their upper edge rather than the default of the center, as illustrated below:

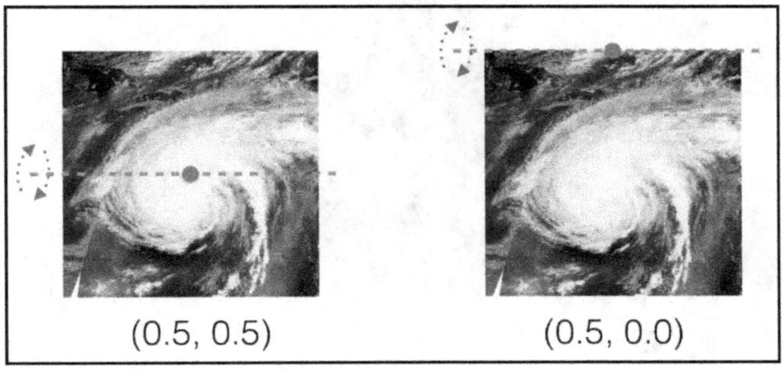

This will make it a lot easer to fan out the images in 3D space.

Build and run your project to see what you've achieved so far:

Hmm — you only see the last image you added to view. That's because all images have the same frame, so you only see the last image you added: Hurricane Irene.

To make it more obvious which hurricane image is being displayed, add the following line at the end of `viewDidAppear(_:)`:

```
navigationItem.title = images.last?.title
```

This code takes the name of the last hurricane image in the collection and sets it as the navigation title of the view controller, like so.

Build and run again to familiarize yourself with Irene:

Notice that you didn't set any perspective transforms on the images; you're going to set a perspective directly on the view controller's view instead.

In the previous chapter you adjusted the transform property on a single view and then rotated it in 3D space. But since your current project has more individual views that you'd care to manipulate in 3D, you can set the perspective of their parent view instead to save yourself a bunch of work.

Add the following code to `viewDidAppear(_:)`:

```
var perspective = CATransform3DIdentity
perspective.m34 = -1.0 / 250.0
view.layer.sublayerTransform = perspective
```

Here you use the layer property `sublayerTransform` to set the perspective of all sublayers of the view controller's layer. The sublayer `transform` is then combined with each individual layer's own `transform`.

This lets you focus on managing the rotation or translation of your subviews without having to worry about perspective. You'll see how this works in more detail in the next section.

Transforming the Gallery

`toggleGallery(_:)` is hooked up to the Browse bar button on the right and is where you'll apply your 3D transform to the four images.

Add the following variable to `toggleGallery(_:)`:

```
var imageYOffset: CGFloat = 50.0
```

Since you don't just rotate all images in place but simply move them around to produce the "fan" animation, you use `imageYOffset` to set the offset of each image.

Next you need to iterate through all the images and run their individual animations.

Add the following code to `toggleGallery(_:)`:

```
for subview in view.subviews {
  guard let image = subview as? ImageViewCard else {
    continue
  }

  // more code here
}
```

Here, you loop through all subviews of the view controller's view and act only on the subviews that are instances of `ImageViewCard`.

Add the following code after the `guard` block you added above, to replace the `more code here` comment:

```
var imageTransform = CATransform3DIdentity

// 1
imageTransform = CATransform3DTranslate(
  imageTransform, 0.0, imageYOffset, 0.0)

// 2
```

```
imageTransform = CATransform3DScale(
  imageTransform, 0.95, 0.6, 1.0)

// 3
imageTransform = CATransform3DRotate(
  imageTransform, .pi / 8, -1.0, 0.0, 0.0)
```

You start by assigning the identity transform to `imageTransform` and then add a series of adjustments to it. This is what each individual adjustment does to the image:

1. Move the image on the y-axis with CATransform3DTranslate; this offsets the image from its default 0.0 y-coordinate as shown below:

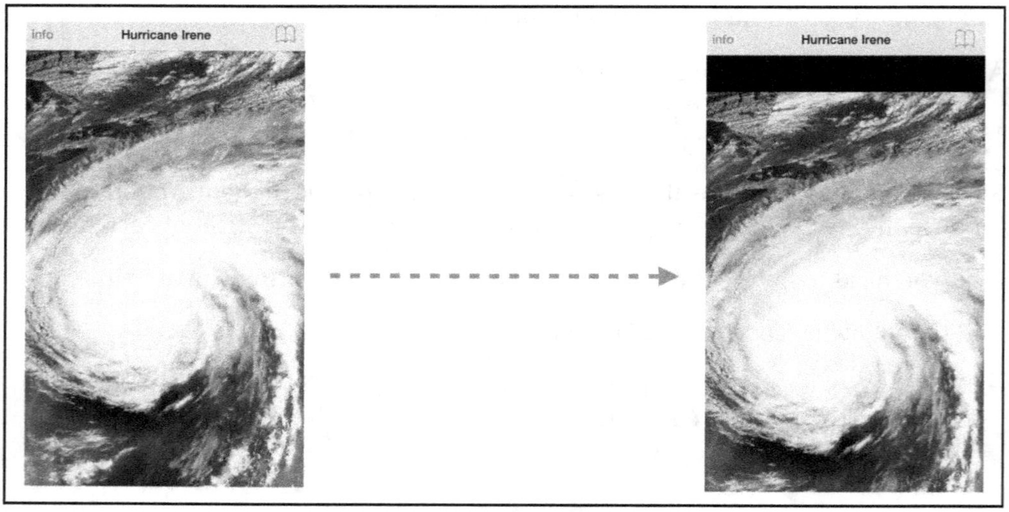

Later, you'll calculate the `imageYOffset` of each image separately; for now all images move by the same amount so you'll still see only the top one for the moment.

2. Scale the image by adjusting the scale component of the transform using `CATransform3DScale`. You shrink the image just a little on the x-axis, but you scale it down to `60%` on the y-axis to enrich the rotation 3D effect:

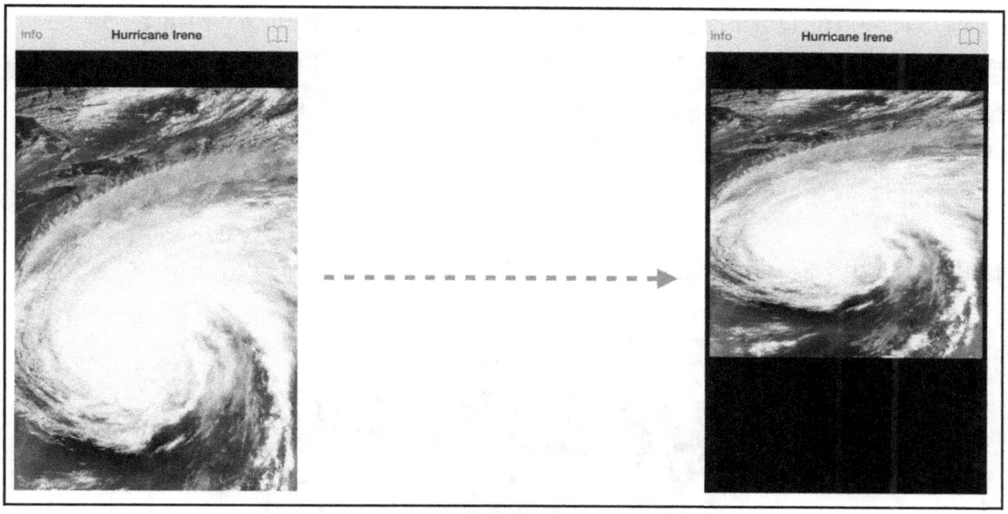

3. Finally, you use `CATransform3DRotate` to rotate the image by `22.5` degrees to give it some perspective distortion as shown below:

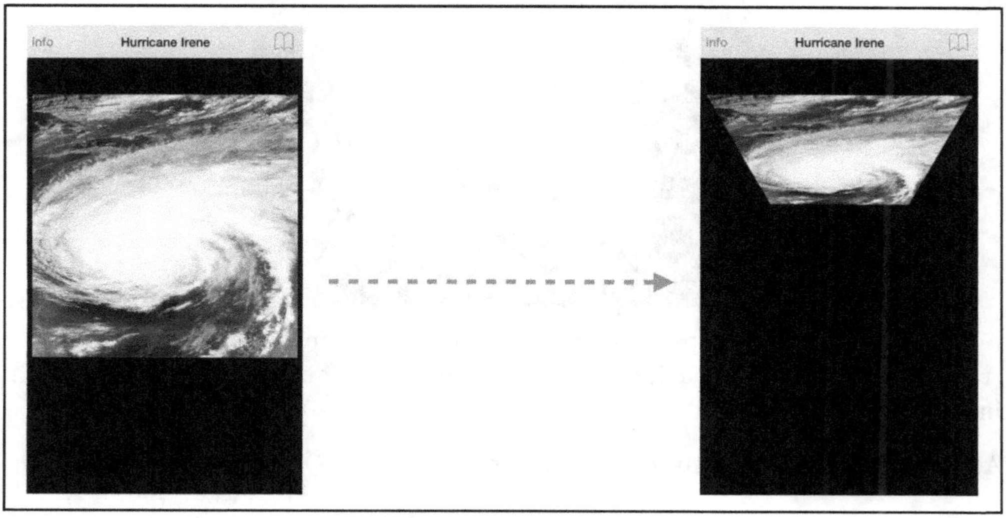

Remember, you already set the anchor point so the image rotates around its top edge.

Now you see the value of setting the m34 value above via view.layer.sublayerTransform; your rotation transform simply re-uses the m34 value from the sublayer transform, without the need to apply it here. That's handy!

Now all that's left is to apply the transform to each image. Add the following line (still inside the for body):

```
image.layer.transform = imageTransform
```

Build and run your project; tap the Browse button to see the result of your transforms:

Again, you only see the top image as all other images behind it have the same transform applied. Now is a perfect opportunity to customize the transform for each image.

Add the following line to the end of the for block:

```
imageYOffset += view.frame.height / CGFloat(images.count)
```

This adjusts the y-offset of each image depending on where it is in the stack. You divide the screen height over the number of images so they distribute themselves evenly over the screen.

Build and run your project to see your views fan out:

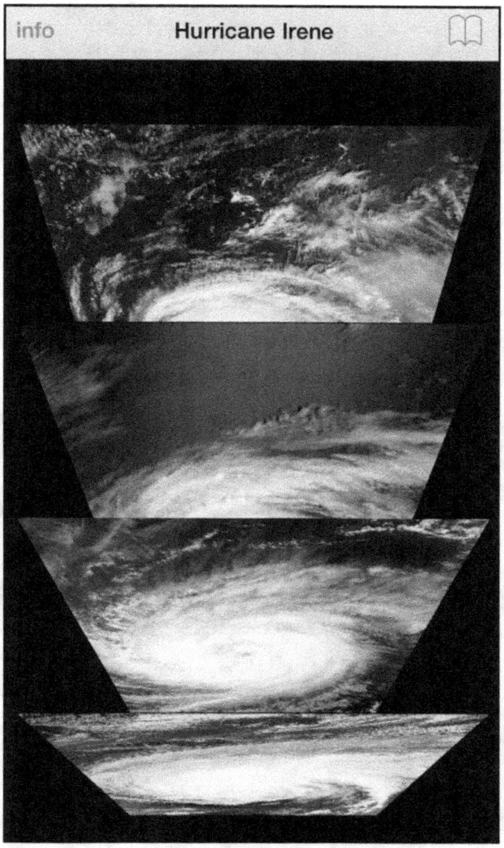

Sweet — the gallery looks just as you intended! But as this is a book about animations, it would be a shame if you didn't animate the transition to the fanned-out view, wouldn't it?

Animating the Gallery

Find the following line in `toggleGallery(_:)` where you set `transform` on each image:

```
image.layer.transform = imageTransform
```

Insert the following code **above that line** to animate transform:

```
let animation = CABasicAnimation(keyPath: "transform")
animation.fromValue = NSValue(caTransform3D:
  image.layer.transform)
animation.toValue = NSValue(caTransform3D: imageTransform)
animation.duration = 0.33
image.layer.add(animation, forKey: nil)
```

This code is definitely familiar: You create a layer animation on the `transform` property and animate it from its current value to the `imageTransform` you designed earlier.

Build and run your project once more; tap the Browse button and enjoy your completed animation:

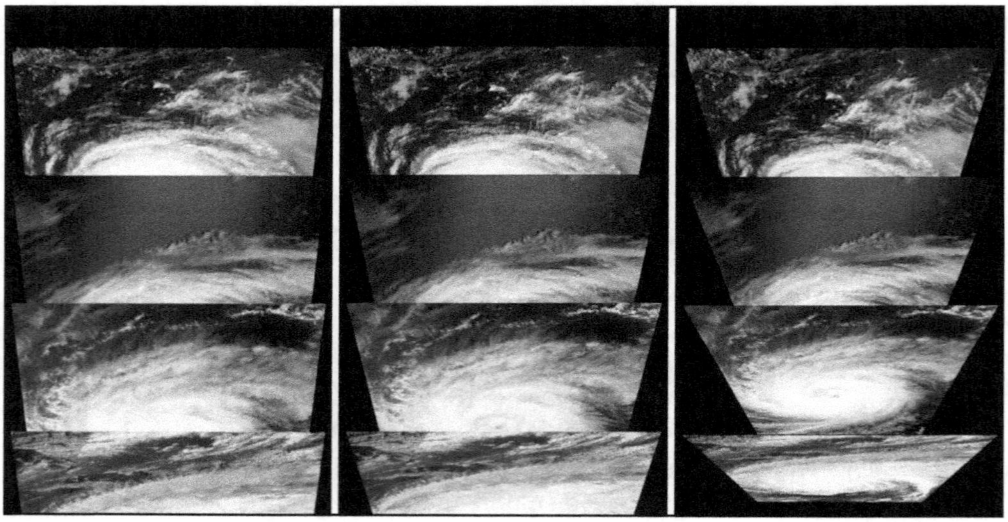

You're finished with the gallery for now; you'll revisit it in the Challenges section when you add the ability to close the fan when the user taps the Browse button.

Bringing an Image to the Front

In this final section, you'll add a bit of interactivity to the image gallery: tapping an image will make it jump in front of the other images so that the user can get a better look at it `ImageViewCard` already features a closure expression property named `didSelect`; this fires when the user taps on the image and receives the tapped image view as an input parameter.

To add this feature, you'll add a method to `ViewController` and assign it to `didSelect` on all the image views.

First, add the following code to `viewDidAppear()`, inside the `for` loop body:

```
image.didSelect = selectImage
```

Xcode will complain that `selectImage` doesn't exist, but you'll fix this in the next step.

Add the following method to `ViewController`:

```
func selectImage(selectedImage: ImageViewCard) {
  for subview in view.subviews {
    guard let image = subview as? ImageViewCard else {
      continue
    }
    if image === selectedImage {
      //selected image
    } else {
      //any other image
    }
  }
}
```

This is the skeleton of `selectImage(selectedImage:)`; when the user taps one of the images, you loop over all subviews and get the `ImageViewCard` instances just like you did earlier. Then you check each `ImageViewCard` to see if it's the selected image.

Now you need two more animations: one to animate the selected image, and another to animate all the other images in the gallery.

You'll tackle this in reverse and fade out the unselected images first.

Replace the `//any other image` comment in `selectImage(selectedImage:)` with the following code:

```
UIView.animate(
  withDuration: 0.33,
  delay: 0.0,
  options: .curveEaseIn,
  animations: {
    image.alpha = 0.0
  },
  completion: { _ in
    image.alpha = 1.0
    image.layer.transform = CATransform3DIdentity
  })
```

This is a simple animation to fade out each image. In the completion block, you reset its transform to the identity transform and alpha to fully opaque. By the time the above animation is done, the selected image will be in front of all others — so transparent or not, you won't see any of the unselected images. Resetting `alpha` here saves you from having to remember to reset it when you want to see the image again.

Build and run your project; open the gallery and tap on an image to see all the other unselected images fade from view.

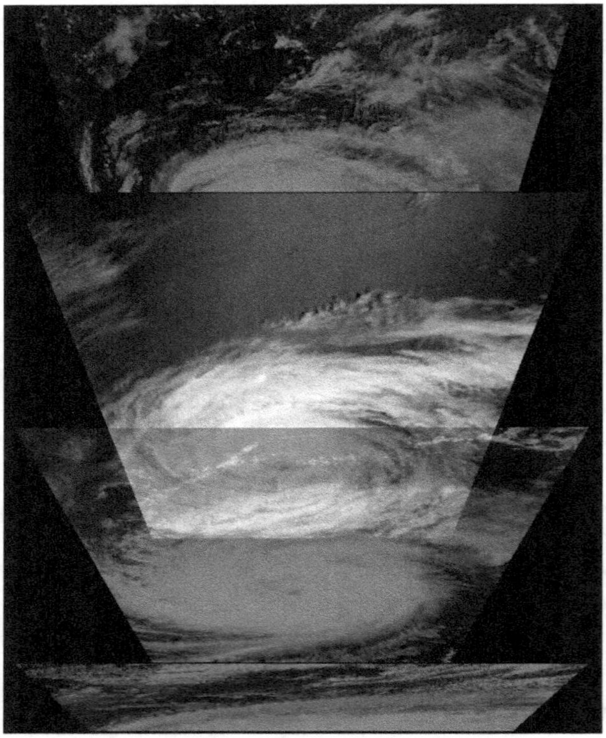

When that animation completes, the view changes back to show the top image at full-screen — because you haven't done anything with the selected image! You'll fix that now.

You'll animate the selected image's `transform` back to the identity transform and pull the image to the front when the animation completes.

Replace the `//selected image` comment in `selectImage(selectedImage:)` with the following code:

```
UIView.animate(
  withDuration: 0.33,
  delay: 0.0,
  options: .curveEaseIn,
  animations: {
    image.layer.transform = CATransform3DIdentity
  },
  completion: { _ in
    self.view.bringSubviewToFront(image)
  })
```

Here, you're un-doing the 3D transform for the animation, and then ensuring the image is at the top of the view stack at the end so it's visible.

Finally, add the following code to the end of `selectImage(selectedImage:)`:

```
self.navigationItem.title = selectedImage.title
```

This will update the navigation bar with the currently selected image title. Build and run your project; tap the various images to see how they zoom to full screen. How does it look? I *thought* you'd enjoy this classy little animation! That's a wrap; there's one small bit of functionality to clean up in the Challenge section below, but other than that, you have a really stunning animation at your fingertips. I suspect you can think of many ways to use it in your own projects!

Key Points

- When you set the 3D perspective via the `m34` property and use the resulting transform to set `sublayerTransform` on a layer, all of its sub-layers can be animated in 3D space.
- You can combine `CATransform3D` layer animations with UIKit view animations and let Core Animation automatically combine and render them on screen.

Challenges

Challenge 1: Toggle the Gallery with the Browse Button

Right now the user must choose an image from the gallery once they open it. In this challenge, you'll make the Browse button work like a toggle to close the gallery view as well. Add a new property to `ViewController` named `isGalleryOpen` and set its initial value to `false`. You need to update the value of this property in couple of places in the code:

- Set it to `true` at the end of `toggleGallery(_:)`
- Set it to `false` at the end of `selectImage(selectedImage:)`

In the for loop in `toggleGallery()`, add a check to see if the gallery is already open. If so, leave `imageTransform` as it is, instead of adding the translate, scale and rotation transforms to it. Don't forget to `toggle()` `isGalleryOpen` at the end of the method.

That's it — if you like, play around with the animations in this project and see what other flashy elements you can add on your own!

28 Conclusion

We hope you're excited about the breadth of animations available to you in iOS! Animations bring life and playfulness to touch-based interfaces; this makes people feel more connected to your interface and creates memorable app experiences for your users.

You're now equipped to use and understand the animation tools available to you, from layers to 3D effects and beyond to SwiftUI. It's up to you now to couple your creativity with the things you've learned in this book and create some impressive effects of your own!

If you have any questions or comments about the projects in this book or in your own animations, please stop by our forums at https://forums.raywenderlich.com.

Thank you again for purchasing this book. Your continued support is what makes the books, tutorials, videos and other things we do at raywenderlich.com possible. We truly appreciate it!

May all your animations be fun and fluid, with furiously high frame rates!

— Marin and Richard

The *iOS Animations by Tutorials* team

www.ingramcontent.com/pod-product-compliance
Lightning Source LLC
LaVergne TN
LVHW080007210926
848481LV00011B/2963
* 9 7 8 1 9 5 0 3 2 5 6 5 8 *